A Rainbow Thread

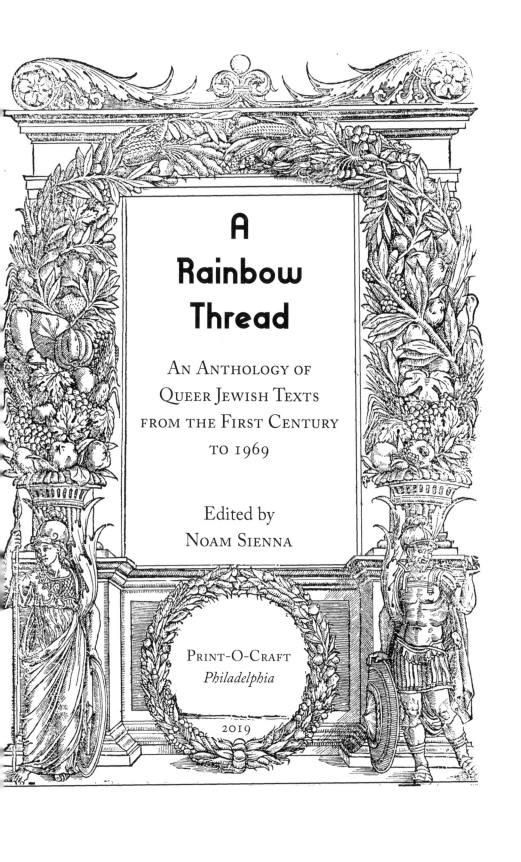

A Rainbow Thread

An Anthology of
Queer Jewish Texts
from the First Century
to 1969

Edited by
Noam Sienna

Print-O-Craft
Philadelphia

2019

A Rainbow Thread:
An Anthology of Queer Jewish Literature
from the First Century to 1969

© 2019 Noam Sienna. All rights reserved.

Cover Illustration: adapted from *Shir ha-shirim* [Brest, Belarus?], 1794,
by the scribe Baruch ben Shemaryah. General Collection, Beinecke
Rare Book Room and Manuscript Library, Yale University.

Book and cover design by David Zvi Kalman.

First edition February 2019

Print-O-Craft Press
P.O. Box 18963
Philadelphia PA 19119

Find us online at www.printocraftpress.com

For bulk order requests or press inquiries, please email gut@shabb.es

Printed in the United States of America
ISBN 978-0-9905155-8-6
Library of Congress Control Number 2018949219

ג ה ז ט י ח ו ד ב   יט כא כג כה כו כח כו כד כב כ

Contents

EARLY MODERN VOICES (1500–1900)

MODERN VOICES (1900–1969)

Foreword

by Judith Plaskow

I cannot remember the particular Jewish conference I was attending—probably in the early 1980s—at which a participant voiced incredulity when told of a workshop on gay and lesbian Jews. "There are no gay and lesbian Jews," she declared—though she was in fact talking to several. Her self-confident erasure of Jewish lesbian and gay existence was in line with a much older Talmudic debate about whether two men may sleep together under the same blanket. While Rabbi Judah forbade it, the majority of sages permitted it on the grounds that Jews are not suspected of homosexual acts. The important 12th century philosopher and Torah scholar Maimonides shared the majority view and codified it in his Mishneh Torah.

This obliteration of the possibility of Jewish gay and lesbian lives, repeated over the course of many centuries, testifies to both the importance and ground-breaking nature of Noam Sienna's anthology of queer Jewish texts throughout the ages. Even in our friendlier time when the active presence of lesbian, gay, bisexual, transgender, and queer Jews is much more difficult to deny—when the existence of numerous LGBTQ synagogues, queer rabbis, a queer Torah commentary, and queer marriage ceremonies means that LGBTQ Jews are much more a part of Jewish communal consciousness—the issue of genealogy has yet to be fully explored. Recognizing the existence of LGBTQ Jews today does not necessarily translate into being able to recognize the queerness of some of our ancestors. To what extent is the existence of queer Jews a relatively new phenomenon, a function of our more tolerant and permissive times, and to what extent have queer Jews always been part of Jewish existence? How would we know, given the bias toward not seeing and therefore the undoubted erasure of most of the sources that might help us to answer that question? And what does it mean even to ask the question, given that the concept of homosexuality emerged only in the nineteenth century and that the use of the term "queer" is of far more recent vintage?

The beauty of *A Rainbow Thread* is that it does not seek to impose contemporary categories on historical documents or come up with some single definition of queer experience. Rather, it imagines Jewish history as a field of fertile possibilities that contains tantalizing clues to a past that LGBTQ Jews generally experience as being denied us. Since history is written by the dominant group in any culture, every marginalized people is faced with the challenge of recovering its past from sources that are at best indifferent to its concerns and at worst deliberately obscure them or render them invisible. Just as Jewish feminists have reread canonical texts with new questions and lenses and greatly expanded the sources on the basis of which to construct a new women's history, so this volume undertakes both to return to mainstream texts with new eyes and to find rich new data for creating a queer lineage. As Elisabeth Schüssler Fiorenza wrote in the early days of feminist biblical interpretation, "the enslavement of a people becomes total when their history is destroyed and solidarity with the dead becomes impossible…" It is therefore essential, she argued, that any marginalized group reclaim the suffering and hopes of its ancestors as subversive or dangerous memory, placing its people at the center of historical reconstruction in ways that allow for solidarity among the past, present, and future.[1]

The task of recovery is especially urgent in the Jewish context because of the central importance of memory in Jewish self-understanding. Again and again in Jewish liturgy and ritual, we are adjured to remember: remember the Sabbath day to keep it holy; remember that we were slaves in the land of Egypt; remember what God did for us when God took us out of Egypt. "We Jews are a community based on memory," Martin Buber said. "A common memory has kept us together and enabled us to survive." This does not mean that Jewish life is based on any one particular past, Buber continues. Rather, it means that each generation hands on to the next a memory that is always growing in scope and that this ever-expanding memory has a power that "sustain[s], [feeds], and quicken[s] Jewish existence."[2] It is in telling the story of our past as Jews that we learn who we are in the present. That is why the sages of the rabbinic period

---

[1] Elisabeth Schüssler Fiorenza, *Bread Not Stone: The Challenge of Feminist Biblical Interpretation* (Boston: Beacon Press, 1984), 19.

[2] Martin Buber, "Why We Should Study Jewish Sources," in his *Israel and the World: Essays in a Time of Crisis* (New York: Schocken Books, 1963), 146.

repeatedly rewrote or embroidered biblical narratives to bring them into alignment with their own practices. And it is why a number of the authors in this volume seek to create a queer Jewish lineage, appealing to biblical or medieval precedents to contextualize their own erotic desires (sources 18, 32, 77, 87, 110). The link between past and present—the continuity between them—is so deeply felt, it is difficult to imagine the full inclusion of LGBTQ Jews in contemporary Jewish life without going back and reading ourselves into Jewish history. Knowing ourselves to be members of the Jewish community in our own time even though there are those who would still like to deny it, we know we have always been part of the Jewish people, whatever forms queerness may have taken in particular eras.

But, again, *how* do we recover our history when the meanings of queerness are constantly shifting even today and so many crucial documents and stories are undoubtedly lost to us? This volume follows the lead of feminist reconstructions of Jewish history in greatly expanding the type and range of sources on which to base an understanding of the past. Canonical texts are not discarded; on the contrary, read through a bent lens, they can yield considerable information. But they are simply one type of literature that might be relevant to queer history, and, significantly, they are not accorded more authoritative status than other forms of documentation. Poetry becomes an important resource; trial records, law and midrash, studies in sexology, newspaper articles all have a place. Sienna draws sources from a wide range of Jewish cultures, from almost every region where Jews have lived, and includes documents translated from more than a dozen languages.

One of the things I find fascinating about the texts collected here is the amount of information available from what we might call "negative" sources—sources that are hostile to homoerotic relations. I know that when, as a young person, I first encountered lists of prohibitions, whether in the Torah or other Jewish texts, I immediately assumed that the behaviors in question were forbidden to Jews and rarely found in Jewish communities. It took some years before I realized that it is unnecessary to condemn practices that no one ever considered within the realm of possibility. When we encounter anti-abortion rhetoric in our own time, for example, we know that its fierceness is connected to the fact that 25% of American women will have had an abortion by age

45. Similarly, numerous sources in this volume from across the centuries that condemn homosexual relations express alarm at the widespread nature of such practices. Philo (source 2) argues that while, in former days, pederasty was not even something that could be mentioned among Jews, in his time (the first century), such behavior had made its way into cities and was even boasted about. Yosef Karo, the sixteenth-century author of the important legal code, the *Shulhan Arukh*, says that while the Talmud teaches that Jews are not suspected of homosexual intercourse, in his own time, sexual licentiousness is widespread (source 38). A nineteenth century Ashkenazi rabbi is appalled by the prevalence of homoerotic activity in the Ottoman Empire (source 55). It is interesting how, like numerous other constructions of a past that never was, many of these sources look back to earlier times or distant places where sexual norms were respected. When we read them all in relation to each other, however, it is hard to see when and where such a time or place might ever have existed!

Negative sources are useful and instructive, but they cannot always be taken at face value, because accusations of sexual dissolution are a common trope used against those perceived as other. For this reason, we need to weigh specific allegations carefully, seeking to discern what else might be going on that triggers a particular accusation. A general condemnation of Jews in "Ishmaelite" lands—especially when contrasted with the purity of European Jews (source 55)—seems more suspect than those interesting instances where homosexual behavior figures into some legal case but appears to be willfully ignored by the rabbinic authorities. A responsum from a rabbi in late 13th century Catalonia (source 31) raises the question of whether two underage boys seen by a Gentile to be engaging in sexual play are liable for their misconduct. The rabbi's ruling focuses entirely on the question of their ages and the status of the Gentile's testimony without any mention of the sexual behavior or warning against it. Similarly, when a Sephardi rabbi in fifteenth century Spain considers whether it is acceptable to continue praying in a synagogue in which the caretaker engaged in sexual relations with a young man (source 35), he addresses only the issue of whether anything can sully the sanctity of a synagogue without ever mentioning the caretaker's offense. Such responsa make one wonder whether Sephardi culture was less anxious about possibility of homoerotic relations than some other parts of the Jewish world.

This supposition is supported by the extraordinarily vivid homoerotic poetry written by some of the major figures of Spanish Jewry. Yehudah Halevi, Shlomo Ibn Gevirol, Moshe Ibn Ezra (sources 20, 22, 25) and others composed poems celebrating the beauty and desirability of young men: the enchanting fawn or gazelle of love. Scholars have debated whether this poetry reflects actual infatuation and sexual experience or is an expression of literary convention, an imitation of Arabic poems on the same theme. Whatever the merits of each position, the willingness of prominent philosophers and poets to use such images certainly suggests a greater elasticity in the Jewish sexual ethos than is generally acknowledged. The fact that some Sephardic rabbis seemingly gave a pass to same-sex relations when accusations were brought before them underscores this point. At the same time, in our contemporary #MeToo moment, it is important to ask about the nature of the sexual relations envisioned in the poetry and involved in some of the court cases as well. What they often celebrate or describe is not consenting sex between equals but the pursuit of a reluctant boy by a much older man. It seems appropriate to make a distinction between evidence for the *existence* of homoerotic relations and the nature and quality of such relations in different contexts. What hierarchies are assumed by different texts, and in what ways do they or do they not provide models for contemporary LGBTQ relationships?

The notion of an often-unrecognized elasticity of Jewish norms applies to the issue of gender as well as sexual relations. Some of the earliest documents in the volume as well as the most recent express an interest in the possibility of gender fluidity that emerges in often-surprising ways. In addition to the well-known Mishnaic source on how the "androginos" is in some ways like women and in some ways like men (source 5), the collection contains a number of fascinating midrashim that play with the gender binary: Adam was an androginos (source 6); Mordekhai nursed Esther himself (source 7); Avraham and Sarah were of indeterminate sex (source 12); Dinah underwent a sex change in the womb (source 14). Whether these texts testify to some awareness among the rabbis of transgender or intersex persons or represent thought experiments ultimately meant to shore up a dimorphic gender grid, the ways they play with the idea of gender malleability provide a foundation for grappling with the challenge of dismantling the gender binary in our own time. Other sources in *A*

Rainbow Thread deal with actual cases of gender dysphoria (source 32), gender transition (sources 51, 73), or intersexuality (sources 68, 108) over the span of many centuries. A Syrian rabbi ruling in 1960 on whether to surgically intervene in the case of an intersex infant bases his response on the Mishnaic text concerning the androginos, simultaneously using an ancient Jewish text to resist modern medical treatment, shoring up a preference for males, and affirming the existence of people with both male and female characteristics (source 108).

I have mentioned just a few of the themes and questions that jumped out at me as I read through this rich collection. At the end of the book, Sienna offers a series of useful thematic links between sources, connecting entries by genre, identity, and geography, but each reader will undoubtedly find texts that are especially compelling to them. The fact that every selection is provided with an introduction and followed by excellent suggestions for further reading means that the book can provide the basis for courses and discussion groups in many different contexts. Mulling over the texts and doing the further readings would leave participants not just with a sense of the presence of queer Jews throughout Jewish history but a deeper understanding of Jewish history and cultures more generally.

This volume, then, offers readers many gifts. For starters, it should certainly silence anyone with the temerity to affirm that LGBTQ Jews do not exist. In fact, it would make a lovely present for anyone who expresses that antiquated conviction! For another thing, it should help LGBTQ Jews feel less alone. The anthology makes clear that we have forbears; we have a lineage. It provides evidence both of the lives of individual LGBTQ Jews, and the ways we have existed in the imagination of the community. Same sex love and gender fluidity, whether anathematized, tolerated, accepted, recognized or played with, were not beyond the boundaries of possibility. They were part of Jewish awareness in many time periods and cultures. But perhaps the most important contribution of *A Rainbow Thread* is this: it greatly enriches our understanding of Jewish history and the complexity and diversity of Jewish communities through the ages. It turns out that not only did we go out of Egypt a mixed multitude, but we have always been a mixed multitude—one that incorporates LGBTQ Jews.

Acknowledgments

I am honored by the scholars, activists, and mentors who offered their assistance with this project, often within the context of their own inspiring work on LGBTQ Jewish history; this book is much stronger for their support. Mara Benjamin and Miryam Kabakov, S. Bear Bergman, Gregg Drinkwater, Shlomo Gleibman, Jill Hammer, Jonathan Ned Katz, Jay Michaelson, and Zohar Weiman-Kelman all showed great enthusiasm for the project from its early stages, and generously provided many helpful suggestions and comments. I also am deeply grateful to the readers who carefully read partial or entire drafts of this anthology and offered their thoughtful feedback: Golan Moskowitz, Miriam-Simma Walfish, Micha'el Rosenberg, and Marc Michael Epstein.

I could not have compiled this anthology without the expertise of many scholars working on the particular topics, figures, places, and periods covered in this anthology. Beyond their published scholarship, I also benefitted greatly from the personal input of many researchers: they suggested texts and characters to include, clarified historical context and biographical data, provided helpful and supportive feedback, shared material from their own archival research, and corrected my many mistakes and misconceptions. Of course, I take responsibility for whatever errors remain. In alphabetical order, I gratefully acknowledge: Yaron Ben-Naeh, Diana L. Burgin, Hinde Burstin, David Caron, Leslie Choquette, Paris Papamichos Chronakis, Julia Philips Cohen, Jonathan Decter, Noach Dzmura, Marc Michael Epstein, Timothy Gilfoyle, Geraldine Gudefin, Shaun Halper, Dan Healey, Heather Hermant, Rainer Herrn, Warren Hoffman, Ofri Ilany, Sarah Imhoff, Barbara Kahn, Yoel Kahn, Adrian Kane, Venetia Kantsa, Clive Kennard, Gerard Koskovich, Eyal Levinson, Laurie Marhoefer, Klaus Mueller, Serena Di Nepi, Ofer Nur, Joshua Picard, Eddy Portnoy, Iris Rachamimov, Ben Ratskoff, Régis Revenin, Bryan Roby, Houman Sarshar, Naomi Seidman, Randall Sell, Karen Sendziak, Abby Stein, Timothy Stewart-Winter, Max Strassfeld, Jennifer Terry, Anna Elana Torres, Tony Trigilio, Ri Turner, Nick Underwood, Sherry Velasco, Mark Wagner, and C Todd White.

My thanks go out to the translators who carefully rendered many of these texts into beautiful English; their names are individually and gratefully acknowledged under each source they translated. I must also thank the librarians and archivists who cheerfully helped retrieve and provide access to a number of sources, including some which were quite obscure. First and foremost, I am very grateful to the wonderful staff at the University of Minnesota Libraries, and particularly its Interlibrary Loan Department, who handled many complicated requests with aplomb. In addition, I thank: Gloria López at the Reference Department of the Arxiu de la Corona d'Aragó / Archivo de la Corona de Aragón, Klaus Mueller and the United States Holocaust Memorial Museum, Zmira Reuveni at the National Library of Israel, Lesley Martin at the Chicago History Museum, Elisa Ho at the American Jewish Archives, Wil Brant at the Gerber/Hart Library, Elizabeth Hyman at the American Jewish Historical Society, Julie Herrada at the Labadie Collection of the University of Michigan, Jacqueline McCoy at the Cook County Clerk Bureau of Vital Records, Alison Darby at the Sheffield City Archives, and June Can at the Beinecke Rare Book & Manuscript Library.

I am especially grateful for the support of Lisa Vecoli, curator emerita of the Jean-Nickolaus Tretter Collection in Gay, Lesbian, Bisexual and Transgender Studies at the University of Minnesota, who not only provided considerable research assistance but also generously shared her own expertise in queer history, and made the Tretter Collection a true home base for my project. She enthusiastically supported this project from the beginning, and I am thrilled and humbled that I am able to begin repaying the favor by expanding the Tretter Collection to include my own research materials. Her successor, curator Rachel Mattson, came into the project at a late stage, but also showed considerable enthusiasm and support.

The writing of this book was supported at a crucial moment by a research award from the Hadassah-Brandeis Institute, and it is an honor to join the outstanding cohort of projects on Jews and gender that they have supported. I also must thank the members of the Workshop on the Comparative History of Women, Gender, and Sexuality in the History department of the University of Minnesota, who read a draft of my introduction with care and rigour, and in particular, Ai Miller for hir generous and helpful feedback. My other colleagues in the History department have all contributed to the supportive environment that has made my time there so enjoyable. I am also very grateful that my advisor patiently accepted this project without questioning how it would affect my dissertation progress.

I was less than a year old when Judith Plaskow published her foundational book *Standing Again at Sinai*; in some sense, then, I have always lived in the world that she has fought for and that she has continued to build. This project could not have come into existence without her work, and so when she agreed to write a foreword to this book, I was deeply honored. Her opening words provide the foundation for all that follows.

I assembled the first iteration of this material for a course at the National Havurah Committee Summer Institute of 2017, and the enthusiasm, passionate questions, and thoughtful insights of my students in that course convinced me that this was an important project. I also tried out presenting different combinations of this material at a number of educational settings in the Twin Cities, including Engage: A Night of Jewish Learning, Telling Queer History at the Hennepin County Library, Mount Zion's Teen Sicha group, the Beth Jacob Shavu'ot Tiqqun, and Mayim Rabim Congregation. I am grateful to all the participants for sharing their thoughts and feedback.

When David Zvi Kalman first approached me to ask about turning my Havurah course into a book, I was nervous, but confident that it would be in the right hands. I chose to publish this book with Print-O-Craft because I believe in their mission of producing original, beautiful, thoughtful, and challenging Jewish books. Working with David Zvi and Print-O-Craft was everything I had hoped for and more. I remain astounded at his ability to engage with content, manage logistics, think creatively, and track down copyright holders without breaking a sweat. His attitude of responding to self-defeating criticisms like "Surely we can't do that" by asking "why not?" continues to inspire me.

Perhaps more than anyone else, my family made this book possible. My siblings, Yonah and Micah, have not only supported me unconditionally but also challenged me, each in their own way, to make this book the clearest and most useful that it could be. The influence of my parents, Baruch and Elyse, is evident on every page of this anthology: my father's love of Jewish history and text, and his careful eye for detail; my mother's passion for inclusive Jewish education, and her insistence that the way forward into a radical, rooted, and intellectually honest Judaism is not to *rewrite* history but to *reread* it. I am so grateful that their loving support for the complexities of my own identity, and their continuing openness to learning more, has accompanied me from my earliest memories.

And finally—as we sing in the Shabbat hymn Lekha Dodi, *sof ma'aseh bamaḥshavah teḥilah*, "although done last, it is thought of first"—this book could not have come into being without the love of Aaron Hodge Greenberg Silver. He is my true *ḥaver*, partner and friend, in the sense defined by Avot deRabbi Natan: one with whom I can eat, drink, and sleep, with whom I can read and study, and with whom I can share all the deepest secrets of my self and my world.

To all those who did not live to see this book: I hope it does honor to your memory. To all those who find themselves in these pages: may it bring you courage to continue living, loving, and fighting for a better future. And to all those who will come after: may the violence and fear present in these stories belong only to the very distant past.

Noam Sienna
Minneapolis, MN

"When I read the Torah, I feel as if I am standing in both the past and the present, and I am keenly aware that I am also part of the future. This book has been the record of my tribe, my clan, my people's way of trying to speak to and about the Divine, for thousands of years. It is mine, more than Shakespeare or fifteenth-century French poetry or any great literature is truly mine. It is my family's spiritual diary, even if I do not like all the entries…[My project] is not about rewriting the Torah. It is about rereading it." Rabbi Elyse Goldstein, ReVisions: Seeing Torah Through a Feminist Lens (1998)

Introduction

This book is an anthology of historical sources relating to queer Jewish history, from the ancient world until 1969. The sources in this book come from all over the world, from almost every region in which Jews have ever lived: the Levant; the Iberian Peninsula; North Africa; Central and South Asia; Western, Central, and Eastern Europe; and the Americas. They were written in more than a dozen languages, including those unique to the Jewish world, like Hebrew, Aramaic, Judezmo, Yiddish, and Judeo-Arabic, along with Greek, Latin, Arabic, Persian, German, Dutch, French, Italian, Russian, English, and more. They belong to diverse bodies and identities: men, women, and people of non-binary gender; cisgender, transgender, and intersex folk; learned rabbis and secular poets, academics and artisans. Over a wide variety of genres—poetry, law, literature, drama, exegesis, journalism, memoir, science, philosophy—they reveal to us a thread woven through countless layers of Jewish history: from the study houses of ancient Babylonia to the gardens of medieval Iberia, the ports of the Ottoman Empire, the cabarets of Weimar Berlin, and the Yiddish tenements of the Lower East Side. While a few of the documents included in this book are well-known, a great number of others have lain long forgotten. Many of the sources in this book are appearing here in English for the very first time.

The significance of this book resides in its recovery of a lineage which has been denied and withheld from the people who have sought it. History is important for everyone, but it takes on a special importance when evidence of one's very existence has been manipulated and censored, forgotten, buried, and destroyed. This is particularly true for queer Jews and others with doubly- and multiply-marginalized identities who so often must fight for recognition and legitimacy on many fronts, both inside and outside the various communities to which they belong. Unfortunately, these efforts at erasure are frequently successful. Even today, queer Jewish individuals can feel like they are the first and only of their kind. One way to fight this feeling is by building horizontal connections across space through activism and education—to find companions and comrades, and to help individuals and communities know that they are not alone. This book offers another resource, by creating connections across time: to feel connected to a legacy, to a history, and to both a past and a future.

At the outset, I would like to note that this book is not a guide to Jewish law; it may not solve Jewish legal and ritual issues relating to queer people and their relationships to their Jewish communities and institutions. I cannot promise that it will "cure" your homophobic/transphobic rabbi, teacher, boss, or grandparent. It is also not an attempt to show that Judaism "really" promotes queer inclusion, or to argue that central Jewish texts might be interpreted to that end. Nor it is a listing of "Famous Gays in Jewish History," and it does not prove that this or that historical figure was actually lesbian or trans—an anachronistic attempt to say "Look! There were [insert-identity-here] Jews in the past!" Instead, this book is intended to do something both deeper and more expansively imaginative. The purpose of this book is to push the reader to re-think what queer Judaism could be, and to encourage them to take a second look at what they assumed they knew about how Jews thought and talked about sexuality and gender over our long history as a people.

An honest engagement with the primary materials of history means allowing what we find to challenge and surprise us. History is not a linear progression or an uninterrupted march towards some universal goal, but a messy, contingent, and complex network of processes, connections, interruptions, and innovations. Encountering primary sources is not always easy: their perspectives can seem incomplete or misguided to us, and their choices about what to tell, and what to leave untold, can be frustrating. Certainly, many of the texts in this book may be painful or uncomfortable to read: the prevalence of un-challenged homophobia and transphobia; the use of sacred texts and spiritual traditions to encourage hatred, fear, and violence towards queer people; the absence of ethical guidelines around age, power, vulnerability, and consent in sexual relationships; the casual disposability of queer bodies and lives.

Other texts might be surprisingly productive: the midrashim that imagine our biblical ancestors with a variety of changing and fluid bodies, for example, might help us imagine new ways to celebrate trans and non-binary identities in Jewish communities today (see sources 6, 7, 12, and 14). The homoerotic poetry of medieval Andalusi rabbis might challenge us to rethink how (and why) male-male desire is intertwined with the central language of Jewish spirituality, (see sources 18–20 and 22–25). The lesbian poetry of Emma Lazarus is an important reminder of how even well-known historical figures have facets of their lives which may be buried or obscured, intentionally or not (see source 61). Queer Jewish identity is so often imagined as existing in spite of—or in opposition to—the world of Jewish text and tradition. Every entry in this book invites us into the process of constantly rereading, reimagining, and revising our understanding of Jewish history.

History as a Field of Possibility

By presenting original primary sources, and allowing readers to engage directly with historical texts, this book challenges us to create a new future through a purposeful reflection on our past. In collecting these texts I have been inspired by scholars like the medievalist Caroline Dinshaw, who has argued that marginalized communities today can link themselves with the past through "shared contemporaneity," which involves imagining ourselves and our ancestors as participating in the same project, across time and space. Drawing on Dinshaw's argument, José Esteban Muñoz suggested in his book *Cruising Utopia: The Then and There of Queer Futurity* (2009) that "queerness exists for us as an ideality that can be distilled from the past and used to imagine a future…Queerness is a structuring and educated mode of desiring that allows us to see and feel beyond the quagmire of the present…[It is] a temporal arrangement in which the past is a field of possibility in which subjects can act in the present in the service of a new futurity." Muñoz is proposing a model of history that focuses not on linearity (where a single original event leads inevitably to its contemporary conclusion) but on multiplicity, on discontinuity, and on simultaneity. This is a history filled with surprises and reversals, with paradoxes and unknowns. Above all, this is a history which is unapologetically entangled with the ongoing negotiations of all of us who are fighting for a better world in the present. This book attempts to facilitate that process, distilling moments from the past that might spark the imagining of other possibilities.

The circular relationship to history that Dinshaw and Muñoz propose, which constantly returns to the past as a "field of possibility" to reshape a new future, is not only characteristic of how queer communities might relate to time (what Muñoz terms "queer futurity"), but also seems deeply Jewish. Many thinkers have suggested that Jewish history, too, can be understood as a non-linear, constantly recurring field of possibility, a sentiment articulated perhaps most famously by Yosef Hayim Yerushalmi. In his book *Zakhor: Jewish History and Jewish Memory* (1982), Yerushalmi proposed that the Jewish world has always structured its own history through a cyclical and mythic imagination pointed towards redemption. He writes: "Those Jews who are still within the enchanted circle of tradition, or those who have returned to it, find the work of the historian irrelevant. They seek, not the historicity of the past, but its eternal contemporaneity." By the "historicity of the past," Yerushalmi refers to the conception of any historical moment as particular and relevant only to its own concrete occurrence; instead, Yerushalmi argues that the "enchanted circle" of Jewish tradition honors the emotional connections that link people and communities across time. All of these frameworks—Yerushalmi's "eternal contemporaneity," Dinshaw's "shared contemporaneity," Muñoz' "field of possibility"—suggest that queer Jewish history must be constructed through an intertwining of past, present, and future.

In an essay in Gregg Drinkwater's pioneering anthology *Torah Queeries* (2009), Jill Hammer connects the same process that Muñoz sees as central to queer identity with the biblical metaphor of recovering Joseph's bones from Egypt before the Exodus, writing: "We must search for the bones of our queer ancestors wherever they are hidden. We cannot leave Egypt without them, for when memories are lost or blotted out, a part of the tribal truth is obscured… The bones of our queer Jewish ancestors lie waiting to be found." We return to the past, we excavate it, and we reassemble it, not only because it has been buried for centuries, but because our own future liberation depends on it. I hope that the stories contained in this book will burst out of its pages to inspire other books and articles, college courses, classroom activities, camp programs, academic lectures, young adult novels, films, paintings, poems, comics, sermons, and whatever else serves the creation of a vibrant queer Jewish future.

What Are "Queer Jewish Texts?"

The sources in this book fall into two categories. Many sources relate to intimate relationships, whether erotic or emotional, between people of the same sex or gender. Other sources are concerned with gender itself: with gender transition, with movement between genders, and with non-binary bodies and identities that do not fit easily into any gender category. The boundary between these two categories is often blurry; for example, the Hellenistic Jewish philosopher Philo of Alexandria speaks of *androgynoi*, or "womanish-men," as men who submit themselves sexually to other men, but he also describes their desire to "imitate" women, and records how some of them modified their bodies to become closer to women (see source 2). This text speaks to Hellenistic ideas about both sexuality and gender; as such, neither "gay man," nor "trans woman"—both modern designations—fully captures the original social setting of this text. Similarly, the gender-bending life of Ben Rosenstein defies our analytic categories (see source 73). Did a young Jewish girl decide to live as a man so that she could live with another woman, akin to what might be seen today as a butch lesbian identity? Was it because he saw himself as a man, akin to what might be seen today as a trans-masculine identity? Because it was the only way they could see a life worth living? Or some combination of all of these? The text does not answer any of these questions, but only confronts us with their life, challenging us: "Understand me on my own terms!"

We must balance between recognizing the shared dimensions of history, on the one hand, and on the other hand allowing space for a diversity of individuals and identities without erasure or homogenization. The life of Ber-el-Beyle (see source 96) might be claimed simultaneously by intersex people, celebrating how he carved out a space to live in his own body; by trans folk, focusing on his movement between genders and its social and political context; and by lesbians, highlighting the continuity of his romantic and erotic relationships with women before and after transition. As Rachel Hope Cleves has written regarding the practice of trans history, this method of holding onto multiple meanings simultaneously "offers a tool not for imposing new stabilities but for fracturing what we think we know about the past." Overlapping resonances do not collapse into a single history, but rather support each other in their infinite variety.

It is essential, above all, to emphasize that the people in this book cannot be assigned a definitive label, and we cannot assume anything about how they saw or would have seen themselves, beyond what is preserved in their writings, and even then we often cannot say whether their writings were meant to correspond to their own lived experience. This project can only excavate fragments of the past which can speak to queer Jews today, fragments which can provide them with a sense of lineage within the Jewish tradition. This is a delicate position to balance in. It is irresponsible to project our identities and understandings onto people in the past; at the same time, it is also irresponsible to ignore the shared practices, behaviors, and experiences that link these stories to other places and times, and that offer clear resonances to our lives today.

Just as the queerness of these texts is complicated, the Jewishness of these sources cannot be pinned down to a single criterion. The Jewishness expressed here is neither homogenous, stable, nor necessarily congruous with our own understandings of Judaism today. This messiness is a reflection of Judaism's own unruly status as a conglomeration of a diasporic people connected through constellations of religion, ethnicity, family, and culture. As a result, this book includes not just "canonical" Jewish sources—Talmudic texts, rabbinic responsa, compendia of halakhah, and the like—but also many literary and documentary sources, including those written in vernacular Jewish languages like Yiddish, Judezmo, Judeo-Arabic and others, which might have only tangential connections to religious practice but which offer a critically-important and often-neglected window into the lived experience of Jewish history.

Furthermore, other sources in this book are connected to Jewish history, even though they might make no reference to Judaism at all, through the author's own biographical and social context: the work of activists like Magnus Hirschfeld, Pearl Hart, and Frank Kameny all draw at least in part from their Jewish heritage, even if that was not made explicit in their writing (see sources 72, 106, and 112). In other texts, like the memoir of Karl M. Baer, the Jewishness of the author may even have been consciously hidden or obscured (see source 68). Nor is this anthology limited to texts from Jewish authors: other sources are included because they discuss Jews or Jewishness, even if their authors or original contexts are from outside the Jewish community. In some instances, only a single sentence or word allows us to connect these texts to Jewish history; for example, we might have had no way of knowing if Jews were involved in early American ball culture had Myles Vollmer not observed that there was "a prevalence of Jews" at the drag ball he attended in Chicago in the 1930s (see source 90).

Several sources also testify to interconnections and conversations across faiths and religious traditions, and at times even movement between them. The medieval Spanish poet Ibn al-Zaqqaq, a Muslim, writes of his love for a Jewish youth (see source 23), while a Sephardi woman was arrested for practicing "Sapphic love" with a Greek Orthodox woman in Salonica (see source 89). The Portuguese ex-converso Rodrigo de Castro was raised in a Christian environment, but returned to open Jewish practice in Hamburg, where he published his study of female sexuality in 1603 (see source 43). Marc-André Raffalovich converted to Christianity the same year he published his book *Uranisme et unisexualité*, and spent the rest of his life in a celibate relationship with his partner, the Catholic convert and priest John Gray (see source 64). We also have glimpses into the lives of figures who lived within multiple traditions simultaneously, like Sarmad Kashani (see source 46) and Esther Brandeau / Jacques La Fargue (see source 51). These are lives which defy categories, demonstrating the futility of capturing the complexity of identities under a single religious label. Honoring the complexities of identity, all the sources in this book are tied to the same protean and unfolding story of Jewish peoplehood.

One central goal of this book is to widen the range of sources that constitute "Jewish history." Starting in the early 1970s, a generation of Jewish feminist writers and theologians (including Rachel Adler, Blu Greenberg, Susannah Heschel, Paula Hyman, Judith Plaskow, and my mother, Elyse Goldstein) argued that relying solely on the extant halakhic tradition, which was created by men and centered around the patriarchal structure that benefitted them, was insufficient to create a Judaism in which people of all genders could be full members. Instead, it became necessary to recover other sources of Jewish knowledge, as Rachel Adler wrote: "the abundance of women's feelings and experiences which have been non-data within the tradition and which Jewish women are only now beginning to recognize and name." The work of writers and thinkers such as these has deepened our understanding of Judaism by recovering these experiences which formed, in Judith Plaskow's phrase, "another world around and underneath the textual tradition." So too, queer Jews have begun to envision themselves as part of a more complex and diverse Judaism, expressed not only in the dry legalities of "thou shalt not," but in areas which were often considered "non-data" for writing Jewish history: poetry and literature, journalism and drama, art and science and music, and all the feelings and experiences which have until now have left little record.

To illustrate why this book is needed, we might consider a responsum written in 1969, the year in which the Stonewall Riots brought a new visibility and urgency to the battle for civil rights for queer people in the United States. In that same year, the noted Reform rabbi Solomon Freehof received a question from a synagogue in Florida (see source 119): "A group in the Temple is planning a discussion program on the question of homosexuality. What is there in Jewish law on this subject?" Freehof responded curtly that "one can say in general that it is remarkable how little place the whole question occupies in Jewish law…The very paucity of biblical and post-biblical law on the matter speaks well for the normalcy and the purity of the Jewish people." In other words, looking only at one particular thread of textual history within the Jewish tradition, Freehof could see no presence of the people he considered "abnormal" and "impure," and therefore denied them any place in the history of the Jewish people. Scholars and activists in the last decades have done much to correct this misconception, but there are still very few collections of Jewish texts easily available in English to a scholar, teacher, rabbi, student, camper, parent, or curious member of the public who might be looking for a connection to queer Jewish history. What is the place of queer people in Jewish history? This book opens the door to imagining a new answer to that question.

What Is Not Here

For every story which has survived to be considered for inclusion in this book, there are hundreds more which did not; we can only guess at that which was never recorded, or which was recorded but lost, through the passage of time or an intentional effort to forget. There is more material in this book from the nineteenth and twentieth centuries than from the previous eighteen centuries combined. The sources which have survived to be included in this book demonstrate that the paucity of records relating to alternative expressions of gender and sexuality is grounded in centuries of erasure and oppression. Even the sources which do survive are often fragmentary, raising more questions than answers. We could wonder, for example: where did Esther Brandeau / Jacques La Fargue go after returning to France (see source 51)? What was in Eve Adams' lost book *Lesbian Love*, confiscated by police in 1926 (see source 82)? Who was the Jewish-American homosexual college student identified as "Tim" in the 1960 *Sex Histories of American College Men* (see source 107)—and did he ever achieve his dream of creating a family, and finding "a happier tomorrow?" There remains much work to do in finding, identifying, recording, connecting, and translating more primary sources for queer Jewish history.

While this anthology was designed to be as comprehensive as possible, a few texts have been excluded for practical reasons. Most conspicuously, I have left out biblical texts, which have been fruitfully explored by many other scholars, and which can be easily accessed in previously published books and articles (see the Bibliography for some recommendations). I have also excluded some rabbinic responsa which simply compile and repeat the prohibitions of earlier centuries. Some texts which explicitly discuss male rape or the sexual abuse of children have also been excluded. This is not to deny the truth of these accounts, but because I consider these behaviors an issue of power, and not a normative or essential component of any sexuality or identity. Other sources were excluded because of their extreme brevity, or their similarity to other sources already present. Finally—and perhaps most glaringly—the nature of this project highlights only textual production: the exploration of the rich queer Jewish identities embodied in music and the visual arts (like the work of Claude Cahun, Gluck, Frances Faye, Aaron Copland, Salim Halali, Max Feldman, Maurice Sendak, and many others), and of the lives of those who devoted themselves to community service and activism without leaving an extensive textual record (like Lillian Wald, Rose Schneiderman, Pauline Newman, Gerry Faier, Bob Basker, Brenda Howard, and many others) must await another study.

The timeframe of this book ends in 1969, the year of the Stonewall Riots. In many ways, Stonewall was neither a beginning nor an ending, especially for queer communities outside the United States. Nonetheless, 1969 was a clear turning point for both Jewish and non-Jewish queer discourse; conversations which had already begun in the 1950s and 1960s exploded with a new energy and visibility in the 1970s. By choosing 1969 as our ending point, this volume leaves out all the transformations in Jewish queer life in the last five decades, including the emergence of queer synagogues and the ordination of queer clergy; the HIV/AIDS crisis and the Jewish responses to it; the debates around same-sex marriage in Jewish and secular contexts; the creation of new rituals for transition, coming out, partnership, mourning, and other significant moments for queer Jews; and the treatment of queer issues in Jewish schools and summer camps. These topics all deserve their own historical accounting, and some of this work has already begun to appear. Similarly, I have also not included material from the large body of oral histories, memoirs, and other reflections on queer Jewish life, which might relate to the timeframe of this book, but which were produced after 1969 (although I did benefit greatly from their insights; see the Bibliography).

Translations, Transliterations, and Terminologies

One of the central issues in queer history is deciding what words to use. As many scholars have demonstrated, words like "homosexual" and "heterosexual," as well as the concepts they describe, have a very recent vintage. This is not to say that people in the past were not able to distinguish between types of sexual activity; of course they were. However, what becomes clear from the textual record is that for much of history, the most important hierarchy for classifying sexual activity was not the binary opposition of the participants' genders ("homosexual" vs. "heterosexual"), but other categories, like licit vs. illicit, natural vs. unnatural, or productive vs. hedonistic. For Hellenistic writers like Philo and Pseudo-Phocylides, non-generative sexual activity with infertile women is just as disruptive to the natural order (*physis*) of gender relations as sex between men or between women (see sources 2 and 3). When Hayyim Vital records the sexual transgressions of the Jews of Damascus in the early seventeenth century, he lists sodomy, adultery, incest, and sexual relations with Gentiles; there is no suggestion that homosexual behavior occupies any independent or coherent category, separate from a category of "heterosexuality" (see source 44). Furthermore, as I noted above, most of the sources in this book do not acknowledge the distinctions we now recognize between physiological and hormonal characteristics ("sex"), behaviors and identities ("gender"), and desires and practices ("orientation"). People who transgressed gender boundaries were understood to also have deviant sexual practices and deviant bodies, and vice versa.

To label anyone in the past who had sex with (or expressed erotic desires for) someone of the same sex as homosexual, lesbian, bisexual, queer, or any other modern label, or similarly to use transgender or genderqueer to speak of people who lived (or wished to live) in a gender different than their birth assignment, is not only anachronistic; it actually prevents us from seeing precisely how people in this different place and time thought about sexuality and gender. In some cases, we do have moments within the primary sources themselves that might seem at first glance to correspond to categories we recognize—see, for example, Philo's *androgynoi* (see source 2), or Rodrigo de Castro's *tribades* and *fricatrices* (see source 43)—although with a closer look these resemblances dissolve. Is de Castro's *tribade* a lesbian? In the sense of a person identified as a woman who engages in sexual contact with another woman, perhaps. But de Castro's understanding of the source of that sexual desire, its relation to the tribade's identity, and the function of the term itself, are all different from what the word lesbian means today.

In other cases, the sources clearly reveal how differently from us their authors understood sexuality, gender, and the bonds of love and friendship—take, for example, Hayyim Vital's impregnating reincarnations (see source 40), Shlomo Ibn Gevirol's coy fawns (see source 20), or the havruta partners who sleep together and share with each other their deepest and most intimate secrets (see source 15). Even in modern visions of sexual orientation and gender identities, there are still many terms which may be unfamiliar: uranists, unisexuals, inverts, and temperamentals (see sources 64, 78, 82, and 104). In writing the prefaces for each entry, I have done my best to balance between respecting the historical and cultural context of each source and drawing links and thematic connections between different times, and between past and present.

With all this in mind, I have chosen—imperfect and uncomfortable as it might be—the term *queer* (a word that, although originating as a derogatory slur, was already used in the early 20th century as a community label; see source 98) to indicate the collective and overlapping communities of people who exist outside, beyond, across, and between normative boundaries of sexuality and gender. I recognize that some readers may reject this term, and that any attempt to find a single unifying word or descriptive category will always be ultimately unsatisfactory. Indeed, I myself have several concerns in using the word queer.

First, I hope to allow each source to speak from its own specificity, rather than suggest that all the stories in this book can be equated to a single experience or subsumed into a single label. Furthermore, too many projects of "queer history" have focused on the stories of gay, white, cisgender, men; my use of the term is accompanied by my commitment to ensuring that marginalized voices, particularly those of women, of trans folks, and of people of color, are not neglected or erased.

Second, I hope to ground this book in the material reality of lived experience, rather than the political abstractions of theory that the term "queer" might imply. This book is not about anyone who might be "queered" by their general resistance to social norms, but about people whose lives were affected in specific and concrete ways by their gendered bodies, their sexual and romantic activities, their emotional attachments, and their choices about how (and with whom) to move through the world.

My final concern stems from my belief that each of the stories in this book carry its own ideas about their identities and communities, whether there was language for them or not. There is a story told of the Ba'al Shem Tov, the eighteenth-century mystic and founder of the Hasidic movement: he was once leading the community in prayer on Yom Kippur, when an illiterate peasant boy joined them. Not knowing the prayers, the boy simply opened the prayer book and said, "Master of the Universe, here are all Your letters! May You rearrange them to say the right thing." This prayer, said the Ba'al Shem Tov, was so powerful that it lifted the whole community through the gates of repentance. I offer a single word here as an imperfect rendering of the myriad lives contained herein—I hope all of you will rearrange it to say the right thing for you.

This anthology contains sources originally written in sixteen languages over the course of two millennia, from almost every corner of the Jewish world. I have provided key terms from the original source language in square brackets; in certain instances, I retain the original term in the main text and give an English rendering in square brackets. Particular care has been taken when dealing with descriptions of sexual practice; for instance, I have translated the Hebrew *mishkav zakhar* (a phrase taken from the prohibition of Leviticus 18:22) and its variants as "homosexual activity" rather than "homosexuality," to emphasize a non-essentialist understanding of pre-modern sexuality—namely, that there is no unchanging essence of something called "homosexuality" that exists outside of cultural context. When dealing with non-Romanized languages (Hebrew, Arabic, Persian, etc.), my transliterations follow the scholarly conventions of the Library of Congress transliteration schema, with some exceptions for the sake of simplicity: e.g. samekh and sin are both transliterated "s," Hebrew quf and Arabic qaf are both transliterated "q," and most vowel diacritics are omitted. Biblically-derived names are generally given in their Hebrew forms (Ya'aqov and not Jacob, Shmu'el and not Samuel, etc.), except in the cases where we know a particular transliteration was used; similarly, some words in general English usage (kibbutz, mitzvah, Torah, etc.) are kept in their most common form. Throughout, I have endeavored to present a system that is consistent and understandable, but which nonetheless does not lull the reader into a false sense of familiarity; as anthropologists are fond of saying, the scholarly mission is "to make the strange familiar and the familiar strange." Encountering primary sources is, at its core, an encounter with a foreign past.

How to Read This Book

There are many ways to read this book. You are invited to read it in order, or not; to start at the end; to concentrate on one group of sources; to scour the index; to follow the notes from one text to another; to open the book to a random page.

The sources in this book are arranged chronologically (as much as is possible), divided into three main sections: *Premodern Voices* (First Century CE–1500 CE), *Early Modern Voices* (1500–1900), and *Modern Voices* (1900–1969). Within these sections, each entry is preceded by a brief introduction offering some background and historical context for the source, and followed by a citation acknowledging its provenance, and a short bibliography offering references for further reading (there is also a complete bibliography at the end of the book).

At the back of this book there is an appendix with lists of suggested combinations that create thematic links between sources from different periods. These tracks connect sources by genre, by identity, and by geography:

- Poetry
- Literature and Drama
- Halakhah (Jewish Law)
- Gender Fluidity and Transition (Trans, Intersex, and Non-Binary Identities)
- Women Loving Women
- Sephardi Lives (Jews of Iberia and its Diaspora)
- Mizraḥi Lives (Jews of the Arab and Persian Worlds)
- Ashkenazi Lives (Jews of Eastern Europe and its Diaspora)

These lists are aimed at assisting readers who wish to use this book in developing a text-based class session, writing a syllabus, or incorporating primary sources in a focused study. These lists are not comprehensive; I have included them in the hope that they open new possibilities for interconnections and creative recombinations. As David Stern has pointed out in his work on anthologies, the arrangement and juxtaposition of sources shapes the reader's experience of interpretation: placing the homoerotic Hebrew poetry of Mordechai Jiří Langer (see source 87) next to that of the medieval poet Shmu'el Hanagid (see source 19) would certainly yield a different effect than reading Langer next to the scientific sexology of his German contemporary Magnus Hirschfeld (see source 72).

An Unfolding Story

Is there anything that all these texts have in common? The overwhelming diversity of languages, cultures, time-periods, genres, and experiences presented in this book might seem overwhelming. At the same time, they are all moments in the larger unfolding story of the Jewish people—a story which is not yet over.

In *Cruising Utopia*, José Esteban Muñoz challenges his readers to use the past to imagine a future for queer people filled with hope: "Queerness is not yet here. Queerness is an ideality. Put another way, we are not yet queer. We may never touch queerness, but we can feel it as the warm illumination of a horizon imbued with potentiality." This sentiment might be anachronistically paralleled in one of the sources in this book, the mystical vision of the Victorian Anglo-Jewish painter Simeon Solomon (see source 58). After describing a world filled with light, where Solomon sees "many whom I knew by name, and who were dear to me," he has a transcendent experience of the Heart of Love, which whispers an ineffable secret to him. "Then all this wondrous vision was fulfilled," Solomon writes, "and again the words of the sage King, *Until the day break and the shadows flee away* (Song of Songs 2:17/4:6); came into my mind." The verse from Song of Songs quoted here speaks of hope, potential, and anticipation. In transforming the richness of Jewish text into support for his own vision of a world of light, of love, and of life just beyond "a horizon imbued with potentiality," Simeon Solomon modeled how to find one's place within the tradition. This book suggests that texts, and Jewish texts in particular, are not just obstacles to be overcome or avoided in the creation of queer Jewish life, but also potential resources waiting to be excavated.

In conclusion, this anthology could be seen not just as a book, but also, following the numerology of Jewish tradition, a life. This book contains 120 primary sources for the study of queer Jewish history: in the Jewish tradition, 120 is the number that symbolizes a full and vibrant life, drawing on the story of Moses, who lived to 120 and, "his eyesight was not dimmed, and his vigor had not left him" (Deuteronomy 34:7). It is traditional in many Jewish communities, upon hearing someone's age or mentioning a birthday, to wish them a good life "until 120." In this way, we could imagine that the 120 texts in this book together represent a full and vigorous queer Jewish life. This thought is especially poignant when one considers how many of the characters and figures in this book were denied that life: Jews who were rejected by their families and communities and who faced legal barriers and social discrimination; Jews for whom the vision of building a family while speaking their truth was unimaginable; Jews who were beaten and imprisoned and killed, by their own hand and by the hands of others, because their world had no place for them to live fully as themselves. Too often, media, art, and literature dealing with queer people focuses on death. This book has death in it, to be sure, and it is painful and tragic and raw—but this book is ultimately about life.

As a Jewish educator, a historian of Jewish culture, and a queer Jew, I myself have long felt the need to document the lives of queer Jews throughout history. Despite coming out as a queer Jew just after my bar mitzvah, in a welcoming family and community, I felt that my identity was still considered an innovation, a novelty; there was no sense that Jews 'like me' had existed for generations. Throughout my Jewish elementary, middle, and high school education, there was no discussion of queer Jews past or present, and no engagement with texts that could have presented possibilities for a Jewish identity beyond cisgender and heterosexual. When I first encountered examples of these texts a decade ago, I cycled through surprise, anger, excitement, sadness, and gratitude. Why had I never known this? Why hadn't this been taught as part of my Jewish heritage? Hearing the language of the Jewish tradition articulate emotions that were familiar to my innermost self filled a part of me I had barely known was empty. My initial goal in preparing this book was to create a resource for other teachers—but far more than expected, this book has ended up teaching me. It is far from the final word, and in so many ways it is only the beginning of the conversation.

Further Reading

Adler, Rachel. "I've Had Nothing Yet So I Can't Take More." *Moment Magazine* 8.8 (1983): 22–26.

Alpert, Rebecca. *Like Bread on the Seder Plate: Jewish Lesbians and the Transformation of Tradition* (Columbia University Press, 1997).

Beck, Evelyn Torton (ed.). *Nice Jewish Girls: A Lesbian Anthology* (Boston: Beacon Press, 1989).

Boswell, John. *Christianity, Social Tolerance, and Homosexuality: Gay People in Western Europe from the Beginning of the Christian Era to the Fourteenth Century* (University of Chicago Press, 1980).

Castle, Terry (ed.). *The Literature of Lesbianism: A Historical Anthology from Ariosto to Stonewall* (Columbia University Press, 2003).

Cleves, Rachel Hope. "Six Ways of Looking at a Trans Man?: The Life of Frank Shimer (1826–1901)." *Journal of the History of Sexuality* 27.1 (2018): 32–62.

Dinshaw, Carolyn, Lee Edelman, et al. "Theorizing Queer Temporalities: A Roundtable Discussion." *GLQ: A Journal of Lesbian and Gay Studies* 13.2–3 (2007): 177–195.

Dzmura, Noach. *Balancing on the Mechitza: Transgender in Jewish Community* (Berkeley: North Atlantic Books, 2010).

Faderman, Lillian (ed.). *Chloe Plus Olivia: An Anthology of Lesbian Literature from the Seventeenth Century to the Present* (New York: Viking, 1994).

Ferry, Anne. *Tradition and the Individual Poem: An Inquiry Into Anthologies* (Stanford University Press, 2001).

Greenberg, Steven. *Wrestling with God and Men: Homosexuality in the Jewish Tradition* (University of Wisconsin Press, 2004).

Kabakov, Miryam (ed.). *Keep Your Wives Away from Them: Orthodox Women, Unorthodox Desires: An Anthology* (Berkeley: North Atlantic Books, 2010).

Katz, Jonathan Ned. *Gay American History: Lesbians and Gay Men in the U.S.A.* (New York: Crowell, 1976).

Kaye/Kantrowitz, Melanie, and Irene Klepfisz (eds.). *The Tribe of Dina: A Jewish Women's Anthology* (Boston: Beacon Press, 1986).

Hammer, Jill. "Uncovering Joseph's Bones: Parashat Vayechi (Genesis 47:28–50:26)." *Torah Queeries: Weekly Commentaries on the Hebrew Bible* (ed. Gregg Drinkwater, Joshua Lesser, and David Shneer, New York University Press, 2009), 68–74.

Muñoz, José Esteban. *Cruising Utopia: The Then and There of Queer Futurity* (New York University Press, 2009).

Plaskow, Judith. *Standing Again at Sinai: Judaism from a Feminist Perspective* (New York: Harper & Row, 1990).

Rose, Andy and Christie Balka (eds.). *Twice Blessed: On Being Lesbian or Gay and Jewish* (Boston: Beacon Press, 1989).

Rubin, Gayle. "Geologies of Queer Studies: It's Déjà Vu All Over Again." In ibid., *Deviations: A Gayle Rubin Reader* (Duke University Press, 2012), 347–356.

Stern, David (ed.). *The Anthology in Jewish Literature* (Oxford University Press, 2004).

Weiman-Kelman, Zohar. *"So the Kids Won't Understand:" Inherited Futures of Jewish Women Writers* (Ph.D. thesis, UC Berkeley, 2012).

Yerushalmi, Yosef Hayim. *Zakhor: Jewish History and Jewish Memory* (University of Washington Press, 1982).

The Sources:
Premodern Voices
(First Century-1500 CE)

1. Sappho and the Torah, Compared by a Hellenistic Philosopher (Alexandria, First Century CE)

The Greek lyric poet Sappho (from the Isle of Lesbos, ca. sixth century BCE) was immensely popular in the ancient world, although only a very small portion of her poetry has survived today. Her love for women has inspired generations of writers, poets, and activists, and is the origin of the terms "lesbian" and "sapphic," which were already used to describe love between women in the early modern period (see sources 43, 81, 89, and 120). While Sappho was not Jewish, there is evidence that some Greek-speaking Jews read and appreciated the homoerotic poetry of Sappho alongside the Hebrew Bible and Greek classics like the epics of Homer: a single line of Sappho's is quoted in a papyrus fragment of an unknown work by the Jewish philosopher Philo of Alexandria (see source 2), found at Oxyrhynchus. Even more telling is the inclusion of a poem of Sappho's in an anonymous treatise, ascribed to a philosopher known only as Pseudo-Longinus. In fact, this poem (known as Fragment 31), which describes Sappho's turbulent emotions watching a man speak with the woman she loves, is preserved nowhere else outside of its citation in Pseudo-Longinus. The exact authorship of this work has been long debated, but most scholars believe that the author was a Greek-speaking Jew from Alexandria. His treatise, "On the Sublime" (*Peri Hypsos*), is a work of literary criticism, most likely dating from the first century CE, which discusses the significance of aesthetics in writing, and highlights examples of great and sublime literature. In this excerpt, he cites both Genesis (in a somewhat adapted form) and Sappho as an example of how literature can bring us to the sublime.

Now, the first of these conditions [of the sublime]—I am speaking of noble-mindedness—ranks highest among them all. In this case also, we must nurture our souls as much as is possible towards greatness in thought, and make them as if they were always pregnant with divine inspiration. But how, you may ask, can this be done? Elsewhere I have written as follows: "The sublime is the echo of a noble mind." This is why a bare idea, by itself and without being spoken, can still evoke wonder for the nobility of mind in itself...

In this way, the lawgiver of the Jews (no ordinary man), bringing forward a worthy expression of the power of the Divine, writes at the very beginning of the Law: "And God said—" What? Let there be light, and there was. [God said] Let there be land, and there was... (cf. Genesis 1:3 and 9)

Now, let us review whether there is anything else that can grant power to words of the sublime. In all things, there exist by nature certain materials which constitute them. Therefore, we necessarily must find one source of the sublime in the selection of the most appropriate of these materials, and the power of how they form in combination a single body. The former process attracts the listener by the substance of the ideas, and the latter by the combination of those elements. Sappho, for example, on every occasion captures the corresponding emotions of erotic passion from those which accompany it in actuality. Where does she demonstrate her excellence? In the skill with which she both selects and joins to one another the most striking, and the most powerful, of those [emotions]:

> to me he seems like the gods
> whoever sits opposite you
> and so close listens closely
> to your sweet voice
>
> and the lure of your laugh
> which rattles my heart in its chest
> since with one flash of a glance at you
> I cannot—no words
>
> like my tongue snapped
> a quick cunning flame runs subdermal
> eyes unseeing
> ears whirring
>
> sweat pours down me
> panic grabs me
> green as a meadow I feel
> I almost died
> (but all of it must be braved)

Are you not amazed at how she, all at once, seeks out soul, body, hearing, speech, sight, color, as if they were foreign to her or long dispersed; at how she is contradictorily warm and cold, unthinking and comprehending? For indeed she appears frightened and nearly dead; we observe in her not just a single emotion but a whole assemblage of emotions. All these things happen to people in love; but it is, as I have said, her selection of the most striking of them, and her combination of them, which brings to completion the poem's pre-eminence.

Pseudo-Longinus, *Peri Hypsos*, sections 9 and 10. Prose adapted by Noam Sienna from the translation of W. Hamilton Fyfe, *On The Sublime* (New York: Putnam and Sons, 1927). Sappho's poem translated from Greek by Yonah Lavery-Yisraeli. Copyright © 2019 Print-O-Craft Press.

Further Reading

Porter, James I. *The Sublime in Antiquity* (Cambridge University Press, 2014).

Rayor, Diane, and André Lardinois. *Sappho: A New Translation of the Complete Works* (Cambridge University Press, 2016).

Royce, James R. "The Oxyrhynchus Papyrus of Philo." *Bulletin of the American Society of Papyrologists* 17:3–4 (1980), 155–165.

2. Philo Condemns "Unnatural Pleasures" (Alexandria, First Century CE)

Philo of Alexandria, who lived in the Roman province of Egypt in the first century CE, was a philosopher and writer from a prominent local Jewish family. His allegorical and philosophical commentaries on the Torah, written in Greek, attempt to explain Jewish law and theology as consistent with Platonic and Stoic philosophical thought. In matters of sexuality, his views were quite severe: he held that the only acceptable purpose of marriage and sexual activity was procreation, and was disturbed by any transgression of gender boundaries. In these passages, we see his vociferous condemnation of male-male sexual contact as "unnatural pleasure," and his disapproval of the contemporary tolerance of such behavior. His concern about gender extends not only to the womanish-man (*androgynos*) who allows himself to be penetrated by other men (and whose gender is suspiciously feminine), but also to the mannish-woman (*gynandros*) who similarly transgresses gendered boundaries and takes an active sexual role. Looking past its violent tenor, it is possible to see in this text a testimony to the awareness of both male and female homosexual activity and gender play in Hellenistic Jewish circles.

I. On the Sacrifices of Cain and Abel

(100) And why should we consider it strange that the uncreated does not deign to use the good which belongs to the created, when even the created itself lays claim to virtues varying according to the different species into which it is divided? Men could not compete with women, nor women with men, regarding the functions which properly belong only to the other sex. But indeed, when those mannish-women [gynandrai] attempt the practices of men, or when those womanish-men [androgynoi] attempt those of women, they will in each case bring the penalty on themselves, and win an ill reputation thereby. And there are some virtues and excellences which nature has so ordained, that not even long practice could make them common property. To sow seed and beget belongs to the man and is his peculiar excellence, and no woman could attain to it. Similarly, welfare in child-bearing is a good thing belonging to women, but cannot be attained by a man's nature [physis].

II. On the Special Laws

(37) Much graver than what is mentioned above [regarding adultery] is another evil, which has ramped its way into the cities, namely the love of boys [paiderastein]. In former days the very mention of it was a great disgrace, but now it is a matter of boasting not only to those who practice it actively, but also to the passive partners [paskhousin], who accustom themselves to endure the disease of femininity, let both body and soul leak away, and leave no ember of their male nature to smolder. In this way, they conspicuously braid and adorn the hair of their heads, and they scrub and paint their faces with cosmetics and pigments and the like, and smother themselves with fragrant unguents. For of all such embellishments, used by all who deck themselves out to wear a comely appearance, fragrance is the most seductive. In fact, the transformation of the male nature to the female is practiced by them as an art and does not raise a blush.

(38) These persons are rightly judged worthy of death by those who obey the law, which ordains that the womanish-man [*androgynos*] who debases the sterling coin of nature should perish unavenged, and should not be permitted to live for a day or even an hour, as a disgrace to himself, his house, his native land and the whole human race.

(39) And the lover of boys himself may be assured that he is subject to the same penalty. He pursues an unnatural pleasure and does his best to render cities desolate and uninhabited by destroying the means of procreation. Furthermore, he sees no harm in becoming a tutor and instructor in the grievous vices of unmanliness [*anandrias*] and effeminacy [*malakias*] by prolonging the bloom of the young and emasculating the flower of their prime, which should rightly be trained to strength and robustness. Finally, like a bad farmer he lets the deep-soiled and fruitful fields lie sterile, by taking steps to keep them from bearing, while he spends his labor night and day on soil from which no growth at all can be expected.

(40) The reason is, I think, to be found in the prizes awarded in many nations to licentiousness and effeminacy. Certainly you may see these womanish-men continually strutting about through the thick of the market, heading the processions at the feasts, appointed to serve as unholy ministers of holy things, leading the mysteries and initiations and celebrating the rites of Demeter. Some of them—who heighten even farther their youthful beauty, desiring to be completely changed into women and going on to mutilate their own genitals—are clad in purple like the great nobles of their native lands, and march in front escorted by a bodyguard, attracting the attention of those who meet them.

(42) But if such indignation as our lawgiver felt was directed against those who do not shrink from such conduct, if they were cut off as public enemies without leniency, each of them a curse and a pollution of his country, many others would be found to take the warning. For relentless punishment of condemned criminals acts as a considerable check on those who are eager to practice the same.

Philo, *De Sacrificiis Abelis et Caini* and *De Specialibus Legibus*. Prose adapted by Noam Sienna from the translations of F. H. Colson and G. H. Whitaker, *Philo: Volume II* and *Volume VII* (Loeb Classical Library, Harvard University Press, 1929 and 1937).

Further Reading

Berkowitz, Beth. *Defining Jewish Difference: From Antiquity to the Present* (Cambridge University Press, 2012).

Brooten, Bernadette. *Love Between Women: Early Christian Responses to Female Homoeroticism* (University of Chicago Press, 1996).

Satlow, Michael. "'They Abused Him like a Woman': Homoeroticism, Gender Blurring, and the Rabbis in Late Antiquity." *Journal of the History of Sexuality*, 5:1 (1994), 1–25.

Szesnat, Holger. "Philo and Female Homoeroticism: Philo's use of γύνανδρος and recent work on 'tribades.'" *Journal for the Study of Judaism in the Persian, Hellenistic, and Roman Period*, 30:2 (1999), 140–147.

3. A Hellenistic Jewish Poet Describes the Sexual Prohibitions of Leviticus (Alexandria, First Century CE)

The *Sentences of Pseudo-Phocylides* is a Greek poetic text, ascribed to the classical philosopher Phocylides of Miletus (sixth century BCE) but actually written by an anonymous Jewish poet, a contemporary of Philo, who likely also lived in Alexandria. The poem attempts to summarize the precepts of Jewish life in the form of Hellenistic educational poetry, drawing mostly from the Torah, but occasionally also the Prophets and Writings. In this excerpt, the author gives his interpretation of the law on sexual activity from Leviticus 18:22, which states that "with a man you shall not lie as with a woman; it is an abomination." Like Philo (see source 2), Pseudo-Phocylides sees same-sex relations as an aberration of natural order (Greek *physis*) and a failure to properly control one's sexual appetite (*eros*). In a world where the essential axis of erotic relationships was not gender but power—between superior (male/penetrating/adult/free) and inferior (female/penetrated/youth/slave)—same-sex relations, whether between two men or two women, disrupted this hierarchy.

(175) Remain not unmarried, lest you perish nameless.
(176) And give something to nature yourself: beget in turn as you were begotten...
(190) Go not beyond natural sexual unions for illicit passion;
(191) unions between males are not pleasing even for beasts.

(192) Let not women mimic the sexual role of men at all.

(193) Be not inclined to utterly unrestrained lust for a woman.

(194) For Eros is no god, but a passion destructive of all.

Pseudo-Phocylides, lines 175–194, as translated in Walter T. Wilson, *The Sentences of Pseudo-Phocylides* (Berlin: De Gruyter, 2005).

Further Reading

Brooten, Bernadette. *Love Between Women: Early Christian Responses to Female Homoeroticism* (University of Chicago Press, 1996).

Satlow, Michael. "'They Abused Him like a Woman': Homoeroticism, Gender Blurring, and the Rabbis in Late Antiquity." *Journal of the History of Sexuality*, 5:1 (1994), 1–25.

Szesnat, Holger. "Philo and Female Homoeroticism: Philo's use of γύνανδρος and recent work on 'tribades.'" *Journal for the Study of Judaism in the Persian, Hellenistic, and Roman Period*, 30:2 (1999), 140–147.

4. A Roman Poet Condemns a Jew for Stealing his Lover (Rome, First Century CE)

Jewish writers like Philo confirm that Jews were well aware of Greco-Roman norms around sexuality, particularly regarding male-male intercourse (see sources 2 and 3). Non-Jewish sources also demonstrate that some Jewish men not only knew of, but participated in, sexual relationships with younger men (in Roman culture, as in Greek culture, age difference between partners was an important part of maintaining social honor; class difference was also crucial). This epigram by the Roman poet Martial (Marcus Valerius Martialis, ca. 40–104 CE) lambasts a Jewish acquaintance whom Martial accuses of two crimes: both plagiarizing and denigrating his poetry, and having sex with one of Martial's favorite boys (*puer*). Focusing on the Jew's circumcised penis, Martial repeatedly calls him *verpa*, which can mean both "circumcised" and "erect" (translated here as "cut-cock"). In Greco-Roman culture, the ideal penis was small and soft, with a long foreskin; an exposed glans and a large erection were considered obscene. The Jewish practice of circumcision was thus both a signifier of Jewish difference, and a mark of scorn. The references to Jerusalem and temples is probably connected to the destruction of the

Temple in Jerusalem some 25 years earlier. In referring to this tragedy, Martial is mocking his Jewish rival, who is unable to swear by his own temple, and reminding him of the temples to Jupiter that were funded by the Jewish tax. Anchialus, the final reference of the poem, is most likely the name of the boy that they were fighting over.

That you are too jealous of me, and always denigrate
    My little poetry books, I can forgive: you're smart enough, for a cut-
cock poet.
Nor do I even care that you pick through my poems
    and steal them: as I said, you're smart enough, for a cut-cock poet.
But what really tortures me is that you—born in Jerusalem itself—
    you bugger my boy, you cut-cock poet: my boy.
And now you deny it, and you swear to me by the temples of Thundering
Jove.
    Well, I don't believe you: swear, O cut one, by Anchialus.

Martial, *M. Valerii Martialis Epigrammaton libri* (ed. Wilhelm Heraeus, Leipzig: Bibliotheca Teubneriana, 1925), Book XI, epigram 94. Translated from Latin by Noam Sienna.

Further Reading

Berkowitz, Beth. *Defining Jewish Difference: From Antiquity to the Present* (Cambridge University Press, 2012).

Cohen, Shaye. *The Beginnings of Jewishness: Boundaries, Varieties, Uncertainties* (University of California Press, 1999).

Roux, Marie. "A Re-Interpretation of Martial, Epigram XI.94." *Scripta Classica Israelica* 36 (2017), 81–104.

Williams, Craig. *Roman Homosexuality*, 2nd edition (Oxford University Press, 2010).

5. The Androginos: A Rabbinic Discussion of Gender Boundaries (Land of Israel, Third Century CE)

The Mishnah is the earliest extant body of rabbinic law, composed in the Land of Israel in the first two centuries of the Common Era as an explanation of the commandments described in the Torah; it covers all areas of Jewish life, including festivals, temple rites, tort law, and agriculture, as well as sexuality and gender. Throughout rabbinic literature the word *androginos*, borrowed from the Greek (see source 2), is used to refer to a person of ambiguous sex. Their gender role was equally ambiguous, as described in this passage from the Mishnah, which attempts to define the legal status of the androginos in relation to the established categories of male and female. At times closer to one category, the other, neither, or both, this passage seems to anticipate modern ideas about the inherent fluid and constructed nature of gender. At the same time, by having the androginos' identity defined entirely in relation to the existing categories of "male" and "female," this text consistently indicates its desire to achieve clarity and fit the androginos into what Charlotte Fonrobert calls "the dual-sex grid holding rabbinic legal thinking in a tight grip." This framework notwithstanding, it is clear that the androginos is seen as a full member of the Jewish community, and in fact their community is involved in the ongoing definition of their gender. The text concludes by recording a minority opinion that the androginos in fact is an independent being of its own— *bri'a bifnei 'atsmah hu*. Like its subject, the history of this text is itself ambiguous; it is recorded differently in different manuscripts of the Mishnah, as well as in a parallel version in the Tosefta, a compilation of rabbinic legal material roughly contemporary with the Mishnah. This translation of the Mishnah's version, by Jewish transgender activist and writer Noach Dzmura, uses a variety of gendered and non-gendered pronouns to highlight the androginos' constantly shifting social position.

[Concerning the hermaphrodite:] There are in him manners equivalent to men, there are in her manners equivalent to women, there are in hir manners equivalent to men and women, and there are in zir manners equivalent to neither men nor women.

Manners equivalent in them to men: he conveys Levitical impurity in semen like men; he may marry but may not be married to a man, like men; like men he may not be alone with women; he may not be sustained with the daughters in matters of inheritance like men; he is obligated to all the mitsvot [commandments] proclaimed in the Torah, like men; he may not put on female clothing or cut [his hair as women do] like men; he may not make himself impure by corpses like men; he may not transgress [the prohibitions of] "you shall not round off [the corners of your hair], and you shall not mar [the corners of your beard]" (Leviticus 19:27) like men.

Manners equivalent in them to women: she may become Levitically impure with menstrual blood like women; she may not be alone with men like women; she may not contract a levitate marriage like women; like women she does not receive a portion [of the inheritance] with the sons; she may not share in the holiest things like women; she is unfit to give any testimony mandated in the Torah like women; if she had prohibited intercourse her sons are prohibited from qualifying for priesthood like women.

Manners equivalent in them to (both) men and women: s/he is obligated for damages incurred as though s/he were a man or a woman; the one who kills hir intentionally is put to death; if unintentionally the murderer receives asylum in the cities of refuge; hir mother will observe, on account of hir birth, the period of blood purification as if she had borne both a female and a male child, and brings an offering on account of the child as though both a male and female child had been born; s/he inherits all (if s/he is an only child) the inheritance like men and women; s/he eats holy things eaten outside of Jerusalem like men and women; if one said, "I am a Nazirite if this is both a man and a woman," then he is a Nazirite.

Manners equivalent in them to neither men nor women: they are not obligated on account of hir uncleanness; they do not burn (an offering) on account of hir uncleanness; zie cannot be subject to valuation like neither men nor women; zie cannot be sold as a Hebrew slave like neither men nor women; and if a person said, "I am a Nazirite if this is neither a man nor a woman," then he is a Nazirite.

Rabbi Yosi says, "Androgynos is a being created in zir own image and the sages could not decide whether he was a man or she was a woman, but *tumtum* [an indeterminate gender category] is judged either a doubtful man or a doubtful woman."

m. Bikkurim 4:1–5, as translated in "Intersexed Bodies in Mishnah: A Translation and an Activist's Reading of Mishnah Androgynos," by Noach Dzmura, from *Balancing on the Mechitza: Transgender in Jewish Community* (North Atlantic Books, 2010), pp. 163–165.

Further Reading

Fonrobert, Charlotte Elisheva. "Regulating the Human Body: Rabbinic Legal Discourse and the Making of Jewish Gender." In *The Cambridge Companion to the Talmud and Rabbinic Literature* (ed. Charlotte Elisheva Fonrobert and Martin Jaffee), Cambridge University Press, 2007, 270–295.

Kukla, Elliot, and Reuben Zellman. "Created by the Hand of Heaven: Making Space for Intersex People." In *Balancing on the Mechitza: Transgender in Jewish Community* (ed. Noach Dzmura), Berkeley: North Atlantic Books, 2010, 182–187.

Lev, Sarra. "The Rabbinic Androginos as the 'Sometimes Jew': Investigating a Model of Jewishness." *Journal of Jewish Identities* 11:1 (2018), 75–85.

Strassfeld, Max. *Classically Queer: Eunuchs and Androgynes in Rabbinic Literature*. Ph.D. dissertation, Stanford University, 2013.

Strassfeld, Max. "Taxonomies of Sex and the Politics of Disambiguation: The *Androginos* in Tosefta Bikurim." *Gender & Jewish Life: Frankel Institute Annual 2014* (University of Michigan, 2014), 52–55.

6. What Was Adam's Sex? A Midrash (Land of Israel, Fifth Century CE)

In this commentary on the creation of the first human in Genesis 1:26, the midrash (rabbinic interpretations of sacred text) presents a number of different opinions regarding the nature of that first being. Connecting the verse in Genesis to another verse in Psalms, the rabbis suggest that the first human was an *androginos*, a doubly-sexed person (see source 5) who was split in two (in a manner recalling the explanation of Aristophanes in Plato's *Symposium*), or a *golem*, an unfinished and non-gendered being who filled the entire world. While this midrash is an imaginative commentary rather than a literal description of any particular community or circumstance, it is clear that the rabbis were comfortable with using gender fluidity and non-conformity to imagine our biblical ancestors (see also sources 7, 12, and 14). Furthermore, the opening verse that connects the creation of humanity to the divine image suggests that the unfolding of gender possibilities presented here reflects how the world and God are united by diversity and multiplicity rather than binary finality. The source of this text, *Bereshit Rabbah*, is one of the earliest collections of rabbinic narrative commentary (*midrash aggadah*), attributed to the third-century Rabbi Oshaya, and probably compiled between the third and fifth centuries CE.

And God said, 'Let us make adam *in our image and our likeness'* (Genesis *1:26*). Rabbi Yoḥanan began [the discussion with the verse] *'You formed me before and behind'* (Psalms 139:5)…

Rabbi Yirmiyah ben El'azar said, "At the moment when the Holy Blessed One created the first *adam*, God created them as an *androginos*, as it is written: '*male and female God created them*' (Genesis 1:27)."

Rabbi Shmu'el bar Naḥman said, "At the moment the Holy Blessed One created the first *adam*, God created them with two faces [and one body], and then God sawed them [apart] and made two backs for them—a back here and a back there." They challenged him: "But is it not written, '*and God took one of his ribs* [tselaʻ]' (Genesis 2:21)?" He answered them, "[here *tselaʻ* means] 'one of his sides,' just as it says elsewhere, '*and for the* tselaʻ *of the Tabernacle*' (Exodus 26:20), which is translated in the Targum as '*and for the side of the Tabernacle*.'"

Rabbi Tanḥuma in the name of Rabbi Benayyah, and Rabbi Berakhiah in the name of Rabbi El'azar, said: "[At the moment when the Holy Blessed One created the first *adam*] God created them as an unformed mass [*golem*] which stretched from one end of the earth until the other, as it is written: '*Your eyes saw my unformed mass* [golmi]' (Psalms 139)."

Rabbi Yehoshuaʻ bar Neḥemiah, and Rabbi Yehudah bar Simon in the name of Rabbi El'azar, said: "[At the moment when the Holy Blessed One created the first *adam*] God created them filling the whole world, from east to west. From where might we learn [that the *adam* filled the world from the east to the west]? As it says, '*You formed me in back and in front*' (Psalms 139:5). From where might we learn [that the *adam* filled the world] from the north to the south? As it says, '*From the edge of the heavens to the edge of the heavens*' (Deuteronomy 4:32). And from where might we learn [that the *adam* filled] the whole space of the world? As it says, '*You placed Your hand* [kapekha] *upon me*' (Psalms 139:5), just as it says elsewhere, '*Withdraw Your hand* [kapekha] *far from me*' (Job 13:21)."

Bereshit Rabbah (ed. Judah Theodor and Hanokh Albeck, Berlin: H. Itzkowski, 1912), parashat Bereshit, 8:1. Translated from Hebrew by Noam Sienna.

Further Reading

Aaron, David H. "Imagery of the Divine and the Human: On the Mythology of Genesis Rabbah 8 §1." *Journal of Jewish Thought and Philosophy* 5:1 (1996), 1–62.

Kessler, Gwynn. "Bodies in Motion: Preliminary Notes on Queer Theory and Rabbinic Literature." In *Mapping Gender in Ancient Religious Discourses* (eds. Todd C. Penner and Caroline Vander Stichele, Leiden: Brill, 2006), 389–430.

7. Mordekhai Nursed Esther Himself: A Midrash (Land of Israel, Fifth Century CE)

Like the passage from Bereshit Rabbah in source 6, where the rabbis present the first human as a multi-sexed being, this section of Bereshit Rabbah presents Mordekhai, a central figure of the Book of Esther, as transgressing (or surpassing) the standard restrictions of gendered bodies. Here, they expand on a teaching that attributes the qualities of "feeding and sustaining" to a number of biblical characters; Rabbi Yudan suggests that in Mordekhai's case, he literally nursed Esther himself (presumably drawing on Esther 2:7, "Mordekhai brought up [*va-yehi omen*] Hadassah, that is, Esther"). A teaching of Rabbi El'azar goes even further, emphasizing the unique physicality of Mordekhai's body that enabled him to nurse Esther. The midrash then records that when one rabbi taught this publicly, he was laughed at by his audience, but he defended his interpretation by referring to a halakhic statement made in the Mishnah to the effect that milk produced by a male (for whatever reason or by whatever process) is still kosher; thus, even seemingly-disruptive bodies and natures can still be made understandable by the rabbinic legal system. Indeed, an actual occurrence of male nursing appears elsewhere in the Talmud (*b. Shabbat* 53b).

The rabbis taught: every [biblical figure whom the text introduces] by saying, "he was," [*hayah*] was one who fed and sustained...Mordekhai [was one of those who] fed and sustained. Really?!* Indeed, Rabbi Yudan said, "One time, he went repeatedly to all the wet-nurses but could not find one for Esther at that moment, and so he nursed her himself." Rabbi Berakhiah and Rabbi Abbahu [said] in Rabbi El'azar's name, "Milk came to him and he would nurse her."

---

*The midrash is responding to its own statement.

When Rabbi Abbahu taught this in public, the congregation laughed at him. He said to them, "Is this not a teaching in the Mishnah? '*Rabbi Shim'on b. El'azar said, "The milk of a male is pure* [tahor]'" (*m. Makhshirin* 6:7)?"

Bereshit Rabbah (ed. Judah Theodor and Hanokh Albeck, Berlin: H. Itzkowski, 1912), parashat Noaḥ, 30:8. Translated from Hebrew by Noam Sienna.

Further Reading

Bregman, Marc. "Mordecai Breastfed Esther: Male Lactation in Midrash, Medicine, and Myth." In *The Faces of Torah: Studies in the Texts and Contexts of Ancient Judaism in Honor of Steven Fraade* (eds. Christine Hayes, Tzvi Novick, and Michal Bar-Asher Siegal, Berlin: V&R Academic, 2017), 257–274.

Kessler, Gwynn. "Bodies in Motion: Preliminary Notes on Queer Theory and Rabbinic Literature." In *Mapping Gender in Ancient Religious Discourses* (eds. Todd C. Penner and Caroline Vander Stichele, Leiden: Brill, 2006), 389–430.

8. Pharaoh Desired to Violate Their Men: A Midrash (Land of Israel, Fifth Century CE)

In this midrash, the rabbis expand on the triumphant Song of the Sea, sung by the Israelites after crossing the Red Sea, imagining how each boast of Pharaoh's was poetically reversed through divine judgment. Pharaoh's desires to pursue and overtake would instead lead to him being pursued and overtaken. The midrash emphasizes the phallic nature of Pharaoh's aggression, implying that the "unsheathing" of his sword expressed his desire to penetrate and rape Israelite men. Other midrashim attribute a similar lust for the penetration of men to other biblical villains, including Ishmael, Esau, and Potiphar. But through divine intervention, Pharaoh's fate was reversed: instead of satisfying his arrogance and humiliating others through sex, he himself would be humiliated and "abused" (sexually) by all the other nations. As scholars like Michael Satlow and Daniel Boyarin have shown, the rabbis saw the act of sexual penetration as an expression of dominance, and thus for a man to penetrate another man was an act of hubris and cruelty. They allow themselves, however, to imagine it as a punishment for Pharaoh, the ultimate symbol of human arrogance. The source of this text, the *Mekhilta deRabbi Yishma'el* (*The Treatise of Rabbi Ishmael*) is an early anthology of rabbinic legal commentary (*midrash halakhah*), on the book of Exodus, probably compiled between the third and fifth centuries CE.

"The foe said, 'I will pursue,' [*I will overtake, I will divide the spoil; My desire shall have its fill of them. I will unsheathe my sword, my hand shall subdue them*]" (Exodus 15:9). "The foe said"—this is Pharaoh. He did not realize what he was saying, [as it says:] *"humans have the heart's preparations, but the tongue's answer is from the Lord"* (Proverbs 16:1). It is not written here, "we will pursue, we will overtake, we will divide the spoil," but, "I will pursue, I will overtake, I will divide the spoil," meaning, "I will be pursued by them, I will be seized by them, I will be driven toward them, I will be delivered to them..."

[Pharaoh said,] "in the past, when you would try to rape [*le'enos*] the [Israelites'] wives and their sons and daughters, I would hold you responsible by the laws of the kingdom. But now, '*I will unsheathe my sword, my hand shall subdue them.*'" Some say: it is not written "*I will use* [eten] *my sword,*" but, "*I will unsheathe* [ariq] *my sword,*" meaning [Pharaoh] intended to rape their males, as it is said elsewhere: it is not written, "*I shall use* [natati] *their swords against your prized shrewdness,*" but, "*they shall unsheathe* [hariqu] *their swords against your prized shrewdness*" (Ezekiel 28:7). Because he was haughty and proud of heart, the Holy Blessed One brought him low, and all the nations abused him.

Mekhilta deRabbi Yishma'el (ed. Jacob Z. Lauterbach, Jewish Publication Society, 1933), Beshalaḥ, parashah 7. Translated from Hebrew by Noam Sienna.

Further Reading

Satlow, Michael. "'They Abused Him like a Woman': Homoeroticism, Gender Blurring, and the Rabbis in Late Antiquity." *Journal of the History of Sexuality*, Vol. 5, No. 1 (1994), 1–25.

Satlow, Michael. *Tasting the Dish: Rabbinic Rhetorics of Sexuality* (Society of Biblical Literature, 2014).

9. The Nations Would Marry A Man to A Man and A Woman to A Woman: A Midrash (Land of Israel, Fifth Century CE)

Explicit rabbinic statements about homosexual activity are rare and generally negative. In this midrash from the *Sifra*—a collection of rabbinic legal commentary (*midrash halakhah*) on the book of Leviticus probably compiled between the third and fifth centuries CE—the rabbis expand on the verse in Leviticus 18:3, which forbids the Israelites from following the practices of the Egyptians and the Canaanites. The midrash explains that since this verse could not be forbidding everything done by another nation, this must refer specifically to their own traditional ways. The narrator then explains what those practices were, focusing on imagined differences in sexual culture: in these foreign nations, the midrash claims, men would marry men and women would marry women, along with polygamy and polyandry. Scholars have suggested that this midrash, along with other similar descriptions of same-sex marriage among Gentile nations (Bereshit Rabbah 26:5, VaYiqra Rabbah 23:9, b. Ḥullin 92a–b), reflect an awareness of contemporary Greco-Roman practices relating to same-sex pairings. At the very least, we can conclude that the rabbis could imagine a same-sex couple desiring to formalize that relationship through marriage, but perceived that possibility as a threat to the divinely-ordained system of gender relations that separated Israel from the other nations.

"*According to the ways of the Land of Egypt…and the ways of the Land of Canaan…you shall not do*" (Leviticus 18:3): Could [this mean] you shall not build buildings, not plant plantings, as they do? Therefore, the verse continues, "*and you shall not walk in their ways* [ḥuqqot]"—I have said [this prohibition only] regarding their ways which are traditional [ḥaqquqim] for them and their fathers and their fathers' fathers.

And what would they do? A man would be married to another man, and a woman to another woman; and a man would marry a woman and her daughter, and a woman would be married to two [men at once]. Therefore, it is said, "*and you shall not walk in their ways.*"

Sifra (ed. Isaak Hirsch Weiss, Vienna: J. Schlossberg, 1862), Aḥarei Mot 9:8. Translated from Hebrew by Noam Sienna.

Further Reading

Berkowitz, Beth. *Defining Jewish Difference: From Antiquity to the Present* (Cambridge University Press, 2012).

Kosman, Admiel, and Anat Sharbat. "'Two Women Who Were Sporting With Each Other': A Reexamination of the Halakhic Approaches to Lesbianism as a Touchstone for Homosexuality in General." *Hebrew Union College Annual* 75 (2004), 37–74.

Moss, Jacob, and Rivka Kern Ulmer. "'Two Men Under One Cloak'—The Sages Permit it: Homosexual Marriage in Judaism." *Journal of Homosexuality* 55:1 (2008), 71–105.

Satlow, Michael. "'They Abused Him like a Woman': Homoeroticism, Gender Blurring, and the Rabbis in Late Antiquity." *Journal of the History of Sexuality*, Vol. 5, No. 1 (1994), 1–25.

10. A Talmudic Rabbi Encounters Two Students Engaged in Intercourse (Land of Israel, Fifth Century CE)

The Talmud is the primary compilation of Jewish legal and exegetical literature from late antiquity, developed orally over generations as a commentary
to the Mishnah (see source 5), and compiled in 63 *masekhtot* (tractates) in
two distinct versions: the Jerusalem (or Palestinian) Talmud, redacted around
400 CE, and the Babylonian Talmud at a later date. In this excerpt from the
masekhet of Sanhedrin, the rabbis conclude a long discussion on false witnesses and mistaken sentencing with a very brief but fascinating anecdote. It
is recorded of the fourth-century Palestinian sage Yudah ben Pazzi that while
he was in the *beit midrash* (House of Study), he came across two men, presumably students, having sexual relations on the roof (we can assume that
the *beit midrash* had a flat roof, as was typical of ancient Mediterranean
buildings, where people could study, eat, or sleep). The two men, apparently concerned that he might try to pursue legal action against them, remind
the rabbi that without other witnesses his testimony would be nullified in any
case. This short episode—the only Talmudic record of homosexual activity as
an actual occurrence rather than a theoretical or metaphorical issue—raises
far more questions than it answers. How did the rabbi react? What happened to the men? How were rabbinic punishments for homosexual behavior enforced in this period, if at all? Despite its brevity, this text indicates that
for at least some men, the House of Study was also a sexualized space, a
dynamic that continued to develop over the following millennium (see sources 48, 52, and 77).

Rabbi Yudah ben Pazzi left to go up to the upper story of the House of
Study, and saw two men coupling with each other. They said to him, "Rabbi,
keep in mind that you are one [witness] and we are two."

y. Sanhedrin 6:3, translated from Aramaic/Hebrew by Noam Sienna.

Further Reading

Greenberg, Steven. *Wrestling with God and Men: Homosexuality in the Jewish Tradition* (University of Wisconsin Press, 2004).

Kosman, Admiel, and Anat Sharbat. "'Two Women Who Were Sporting With Each Other': A Reexamination of the Halakhic Approaches to Lesbianism as a Touchstone for Homosexuality in General." *Hebrew Union College Annual* 75 (2004), 37–74.

Satlow, Michael. *Tasting the Dish: Rabbinic Rhetorics of Sexuality* (Society of Biblical Literature, 2014).

11. The Rabbis of the Talmud Discuss Sexual Contact Between Women (Babylonia, Sixth to Eighth Centuries CE)

This brief passage, which appears in both the Jerusalem and Babylonian Talmuds, contains the only explicit discussion regarding female same-sex eroticism in the Talmud. In the Jerusalem Talmud, it is recorded as a dispute between the first-century schools of Hillel and Shammai, where Hillel permits a woman who sports (*mesalledet*) with another woman to marry a *kohen*, while Shammai forbids it (*y. Gittin* 8:8); in the Babylonian Talmud the latter opinion is attributed to Rav Huna. The larger context is a discussion of which types of women's adornment are permitted or forbidden on Shabbat. The Talmudic narrator juxtaposes the Mishnah's teaching with the father of Shmu'el, Abba, who, among other things, did not permit his daughters to sleep together. The narrator wonders whether this might support the opinion of Rav Huna (one of Shmu'el's students), who taught that women who "rub together" (*mesollelot*) are disqualified from marrying a *kohen* (who may not marry a divorced woman); but they conclude that in fact this was not Abba bar Abba's main concern. In Tractate Yevamot, Rav Huna's teaching is quoted again, but Rabbi El'azar disagrees, saying that erotic activity between women is merely licentiousness (*pritsuta*) and does not disqualify them from marriage. In any case, it is clear that the rabbis of the Talmud did not treat sexual contact between women as desirable or approved; at the same time, they did not see it as a particularly serious or pressing issue.

MISHNAH: *Young girls may go out* [*on Shabbat*] *wearing ribbons.* The father of Shmu'el did not permit his daughters to go out wearing ribbons, and he did not allow them to sleep together, and he made *miqva'ot* for them in the days of Nisan, and had mats placed [in the river] in the days of Tishre.

"He did not permit them to go out wearing ribbons"—but we [just] learned [in the Mishnah], "young girls may go out [on Shabbat] wearing ribbons!" The daughters of Shmu'el's father had colored ones [and so they might have been tempted to remove them to show others].

"He did not permit them to sleep together"—could we say that this supports the opinion of Rav Huna? For Rav Huna said, "Women who rub [*mesollelot*] with one another are unfit for [marrying into] the priesthood." No, this was not [the motivation]; rather it was so that they should not become accustomed to [sleeping with] a foreign body.

b. Shabbat 65a–b, translated from Aramaic/Hebrew by Noam Sienna.

Further Reading

Brooten, Bernadette. *Love Between Women: Early Christian Responses to Female Homoeroticism* (University of Chicago Press, 1996).

Kosman, Admiel, and Anat Sharbat. "'Two Women Who Were Sporting With Each Other': A Reexamination of the Halakhic Approaches to Lesbianism as a Touchstone for Homosexuality in General." *Hebrew Union College Annual* 75 (2004), 37–74.

12. Avraham and Sarah were Tumtumim: A Midrash (Babylonia, Sixth to Eighth Centuries CE)

In this excerpt from Tractate *Yevamot*, the rabbis present one midrashic understanding of why Avraham and Sarah were childless for so long, as part of a larger discussion of the barrenness of the matriarchs and patriarchs. Rav Ammi suggests, drawing on a pair of verses from Isaiah 51, that Avraham and Sarah were in fact *tumtumim*, and Rabbi Naḥman further imagines that Sarah was an *aylonit*. The *tumtum* and the *aylonit*, like the *androginos* (see source 5), are Talmudic categories of sex that have no exact equivalent in English. While the *androginos* has both male and female sexual characteristics, the *tumtum* is not clearly identifiable as either male or female. The *aylonit* is someone assigned female at birth, but who does not show signs of (female) sexual development, and who is unable to bear children. As in other midrashim (see sources 6, 7, and 14), the rabbis here show their comfort in applying their observations on the variations in sex and gender to our biblical ancestors.

Rabbi Ammi taught: "Avraham and Sarah were *tumtumim*, as it is said, '*Look to the rock from where you were hewn, and to the hole of the pit from where you were dug out*' (Isaiah 51:1) and [following that] it is said, '*Look to Avraham your father, and to Sarah that bore you* (Isaiah 51:2).'"

Rabbi Naḥman taught, in the name of Rabbah bar Abbuha, "Our mother Sarah was an *aylonit*; as it is sad, '*And Sarai was barren; she had no child* [vlad]' (Genesis 11:30)—she did not even have a womb [*beit vlad*]."

b. Yevamot 64a–b, translated from Aramaic/Hebrew by Noam Sienna.

Further Reading

Kessler, Gwynn. "Bodies in Motion: Preliminary Notes on Queer Theory and Rabbinic Literature." In *Mapping Gender in Ancient Religious Discourses* (eds. Todd C. Penner and Caroline Vander Stichele, Leiden: Brill, 2006), 389–430.

Kukla, Elliot, and Reuben Zellman. "Created by the Hand of Heaven: Making Space for Intersex People." In *Balancing on the Mechitza: Transgender in Jewish Community* (ed. Noach Dzmura, Berkeley: North Atlantic Books, 2010), 182–187.

Lev, Sarra. "How the 'Aylonit Got Her Sex." *AJS Review* 31:2 (2007), 297–316.

Strassfeld, Max. *Classically Queer: Eunuchs and Androgynes in Rabbinic Literature.* Ph.D. dissertation, Stanford University, 2013.

13. The Robber and the Rabbi: Rabbi Yoḥanan and Resh Laqish (Babylonia, Sixth to Eighth Centuries CE)

This enigmatic and well-known Talmudic passage portrays the relationship between two third-century Palestinian rabbis: Rabbi Yoḥanan bar Nappaḥa and Rabbi Shim'on bar Laqish, or "Resh" Laqish. Rabbi Yoḥanan is described as beautiful beyond all others—in particular as lacking a beard—and thus effeminate rather than virile. Resh Laqish is described as strong and violent, and elsewhere in the Talmud it is suggested he was a soldier or even a gladiator. Several scholars, beginning with Daniel Boyarin, have interpreted this passage as articulating a rabbinic discomfort with Roman ideals of masculinity and claiming a spiritual and intellectual excellence that exceeds that of the body. The end of the story, however, retains a deep ambivalence about just how transformative the power of rabbinic learning is, and whether the actions taken by Rabbi Yohanan—or indeed, any of the actors in the story—were correct. The relationship between Rabbi Yohanan and Resh Laqish, while not explicitly sexual, is clearly an intense emotional bond that mirrors the eroticized educational relationships of ancient Greece and Rome, although here inverted (a young, beardless man who takes an older virile man under his wing and educates him, rather than vice versa). The tensions in this story between heterosexual family life and the homosocial (and homoerotic) space of the House of Study continued to operate throughout the Jewish world for centuries (see sources 48, 52, and 77).

Rabbi Yohanan would say, "I alone have survived from the beautiful ones of Jerusalem." If one wished to see the beauty of Rabbi Yohanan, they could take a new silver goblet, fill it with red pomegranate seeds, and adorn it with a garland of red roses and set it between the sun and the shade; that radiance is a taste of the beauty of Rabbi Yohanan. But is this true? Isn't it said, "The beauty of Rav Kahana is a taste of the beauty of Rabbi Abbahu, and the beauty of Rabbi Abbahu is a taste of the beauty of our father Ya'aqov, and the beauty of our father Ya'aqov is a taste of the beauty of the first Adam"—and Rabbi Yohanan is not mentioned? Rabbi Yohanan was different, for he did not have "splendor of face" [i.e. a beard].

Rabbi Yohanan would go and sit at the gates of [the baths of] immersion, and he would say, "As the women of Israel are coming out from their ritual immersions, they will look at me, and so have children as beautiful as I am." The rabbis asked him, "Are you not afraid of the Evil Eye?" He replied, "I am from the seed of our father Yosef, over whom the Evil Eye has no power, as it is said, 'Yosef is a fruitful vine, a fruitful vine by the fountain,' (Genesis 49:22) and Rabbi Abbahu taught, 'Do not read "by the fountain" ['alei 'ayin], but "over the Eye" ['olei 'ayin]...'"

One day, Rabbi Yohanan was swimming in the Jordan. Resh Laqish saw him [*some manuscripts add here:* and thought he was a woman] and jumped in the Jordan after him. [Rabbi Yohanan] said to him, "Your strength for Torah!"

[Resh Laqish] said to him, "Your beauty for women!" [Rabbi Yoḥanan] said to him, "If you return, I will give you my sister, who is more beautiful than I." He accepted it; he then wished to return to get his belongings, but he was not able to return. [Rabbi Yoḥanan] taught him Bible and Mishnah, and made him a great man [*gavra rabba*].

One day, there was an argument in the House of Study [about the following ruling]: "The sword, knife, dagger, spear, handsaw, and sickle—when [in the process of making them] do they become susceptible to ritual impurity? Once their manufacture is completed" (*m. Kelim* 13:1).

But when is their manufacture completed? Rabbi Yoḥanan said, "When they are hardened in the furnace." Resh Laqish said, "When they are tempered in water." [Rabbi Yoḥanan] said to him, "A robber would know of robbery." [Resh Laqish] said to him, "So what good have you done me? There they called me master [*rabbi*], here they call me master." [Rabbi Yoḥanan] said to him, "I have done you good by bringing you under the wings of the Divine Presence!" Rabbi Yoḥanan's mind weakened, and Resh Laqish weakened, too. [Rabbi Yoḥanan's] sister came and wept, saying, [*some manuscripts add:* "Look at me!" He ignored her. She said] "Do something for the sake of my children!" He said to her, "*Leave your orphans, and I will raise them*" (Jeremiah 49:11). [She said,] "Do something for the sake of my widowhood!" He said to her, "*and let your widows trust in Me*" (Jeremiah 49:11).

Resh Laqish died and Rabbi Yoḥanan became greatly distressed over it. The rabbis said, "Who will go to relieve his mind? Let Rabbi El'azar ben Pedat go, for his statements are sharp." He went and sat with him; for every argument that Rabbi Yoḥanan made, he would say, "Yes, there is a teaching that supports you." [Rabbi Yoḥanan] said, "Are you like Resh Laqish? Resh Laqish would challenge everything I said with 24 objections, and I would respond with 24 answers, and thus we would settle the issue. And [all] you say is that there is a teaching that supports me? Don't I know that what I said is right?" [Rabbi Yoḥanan] tore his clothes and wept, saying, "Where are you, Resh Laqish? Where are you, Resh Laqish?" He cried out until his mind slipped [from him]. The rabbis prayed for mercy for him, and he died.

b. Baba Metsia' 84a, translated from Aramaic/Hebrew by Noam Sienna.

Further Reading

Boyarin, Daniel. *Unheroic Conduct: The Rise of Heterosexuality and the Invention of the Jewish Man* (University of California Press, 1997).

Boyarin, Daniel. "Why is Rabbi Yoḥanan a Woman? or, A Queer Marriage Gone Bad: 'Platonic Love' in the Talmud." In *Authorizing Marriage?: Canon, Tradition, and Critique in the Blessing of Same-Sex Unions* (ed. Mark D. Jordan, Princeton University Press, 2006), 52–67.

Kosman, Admiel. "Johanan and Resh Lakish: The Image of God in the Study Hall: 'Masculinity' Versus 'Femininity.'" *European Judaism* 43:1 (2010), 128–45.

Satlow, Michael. *Tasting the Dish: Rabbinic Rhetorics of Sexuality* (Society of Biblical Literature, 2014).

Siegal, Michal Bar-Asher. *Early Christian Monastic Literature and the Babylonian Talmud* (Cambridge University Press, 2013).

14. Dinah's Sex is Changed: A Midrash (Land of Israel, Sixth to Eighth Centuries CE)

This remarkable teaching, from a midrashic collection known as *Tanḥuma-Yelammedenu*, comments on the biblical account of the birth of Dinah, the daughter of Ya'aqov and Leah. The rabbis explain that Dinah was originally male, but transformed into a girl at Leah's request. (This tradition is recorded in several places; see *Bereshit Rabbah 72:6* and *y. Berakhot 9:3.*) Drawing on a passage in Jeremiah where God is compared to a potter who can make and remake vessels at will, human sex is portrayed as equally malleable. "It is not difficult for the Holy Blessed One," one rabbi says, "to convert females into males and males into females," even at the moment of birth. *Tanḥuma-Yelammedenu* is one of three early midrashic collections attributed to the fourth-century Rabbi Tanḥuma bar Abba; it is called Yelammedenu because many of its sections begin with *yelammedenu rabbenu*, "Let our master teach us." It was probably compiled and edited in the Land of Israel between the sixth and eighth centuries.

"*And God remembered Raḥel*" (Genesis 30:22). Let our master teach us: if a man's wife is pregnant, may he pray, "may it be Your will that my wife give birth to a son?" Thus our masters teach us: the man whose wife is pregnant and who prays "may it be Your will that my wife give birth to a son"—this is a prayer in vain. Rav Huna, however, said in the name of Rabbi Yose: "Even though we have been taught that the husband of a pregnant woman who prays, 'May it be Your will that my wife give birth to a son,' is saying a prayer in vain, this is not the case; rather, he may pray for a son even as she commences labor. For it is not difficult for the Holy Blessed One to convert females into males and males into females." Thus it is explained by Jeremiah: "*I went down to the potter's house, and there he was, working at the wheels. And when the vessel he was making of clay was spoiled in the hand of the potter, he made another vessel, as it seemed good to the potter to make it*" (Jeremiah 18:3–4). And then did not the Holy Blessed One say to Jeremiah: "*Cannot I do with you as this potter, O house of Israel? declares the Lord*" (Jeremiah 18:6)?

And thus you find this with Leah: after she had given birth to six sons, she saw in a prophecy that twelve tribes would be established from Ya'aqov. She had already given birth to six sons and was pregnant with her seventh and the two handmaidens had each had two sons, making ten sons in all; so Leah arose and pleaded with the Holy Blessed One, saying, "Master of the Universe, twelve tribes are to come from Ya'aqov, and since I have already given birth to six sons, and am pregnant with a seventh, and each of the handmaidens has had two sons, this is already ten. If this child [within me] is a male, my sister Raḥel will not have as many [sons] as one of the handmaidens." Immediately the Holy Blessed One heard her prayer and converted the fetus in her womb into a female, as it is said, "*And afterwards* [aḥar] *she bore a daughter and called her Dinah*" (Genesis 30:21)—it is not written *aḥeret* [in the feminine form] but *aḥar* [in the masculine]. And why did Leah call her Dinah? Because the righteous Leah had stood for justice [*din*] before the Holy Blessed One, who said to her, "You are merciful, and so I too shall be merciful to her." Immediately, "*God remembered Raḥel*" (Genesis 30:22).

Tanḥuma-Yelammedenu (Vienna, 1863), VaYetse 8. Translated from Hebrew by Noam Sienna.

Further Reading

Kessler, Gwynn. "Bodies in Motion: Preliminary Notes on Queer Theory and Rabbinic Literature." In *Mapping Gender in Ancient Religious Discourses* (eds. Todd C. Penner and Caroline Vander Stichele, Leiden: Brill, 2006), 389–430.

Weiss, Dov. "Lawsuits against God in Rabbinic Literature." In *The Divine Courtroom in Comparative Perspective* (eds. Ari Mermelstein and Shalom E. Holtz, Leiden: Brill, 2014), 276–288.

15. A Midrash on the Bond Between Study Companions (Babylonia, Seventh to Ninth Centuries CE)

The *Avot deRabbi Natan* is a midrashic collection that expands on the teachings in *Pirqei Avot*, one of the tractates of the Mishnah. This teaching expands on the statement in *Pirqei Avot* 1:6, "Appoint for yourself a teacher, and acquire for yourself a companion." Describing the character of an ideal companion (*ḥaver*), the midrash explains that one should eat, drink, study, and sleep with one's companion, and reveal to them all secrets. In other words, the *ḥaver* is portrayed here as a man's most emotionally and socially intimate partner; while one's wife is necessary for rearing a family, it is the same-sex bond between study partners (*ḥavruta*) which was, for the rabbis, their most significant relationship. Indeed, several ancient and modern sources confirm that this was true in many actual cases (see sources 13, 49, 52, and 77). While the text preserves some older material, *Avot deRabbi Natan* most likely took its final form during the geonic period, between the seventh and ninth centuries CE.

"*And acquire for yourself a companion* [ḥaver]" (*m. Avot* 1:6). How [is this to be done]? This teaches that a man should acquire for himself a companion and that he should eat with him, drink with him, read with him, study with him, sleep with him, and reveal to him all his secrets: the secrets of Torah and the secrets of worldly matters [*derekh erets*]. For when they sit and occupy themselves with Torah and one of them makes an error in a matter of legal reasoning or in recalling a citation, or if he declares an impure thing to be pure or a pure thing impure, or a forbidden thing permitted and a permitted thing forbidden, then his companion will return him [to the correct reasoning]. And from where [in Scripture can we learn] that when his companion guides him and studies with him, that they receive a good reward for their labor? As it is said, "*Two are better than one, for they have a good reward for their labor*" (Ecclesiastes 4:9).

Avot deRabbi Natan (ed. Solomon Schechter, Ch. D. Lippe: Vienna, 1887) 8:3, translated from Hebrew by Noam Sienna.

Further Reading

Boyarin, Daniel. *Carnal Israel: Reading Sex in the Talmud* (University of California Press, 1993).

Gleibman, Shlomo. "The Jewish Queer Continuum in Yeshiva Narratives." *Shofar: An Interdisciplinary Journal of Jewish Studies* 35:3 (2017), 1–31.

Greenberg, Steven. *Wrestling with God and Men: Homosexuality in the Jewish Tradition* (University of Wisconsin Press, 2004).

16. Sa'adia Gaon Describes the Danger of Homoerotic Love (Baghdad, 933 CE)

Sa'adia ben Yosef al-Fayyumi (882–942 CE) was born in Egypt, but spent much of his life in Babylonia as the *gaon* (head of the Babylonian Talmudic academy) of Sura; he was one of the most important Jewish philosophers and theologians of the geonic period, and defended rabbinic Judaism fiercely against Islamic and Karaite charges. In this excerpt from his Judeo-Arabic work *Kitab al-Amanat wa'l-I'tiqadat* (The Book of Beliefs and Opinions), Sa'adia discusses the notion of '*ishq*, passionate or erotic love, which he argues should be controlled strictly and not indulged in. He uses the example of two hypothetical men, Zayd and 'Amr (in the Hebrew translation, Re'uven and Shim'on) who love each other. He refutes the idea that their love is determined astrologically, as well as the Greek-inspired myth of a person looking for their lost 'other half,' but interestingly, he does not comment on the possibility of love between two men itself. Instead, Sa'adia focuses on the inflammatory danger of love, the human ability to control it, and his belief (later emphasized by Maimonides) in the importance of moderation. In fact, his account of the passionate but turbulent relationship between a lover and his male beloved has clear parallels to the standard descriptions of homoerotic love in medieval Hebrew prose and poetry (see sources 18–25 and 29). As an interesting postscript, it should be noted that Sa'adia himself was accused of engaging in inappropriate sexual behavior with young men from the yeshiva of Pumbedita, in a pamphlet by Khalaf Aharon ibn Sarjada, a student of the exilarch David ben Zakkai (as published by Harkavy), who claimed that "he [Sa'adia] had been caught with the young men, and witnesses testified to that, and said to him...'Reliable men saw you in the alleyway of Darb al-Baqr [the Street of Cattle], underneath the young men, in the presence of holy books. Surely the young men of Nehardea are tired from pursuing you!'"

This chapter, even though it is shameful [*qabiḥ*] to mention it, is no more shameful than discussing the opinions of heretics; and so, just as we discussed those in order to refute them and strengthen hearts [against them] etc., here, too, we will discuss this in order to refute it and strengthen hearts [against it].

To wit: there are some who believe that erotic love [*'ishq*] is the best of all things for a person to engage in, and they imagine that it makes the spirit gentle, and softens the temperament, until the soul becomes very refined in its gentleness, in a state of intense delicacy. They explain it as a natural process: a matter, originating in a glance, enters into the heart; then, desire [*ṭama'*]; then, it takes control [*tamakkun*]; then, other matters are added to it; until finally it is firmly established. And they go further than this, explaining it by the actions of the stars; they say that if two people are born under the ascendant of two stars, facing each other by thirds or sixths [i.e. in full or in part], and a single star rules over their love sign, then by necessity there will be love and friendship between them.

And they go even further, explaining this as the action of the blessed and exalted Creator. They claim that God created people's spirits as round spheres, and then split them into halves, and then placed a half in each human being. Therefore, when the soul finds its [other] half, it cleaves to it. From this, in fact, they go even further yet, making it [i.e. passion] into a commandment [*farḍ*], saying that the servants of God are tested with this matter in order to teach them how to submit to love, so that they might submit to their Lord and serve God. But those who discuss all this are fools without any sense. I see fit, therefore, to refute them in this matter, first providing a clear response to what they mistakenly believe, and then demonstrating the dangers in the beliefs they cling to.

I say, regarding what you claim about our exalted and glorious Lord: it cannot be that God would test us with something that God warned against, as it is written, "*God does not ordain foolishness*" (Job 24:12), and also, "*You are not a God who desires wickedness, and evil does not reside with You*" (Psalms 5:5). And as for the belief in the division of the spheres which they cling to, we have already refuted that with what we said earlier* regarding the existence of *ruḥaniyyat* [spiritual beings], and we established clearly that each human soul is created with a complete form; therefore, this matter is null and void. As for

---

* *The Book of Beliefs and Opinions*, Chapter 5, Gate 8.

their opinion regarding the influence of the stars and the alignment of their ascending signs and constellations—if it were as they said, then it would be impossible for Zayd to love 'Amr without 'Amr also loving [Zayd] in return, for their [signs] are equal; but we do not find that to be the case.

And as for what they discussed regarding its origin in a glance, and then the occurrence of desire in the heart—I say that indeed, for this very reason, our exalted and glorious Lord commanded us to join our eyes and hearts in service, as it is written, "*my son, give your heart to Me, and let your eyes watch My paths*" (Proverbs 23:26); and God forbade us to rebel with them, saying, "*and do not follow after your hearts and your eyes, after which you go astray* [zonim]" (Numbers 15:39). This [warning] refers to when this emotional state takes control of the heart, until it controls [the subject] and rules over him; such a man abandons eating and drinking and other basic necessities until his body wastes away and his flesh withers, and severe illnesses approach him. And what of all the in-flaming, and fainting, and pulsating, and anguish, and upheaval, and agitation? Of this, [Scripture] says, "*they have prepared their hearts like an oven, while they wait*" (Hosea 7:6).

This [emotional upheaval] is sometimes carried into the brain, where it weakens the imagination, thought, and memory, and can even nullify the body's senses and movements. It is possible that when he sees his beloved, he would fall into a faint, and his soul would leave his body temporarily. It is even possible that the mere sight of his beloved, or hearing a mention of him, would cause him gasp his last breath and actually die. This would prove the truth of the proverb, "*For she has felled many victims, and she has slain a great host*" (Proverbs 7:26). How can it be that a person and his intellect be imprisoned [by passion], to the point that he does not know anything—his Lord, or his strength, or this world and the next—except [his beloved]? As it says, "*the impious at heart become angry; they do not cry for help when they are imprisoned*" (Job 36:13).

And what of all the groveling, and the submission to the beloved and those around him, and the sitting at the gates and waiting for him around every corner? As it says, "*Lift up your eyes to the hills, and see: where have you not been slept with? At the crossroads you have sat* [for your lovers]" (Jeremiah 3:2). And what of all the vigils at night, and the waking at dawn, and the hiding from whoever might find you, and the deaths one dies for every embarrassment? As it says, *"the eye of the adulterer waits for dusk, saying 'no eye will see me,' and covers his face"* (Job 24:15). And what of the murder of the lover or the beloved, or one of those around them, or both of them and those around them, and many others along with them? As it says, *"for they have committed adultery, and indeed blood is on their hands"* (Ezekiel 23:45).

Finally, if he ever succeeds in attaining what he desires, and satisfies that for which his soul has struggled, he might then regret [what he had done], and hate what he had loved more strongly than he had loved it. As it says, *"and Amnon hated [Tamar] with great hatred, and his hatred of her was stronger than the love he once had for her"* (II Samuel 13:15).

It should therefore be clear to a person [who gives in to his passion] that he has sold his soul, and his faith [*din*], and all his senses, and his reason [*'aql*]; for once this arrow has been released it cannot be taken back. As it says, *"until an arrow strike his liver, like a bird runs to the snare"* (Jeremiah 7:23). Thus, this [emotional] state is only proper in the matter of a man's marriage. He should be affectionate with [his wife], and she should be affectionate with him, [only] for the purposes of building the world [i.e. having children]. As it says, *"A lovely deer and a graceful doe—her lovemaking shall always satisfy you"* (Proverbs 5:19). A husband should satisfy his passion for his wife, according to reason and faith, to the extent necessary to bind them together; but he should restrain it beyond that to the best of his abilities and strength.

Sa'adia Gaon, *Kitab al-Amanat wa'l-I'tiqadat* (ed. Samuel Landauer, Leiden: Brill, 1880), Chapter 10, Gate 4. Translated from Judeo-Arabic by Noam Sienna.

Further Reading

Harkavy, Avraham (ed.). *Maḥberet Khalaf Aharon ibn Sarjada*. In Avraham Harkavy, *Leben und Werke Saadia's Gaon*, vol. 1 (Berlin: M'kize Nirdamim, 1891).

Harvey, Steven. "The Meaning of Terms Designating Love in Judaeo-Arabic Thought and Some Remarks on the Judaeo-Arabic Interpretation of Maimonides." In *Judaeo-Arabic Studies* (ed. Norman Golb, Amsterdam: Harwood, 1997), 175–196.

Rosenblatt, Samuel (ed. and trans.). *The Book of Beliefs and Opinions* (Yale University Press, 1948).

Roth, Norman. "'Fawns of My Delight': Boy-Love in Arabic and Hebrew Verse." In *Poetics of Love in the Middle Ages* (ed. Moshe Lazar and Norris Lacy, George Mason University Press, 1989), 96–118.

17. A Babylonian Gaon Forbids Singing Homoerotic Poetry in Arabic (Baghdad, Late Tenth Century)

With the rapid spread of Islam in the two centuries after its founding, Jews living under Islamic rule quickly began participating in its vibrant intellectual, literary, and cultural environment. This responsum of Hayy ben Sherira (939–1038), *gaon* (head of the Babylonian Talmudic academy) of Pumbedita, deals with the question of Arabic music and poetry, and is addressed to two rabbinic scholars of the city of Qabis (Gabès) in modern-day Tunisia. He protests against the growing popularity of using the tunes of Arabic songs for liturgical music, and declares specifically that the Talmudic prohibition on music (b. *Gittin* 7a) applies not to synagogue music but to the Arabic poems known as *ash'ar al-ghazal* (love songs), like "songs of a man's love for his [male] companion, or to praise a beautiful one for his beauty, and to praise a strong one for his strength." Nonetheless, the genre of homoerotic poetry, in both Hebrew and Arabic, remained popular in Jewish communities for centuries (see sources 18–20, 22–25, 33, 39, and 47).

These questions were asked before us by the joy of our eyes, the esteemed Rabbi Nehemiah bar Ovadiah, and the esteemed Rabbi Moshe bar Shmu'el Bar Nama' of blessed memory, and the [other] rabbis and students of the city of Qabis in the region of the Maghreb…

[Regarding the passage] "A question was once sent to Mar 'Uqba: from where [in Scripture] is it shown that music is forbidden, etc. (b. *Gittin* 7a)." We have seen that the custom of all Jews, whether at feasts generally or in the house of a bride and groom in particular, is to celebrate with joyous voices, and recite words of poetry and praise before God, and recall God's wonders and kindnesses for the people of Israel in times past, and the hopes for the revelation of God's kingdom, and the promises of goodness and tidings of comfort which the prophets proclaimed to the people of Israel, and many *piyyutim* [poems] on these subjects and similar things, in a musical melody, and in the houses of brides and grooms, and celebrations, and to recall marriage canopies and [give] blessings of success and prosperity—there is nobody among the people of Israel who refrains from all these.

But [when the Talmud says that] Mar 'Uqba forbade music, [what was intended are] things that are not of this nature, but rather the songs of a man's love for his companion, or to praise a beautiful one for his beauty, and to praise a strong one for his strength, and other things like this, such as those of these Ishmaelites [i.e. Arabs], which are called *ash'ar al-ghazal* [love songs]. These songs are not only forbidden, but they are forbidden even when they are sung with the voice only [and no instruments].

Teshuvot HaGe'onim. As published by Avraham Harkavy, *Responsen der Geonim*, vol. 4 (Berlin: H. Itzkowski, 1887). Translated from Hebrew by Noam Sienna.

Further Reading

Lewin, Benjamin Menashe. "Teshuvot Rav Hayy Gaon Leqabes." *Ginzei Qedem: me'asef mada'i litqufat hage'onim* 5 (1923), 33–35.

Lowin, Shari. *Arabic and Hebrew Love Poems in Al-Andalus* (Routledge, 2014).

Roth, Norman. "Religious Constraints on Erotic Poetry among Muslims and Jews in al-Andalus." *Maghreb Review* 19:3–4 (1994), 194–205.

18. Poetry of Yitshaq Ibn Mar Sha'ul (Spain, Eleventh Century)

Yitshaq Ibn Mar Sha'ul, born in Lucena (southern Spain) in the final decades of the tenth century, was a respected Hebrew grammarian and liturgical poet. He is believed to have been the first to introduce the literary tropes of Arabic homoerotic poetry, such as the figure of the gazelle, into Hebrew poetry, creating a genre which flourished for the next three centuries (see sources 19, 20, 22–25, 39, and 87). For decades, scholars have argued over how to interpret these poems: as evidence of genuine experience, poetic exercises, descriptions of platonic friendships, or metaphorical philosophy. It is clear that, at the very least, the expression of homoerotic desire was valued as beautiful and seen as the subject of choice for generations of Hebrew poets, who drew on both the literary conventions shared with Arabic poetry and the depths of the Jewish biblical and literary traditions. In this poem, Ibn Mar Sha'ul describes the emotion of lovesickness caused by the sight of his beloved, who is compared to beautiful male figures from the Bible like Joseph and David.

Gazelle desired in Spain,
   wondrously formed,
Given rule and dominion
   over every living thing;
Lovely of form like the moon
   with beautiful stature:
Curls of purple
   upon shining temple,
Like Joseph in his form,
   like Adoniah his hair.
Lovely of eyes like David,
   he has slain me like Uriah.
He has enflamed my passions
   and consumed my heart with fire.
Because of him I have been left
   without understanding and wisdom.
Weep with me every ostrich
   and every hawk and falcon!
The beloved of my soul has slain me—
   is this a just sentence?
Because of him my soul is sick,
   perplexed and yearning.
His speech upon my heart
   is like dew upon parched land.
Draw me from the pit of destruction
   that I go not down to hell!

As translated in Norman Roth, "'Deal Gently with the Young Man': Love of Boys in Medieval Hebrew Poetry of Spain." *Speculum* 57 (1982), 20–51. Copyright 1982 by The Medieval Academy of America.

Further Reading

Cole, Peter. *The Dream of the Poem: Hebrew Poetry from Muslim and Christian Spain, 950–1492* (Princeton University Press, 2007).

Lowin, Shari. *Arabic and Hebrew Love Poems in Al-Andalus* (Routledge, 2014).

Roth, Norman. "'Fawns of My Delight': Boy-Love in Arabic and Hebrew Verse." In *Poetics of Love in the Middle Ages* (ed. Moshe Lazar and Norris Lacy, George Mason University Press, 1989), 96–118.

Scheindlin, Raymond. "Merchants and Intellectuals, Rabbis and Poets: Judeo-Arabic Culture in the Golden Age of Islam." In *Cultures of the Jews: A New History, Vol. 2* (ed. David Biale, Knopf, 2010), 11–86.

Schippers, Arie. *Spanish Hebrew Poetry and the Arabic Literary Tradition: Arabic Themes in Hebrew Andalusian Poetry* (Brill, 1994).

Schirmann, Jefim. "The Ephebe in Medieval Hebrew Poetry." *Sefarad* 55 (1955), 55–68.

19. Poetry of Shmu'el Hanagid (Spain, Eleventh Century)

These poems, by the Granadan poet and politician Shmu'el Hanagid (993–1056), are love songs dedicated to a beautiful youth, referred to as a fawn (*tsvi* or *'ofer*) and in the final poem unusually as *gozal* (chick), which puns both on the Arabic *ghazāl* (gazelle) and *ghazal* (love poem). In the first poem, it seems that the lovers are about to kiss, as the poet focuses closer and closer, from the garden to the glass to his lips...but then he pivots to the moon in the night sky, and we are left to imagine what then transpired. The second and third poems present the beloved, as is typical in this style, as flirtatious, quarrelsome, fickle, and ultimately elusive. Shmu'el Hanagid, or Samuel ibn Naghrillah, fled the sacking of Cordoba in 1013 for Granada, where he served both as *nagid*, head of the local Jewish community, as well as the vizier and general to the *amir*—one of the highest political positions achieved by a Jew in medieval Europe. For other examples of the genre of *tsvi* poems, see sources 18, 20, 22–25, and 39.

I.

I'd sell my soul for that fawn
of a boy   night walker
to sound of the 'ud & flute playing
who saw the glass in my hand   said
"drink the wine from between my lips"

& the moon was a yod drawn on
the cover of dawn—in gold ink

II.

That's it—I love the fawn
plucking roses from
your garden—
you can put the blame on me
but if you once looked at my lover
with your eyes
your lovers would be hunting you
& you'd be gone
that boy who told me: pass
some honey from your hive
I answered: give me some back
on your tongue
& he got angry, yelled:
shall we two sin against the living God?
I answered: let your sin,
sweet master, be with me

III.

Change, my God, the heart of that chick that checked
My sleep, and make him give it back to me;
A fawn who swore by Your name to give
His love to me, a gift of his own free will,
And then betrayed me; lovers all betray.
Forgive his sin—or wipe me out, I pray.

"I'd sell my soul for that fawn" and "That's it—I love the fawn" as translated by Jerome Rothen-
berg and Harris Lenowitz, from *Exiled in the Word: Poems and Other Visions of the Jews from
Tribal Times to the Present* (Copper Canyon, 1989). "Change, my God, the heart of that chick,"
reproduced from Raymond Scheindlin, *Wine, Women, & Death: Medieval Hebrew Poems on the
Good Life* (JPS, 1986).

Further Reading

See bibliography for source 18.

20. Poetry of Shlomo Ibn Gevirol (Spain, Eleventh Century)

These poems, by the poet and philosopher Shlomo Ibn Gevirol (ca. 1021–1058?), are love songs dedicated to a beautiful youth (*tsvi*). The first poem, "Say to him," is dedicated to a youth whose beard has begun to grow ("him whose hair embraces his cheek")—a popular theme in both Hebrew and Arabic poetry. The name "Agur" references a biblical epithet for King Solomon (Shlomo), and is thus an allusion to the poet himself. The other two poems present a common theme of the beloved's cruelty in ignoring his lovers, "his cheeks...like marble slabs all smeared with lovers' blood." Beyond his secular and liturgical poetry, Shlomo Ibn Gevirol is also known for his philosophical composition, *Fons Vitae* (Fountain of Life), a Neo-Platonic dialogue on the nature of Creation preserved only in its Latin translation. For other examples of the genre of *tsvi* poems, see sources 18, 19, 22–25, and 39.

I.

Say to him whose hair embraces his cheek:
    How can noon embrace the morning!
Do not consider it a sin to Agur in saying
    That beauty is vanity and grace a lie.
It is sufficient that your cheeks testify the truth,
    For the deeds of God are unfathomable.

II.

He wounds me, whose necklace is the Pleiades
    and whose neck is [white] like the light of the moon.
In opening the loops of his mouth he reveals
    the light of his pearls like the sun from its abode.
I answered him: "Take my soul and slay [it]; or if not, heal me, please heal!"
    He replied with the sweetness of his mouth: "There is no cure for an old wound."
"Is my wound old, my friend?

It is fresh—not more than a year old."
He answered: "Drink my cup, and sing to me
  as on a day of parting, let there be no exaltation."
And my beloved sang to me in Arabic:
  "In memory of the man whose appearance I love."

III.

That fawn of love! I'd sell my soul for him.
  The sight of him cheers even brooding men.
His cheeks are white and red, like marble slabs
  all smeared with lovers' blood.
His teeth are lances ranged behind his lips. His eyes
  transfix his lovers' hearts like spears.

"Say to him" and "He wounds me" as translated in Norman Roth, "'Deal Gently with the Young Man': Love of Boys in Medieval Hebrew Poetry of Spain." *Speculum* 57 (1982), 20–51. Copyright 1982 by The Medieval Academy of America. "That fawn of love" as translated in Raymond Scheindlin, *Vulture in a Cage: Poems by Solomon Ibn Gabirol* (Archipelago Press, 2016). Reprinted by permission of Archipelago Press.

Further Reading
See bibliography for source 18.

21. Two Amorous Men Cause A Brawl in the Synagogue (Jerusalem, 1052)

This fascinating and puzzling letter was preserved in the Cairo Genizah, a large repository of medieval Jewish documents stored in the Ben Ezra synagogue in Fustat, or Old Cairo. Written by a Jewish pilgrim named Ḥassan ben Mu'ammal, the letter describes his pilgrimage to Jerusalem for the High Holidays, Tishrei 4813 (September, 1052 CE), and an "altercation" that had happened in the synagogue. Apparently, on Yom Kippur, many pilgrims had gathered from around the Mediterranean, and two men—one from Tyre (in southern Lebanon) and one from Tiberias (in the Galilee)—began engaging in amorous activities, causing a brawl to break out between the other pilgrims from Tyre and Tiberias. It is not made explicit whether the brawl was sparked by the homosexual nature of their affections, and the off-hand tone with which it is mentioned suggests that it was actually the rivalry between Tyre and Tiberias that was the more inflammatory aspect of the event. Ḥassan goes on to report that the altercation led to the (non-Jewish) authorities getting involved, and eventually to a reconciliation between the local heads of the Palestinian and Babylonian communities; he concludes the letter with best wishes to the recipients, his brother Abu Naṣr and family.

[Recto:] In the name of God [this is] my letter to you, my brother and master, may God lengthen your life and establish your glory, protection, peace, and sweetness. From Ramla, the end of Tishrei, may God teach you blessing, and the blessing of the blessed holidays, and may God grant you long life.

I inform you that we had such lovely holidays, more than has ever been. I've already said that you should come on the pilgrimage, and [if you did] I would praise you to no end. Al-Da'udi asked about my lord and I [told] him: he could not come because of the circumstance of the altercation, and Ibn Shua' had done things [...] and the first thing that happened was that on the day of the Fast of Kippur, a man from [Tyre] and a man from Tiberias became involved in love, and the Tiberian began embracing the Tyrian in the sight of [the people] and those from Tiberias and those from Tyre began to fight with one another and went out to [...] and they brought the chief of the police to the synagogue and [...] until the people calmed down.

Then Yosef [HaKohen ben Shlomo, the Palestinian gaon] said to Daniel [ben 'Azaryah, the Babylonian gaon], "this is [...], for such is the behavior of these people every day." So they reached an agreement regarding their leadership and they [went] with the people to the [Temple] Mount, and they spent all the rest of the festivals [together] and [Yosef pr]ayed for Daniel to be rosh yeshiva and Daniel prayed for Yosef to be the head of the *beit din* of the yeshiva—a beautiful prayer. I send you greetings, and to Abu al-Faraj greetings, and to Far[...].

[Verso:] To Abu Naṣr the cockeyed Ibn Siba' from his brother Ḥassan ben Mu'ammal, at the Red Street, may God lengthen his life. Ḥusayn ben Naja [...]

T-S 8J22.25, translated from Judeo-Arabic by Noam Sienna.

Further Reading

Assis, Yom Tov. "Sexual Behaviour in Mediaeval Hispano-Jewish Society." In *Jewish History: Essays in Honour of Chimen Abramsky* (ed. Ada Rapoport-Albert and Steven Zipperstein, Peter Halban, 1988), 25–60.

Goitein, Shlomo Dov. "The Sexual Mores of the Common People." In *Society and the Sexes in Medieval Islam* (ed. A. L. al-Sayyid Marsot, Udena Publications, 1979), 43–61.

22. Poetry of Yehudah Halevi (Spain, Twelfth Century)

These poems, by the poet and philosopher Yehudah Halevi (ca. 1075–1141), are love songs dedicated to a beautiful youth (*tsvi*). The first poem, "Once when I fondled him," is actually an adaptation of an Arabic poem by the Iraqi poet Aḥmad al-Mutanabbi (915–965), originally addressed to a young woman. Halevi's transformation of the beloved's gender indicates that there was some conscious choice or meaning in composing homoerotic poetry, not just literary convention. The final poem, "O you, my gazelle," is in the form known as *muwashshaḥ*, or a girdle poem, closed by a final couplet (*kharja*) in Arabic. In this *muwashshaḥ*, he cleverly describes the blushing youth as "an Aramean by name," who has become an Edomite; this pun refers to the biblical figure of Lavan the Aramean, whose name means "white," and to the nation of Edom, which also means "red." Yehudah Halevi is one of the most well-known Jewish intellectuals of medieval Spain, famous for his philosophical defense of Judaism (the *Kuzari*). For other examples of the genre of *tsvi* poems, see sources 18–20, 23–25, and 39.

I.

Once when I fondled him upon my thighs
    He caught his own reflection in my eyes
And kissed my eyes, deceitful imp; I knew
    It was his image he kissed, and not my eyes!

II.

O you, my gazelle, O you, my lord,
May my grief be dear in your eyes

Lest my ruin too soon come upon me—
    Soft, soft, soft with my soul!
    For my welfare is held in your hands
May your heart be soft for the wretch
Who fasts and who weeps from your rage
Who awaits your desire as his manna
    Sate, sate, sate me with manna
    And pay me my due every day
Though you celebrate o'er my sickness
To you I will yet turn my cheek
But somehow you answer me: "Faith! By my life!
    None, none, none have been snared in my net
    Save those who were felled by my virtue."
I feud in my soul with the miser
If only he'd fear me enough
To restore my lost years, and perhaps he might then
    Fly, fly, fly through my sleep
    And be caught in the weave of my dreams
If I ask for the wine of his lips
He turns red like the sun as it sets
Until from his visage I see,
    How, how, how an Aramean by name
    Can turn out to be Edomite
His sweet song will split my own sorrows
And his voice will arouse my bright flame
My dear, kiss my lips and so be sufficed:
    Kiss, kiss, kiss my two lips
    Spurn the black of your woe, my true love!

"Once when I fondled him," reproduced from Raymond Scheindlin, *Wine, Women, & Death: Medieval Hebrew Poems on the Good Life* (JPS, 1986). "O you, my gazelle" translated from Hebrew by Michael Yaari.

Further Reading
See bibliography for source 18.

23. Poetry of Ali ibn 'Aṭṭiyah Ibn al-Zaqqaq (Spain, Twelfth Century)

Medieval Hebrew and Arabic literature also includes examples of erotic attraction and encounter across religious and ethnic communities. This poem, by the Andalusi poet 'Ali ibn 'Aṭṭiyah Ibn al-Zaqqaq (ca. 1096–1134), depicts the poet celebrating his love for the Jewish youth who would spend Shabbat with him. Even though Ibn al-Zaqqaq describes himself as "a Muslim, and a pious one [taqiyy; in another version, he uses the term ḥanif, 'righteous']," he declares that he loves the Jewish Sabbath (yawm al-sabt) for its connection with his love. This poem was anthologized in the seventeenth-century Maghrebi compilation Nafḥ al-ṭib min ghuṣn al-Andalus al-raṭib (The Perfumed Breath from the Green Branch of al-Andalus) of Aḥmad Muḥammad al-Maqqari (ca. 1578–1632), where al-Maqqari summarizes its content as "regarding a Jewish youth [ghulam] who would sit with him as a cup-companion [nadim] on the day of the Sabbath."

And I have come to love the Sabbath day, for on it
    he accompanies me—the one whom I love.
This is among the most wondrous things: for I am a Muslim,
    and a pious one—but of all days, the sweetest for me is the Sabbath.

'Ali ibn 'Aṭṭiyah Ibn al-Zaqqaq, *Diwan* (ed. 'Afifah Mahmud Dayrani, Beirut: Dar al-Thaqafah, 1964). Translated from Arabic by Noam Sienna.

Further Reading

Assis, Yom Tov. "Sexual Behaviour in Mediaeval Hispano-Jewish Society." In *Jewish History: Essays in Honour of Chimen Abramsky* (ed. Ada Rapoport-Albert and Steven Zipperstein, Peter Halban, 1988), 25–60.

Crompton, Louis. "Male Love and Islamic Law in Arab Spain." In *Islamic Homosexualities* (eds. Stephen O. Murray and Will Roscoe, NYU Press, 1997), 142–157.

Lowin, Shari. *Arabic and Hebrew Love Poems in Al-Andalus* (Routledge, 2014).

Monroe, James. "The Striptease That Was Blamed on Abu Bakr's Naughty Son: Was Father Being Shamed, or Was the Poet Having Fun? (Ibn Quzman's zajal no. 133)." In *Homoeroticism in Classical Arabic Literature* (eds. Jerry Wright & Everett Rowson, Columbia University Press, 1997), 94–139.

24. Poetry of Yehudah al-Ḥarizi (Spain, Twelfth Century)

These poems are taken from the 50th and final chapter of the *Taḥkemoni*, the foremost Hebrew example of the genre of a *maqamah* collection: a frame tale of narrated episodes in rhymed prose (interspersed with poetry). In this episode, the narrator demonstrates his prowess in a poetry contest, sharing a long sequence of his poems written over the course of his adventures, including love poems addressed to both boys and girls. He then describes one homoerotic poem which he had heard in Baghdad, where the speaker claims that if Moses had seen this beautiful boy he would not have written the Levitical law forbidding sexual intercourse between men ("*lo ḥaq betorato ve'et zakhar*"). The narrator declares this poem to be "full of filth and impurity," and explains that he gathered ten other poets to compose responses, presenting those ten derogatory poems (of which the first is presented here), which all share the same rhyme scheme as the original, centered on the Hebrew word *zakhar* (male). What is it about this poem that crossed the line—its allusion to actual sexual contact? Or perhaps its willingness to blaspheme against the Torah? Whether this is meant as poetic one-upmanship, or as a commentary on homoerotic poetry itself, it demonstrates the complexities facing Hebrew poets writing and sharing homoerotic verse. The author of the *Taḥkemoni*, Yehudah al-Ḥarizi (1165–1225), was also a prolific translator, translating into Hebrew the Arabic *maqamat* of Abu Muhammad al-Qasim al-Ḥariri of Basra (1054–1122), and Maimonides' *Guide to the Perplexed* (among others).

I.

In days of youth, I wrote these songs about desire [*ḥesheq*]:
    My darling fawn—his cheeks
sparkle with sapphires.
Lightning crackles
when his eyes turn to me.
His lips are nectar, his face a garden.
His teeth are pearls and his mouth drips
with honey. As we watch each other,

my eyes delight in the garden of his cheeks.
But my soul is scorched and scoured
in the flame of his desire:
my eyes are in Eden
but my heart is in hell…

II.

A man of Baghdad crafted this song of perversion:
    If Amram's son had seen my lover's face—
ruddy as the hour when he drank—
his graceful locks, the splendor of his grace,
he couldn't have forbade two men a lover's embrace.
    When I gathered ten men of wit and wisdom who'd heard the song,
we censured him with his own rhyme:
    God will whip His sword of vengeance against
the impure one who brought His teaching to disgrace.
The mouth that opened to curse
the Lord, soon will be drunk with blades.
He who sells God's holiness for impurity,
will swiftly land before the executioner's face…

Yehudah al-Ḥarizi, *Sefer Taḥkemoni* (ed. Aharon Kaminka, Warsaw: Shuldberg Bros., 1899). Translated from Hebrew by Emily Jaeger.

Further Reading

See bibliography for source 18, and in addition:

Decter, Jonathan. *Iberian Jewish Literature: Between al-Andalus and Christian Europe* (Indiana University Press, 2007).

Segal, David Simha (trans. and ed.). *The Book of Taḥkemoni: Jewish Tales from Medieval Spain.* (Littman Library of Jewish Civilization, 2001).

25. Poetry of Moshe Ibn Ezra (Spain, Twelfth Century)

These poems, by the Granadan poet and linguist Moshe Ibn Ezra (ca. 1055– after 1138), are love songs dedicated to the beautiful youth, referred to as a fawn (*'ofer*), a stag (*tsvi*), and in one poem, described as a cupbearer (*saqi*) at a courtly wine party. In that poem ("The saki"), Ibn Ezra emphasizes that this youth inspires both "chaste" and "lecherous" devotion; he and his companions resign themselves to gazing on his beauty "with eyes alone." But in "My heart's desire" and "These rivers," however, he alludes to more intense erotic encounter, speaking of stripping off clothes and making love all night. The first poem, "In the fawn's hand," is a short ode using the poetic technique of *tajnis*, a type of pun where the same word is repeated with different meanings: in this case, the word *'adi*, which means both "mouth/lips" and "jewel." The final two poems, "My heart's desire" and "These rivers," are in the form known as *muwashshah*, or girdle poems, closed by a final couplet (*kharja*), in Hebrew in the former, and Arabic in the latter. In all these poems, as is typical of this genre, the beloved youth is either distant and unreachable, or cruelly fickle. For other examples of the genre of *tsvi* poems, see sources 18–20, 22–24, and 39.

I.

In the fawn's hand the glass will rise like a star
    and the West he shall make like his jewel.
And its lights shall shine bright on his cheek, beautified
    in its splendor by his lips' dazzling glory.

II.

The saki has a weakling's lisp, and yet
    Brave soldiers fall before the words he speaks
His eyes are widened not with paint, but charm;
    Abundant loveliness they have, and magic power.
Sometimes they deal out life and sometimes death
    According as their glance is firm or weak.
They show the path of chasteness to the pure;
    To wicked men they teach the lecher's way...
With our imaginary mouths we kiss his lips:
    With eyes alone we pluck his beauty's buds;
We sate our eyes on his abundant grace
    Our lips the while are faint with famine's pangs.

My heart's desire, my eyes' delight—
The cup in my hand, the fawn beside me!
My opponents are legion, yet I hear them not,
Come, my gazelle, and I shall vanquish them,
Time shall put an end to them, death shall shepherd them away.
    Come, my gazelle, arise and restore me,
    And with your lips' nectar please sate me!
Why, oh why must they deter my heart?
If it was in the name of sin, for the sake of guilt
That I devoted myself to your beauty—let God be the judge!
    Let your heart not heed the words of he who torments me,
    That stubborn man! Come, now test me!
He was seduced, and we left for his mother's house,
And his back yielded beneath the weight of my yoke,
Night and day, I am with him only.
    I strip off his clothes—and he strips me,
    I suck at his lips, and he suckles me.
But once my heart was locked in his eyes,
The yoke of my sins was bound by his hand—
He turns to enmity, summons his wrath,
    Angrily shouting, "Enough of you! Leave me,
    Do not push me off course, do not mislead me!"
Do not rage at me, my gazelle, as if to destroy me,
But dazzle me with your desire,
Kiss your beloved, fulfill his ardor,
    If there's life in your soul, then revive me,
    But if you would rather kill me—then kill me!

IV.

These rivers reveal for the world to see
The secret love concealed in me.
    You who blame me, Ah! be still.
    My love's a stag who's learned to kill,

Arrogant, with stubborn will.
Passion has disheartened me—
Cruel of him to part from me.
    A fawn is he with slender thighs.
    The sun goes dark when it sees him rise.
    Darts are flying from his eyes.
Stole my sleep away from me,
Altogether wasted me.
    Never will I forget the night
    We lay together in delight
    Upon my bed till morning light.
All night he made love to me,
At his mouth he suckled me.
    Charming even in deceit;
    The fruit of his mouth is like candy sweet.
    Played me false, that little cheat!
Deceived me, then made fun of me;
I did him no wrong, but he wronged me.
    One day when my eyes were filled to the brim
    There came to my ears this little hymn,
    So I sang my doleful song to him:
    "How dear that boy is to me!
    Maybe he'll come back to me."

"In the fawn's hand" and "My heart's desire" translated from Hebrew by Michael Yaari. "These rivers" and "The saki" reproduced from Raymond Scheindlin, *Wine, Women, & Death: Medieval Hebrew Poems on the Good Life* (JPS, 1986).

Further Reading
See bibliography for source 18.

26. A Tale of Lovers Martyred During the First Crusade (Germany, 1140)

The Jews of the Rhineland, known as Ashkenaz in medieval Hebrew sources, did not leave behind extensive homoerotic literature and poetry as did their counterparts in the Islamic world. Nonetheless, the existing textual evidence demonstrates that some medieval Ashkenazi writers glorified a vision of intimate male-male friendship, which was apparently also part of Ashkenazi Jewish daily life. One example is this moving story, which celebrates the love of two young men named Shmu'el and Yeḥiel, martyred during the antisemitic massacres of the First Crusade in 1096 in the fortified town of Wevelinghoven in the Cologne region, in western Germany. The report comes from a text known as *The Chronicle of Solomon bar Samson* (Shlomo Bar Shimshon), written around 1140 in Mainz. In this text, the story of Shmu'el and Yeḥiel is memorialized, alongside other emotional tales of the heroic martyrdom of parents together with their children, of elderly men and women and of young married couples, as part of the tragedy that befell the Jews of Ashkenaz during the high and late Middle Ages.

And on that day, Tuesday, the enemies of God came to one city and by evening [the inhabitants] had martyred themselves for the Divine Name— beautiful brides and grooms, elders, young men and women, stretched out their necks and slaughtered each other themselves, giving their souls for the sanctification of the Name by the lakes near the city. When the enemies came to the city, some of the pious ones climbed up the tower and threw themselves into the river of the Rhine that went around the city, and drowned themselves in the river, and they all died.

There were just two bachelors who were not able to die in the water: the betrothed Rabbi Shmu'el, son of Rabbi Gedalyah, and Yeḥiel, son of Rabbi Shmu'el. "*They were cherished in their lives,*" for they loved each other greatly, "*and in their death they were not divided*" (II Samuel 1:23). When they decided to throw themselves into the water, they kissed one another and grasped one another and embraced one another by their shoulders, and wept, saying, "Woe for our youth, that we did not merit to see generations issuing from us, and that we did not reach old age! Even so, '*let us fall now by the hand of God*' (II Samuel 24:14), who is the faithful and merciful King. It is best for us to die here for the sake of God's great name, and we will walk with the saints in the Garden of Eden, and these unclean and uncircumcised ones will not capture us against our will in their wicked waters."

After this, those that had remained in the city and did not go up to the tower saw all those who had drowned, and they found these two good and saintly companions, clasped tightly together. When the pious Shmuel saw his son Yeḥiel, who had thrown himself into the river but had not yet died—and he was a beautiful youth, with *"an appearance like Lebanon"* (Song of Songs 5:15)—he cried out, "Yeḥiel, my son, my son! Stretch out your neck before your father, and I will offer you, the soul of my son, as a sacrifice to God; I will say the blessing for the slaughter and you answer amen." And the saintly Rabbi Shmuel did this, and slaughtered his son with his knife in the water.

And when the betrothed, Rabbi Shmuel son of Rabbi Gedalyah, heard that his companion, the saintly Yeḥiel, had been convinced by his father to be slaughtered in the water, he decided that he would do the same. He called to Menaḥem, the *shammash* of the synagogue in Cologne, and said to him: "By your life, take your sharp knife and check it well, so that there are no nicks in it, and slaughter me also, so that I will not see the death of my companion. Say the blessing for the slaughter, and I will answer amen." These pious ones did so, and as they were slaughtered together, before their souls left them they clasped their hands together and died together in the river; thus they fulfilled the Scripture, *"in their death they were not divided"* (II Samuel 1:23).

Sippur Hagzerot Lerabbi Shlomo BaR Shimshon (*4856 = 1096 CE*), as published by Abraham Meir Habermann, *Sefer Gzerot Ashkenaz Vetsarfat* (Jerusalem: Tarshish, 1946). Translated from Hebrew by Noam Sienna. I thank Eyal Levinson for pointing me toward this source and clarifying its historical context.

Further Reading

Chazan, Robert. *God, Humanity, and History: The Hebrew First Crusade Narratives* (Berkeley: University of California Press, 2000).

Cohen, Jeremy. *Sanctifying the Name of God: Jewish Martyrs and Jewish Memories of the First Crusade* (University of Pennsylvania Press, 2004).

Levinson, Eyal. "'The Friend Visits Him Frequently and Reveals His Secret': Hasidei Ashkenaz and Male Friendship." Paper presented at the conference "Sefer Hasidim in Context," National Library of Israel, March 19–22, 2017.

27. Maimonides Codifies Laws on Homosexual Activity (Egypt, Mid-Twelfth Century)

Moses Maimonides, or Moshe ben Maimon (1135–1204), is one of the most well-known figures of medieval Jewish history, a renowned philosopher, doctor, and rabbinic authority. Born in Cordoba, Maimonides studied medicine in Fes before settling in Egypt, where he compiled several core texts of Jewish theology, philosophy, exegesis, and law, including his magnum opus of Jewish law, the *Mishneh Torah* (written while he was serving both as *nagid* [leader] of the local Jewish community, and court physician to the Ayyubid sultan Saladin). The excerpts presented here, from Maimonides' *Commentary on the Mishnah* and his *Mishneh Torah*, affirm the death penalty for anal same-sex penetration between men. Interestingly, Maimonides is content with the simple statement of prohibition, but seems more concerned with emphasizing the issue of same-sex activity among women, perhaps precisely because it is not biblically prohibited and thus needs to be reinforced. Maimonides repeats the Talmudic language of *nashim mesollelot* and forbidden foreign practices (see sources 9 and 11) but adds that there were women who were "known for this," and that a man should prevent his wife from associating with them. His legal position goes much further than the rabbinic texts he draws on, and is almost exactly parallel to the discussions of lesbianism in Islamic law among his contemporary Arab peers.

I. *Commentary on the Mishnah*, Sanhedrin 7:4

Similarly, this shameful practice which occurs among women, namely sexual intercourse between one woman and another, is a detestable [*makruh*] practice. However, there is no punishment for it mandated by either the Torah or the rabbis, and no woman who does this is called a prostitute* and she is not forbidden from her husband, nor from [marrying into] the priesthood. And this is what the sages call women who rub with one another [*nashim mesollelot zo bazo*], which is derived from *maslul*, which means "path."

---

* *Zonah*. This is a legal status which affects whom she can marry.

Although there is no punishment for this practice, it is considered to be among the abominations of Egypt, and [our Sages] said in explaining "*the deeds of the land of Egypt*" (Leviticus 18:3): "And what would they do? A man would be married to another man, and a woman to another woman, and a woman would be married to two [men at once]" (*Sifra*, Aḥarei Mot 9:8).

II. *Mishneh Torah*, Laws of Sexual Prohibitions

[1:14:] Regarding one who penetrates [another] man, or who allows another man to penetrate him—if they are both adults, they are stoned to death, as it says, "*With a male you shall not lie*" (Leviticus 18:22), whether he was active or passive. If he was a minor over the age of nine and one day, then the adult who penetrated him or who allowed himself to be penetrated is stoned, but the minor is exempt [from stoning]. If he was a minor under the age of nine, then they are both exempt [from stoning], but it is appropriate for the court to administer lashes to the adult, since he lay with a male, even if he was younger than the age of nine.

[21:8–9:] Women who rub [*mesollelot*] one another—[this is] forbidden, and it is considered "a practice of Egypt" against which we were warned, as it says, "*According to the ways of the Land of Egypt...you shall not do*" (Leviticus 18:3). And [furthermore] the sages said, "And what would they do? A man would be married to another man, and a woman to another woman, and a woman would be married to two [men at once]" (*Sifra*, Aḥarei Mot 9:8). However, even though this act is forbidden, one is not [obligated by Torah to] administer lashes for it, since it is not [addressed] by a specific prohibition, and since indeed there is no actual penetration.

Therefore, [these women] are not forbidden from [marrying into] the priesthood because of adultery [*zenut*], nor is a woman forbidden from [remaining with] her husband for this, since there is no adultery here. Nonetheless, it is appropriate for the rabbinic court to administer lashes, since they have still done a forbidden act. And a man should be careful to be strict with his wife regarding this matter, and prevent the women who are known for this to enter [the house] to join her, and [prevent] her from going out to join them.

Maimonides, *Mishneh Torah* (New York: E. Grossman, 1957) and *Commentary on the Mishnah* (ed. Yosef Qafiḥ, Jerusalem: Mossad Rav Kook, 1963). Translated from Hebrew and Judeo-Arabic by Noam Sienna.

Further Reading

Alpert, Rebecca. *Like Bread on the Seder Plate: Jewish Lesbians and the Transformation of Tradition* (Columbia University Press, 1997).

Amer, Sahar. "Medieval Arab Lesbians and Lesbian-Like Women." *Journal of the History of Sexuality* 18:2 (2009), 215–236.

Kosman, Admiel, and Anat Sharbat. "'Two Women Who Were Sporting With Each Other': A Reexamination of the Halakhic Approaches to Lesbianism as a Touchstone for Homosexuality in General." *Hebrew Union College Annual* 75 (2004), 37–74.

Omar, Sara. "From Semantics to Normative Law: Perceptions of *Liwāṭ* (Sodomy) and *Siḥāq* (Tribadism) in Islamic Jurisprudence (8th–15th Century CE)." *Islamic Law and Society* 19 (2012), 222–256.

28. A Love Amulet Between Two Men (Egypt, ca. 1200)

The Cairo Genizah preserved not only sacred texts, but also thousands of documents that shed light on ordinary life in medieval Egypt, including business correspondence, shopping lists, schoolbooks, personal letters, poetry, and magical amulets (see source 21). This example is an amuletic text with a spell to ensure love between two men. It is undated but probably comes from the late twelfth century and was made for a prominent local scholar and contemporary of Maimonides, Yehudah bar Yoshiyah. Like other love spells from the Genizah, Yehudah here appeals to the power of angelic and divine names to inflame the heart of a man named Hodayah bar Shlomo, reworking verses from Psalms and Song of Songs to include their names. The back of the amulet contains another magical spell, asking for favor in the eyes of rulers and scholars, and protection from enemies.

[Yehud]ah bar [...]

YH[VH] Shaddai Ehye / ABG YTS QR' MSN NGD Y[KS...]*

I [demand] from you and ask of you, the names [...]

I [adjure] you to inflame Hodayah bar [Sh]lomo [for] Yehudah bar Yoshiyah. *Many waters cannot quench love and rivers cannot wash it away. If* Hodayah bar Shlomo *were to give all the wealth of his house* to Yehudah bar Yoshiyah, *he would be utterly scorned* (Song of Songs 8:7). *As the deer pants for streams of water,*

*These letters form a mystical 42-letter divine name widely used in medieval amulets.

so the soul of Hodayah bar Shlomo *pants for you,* Yehudah bar Yoshiyah (Psalms 42:2).* And he shall come to him swiftly and speedily. A[men] A[men] Selah. Finished.

This great secret is designated to be as a sharp sword in the hand of Yehudah bar Yoshiyah, born of [MYAM?], in the name of the Lord of Hosts who is enthroned between the Cherubim, I Am That I Am Adiraron Akatriel…

JTS ENA 3296.16/3319.3, translated from Judeo-Arabic by Noam Sienna.

Further Reading

Bohak, Gideon. "Reconstructing Jewish magical recipe books from the Cairo Genizah." *Ginzei Qedem* 1 (2005), 9–29.

Goitein, Shlomo Dov. "The Sexual Mores of the Common People." In *Society and the Sexes in Medieval Islam* (ed. A. L. al-Sayyid Marsot, Udena Publications, 1979), 43–61.

Saar, Ortal-Paz. "Success, Protection and Grace: Three Fragments of a Personalized Magical Handbook." *Ginzei Qedem* 3 (2007), 101–135.

Saar, Ortal-Paz. "'Let His Heart Burn for Her': The Motif of Fire in Love Spells from the Cairo Genizah." *Pe'amim* 133 (2013), 209–240.

29. The Tale of Sapir and Shapir (Spain, 1233)

Homoerotic motifs are found not only in the Hebrew poetry of the Middle Ages, but also in other literary compositions. Beginning in the twelfth century, Jewish authors began composing a genre of literary fiction known in Arabic as *maqamah* (and in Hebrew *maḥberet*)—a narrative in rhymed prose of short episodes, incorporating interspersed poems (see source 24). One trope in *maqamah* literature, in both Arabic and Hebrew, is a scene sometimes called "the pederast tale," the story of a man's frustrated pursuit of a beautiful young man. This example comes from the collection of the writer and translator Ya'aqov Ben El'azar (ca. 1170–1233) of Toledo, called *Sefer Hameshalim* (Book of Fables). Its ten tales include a number of allegorical love-stories, both between two men and between men and women, in dialogue with contemporary Arabic and Romance literary models. The fifth chapter tells the story of how Sapir ("Sapphire") and Shapir ("Beauty") fall in love, and defend themselves against Birsha, who shares the name of a

*In both of these verses, the writer has modified the text to insert these two names.

king of Gomorrah. The old "pederast" Birsha attempts to plead his case with a judge, but he is condemned to death, and Sapir and Shapir kill themselves. As Jonathan Decter has observed, it is not clear why Birsha's pursuit of Shapir is condemned while Sapir's is sanctioned. Is it the greater age gap between them? Birsha's false piety? His violence in kidnapping Shapir? It is likely some combination of these elements which leads Ben El'azar to cast the villain Birsha, through numerous textual allusions, as connected to Sodom—the charge of "sodomy" as a category of forbidden sexual activity between men had already emerged in Latin Christendom over the previous two centuries (see source 34).

[From among the male and female gazelles, Sapir] placed [Shapir] in his command, laid him down in his lap, fed him from his bread, placed the gazelle in his trap and caught him in his snare. His desire continued to grow such that when he was apart his soul departed, for it was bound to his soul. In his cheek his sun rose; his night was the hair on his head. His love began to trouble and oppress him and he said, "How my desire has weakened me! Was I not only dallying?"

The tent-pegs of desire that had pierced his heart tortured him and the nails of love became fixed in his soul and he said, "From the beginning you were faint, now your strength is small and you suffer. If once you dallied with love, now love dallies with you many times over..."

[An old man named Birsha Ben Mesha kidnaps Shapir, but Sapir follows them.]

[When Shapir sees Sapir, he says to him:] "I am but a youth, so do not think I have transgressed! I saw his beard and white hair, and heard his words smooth like a woman's! He stole me with his smooth speech. I did not know that his beard was shame and that he would hunt me thrust upon thrust."

[Sapir and Shapir escape to a nearby spring.]

And [Birsha] rose up against Sapir the hunter and the two of them wrestled in the field. Birsha said, "Let there be no strife between us. *'Behold, there is a city nearby,'* (Genesis 19:20) where there is a judge of truth who can testify against the living that he was murdered by the dead! *'He will decide between us, lay his hand on both of us [in judgment]'* (Job 9:33). His name is Arioch and he spills the blood of the innocent." They came to the city, which was called "Foolishness" since there are no men there. They came to the judge who subverts the rights of the stranger and the orphan. Each told his story and what had happened to him. [The judge] became full of wrath, *"struck his hands together"* (Numbers 24:10) and rebuked Birsha by saying, "Get away from me, you despicable and contemptible man! This man deserves the death penalty!" He called out in a loud voice, *"'Because of this the Earth bears guilt!'"* (Hosea 14:1) He is guilty; he has incurred guilt. Because of this the lad will not go with you and you will go on your way."

When Birsha heard [the judge] say, "Forfeit the boy!" he said, *"'He came here as a foreigner and now he acts as judge!'"* (Genesis 19:9) The boy is my son; I begat him and he is my only son, and you have snatched him from my hand." When Sapir heard [Birsha] lording himself over the youth, his spirit departed and he was despoiled, he acted like a madman and languished, he spoke senselessly and blasphemed and cursed more than a woman in travail. He fell to the ground and flailed about; he was poured out like water. The gazelle [Shapir] called out to him, "My love, my love," but there was no sound, no one to answer, no one to behold, and no one to turn (in attention). The gazelle Shapir took a handful of the water of love and sprinkled it on [Sapir's] face. The burning subsided and he opened his eyes. He took the hand of the gazelle Sapir and shouted because of his great passion, and the gazelle wept with him. He recited:

> Brothers in desire are brothers in sickness! They alone are brothers of ruin.
> In their hearts, birds grow new wings each day,
> For my heart is like a darting bird, flying in every direction.—
> Lovesick, liver-stricken, apart from him [I am] like a passing shadow.

[He recited such that] even the brutish man could understand. But what happened to the youth? The gazelle Shapir said, "Have you seen the beard of Birsha, that it is a beard of wickedness? For all its length and breadth, the best of it is trouble and sorrow! It holds the venom of asps! This, my lord, is what fooled me. The wearer of the beard stole me, he enticed me." The judge pitied Sapir and his beloved, and placed [Birsha] in his charge. They beat Birsha and wounded him severely. They pressed him between the doors. He died; they dragged [his corpse] and tossed it upon the dung heap.

Yaʻaqov Ben Elʻazar, *Sefer Hameshalim*, as translated in Jonathan Decter, "A Hebrew 'sodomite' tale from thirteenth-century Toledo: Jacob Ben Elʻazar's story of Sapir, Shapir, and Birsha," *Journal of Medieval Iberian Studies* 3:2 (2011), 187–202. Reprinted by permission of Taylor & Francis Ltd, http://www.tandfonline.com.

Further Reading

Assis, Yom Tov. "Sexual Behaviour in Mediaeval Hispano-Jewish Society." In *Jewish History: Essays in Honour of Chimen Abramsky* (ed. Ada Rapoport-Albert and Steven Zipperstein, Peter Halban, 1988), 25–60.

David, Yonah (ed.). *Sippure Ahavah shel Yaʻaqov ben Elʻazar* (Tel Aviv University, 1993).

Decter, Jonathan. *Iberian Jewish Literature: Between al-Andalus and Christian Europe* (Indiana University Press, 2007).

Huss, Matti. "Maḥberet 'Shaliaḥ Hatsibbur': lishe'elat meqoroteha veziqatah lesifrut haʻivrit hahomoʻerotit biyemei habenayyim." *Tarbits* 72 (2003), 197–244.

30. Avraham Maimonides Disapproves of Gender-Nonconformity (Egypt, Early Thirteenth Century)

Avraham ben HaRambam, or Abraham Maimonides (1186–1237), succeeded his father Maimonides (see source 27) as *nagid*, head of the Egyptian Jewish community. In this responsum he attacks a contemporary practice of having cross-dressing and gender play as part of wedding celebrations, including arming the bride with weapons and adorning the groom with feminine cosmetics. He adds a further note voicing his displeasure with young boys who were similarly decorated with henna and dressed with feminine adornments, and who apparently served as entertainment at celebrations and holidays. Despite Avraham's disapproval of these feminine dancing youths, perhaps the same ones who are praised in the homoerotic poetry of his time, they remained a popular feature of Jewish (and non-Jewish) societies throughout the Middle East, in some places surviving to the present day (see sources 49 and 74).

Although Jewish women are largely guarded from this sin (may the Merciful protect us) of the prohibition of "[*wearing*] *men's clothing*" (Deuteronomy

22:5), some of them do indeed fall into this [sin] because of their folly. At their weddings, they impersonate non-Jewish [men] and the woman will wear a turban or a hat, and takes a sword in her hand, and goes out in dance in front of the men, and the other women [are with her] in this abomination. One cannot think that because she is a bride, she has been permitted a biblical prohibition…

And it has long been the custom in Egypt, and even great people have fallen in this, until we abolished it and erased its memory. Similarly, the groom would go out [dressed] as a woman, adorned by the cosmetician, and this is entirely [a violation of the prohibition against wearing] a woman's ornament and it is forbidden to do it. It is good to be careful of this and not rely on women who have neither sense nor wisdom; and the one who fears Heaven will himself be scrupulous regarding this, so that they do not fall into this sin, lest he also be caught in their sin.

And thus also [with regards to] the little boys, who are sometimes adorned with women's ornaments and their hands are dyed with the color that women dye their hands with—this is the opposite of what is commanded by the blessed transmitters of tradition…This is a crooked path and the path of sinners, that they do this in public, in the synagogues, in the midst of the congregation and community of Israel, on holidays, and no one takes any heed.

Qovets Teshuvot HaRambam Ve'iggerotav (ed. Avraham Likhtenberg, Leipzig, 1859), Ḥiddushei HaRambam 1:51a. Translated from Hebrew by Noam Sienna.

Further Reading

Assis, Yom Tov. "Sexual Behaviour in Mediaeval Hispano-Jewish Society." In *Jewish History: Essays in Honour of Chimen Abramsky* (ed. Ada Rapoport-Albert and Steven Zipperstein, Peter Halban, 1988), 25–60.

Roth, Norman. "'Fawns of My Delight': Boy-Love in Arabic and Hebrew Verse." In *Poetics of Love in the Middle Ages* (ed. Moshe Lazar and Norris Lacy, George Mason University Press, 1989), 96–118.

31. A Rabbi Rules on Sexual Behavior between Boys (Catalonia, Late Thirteenth Century)

This unusual legal responsum concerns two underage boys who were seen by non-Jews to be engaging in sexual activity. The rabbi addressed by the question, Shlomo Ibn Aderet (1235–1310), also known as the Rashba, was one of the greatest rabbinic authorities of the medieval Christian kingdoms of Aragón-Catalonia. The boys are pardoned on two counts: both because they are under the age of Jewish legal majority—namely, one day over the age of thirteen—and because non-Jews are not eligible to testify as witnesses in a Jewish court. The nature of this "sex play" is not clear from the text, and indeed, while the precise ages of the boys seem to fluctuate in the responsum, they are certainly quite young. Nevertheless, it is astonishing that Ibn Aderet does not address the particular issue of sex between two boys, does not warn them to prevent this kind of behavior, and bases his legal ruling entirely on Talmudic texts that discuss the age limits for sexual activity with girls (rather than, for example, Maimonides' explicit ruling on male-male sexual activity—see source 27).

QUESTION: Regarding two Jewish youths, one eleven years old and the other twelve years old—a group of about twenty Gentiles testified against them, that they were fooling around with each other. Please enlighten us whether they are exempt or liable according to the Gentiles' testimony. And if, Heaven forbid, the matter is true, are they exempt or liable? And similarly, enlighten us what their judgement should be, if the older one is older than thirteen years old, according to Jewish law, and what their punishment should be.

RESPONSE: Why are you asking me about Gentile testimony? This requires neither a question nor an answer [since such testimony is automatically disqualified]. And if the matter is true, as you asked me, what should their judgement be? You should know that a male minor under the age of thirteen and a day, and a female minor under the age of twelve and a day, are not liable for punishment and cannot be sentenced to death by a Jewish court, even if there were witnesses there who saw it, for this is as we learned in Tractate *Niddah* [44b]…

And in that same *mishnah* which we referenced above, you can also learn about what you asked regarding [what should happen] if one was older than thirteen and a day and the other was ten [or eleven] years old: the older one is liable [if he were penetrated by] the younger one, and the younger one is exempt, as we have learned…

You can learn from this that the older one is punished if he is penetrated by the younger one, but the younger one is not punished if he is penetrated by the older one, since a minor is not liable for punishment…And in any case, you should already know that even the older one cannot be sentenced to death by a Jewish court unless there were two [Jewish] witnesses who saw the act, and this needs no further explanation.

Sefer She'elot Uteshuvot HaRaShBA, Vol. 4 (Jerusalem, 1960), §166. Translated from Hebrew by Noam Sienna.

Further Reading

Assis, Yom Tov. "Sexual Behaviour in Mediaeval Hispano-Jewish Society." In *Jewish History: Essays in Honour of Chimen Abramsky* (ed. Ada Rapoport-Albert and Steven Zipperstein, Peter Halban, 1988), 25–60.

32. Poetry of Qalonymos ben Qalonymos (Provence, 1323)

Qalonymos ben Qalonymos, born in 1286 in Arles (southern France), was a Provençal Jewish writer, philosopher, and translator. This fascinating and puzzling poem (originally written in rhymed prose) is taken from Qalonymos' book *Even Boḥan* (Touchstone), a carnivalesque and satirical reflection on fourteenth-century Jewish life in Catalonia and Provence, which skewers the hypocrisies of Jewish society and presents critical parodies of local scholars and holiday celebrations. The speaker describes at great length their deep dissatisfaction with masculinity and their dream of becoming female, drawing on biblical miracles of transformation and midrashic accounts of sex change (see source 14). In the end, they conclude that if it is not to be, they will suffer their fate with bitter dignity. It is not clear whether this text is meant to present a comedic reversal of gender stereotypes, a gentle parody of male chauvinism, or perhaps even an ironic response to women reciting, "Who has made me according to Your will" during the morning blessings—a custom first documented among Sephardi Jews in the early fourteenth century (for another, later, response to the morning blessings, see source 65). While it most likely cannot be taken as a personal confession of the author, the depth and authenticity of its feeling is still moving, and provides an example of how medieval Jews could imagine and articulate a desire for gender transition.

What an awful fate for my mother
that she bore a son. What a loss of all benefit!…
Cursed be the one who announced to my father: "It's a boy!"…
Woe to him who has male sons.
Upon them a heavy yoke has been placed, restrictions and constraints.
Some in private, some in public,
some to avoid the mere appearance of violation,
and some entering the most secret of places.
Strong statutes and awesome commandments,
six hundred and thirteen.
Who is the man who can do all that is written,
so that he might be spared?
Oh, but had the artisan who made me
created me instead—a fair woman.
Today I would be wise and insightful.
We would weave, my friends and I,
and in the moonlight spin our yarn,
and tell our stories to one another, from dusk till midnight.
We'd tell of the events of our day, silly things,
matters of no consequence.
But also I would grow very wise from the spinning,
and I would say, "Happy is she who knows how to work with combed
flax and weave it into fine white linen."
And at times, in the way of women,
I would lie down on the kitchen floor,
between the ovens, turn the coals, and taste the different dishes.
On holidays I would put on my best jewelry.
I would beat on the drum
and my clapping hands would ring.
And when I was ready and the time was right,
an excellent youth would be my fortune.
He would love me, place me on a pedestal,

dress me in jewels of gold,
earrings, bracelets, necklaces.
And on the appointed day,
in the season of joy when brides are wed,
for seven days would the boy increase my delight and gladness.
　　Were I hungry, he would feed me well-kneaded bread.
Were I thirsty, he would quench me with light and dark wine.
He would not chastise nor harshly treat me,
and my [sexual] pleasure he would not diminish.
　　Every Sabbath, and each new moon,
his head would rest upon my breast.
The three husbandly duties he would fulfill,
rations, raiment, and regular intimacy.
And three wifely duties would I also fulfill,
[watching for menstrual] blood, [Sabbath candle] lights, and bread.
　　Father in heaven, who did miracles for our ancestors with fire and
water,
You changed the fire of Chaldees so it would not burn hot,
You changed Dinah in the womb of her mother to a girl,
You changed the staff to a snake before a million eyes,*
You changed [Moses'] hand to [leprous] white**
and the sea to dry land.
In the desert you turned rock to water,
hard flint to a fountain.
　　Who would then turn me from a man to woman?
Were I only to have merited this, being so graced by goodness.
　　What shall I say? Why cry or be bitter?
If my Father in heaven has decreed upon me
and has maimed me with an immutable deformity,
then I do not wish to remove it.
And the sorrow of the impossible
is a human pain that nothing will cure
and for which no comfort can be found.

---

*Exodus 7:8–13.
**Exodus 4:6–7.

So, I will bear and suffer
until I die and wither in the ground.
And since I have learned from our tradition
that we bless both the good and the bitter,
I will bless in a voice, hushed and weak,
Blessed are you, O Lord,
who has not made me a woman.

Qalonymos ben Qalonymos, *Even Bohan*, as translated in Greenberg, Steven, *Wrestling With God And Men.* © 2004 by the Board of Regents of the University of Wisconsin System. Reprinted by permission of the University of Wisconsin Press.

Further Reading

Cole, Peter. *The Dream of the Poem: Hebrew Poetry from Muslim and Christian Spain, 950–1492* (Princeton University Press, 2007).

Rosen, Tova. *Unveiling Eve: Reading Gender in Medieval Hebrew Literature* (University of Pennsylvania Press, 2003).

33. Todros Abulafia's Defense of Erotic Poetry, and Poems (Spain, Early Fourteenth Century)

Several Hebrew poets of medieval Iberia wrote defenses of their love poetry (whether homosexual or heterosexual); while they did not deny the content of these poems, they argued that their erotic poetry was a literary exercise rather than a description of experience, and emphasized its allegorical meanings. In this excerpt from the introduction to his *diwan* (poetry collection), Todros Abulafia (1247–after 1300) explicitly declares that his erotic poems, which were written about both boys and girls, are not meant to be understood literally as matters of transgression; rather, they are his demonstration that Hebrew is equally capable of expressing poetic conventions as contemporary Arabic poetry. Abulafia was born and raised in Toledo, and he was a prominent poet in the courts of the Castilian rulers Alfonso X and his son Sancho IV; his poetry is often ironic, candid, and frank, including erotic poetry in praise of both boys and girls, but especially Arab and Christian girls. In this unusual poem, he describes his longings for an Arab girl who spent her time "in the company of other young women, all kissing one another." Unlike Qalonymos ben Qalonymos' poem in *Even Bohan*, which narrates a sincere desire for womanhood (see source 32), here Abulafia playfully suggests that it would have been better for him to be a woman, since he would then have a better chance at winning this woman's love. While there are a number of medieval Arabic texts from the Mediterranean and the Middle East that portray romantic and sexual relationships between women (often termed sahq, "rubbing, grinding"), such depictions are almost unknown in medieval Hebrew literature.

I.

And if one might find in [my book] erotic matters and the praise of boys and girls—I swear by the heavens and the earth as my witnesses, that [this is] not for any matter of transgression, and Heaven forbid that I intend any evil; it is not for any sin or pride, but rather to reveal secrets in the ways of poetry, and to demonstrate that the Holy Tongue can be as sweet in poetry as Arabic, and that lofty things can be spoken of with it. For custom [*minhag*] is the bond of prophets and the commandment of learned men (cf. I Samuel 10:5 and Isaiah 29:13)...

II.

Concerning an Arab girl whose love was sweet to me, whom I saw in the company of other young women, all kissing one another:

> I have not given birth, though in love I travail,
>   Being caught in the snare of this Arab gazelle.
> My own soul so desires to kiss her sweet lips
>   That I long to be female, to no avail—
> For she's perfectly willing to kiss other girls,
>   Oh, how I've missed out, being born a male!

David Yellin (ed.), *Gan Hameshalim Vehahidot: osef shire Todros ben Yehudah Abu Al'Afia* (Jerusalem: Weiss Press, 1934). Prose translated from Hebrew by Noam Sienna. Poetry translated from Hebrew by Michael Yaari.

Further Reading

Amer, Sahar. "Medieval Arab Lesbians and Lesbian-Like Women." *Journal of the History of Sexuality* 18:2 (2009), 215–236.

Rosen, Tova. *Unveiling Eve: Reading Gender in Medieval Hebrew Literature* (University of Pennsylvania Press, 2003), esp. 30–63.

Roth, Norman. "Religious Constraints on Erotic Poetry among Muslims and Jews in al-Andalus." *Maghreb Review* 19:3–4 (1994), 194–205.

34. Issach Salamó is Executed for Sodomy (Perpignan, 1403)

Starting in the mid-eleventh century, Christian legal scholars formulated the notion of sodomy (*sodomia*), a "crime against nature" that could refer to bestiality (*sodomia ratione generis*) and non-procreative heterosexual sex (*sodomia ratione modi*) as well as intercourse between people of the same sex (*sodomia ratione sexus*). Punishments included beatings, confiscation of property, exile, castration, and death. In many codes, sodomy was also closely connected to religious heresy and to improper relationships between Christians and Jews or Muslims. In spite of this legislation, in many areas of Europe there were not significant numbers of sodomy trials until the fourteenth or even fifteenth centuries. This case records the trial of a Jew named Issach Salamó, who was tried and condemned for sodomy in Perpignan in the winter of 1402. Originally from the Aragonese town of Calatayud, Salamó was living in the small town of Tuïr (Thuir) near Perpignan, in what was then the Catalan province of Rosselló (now called Roussillon; it has been a part of France since the Treaty of the Pyrenees was signed in 1659). Salamó was burnt at the stake on the twelfth of January, 1403; according to this notarial record, the total expense of his execution came to 38 sous and 4 diners.

On January 12, I paid the executioner Alfonso for cord and gloves which served to burn Issach Salamó of Calatayud, a Jew, who was convicted of the sin of sodomy: 6 sous.*

On the same day, following the order of the bailiff given to me by the messenger Johan Sola, I paid Joffrena de Garius for renting out her horse, which carried Issach to the place where he was burned: 2 sous, 6 diners.

---

*A medieval coin, equivalent to 12 diners.

I paid Pere de Castres, vice-bailiff, for one *somada* [approximately 300 lbs.] of olive tree wood, which he purchased for [the purpose of burning] the said Issach.

I paid Bonfil Tauler for 8 *quintals* [approximately 100 lbs.] of wood, which are equivalent to two *pes* bought by the aforementioned vice-bailiff for the same purpose: 8 sous.

I paid Arnau Joan, blacksmith, for one *pes* of wood, which is 4 *quintals*, which the said vice-bailiff purchased for the same purpose, at a rate of 14 diners per *quintal*: 4 sous 8 diners.

I also paid the said vice-bailiff for one small bundle of wood, which he purchased from a porter for the same purpose: 1 sous.

I also paid the vice-bailiff 3 sous which he had paid to one carpenter for the pole which he purchased, on which the Jew was bound. And I also paid him another 2 sous which he had paid to 2 porters who helped him, for the same purpose: 5 sous.

I paid Posset and Arnanto, messengers, for going to Thuir to bring the said Jew who had been arrested, and they stayed there two days: 6 sous.

On January 15th, I paid Manresa, a messenger, who brought the Jew's brother Bonet, and Abram Cota, [both accused of the same] crime, but then it was found that they did not deserve punishment.

Archivo de la Corona de Aragón, Real Patrimonio, Mestre Racional, Volúmenes, Serie General, 1682, fol. 83v–84r. Translated from Catalan by Dr. Natalie Oeltjen, with the generous assistance of Dr. Neil Manel Frau-Cortes. Copyright © 2019 Print-O-Craft Press. I am grateful to Dr. Michael Ryan for his additional help in contextualizing this source and to Gloria López and Félix Hernández Durán of the ACA for their efforts in locating and digitizing this document.

Further Reading

Assis, Yom Tov. "Sexual Behaviour in Mediaeval Hispano-Jewish Society." In *Jewish History: Essays in Honour of Chimen Abramsky* (ed. Ada Rapoport-Albert and Steven Zipperstein, Peter Halban, 1988), 25–60.

Jordan, Mark. *The Invention of Sodomy in Christian Theology* (University of Chicago Press, 1997).

Mills, Robert. *Seeing Sodomy in the Middle Ages* (University of Chicago Press, 2015).

Riera i Sans, Jaume. *Sodomites Catalans: Història i vida, segles XIII–XVIII* (Barcelona: Editorial Base, 2014).

Telechea, Jesus Angel Solorzano. "*Fama publica*, infamy and defamation: judicial violence and social control of crimes against sexual morals in medieval Castile." *Journal of Medieval History* 33:4 (2007), 398–413.

35. A Romaniote Rabbi Rules on Homosexual Activity in the Synagogue (Constantinople, Late Fifteenth Century)

This astonishing legal response comes from Eliyah Mizraḥi (1455–1526), a scholar of Romaniote origin who was one of the foremost rabbinic authorities in the Ottoman Empire. In general, he strove to promote inter-communal tolerance, both between Karaites and Rabbanites and between Romaniotes and Sephardim. This responsum, while undated, must come from before the 1492 expulsion of the Jews from Spain, since it refers to a Jewish community in Aragon. The situation presented is that the caretaker of a local synagogue was apparently witnessed engaging in homosexual activity with a young man and some people were reluctant to continue attending the synagogue as a result. Remarkably, Mizraḥi condemns this attitude and declares emphatically that there is absolutely no issue or prohibition in continuing to attend the synagogue—in fact, he has nothing at all to say about the nature of the transgression. Instead, he explains that even idolatry, which is "more severe and more disgusting" than homosexuality, cannot undo the holiness of a synagogue, and therefore there is nothing to be concerned about regarding this more minor transgression. Like the responsum of Ibn Aderet two centuries earlier (see source 31), this text is a clear indication that at least in some cases, the homoeroticism expressed in medieval Iberian Hebrew literature was based in actual behavior, and it illustrates the relative lack of concern with which it was received.

QUESTION: Regarding a transgression that was committed in the community of Aragon, where reliable witnesses saw the caretaker [*shammash*] of the synagogue playing around with a certain young man in the sanctuary itself. Is it permissible to [continue to] pray in that synagogue, or not?

RESPONSE: Since I have already heard that a number of our people have raised concerns about this synagogue, saying that a great transgression has been committed in it and thus it is not fitting to pray in it or recite prayers of holiness or place a Torah scroll in it, I have therefore come forward to publicize and demonstrate their errors. For this matter is not at all as they think; rather, they are certainly completely mistaken and in error, and it is not fitting for them to say this. For according to their erroneous opinion, it would not be fitting to pray in any house of the Byzantines or Franks, since even they practice idolatry in their very homes, and not only in an accidental manner but in a purposeful way, since this is the way of Gentiles—they always place in their homes images of Jesus, and his mother, and underneath them a lit candle and burning incense, which is clear idolatry. And our rabbis of blessed memory taught explicitly [in *b. 'Avodah Zarah* 20b–21b] that while one may not sell houses to Gentiles in the Land of Israel, outside the Land we may sell them houses.

And even where it is permitted to lease houses to them, it is not permitted for them to live in it, since the Gentile will bring idolatry into it, and it is said, *"you shall not bring a taboo* [to'evah] *into your home"* (Deuteronomy 7:26), so [it is permissible] only to lease a house to them for the purposes of storage. Here you have a clear and explicit teaching that the homes of Gentiles themselves are places of idolatry, which is more severe and more disgusting than any other transgression, and yet with all this, we sell and buy homes from Gentiles and we pray in them in all the areas of our dispersion, and there is no one who speaks up or opens their mouth to protest about this. Therefore, anyone who dares protest about this matter is simply mistaken.

And what of our Temple, which was the Divine Sanctuary, the Holy of Holies where the Divine Presence dwelt? Our prayers were not forbidden there, even when they performed idolatry in it, as is taught in Tractate *'Avodah Zarah* [52b]: "in the northeast [chamber of the Temple] the Hasmoneans hid the altar stones which the Greek kings had defiled. Rav Sheshet added: which they had defiled through idolatry." But even then, the Temple returned to [a state of] holiness, as our rabbis said in the prayer of *'Al HaNissim:** "and afterwards, Your children came to Your sanctuary and cleared Your Temple, etc…" In our synagogues, which are only a sanctuary in miniature, we are lenient regarding some things which were forbidden in the Temple—how much more so [we should be lenient in this case]!

---

* This prayer is said on Hanukkah.

And do not think to reply that even though idolatry is a more severe transgression, it is not disgusting , while this [transgession] is disgusting; see, [a place of idolatry] is like a place of filth, or a bathhouse, or an outhouse, where it is forbidden to pray! So indeed, one should say that idolatry is also disgusting… And therefore, there is no prohibition in this matter. Signed, the humble Eliyah Mizraḥi.

Mikhl-Yitskhak Rabinovitch (ed.), *Sefer She'elot Uteshuvot Rabbenu Eliyahu Mizraḥi* (Jerusalem: Darom Press, 1938). Translated from Hebrew by Noam Sienna.

Further Reading

Assis, Yom Tov. "Sexual Behaviour in Mediaeval Hispano-Jewish Society." In *Jewish History: Essays in Honour of Chimen Abramsky* (ed. Ada Rapoport-Albert and Steven Zipperstein, Peter Halban, 1988), 25–60.

Ben-Naeh, Yaron. "Moshko the Jew and his Gay Friends: Same-Sex Sexual Relations in Ottoman Jewish Society." *Journal of Early Modern History*, 9:1–2 (2005), 79–105.

Roth, Norman. "'Fawns of My Delight': Boy-Love in Arabic and Hebrew Verse." In *Poetics of Love in the Middle Ages* (ed. Moshe Lazar and Norris Lacy, George Mason University Press, 1989), 96–118.

The Sources:
Early Modern Voices
(1500–1900)

36. Enforcing a Punishment for Homosexual Activity in Ottoman Palestine (Tsfat, Early Sixteenth Century)

This responsum is one of the few descriptions of an early modern Jewish community enforcing a punishment for homosexual activity (see also source 57 for a nineteenth-century example). The scene is the city of Tsfat (Safed), then in Ottoman Palestine, sometime in the 1520s or 1530s; a certain married man is caught pursuing homosexual liaisons and is handed over to the non-Jewish authorities to be beaten and imprisoned. He finally makes a deal with the lay leadership of the Jewish community that he would grant his wife a divorce in return for his bail money; once freed, he is banished from the city. The case was recorded by Rabbi Moshe MiTrani (Moses di Trani, or the Mabit), a Sephardi scholar who became one of the leading rabbinic figures of sixteenth-century Tsfat, and who served as the legal authority in this decision.

I was called to the assembly of the sages of Tsfat, with its advisors and leaders, to [deal with] the issue of Ya'aqov Zarqon, who had been tainted with heresy and also engaging in homosexual activity. We granted authority to the leaders of the community to let him be punished by the Gentile [authorities]. He was seized by them and beaten as was fitting for him, until he begged for mercy and was bellowing with tears, [asking the Jewish community] to look into his affairs and try to save him from his captors. The [Jewish] leaders said to him, "We want you to leave this city, so that you will not pollute the land with your evil deeds" (cf. Numbers 35:34). When the family of his wife heard this, they said, "How can you expel him from the city, and leave this poor woman an *agunah* [unable to remarry]?" Then the leaders said to him, "If you want to be free of your captors, divorce your wife and we will provide what is needed by the city authorities." Then they put forward one of the leaders as guarantee, until they collected the money.

Then they assembled in the house of one of the leaders, sent for me, and told me to arrange the manner of presenting the *get* [divorce document] which this aforementioned Ya'aqov wanted to give to his wife. I asked him, "Do you want to give this *get* to your wife?" He said, "I would have wanted only to give a temporary *get*." The leaders said, "It is not our desire to pay for your freedom, unless you give her a full *get* of separation." He replied that they should give him all his clothing and belongings; I ordered immediately that they should supply him with all his clothing and belongings, exactly as they were accounted for. Then he forfeited whatever objections he had raised regarding the *get* and performing the ceremony of giving the get, and he instructed the scribe to write it and the witnesses to sign it. [The *get*] was written and signed in our presence, and they took it and gave it to his wife according to the law. Immediately he returned with the leaders who were serving as his guarantors, and his wife gave some of what was required to pay to the city authorities, and the leaders supplied the rest of what they had agreed to with the authorities, and freed him, and he left.

After some time, after he saw that these leaders had been slow to expel him, he began to spread slander about the *get*, saying that he had been forced to give it, and that they had beat him until he would divorce his wife. He would go from sage to sage to strengthen his case, and indeed some of them would listen sympathetically. Therefore, I was forced to write down on a roll all the proofs that I used in writing the *get* in a way befitting the law...And in the responsa of Rabbi Yosef Colon [Trabotto, ca. 1420–1480] of blessed memory, he cited the teaching of Rabbenu Tam [i.e. Jacob ben Meir, 1100–1171] that if a man betroths a woman according to Jewish law, but in the end the woman does not desire him, he cannot be compelled [to marry] by either Jewish or Gentile authority, but if he is imprisoned by Gentiles for taxes or some other offence, it is permissible to say to him, "We will not free you from your captors unless you divorce your wife with a kosher *get*." This is not coercion, since they are not doing anything bad to him directly, but just refraining from helping him, and refraining from doing a favor is not considered coercion.

Such is the teaching of Rabbi Yosef Colon of blessed memory, and this is precisely our circumstance: this man was arrested for the matter of pursuing [homosexual] impropriety [*zenut*], but they were lenient with the punishment imposed on him, to divorce his wife in exchange for the money that they would give him to pay his fees, as described above. After this, the great Rabbi Ya'aqov Berav [1474–1541] came and I consulted with him regarding all this, and he agreed with me as well. Signed, the young Moshe, the son of Rabbi Yosef, of blessed memory, di Trani.

Moshe Mitrani, *She'elot Uteshuvot Meharav Moshe Mitrani* (Lvov, 1861), 1:22. Translated from Hebrew by Noam Sienna.

Further Reading

Ben-Naeh, Yaron. "Mishkav Zakhar Baḥevrah Hayehudit Ha'Othomanit." *Zion* 66 (2001), 171–200.

Ben-Naeh, Yaron. "Moshko the Jew and his Gay Friends: Same-Sex Sexual Relations in Ottoman Jewish Society." *Journal of Early Modern History* 9:1–2 (2005), 79–105.

Lamdan, Ruth. "Stiyyot Minormot Hamussar Hamequbbalot Baḥevrah Hayehudit Be'erets Yisra'el Uvamitsrayyim Bame'a Ha-16." In *Sexuality and the Family in History: Collected Essays* (eds. Israel Bartal and Isaiah Gafni, Jerusalem 1998), 119–130.

37. Moshko's Sexual Escapades Are Revealed in Court (Arta, 1561)

This fascinating responsum records at great length the sexual escapades of a certain Jew named Moshko ("little Moses") Kohen, from the city of Arta in northwestern Greece, then part of the Ottoman Empire. The accounts of sexual behavior in this responsum are completely unparalleled for their extensiveness and specificity. It is perhaps even more astonishing that they are brought in only as a side-note to the main question, which concerns the validity of a betrothal with conflicting accounts of what was offered, what the young man said, and what the young woman replied. As a way of undermining the case, a number of citizens inform the judges of the disqualifying character of the witnesses to the betrothal. The first, Yehudah Kohen, is shown to be a serial gambler, and thus ineligible for testimony in a Jewish court.* Moshko, on the other hand, is well known in the local community for his sexual activity with men, and numerous witnesses come forward to attest to his liaisons with Jewish and non-Jewish men. His testimony is disqualified, and in the end both the witnesses and the original "groom" confess to having fabricated the whole affair; the marriage is declared null and void, and there is no reference to any repercussions or follow-up investigation of Moshko's behavior, which was clearly openly known already. The adjudicating rabbi, Shmu'el ben Moshe de Medina (or Maharashdam, 1505–1589), was born and raised in Salonica, and was one of the chief rabbinic authorities for the Sephardi community there.

---

*See *b. Sanhedrin* 24b.

We, the undersigned, convened as the three judges of a single *beit din* [Jewish court], when Yeshua', son of the honored Rabbi Avraham, came before us and told us, "You should know, my masters, that seventeen days ago (which was a Friday), I left my house at dusk and found these two bachelors, namely: Yehudah, son of Yitshaq Kohen, and Moshko Kohen. I said to them, 'Come with me!' and we all left our building and entered the courtyard of this [other] building. I called for the young woman, Flori, daughter of the rabbi, Yosef. When she came down to us, I took out one new Venetian *zecchino*.** I said to her, 'Take this as your marriage payment,' and to [Yehudah and Moshko], 'You will be my witnesses.' She reached out her hand and took it." Afterwards, the aforementioned Moshko came before us and testified as a witness [to these events]…[However, the judges suspected that this engagement was fraudulent and began interrogating the witnesses' stories. Finally, the reliability of the witnesses themselves is called into question.]

At a later session [of the court], Leon, son of the honorable Rabbi Simo, came before us and testified that he saw the aforementioned Yehudah Kohen gambling, at a time when there was a *herem* [ban] in the community on gambling anytime other than a holiday, or on the Fast of Esther and Purim; but he was gambling nonetheless [and thus disqualified]! This Yehudah claimed that because he came here to Arta from another country, he did not accept the *herem*, but we know that it has already been two years since he began living here with his father and mother and brother, and he has no intention of returning to the place where he came from. And Ya'aqov, son of the honorable Rabbi Moshe Barzilai, testified to the same effect, that the aforementioned Yehudah was gambling as described above, and [the report] was affirmed.

At this session, Rabbi Yosef Marato came before us and told us: "You should know, my masters, that I have witnesses [who can testify] against Moshko, for he is disqualified from testimony because of the transgressions he has committed. Now, call these witnesses, and bring [Moshko] to the *beit din*, and they will testify against him." We, the court, called for [Moshko] several times and he did not want to come. We then sent an agent of the court, who warned him, in front of witnesses, but he still did not want to come. The witnesses then came and testified before us regarding this warning, and they were: Rabbi

---

** A gold coin.

David bar Mordekhai, and Rabbi Moshe Tsoref, and Rabbi Yosef and Rabbi Yisrael Berakhah. Since we saw that [Moshko] did not want to come, we accepted the testimony of the witnesses [against him].

First, Rabbi Ḥayyim Gabi came and testified that he saw the aforementioned Moshko wasting seed on Yom Kippur. Then David bar Nissim came and testified how, this past summer, he was traveling through a village with a certain Turk and they crossed through an orchard to ask the owner to sell them some fruit; there they saw this Moshko with a certain bachelor, and he was being sexually penetrated by him. When [Moshko and the bachelor] saw them, they fled and separated from each other, and ran away with their pants undone.

Then, Ḥayyim bar Matityah came and testified how once he was traveling by the place with the large, smooth boulder, and there he saw the aforementioned Moshko, and a certain Turk was penetrating him with his consent—this deed was around two months ago. Then, the bachelor Avraham di Mili came and testified that [Moshko] pursued him to force him into penetrative sex, but he did not want to. Then, the bachelor Eliʿezer bar Avraham came and testified how he heard so many rumors about Moshko when he was in Ioannina, namely that he was having sex with this Turk, that it gave him a bad reputation and they would call him a disgraceful epithet. [This report] was sustained.

At this session, Rabbi Yudah Tsuri came before us and testified, "Around two years ago, I went with some other bachelors to Moshko's house and we ate and drank. After the meal, all the bachelors began to head to their homes, and I myself saw the aforementioned Moshko being penetrated by Yaʿaqov Mazal-Tov." [This report] was sustained. And at a later session, Avraham bar Mar David came and said, "About a year and a half ago, I was in the house of the aforementioned Moshko and I saw him penetrating a certain bachelor." All these testimonies were given under the threat of a *ḥerem* [ban] that we instituted, in order to ascertain the truth, and they were sustained...

At a later session when we convened as a court, the bachelor Yeshuaʿ, the son of Avraham, came before us and confessed the transgression that he had committed, regarding what he had claimed before the court: namely, that he had been betrothed to the young woman Flori, daughter of the honorable Rabbi Yosef; for it had all been lies and falsehoods, and he had never been betrothed to this young woman. In our presence he admitted how he had sinned a terrible sin in spreading this rumor, and told us what things had brought him to do this. He asked forgiveness from Rabbi Yosef, the father of the young woman, falling to the ground and kissing his feet so that he would forgive him and so that God could absolve him of his transgression.

At this session, the bachelors Moshko and Yehudah Kohen, who had testified to this marriage, came before us and confessed their transgression, that they had transgressed and sinned in what they had testified regarding this marriage, since it was all lies and falsehoods. They told us the circumstances that had led them to do this, and asked forgiveness from God to absolve their transgressions, and this was sustained.

Shmu'el ben Moshe de Medina, *She'elot Uteshuvot Maharashdam* (Lvov, 1862), §50. Translated from Hebrew by Noam Sienna.

Further Reading

Ben-Naeh, Yaron. "Mishkav Zakhar Baḥevrah HaYehudit Ha'Othomanit." *Zion* 66 (2001), 171–200.

Ben-Naeh, Yaron. "Moshko the Jew and his Gay Friends: Same-Sex Sexual Relations in Ottoman Jewish Society." *Journal of Early Modern History* 9:1–2 (2005), 79-105.

Greenberg, Steven. *Wrestling with God and Men: Homosexuality in the Jewish Tradition* (University of Wisconsin Press, 2004).

38. Yosef Qaro Rules on "Licentiousness in Our Generation" (Tsfat, Mid-Sixteenth Century)

Yosef Qaro, born in Toledo in 1488, was one of the greatest rabbinic authorities of early modern Jewry. His family moved to the Ottoman Empire after being expelled from the Iberian Peninsula; Qaro made his way to the Land of Israel, eventually settling in Tsfat (Safed). His master work, the *Shulḥan Arukh* (The Set Table), is a comprehensive summary of Jewish law which quickly became one of the most widely-influential legal codes in the Jewish world. In the excerpt presented here, Qaro asserts that despite the Talmudic declaration that Jewish men should not be suspected of improper activity, he believed that sexual licentiousness was widespread in his own time, and that more intense supervision was needed. This belief was clearly rooted in his own experience; indeed, in his responsa he himself records an episode that substantiated his fears of what young unchaperoned men might be tempted to do. As part of a lengthy saga involving the inter-communal struggles between the Sephardi communities of Manisa (western Turkey) during the 1560s, the questioners report that certain young men of the community would spend Shabbat afternoons travelling unsupervised in the forests outside the city, where they would engage in improper sexual behavior, and in the end it took a great deal of rabbinic intervention to finally put an end to this practice.

I. *Shulḥan Arukh*, Even Ha'ezer 24:1

[The Talmud teaches, *b. Qiddushin* 81b]: "Jews are not suspected of homosexual intercourse or bestiality." As a result, there is no prohibition [for two men, or a man and an animal] to be alone together. However, a man who nonetheless distances himself from another man or animal—this is praiseworthy. Indeed, the greatest of our sages would separate themselves from an animal in order that they should not be alone with it. And in these generations, when licentious men are prevalent, a man should distance himself from being alone with another man.

II. *Avkat Rokhel*, §206

[The question first describes how a number of communities of Iberian exiles in Manisa have created a unified community council, but the Jews of Toledo oppose the appointment of a particular leader.]

Regarding everything that these leaders declared and established at this time, along with the treasurers and teachers—they all swore a grave oath to uphold it and took the content of these agreements upon themselves; the leaders and treasurers, as well as the leading scholar [of the community], all signed their names. On the advice of this sage, the leaders and treasurers established one particular decree and agreement, which was an exigency ruling: since they had seen the sins of this licentious generation—and especially how bachelors and young men would travel out of the city on Shabbat to particular places, where they would commit serious and evil transgressions—they agreed that [young men] would not be permitted to travel on Shabbat outside the city to those particular places. They announced this agreement in all the congregations, [sending] respected sages to announce it, and all the congregations agreed to uphold it.

But, later one Shabbat, a group of young men from the Toledo congregation* violated this agreement, and went out to travel; they said that they had only heard one particular place [mentioned in the agreement] and not the other places to which they had traveled. The sage, along with the other leaders, told them that the agreement applied to all these places; he then warned them, telling them that since they claimed they had not heard [the full agreement] their transgression was accidental, but from now on they had been warned. If they went [to any of these places] they would be violating the agreement and be subject to excommunication [ḥerem], Heaven forbid. Some from the congregation said that they did not want to accept [this condition], and the sage answered them that they could not undo the agreement which they had already accepted and which had been proclaimed; but they continued to gossip [about it].

The [young men] did not go out to any of these places for two or three Shabbats, but on the day of Shabbat Zakhor,** certain rebellious men came forth and said that the sage had given permission to travel [anywhere] with the exception of this one particular place. Many bachelors and young men followed them, along with other reckless and irresponsible men; they went traveling and violated the agreement. The leaders and treasurers came together to punish them, and those from the Lorca congregation accepted the rebuke, and left the synagogue asking for forgiveness; they were forgiven for what they had done in transgression. But those from the Toledo congregation did not want to accept the rebuke, saying that they did not violate the agreement, and that the authority of their leader and treasurer would support them.

---

* That is, the congregation comprising Toledo expatriates.
** The Shabbat immediately preceding the holiday of Purim.

Their claim—that the sage had given them permission—was found to be false, since he would have been unable to give permission [by himself] without the other treasurers, but after that they still insisted that they had not accepted [that the agreement applied] to any place other than this one, even though the sage and the other leaders explained that the agreement applied to everything and that they had agreed to all of it, and so they had violated the agreement. They dared to object to the sage, saying that they would not accept his authority, and that they would take their case to the great sage, the honored physician Shmu'el Zabi (may the Merciful protect and redeem him). The [other] congregations were satisfied with this, in order to prevent disputes from multiplying among the community. The sage himself put his pride aside, even though there is no greater shame than this.

Yosef Qaro, *Shulḥan Arukh* (Vilna: Romm, 1911), and *Sefer Avkat Rokhel* (Leipzig: Leopold Schnauss, 1859). Translated from Hebrew by Noam Sienna. I thank Dr. Yaron Ben-Naeh for his assistance in understanding and contextualizing this source.

Further Reading

Ben-Naeh, Yaron. "Mishkav Zakhar Baḥevrah HaYehudit Ha'Othomanit." *Zion* 66 (2001), 171–200.

Ben-Naeh, Yaron. "Moshko the Jew and his Gay Friends: Same-Sex Sexual Relations in Ottoman Jewish Society." *Journal of Early Modern History* 9:1–2 (2005), 79–105.

Greenberg, Steven. *Wrestling with God and Men: Homosexuality in the Jewish Tradition* (University of Wisconsin Press, 2004).

Lamdan, Ruth. "Sṭiyyot Minormot Hamussar Hamequbbalot Baḥevrah HaYehudit Be'erets Yisra'el Uvamitsrayyim Bame'a Ha-16." In *Sexuality and the Family in History: Collected Essays* (eds. Israel Bartal and Isaiah Gafni, Jerusalem 1998), 119–130.

39. Poetry of Menaḥem Egozi (Turkey, Mid-Sixteenth Century)

Homoerotic Hebrew poetry—like secular Hebrew poetry in general—was transformed during the final two centuries of Christian rule over the Iberian Peninsula, from the thirteenth through the fifteenth centuries, and yet again after the expulsion of the Jews at the end of the fifteenth century. Nonetheless, it did not disappear; poets in North Africa and the Ottoman Empire continued to write Hebrew poetry in the Sephardi tradition, including the same celebrations of beautiful youths that had flourished in Iberian Hebrew poetry since the eleventh century (see sources 18–20 and 22–25). Little is known about the poet Menaḥem ben Moshe Egozi (d. 1570), whose poems are presented here. The Egozi family (literally, "walnut"—they also used the name Qaridi, from the Greek for walnut, *karydi*) was a Turkish rabbinical family of the Greek Romaniote tradition. A book of Menaḥem Egozi's sermons on Genesis, *Gal shel Egozim*, was printed posthumously in 1593, at the famous press of Doña Reyna Nasi in Ortaköy, just outside Constantinople. The original manuscript of his poetry and other writings, titled *Ginnat Egoz*, is preserved in a manuscript in the British Library; these poems, like their earlier precedents, celebrate the beauty of the young man described as a "gazelle."

Like the glare of the moon, this dusky gazelle
    Spreads his dark o'er the white of the skies;
He is dark that his lovers and lusters might see
    Without searing the sight from their eyes.

Your heads, North and South, you should bow towards the West
    For it's there my gazelle now abides;
Than the East he is grander and brighter by far—
    The sun dims in its shame, the moon hides.

Had the font of my tears not extinguished the flame
    Of this wanton gazelle, I would burn in his fire;
Had the heat of his passion not dried my tears' sea,
    I'd be carried away in its gyre.

Menaḥem Egozi, *Ginnat Egoz* (BL Or. 11.111), as published in A. M. Habermann, *'Af'apei Tsvi: me'ah shirei ḥesheq shel meshorrerim 'ivriyyim asher bisefarad uve'artsot hamizraḥ* (Jerusalem: Tarshish, 1943). Translated from Hebrew by Michael Yaari.

Further Reading

Galanté, Abraham. *Histoire des Juifs d'Istanbul depuis la prise de cette ville en 1453* (Istanbul: Hüsnütabiat, 1942).

Roth, Norman. "'Fawns of My Delight': Boy-Love in Arabic and Hebrew Verse." In *Poetics of Love in the Middle Ages* (ed. Moshe Lazar and Norris Lacy, George Mason University Press, 1989), 96–118.

40. Ḥayyim Vital Describes Male Souls in Female Bodies (Tsfat, Mid-Sixteenth Century)

One of the most unusual innovations of Kabbalistic theology, and one which was especially developed in the mystical circles of sixteenth-century Tsfat, was the concept of *gilgul nefashot*, or the "transmigration," or "reincarnation," of souls. The human soul, in this theory, is an eternal spark of divine holiness, which in each lifetime undergoes a new transformative journey in the hopes of repairing the damage of its previous incarnation. Here Ḥayyim Vital (1542–1620), one of the most important disciples of the great Kabbalist Yitsḥaq Luria (1534–1572; see sources 41 and 44), explains that these reincarnated souls can also affect a person's gender: a male soul that has entered the body of a woman will render her unable to conceive, unless another female soul also enters this body—not as a *gilgul*, but as a kind of psychic impregnation, called an *'ibbur*, which then exits through the birth of a child. Vital later gives examples of actual individuals who had been "diagnosed" with a soul that has reincarnated across genders, including his own wife Hannah, whom Luria identified as the reincarnation of Kalba Savua', the father-in-law of the Talmudic sage Rabbi Akiva.

Know that sometimes a man may reincarnate into the body of a woman because of a transgression, such as homosexual activity or something similar. This woman, who has received the soul of a man, will not be able to conceive and become pregnant…This woman will need great merit to enable her to become pregnant and give birth. The only way it can be done is that some other feminine soul must enter her as an *'ibbur* [incubating soul]…

However, she cannot give birth to sons, for two reasons. The first is, since Scripture says, "*If a woman gives seed* [tazria'], *and a male child is born*" (Leviticus 12:2).* But in this case, the woman is male, just as her husband; so there is no way for her to conceive a male child, and she will have only female children.

---

*This is interpreted by the Talmud (*b. Berakhot 60a* and *b. Niddah 31b*), to mean that when a woman is the first to "give seed," i.e. climax, the child conceived will be male, but if the man "gives seed" first, the child will be female.

The second reason is that the feminine soul that has entered her does so only as an *'ibbur* in order to help her become pregnant and give birth. Once this woman gives birth, that soul does not need to stay there without a reason, so at the time that she gives birth, that [feminine] soul fully enters into the fetus as an actual reincarnation and not as an *'ibbur*, like it was at first. That is why the child that is born must be female and not male. And it is the case that every woman whose soul is a male soul, as described above, cannot give birth to male children, but only female ones. Moreover, the female child that she births is that very same female soul which had entered her at the beginning as an *'ibbur*, in order to help her, as was described.

Ḥayyim Vital, *Sha'ar Hagilgulim* (Jerusalem, 1903), 9:2. Translated from Hebrew by Abby Stein; I thank her for bringing this source to my attention.

Further Reading

Fine, Lawrence. *Physician of the Soul, Healer of the Cosmos: Isaac Luria and His Kabbalistic Fellowship* (Stanford University Press, 2004).

Magid, Shaul. "Constructing Women from Men: the Metaphysics of Male Homosexuality Among Lurianic Kabbalists in Sixteenth-Century Safed." *Jewish Studies Quarterly* 17 (2010), 4–28.

Michaelson, Jay. "Kabbalah and Queer Theology: Resources and Reservations." *Theology and Sexuality* 18:1 (2013), 1–18.

41. The Kabbalistic Tiqqun of Yitsḥaq Luria for Homosexual Activity (Tsfat, Mid-Sixteenth Century)

Yitsḥaq Luria (1534–1572), also known as the Ari or Arizal, led a transformation in the development of the mystical tradition of Kabbalah, becoming father to what has come to be known as Lurianic Kabbalah. Luria left almost no writings himself; his foremost disciple, Ḥayyim Vital (see sources 40 and 44), gathered Luria's teachings from his notes and from the notes of others, organizing them into eight "Gates." In this excerpt from the seventh Gate, *Sha'ar Ruaḥ HaQodesh* (The Gate of the Holy Spirit), Vital shares a Lurianic mystical remedy, or *tiqqun*, for the sin of male-male sexual intercourse. The remedy establishes a system of fasts and self-mortifications to restore balance to the harmony of divine emanations (*sefirot*) which have been damaged by this sin. Luria also advises similar treatments to repair other sexual activities seen as spiritually harmful, including masturbation, sex with a non-Jewish woman, sex with a menstruating woman, and adultery. Interestingly, Vital explains that Luria had prescribed this *tiqqun* to three people. Although he does not specify whether they were members of Luria's circle or other Jews living in Tsfat, it is clear that this was a practical concern rather than a theoretical one.

The 22nd *tiqqun* [remedy]. This is for one who had sex with another man. I saw that my teacher of blessed memory [Yitshaq Luria] gave this *tiqqun* to three people, but I do not know if it is the same [*tiqqun*] for all people, since I did not receive this matter from him directly, but from the three people who performed this *tiqqun*…

The *tiqqun* for this is to perform 233 [days of] fasting, the numerical value of *regel* [foot] as indicated,* [which is also] the numerical value of the sin of *zakhur* [male]…And here is the *kavvanah* [intention] for this matter: he should intend every day to raise up the [divine] names, from below in the "feet" of the cosmic male [*ze'ir anpin*] to a higher elevation. How? For the first ten days, he should focus his intent on the first *yod* of the Tetragrammaton, and he should continue to do this until he has completed 72 fasts. Then he has repaired the damage to [the divine configuration of] Abba ["Father," i.e. the *sefirah* of *Hokhmah*]. Then he should perform 161 fasts, which will repair the damage to [the divine configuration of] Ima ["Mother," i.e. the *sefirah* of *Binah*]. And every day, he should focus his intent on whichever letter of the Divine Name he has reached, and repair it then.

With regards to this *tiqqun*, it is necessary that these fasts be performed during the winter, when the snow falls, and he should immerse in it. It does not matter, with regards to the snow, whether it is at the beginning of the fasts, or at their end, only that it happens on some day out of these 161 fasts and not on any other day. With regards to the snow: you should take off your clothes, remain totally naked, and then roll yourself in the snow, forward and back; then get up and return. Do this nine times. If there is a *miqveh*

---

*Vital is here using the numerological system known as *gematria*. In this system, both *regel* and *zakhur* have the value 233.

[ritual bath] into which snow falls, and you immerse in it nine times, that is sufficient.

Ḥayyim Vital, *Sha'ar Ruaḥ HaQodesh* (Jerusalem: Isaac Goscinny, 1874), *tiqqun* 22. Translated from Hebrew by Noam Sienna.

Further Reading

Fine, Lawrence. *Physician of the Soul, Healer of the Cosmos: Isaac Luria and His Kabbalistic Fellowship* (Stanford University Press, 2004).

Magid, Shaul. "Constructing Women from Men: the Metaphysics of Male Homosexuality Among Lurianic Kabbalists in Sixteenth-Century Safed." *Jewish Studies Quarterly* 17 (2010), 4–28.

Michaelson, Jay. "Kabbalah and Queer Theology: Resources and Reservations." *Theology and Sexuality* 18:1 (2013), 1–18.

42. The Inquisition Arrests a "New Christian" For Sodomy and Judaizing (Brazil, 1593)

The Portuguese Inquisition formally began in 1536, modelled after the Tribunal of the Holy Office of the Inquisition in Spain (first established in 1478). The Portuguese Inquisition, like its Spanish counterpart, aimed to root out anyone who deviated from orthodox Catholic doctrine, in particular Jews (and their descendants) who had converted to Christianity but who maintained secret Jewish affiliations and practices, known as *cristãos-novos* (New Christians) or *conversos*. The Inquisition was also concerned with witchcraft, heresy, and especially sodomy, which was the second most common category of trials after the crime of Judaizing (returning to Jewish practice, and/or encouraging others to do so). The work of Luiz Mott has shown that if a defendant was accused of both Judaizing and sodomy, they were three times as likely to receive a death sentence than if they were accused of only one of those two crimes. This document records the trial of a 33-year-old merchant named João Batista (Joam Bautista), who lived in Brazil. His parents were Iberian *conversos* who had fled to the Ottoman Empire and returned to open Jewish practice there; Batista himself had been previously investigated by the Inquisition for Judaizing. Batista confesses to his many homosexual encounters with Jews, New Christians, and non-Jews, including in Italy, the Ottoman Empire, Portugal, and the African island of São Tomé. In Brazil, where he had been for the last five years, Batista named two sexual partners, both also members of the New Christian community in Bahia: Pero de Leão and Gonçalo Pires, who were themselves later investigated by the Inquisition. Batista's life trajectory exemplifies the networks of Iberian Conversos who established diaspora communities throughout Western Europe, the Ottoman Empire, and the New World.

On August 12, 1593, in this city of Salvador Bahia of all Saints, in the place of residence of the Senhor Visitador [Inspector] from the Holy Office, Senhor Furtado de Mendoça, a man appeared before him named Joam Bautista [João Batista]. Wanting to confess his sins, he received a sentence from the Holy Officers who instructed him to put his right hand under oath, promising to say the truth. He said he was a New Christian, son of Francisco Roiz Montemor and his wife, Felipa Carlos,* deceased, [who were] New Christians, Jews in Salonica, the *juderia* [Jewish quarter] of Turkey. From there the confessant, being a Jew, fled for Rome, and from Rome fled for Lisbon where he was reconciled with the Holy Inquisition. [He is now] a natural of Lisbon, a bachelor merchant, about 33 years old, more or less.

Being in this city [of Bahia] and confessing, this Jew said that in Turkey, [when he] was about 18 years old, he committed the nefarious sin of sodomy three or four or five times, either as active or as passive with Turks and Syrian Jews, whose names have not been remembered. He had his dishonest virile member in their back vessels, having pollution in them, and himself consenting for them to do it to him in the above-mentioned way. Then he was in Venice for ten or twelve years, spending the nights in his bed with a young lad whose name he doesn't remember, who was also a Jew who had become a Christian; he did the above-mentioned sin two or three times with him completely, the confessant being always passive. The young lad remained in Venice and he doesn't know more of his encounters.

After these ten or so years he was [traveling] through Rome; going to his bath he came across a young Italian lad whose name and encounters he doesn't know, and he also did the above-mentioned sin with him, having completed

---

*Transcribed incorrectly in the manuscript testimony as Calros.

pollution in his backside. After this the confessant was on the island of São Tomé, and in this city he did and completed the mentioned nefarious sin of sodomy with some Black women, not knowing how many, doing it with them and penetrating their backsides with his dishonest member as if they were doing it in the front, as is natural. With these Black women he did it at least fifteen times more or less.

He confessed further that for [the past] sixteen years, more or less, he had stayed in Lisbon in the house of his uncle Manuel Drago, a merchant, and this uncle had in his house a shop assistant named Pero de Leam [Leão], a young lad that was then bearded under his chin and on his legs or arms, married to a strong woman, the only daughter of a goldsmith. Both being in the above-mentioned house of his uncle, they both slept together in the same bed of Pero de Leam some nights. It isn't affirmed how many nights the confessant did and completed the nefarious sin with the mentioned Pero de Leam, [and] it isn't affirmed how many times the confessant was always the active, penetrating with his virile member the back vessel of the mentioned Pero de Leam and finishing in him and doing it with him from behind like one does with a woman from the front.

He confessed further that for the last five years, more or less, while he has been in this city, [that] coming to his house [was] Gonçalo Pires, a young lad who had just begun to show signs of spotty facial hair that […] stayed a night in his house, and both laid down in the bed of the confessant and with the confessant the mentioned Gonçalo Pires did and completed the mentioned nefarious sin, being active in the above-mentioned manner, and the confessant being passive. And this sin completed as described, the two did it just once and the confessant wanted to do the same with him being active, [but] he did not consent to it, so it did not happen more than what has been said.

And for all these sins, he said that he is very repentant, and he asked forgiveness from God our Lord with signs of repentance, and said that he already confessed them to his spiritual parents and he completed the penitence that they gave him. Later the Senhor Visitador showed him much compassion, [instructing him] that from today forward he would not do such horrible and nefarious sins, and if he […] the conversion of the mentioned persons and with all the others that he could have [had] the chance of such dirtiness, because doing the opposite will be gravely punished. He was ordered to confess to the College of Jesus and bring a written confession [of] that [which] he confessed at this table, and he promised to complete it, and questioned about the custom with the different accomplices, he said nothing, and he promised secrecy.

Signed with the Senhor Visitador here: Manoel Francisco, honorary of the Holy Office in this visit, the scribe, [and] Heitor Furtado de Mendoça, [and] Joam Bautista. About which confession I, Manoel Francisco, notary of the Holy Office on this visit, translated well and faithfully on my own and with certainty, the Senhor Visitador agreeing with good word, we both sign here: [signed] Manoel Francisco, notary of the Holy Office on this visit and the scribe; [signed] Mendoça.

Arquivo Nacional da Torre do Tombo, Inquisição de Lisboa, Processo 4307, August 20, 1593. Translated from Portuguese by Dr. Matthew Barrile, with the assistance of Michael Waas in transcription. Copyright © 2019 Print-O-Craft Press.

Further Reading

Graizbord, David. *Souls in Dispute: Converso Identities in Iberia and the Jewish Diaspora, 1580–1700* (University of Pennsylvania Press, 2004).

Mott, Luiz. "Crypto-Sodomites in Colonial Brazil." In *Infamous Desire: Male Homosexuality in Colonial Latin America* (ed. Pete Sigal, University of Chicago Press, 2003), 168–196.

Mott, Luiz. "Filhos de Abraão & de Sodoma: Cristãos-novos Homossexuais nos Tempos da Inquisição." In *Ensaios sobre a intolerância: inquisição, marranismo e anti-semitismo* (ed. Maria Luiza Tucci Carneiro and Lina Gorenstein, São Paulo: Associação Editorial Humanitas, 2005), 23–63.

Vainfas, Ronaldo. "The Nefarious and the Colony." In *Pelo Vaso Traseiro: Sodomy and Sodomites in Luso-Brazilian History* (eds. Harold Johnson and Francis A. Dutra, Tucson: Fenestra Books, 2006), 337–368.

43. A Converso Doctor Describes the Origin of Lesbianism (Hamburg, 1603)

A new awareness of the idea of lesbianism—that is, the possibility of love between women—emerged in early modern Europe in the mid-sixteenth century, associated with the rediscovery of the accounts of female same-sex love of classical antiquity, including not just Sappho but also Ovid, Martial, and Juvenal. Literature and poetry featuring love between women flourished throughout Europe; medical and scientific authorities also reckoned with the figure of the lesbian, named variously as lesbian, sapphic, tribade, fricatrice, sodomite, rubster, and innumerable slang terms both self-invented and derogatorily imposed. Here Rodrigo de Castro (1546–1627), a Portuguese converso physician, describes how lesbianism emerges from physiological deformity, claiming that an "unnaturally" large clitoris drives women to pleasure one another. He supports his case not only with classical authorities (Aurelianus, Plautus, Martial), but also the experience of his colleague and fellow converso Amatus Lusitanus (João Rodrigues de Castelo Branco, 1511–1568), who had encountered lesbians in Ottoman Thessaloniki, as well as his own experience seeing lesbians tried and sentenced in Lisbon. De Castro was born in Lisbon to a Sephardi family which had converted to Christianity under the Inquisition. He studied medicine at the University of Salamanca before leaving Iberia and settling among the Portuguese Jewish community in Hamburg (a significant haven for Iberian conversos) where he returned openly to Judaism and took the name David Nahmias. This excerpt is from his 1603 work *De Universa Mulierum Morborum Medicina* (On The Universal Treatment of Women's Diseases), a widely-acclaimed textbook of gynecology.

For in this [clitoris], an extraordinary itching is produced; it is therefore thought to be the particular seat of female pleasure, when they make love…In fact, this protuberance sometimes exceeds its natural size, and grows to such magnitude that, hanging down beyond the uterus, it brings on deformity together with shame. Being continuously rubbed by clothing, it provokes their desire to such a degree that they can no longer hold it back; these women, whose erections resemble men's in this part, rush into lovemaking, polluting themselves with the mutual intercourse of incubi and succubi [i.e. both active and passive].

This is what Amatus [Lusitanus] reports of two Turkish women of Thessaloniki; and we, in Lisbon, have seen some women punished publicly for a similarly disgusting crime. They are called *tribades* by Caelius Aurelianus,* by

---

*Caelius Aurelianus of Sicca, ca. fifth century CE.

Plautus* *subigatrices* [dominatrices], and Martial says of a certain Bassa, "you have invented a riddle worthy of the Theban sphinx—here where there is no man, there is yet adultery..." ("For Bassa, a Tribade," *Epigrams*, I.90).

Virgins who have never experienced intercourse do not desire it that much, since it is only an annoyance to be done with; other women desire that activity, not only for this cause, but also since they can remember past pleasures. How much more so with those [women] who are called *tribades* or *fricatrices*, who love only rubbing each other, and so mutually practice this disreputable act [*actum infamem*] with each other. Of them—some of whom were accused of this crime [*flagitium*], and who were sent together into exile—we have already spoken.

Rodrigo de Castro, *De Universa Mulierum Morborum Medicina* (Hamburg: Philipp Ohr, 1603), 6 and 56. Translated from Latin by Noam Sienna.

Further Reading

Arrizabalaga, Jon. "Medical Ideals in the Sephardic Diaspora: Rodrigo de Castro's Portrait of the Perfect Physician in early Seventeenth-Century Hamburg." *Medical History Supplement* 29 (2009), 107–124.

Borris, Kenneth (ed.). *Same-Sex Desire in the English Renaissance: A Sourcebook of Texts, 1470–1650* (Routledge, 2004).

Castle, Terry (ed.). *The Literature of Lesbianism: A Historical Anthology from Ariosto to Stonewall* (Columbia University Press, 2003).

Velasco, Sherry. *Lesbians in Early Modern Spain* (Vanderbilt University Press, 2011).

44. A Spirit Reveals the Prevalence of Homosexual Activity to Ḥayyim Vital (Damascus, 1609)

Beyond preserving and disseminating the philosophy of his teacher Yitsḥaq Luria (see source 41), Ḥayyim Vital also recorded his own mystical experiences, including in an autobiographical diary, *Sefer HaḤezyonot* (The Book of Visions). In this excerpt, Vital describes his dealings with a *ruaḥ*, the spirit of a deceased rabbi named Ya'aqov Piso, who had possessed the young daughter of Rabbi Rafa'el Anav of Damascus. Vital and Rabbi Ya'aqov Abulafia both worked with the *ruaḥ*, Rafa'el's daughter acting as a kind of

---

* Ca. third century CE.

medium. In the process of demonstrating their otherworldly knowledge, the *ruaḥ* revealed the many sins of the local community, including various sexual transgressions (a common theme in Jewish stories of spirit possession). Homosexual activity is included along with adultery, and sex with non-Jewish women, and in fact some of the same individuals are named as having sinned in all these ways. We might wonder whether this text, like other incidents of spirit possession, should be understood as a condemnation of the hypocrisy of the rabbinic establishment (coming, as it did, from the mouth of a young woman); or perhaps it was a tool of the establishment to use shame and fear to encourage wide-scale confessions and repentance. Most notable among those named by the *ruaḥ* is Yisrael Najarah (ca. 1555–ca. 1625), well-known for his liturgical poetry (such as the Shabbat standard *Yah Ribbon*), but here presented as an incorrigible drunkard and sexual glutton who, according to the spirit of Rabbi Piso, should be shunned. This controversial passage, along with several others, was censored in earlier published versions of this text.

Rosh Ḥodesh Kislev, 5370 [November 27, 1609]…The spirit said to [Abulafia]: "Behold, you and the [other] inhabitants of Damascus have no place in the World to Come, Heaven forbid, for several reasons…Your wives go out dressed provocatively, in shameful clothing and jewelry, like these silk brocades on their heads, and with their uncovered breasts filling their bosom, their clothing exposing the size of their breasts, trailing [only] flimsy shawls and veils that show off their bodies. They perfume themselves with citrus oils and spices and other scents, to arouse the evil inclination in men. And they do all this in the marketplaces and public squares, to show their beauty to the world. You must also rebuke your sons, and prevent them from sinning. Indeed, there are 48 men who are sinning through sex with non-Jewish women, married women, and with other men, not to mention their other sins."

And [the spirit] listed them all, and emphasized these ones to me: "Eliyahu Ḥafets and the sons of Gandor and the son of Qureidi and Avraham Mutseiri [Mosseri] are sleeping with non-Jewish women. The daughter of Qumeiri, the apostate, has illicit relations with Yehoshua' Qureish, and many other men. Rabbi Ya'aqov Monidas has sex with Natan Khuleif, and now he has given him his daughter [in marriage], but he is still having illicit relations with him! Woe to Ya'aqov, for his face is as black as tar in the World to Come from all his sins, and he has no place in the World to Come."

[...]

"And now, with regard to Rabbi Yisrael Najarah: it is true that the poems that he has composed might be good in themselves; but it is forbidden for anyone to speak to him, or to recite the poems that he has composed, for he always uses profanities and has been a drunkard his whole life. Indeed, he once held a festive meal during the mourning period between the fasts* at a certain time at the home of Ya'aqov Monidas. He put his hat on the ground and sang songs in a loud voice, ate meat and drank wine and became drunk. How could he call for vigils in Jobar, and ask people to repent?"

I myself, Hayyim, told him of this matter, and he admitted that it was true. Even now, while he is fleeing the plague, he has sex with men in his drunkenness. On Shabbat, he committed two more sins. First, he quarreled with his wife and threw her out of the house. The second is that afterwards a certain non-Jewish woman came to his house to light a fire, and afterwards he slept with her. Therefore it is forbidden to employ him or ask him to write a certificate of marriage or divorce; indeed, it is almost worthy to invalidate [the ones he has already written]...Indeed, homosexual activity is very common in this country, and the perversion and delaying of justice is common in this country as well.

Hayyim Vital, *Sefer HaHezyonot* (ed. Morris Faierstein, Jerusalem: Ben Zvi Institute, 2005), 65–69. Translated from Hebrew by Noam Sienna.

Further Reading

Ben-Naeh, Yaron. "Mishkav Zakhar Bahevrah HaYehudit Ha'Othomanit." *Zion* 66 (2001), 171–200.

Ben-Naeh, Yaron. "Moshko the Jew and his Gay Friends: Same-Sex Sexual Relations in Ottoman Jewish Society." *Journal of Early Modern History* 9:1–2 (2005), 79–105.

Greenberg, Steven. *Wrestling with God and Men: Homosexuality in the Jewish Tradition* (University of Wisconsin Press, 2004).

Lamdan, Ruth. *A Separate People: Jewish Women in Palestine, Syria, and Egypt in the Sixteenth Century* (Brill, 2000).

---

*I.e. between the 17th of Tammuz and the 9th of Av, an annual period of mourning.

Magid, Shaul. "Constructing Women from Men: the Metaphysics of Male Homosexuality Among Lurianic Kabbalists in Sixteenth-Century Safed." *Jewish Studies Quarterly* 17 (2010), 4–28.

45. Three Jewish Men Are Accused of Sodomy (Rome, 1624)

Numerous sources testify to a flourishing culture of homoeroticism in the urban centers of Renaissance Italy, including Rome, Florence, Mantua, Bologna, and Venice; according to the research of Michael Rocke, two out of every three men in Florence in the fifteenth century were implicated in homosexual activity at some point in their lives. At the same time, religious and legal authorities were anxious to root out this "abominable vice," and surveillance, prosecution, and harsh punishment of sodomy became increasingly common between the fifteenth and seventeenth centuries. We know that Italian Jews in this period also participated in homosexual activity, although we have only a few legal sources which document it. The excerpts presented here are testimonies from a trial that took place in Rome in the spring of 1624, a rare and lengthy example (the original records for this case in the municipal archives of Rome stretch over 200 double-sided pages) of the prosecution of Italian Jews for sodomy. Rumors had been spreading that two Jewish cloth merchants—Leone di Montefiore and Lazzaro Abbina—were living together in the Jewish ghetto of Rome with their teenaged apprentice Simone del fu Giuseppe di Pesaro, and practicing sodomy. The investigating officer found two men half-naked in bed together and a third in the room, and arrested them all, confiscating the sheets as evidence. However, despite the testimonies of several witnesses, the evidence of semen-stained sheets, and the opinion of 10 barber-surgeons who examined Simone and found evidence of anal penetration, the judge concluded that there was not enough direct evidence of sodomy and allowed the men to be freed.

[Testimony by captain Jacobus Spellatus, March 15, 1624:]

Having been directly ordered to inspect the house of Stella [daughter] of Dattiluccio, a Jew, and of Sabbato, another Jew in the ghetto, to see if

Leone, another Jew, was sleeping in the same bed as the Jew Simone son of Giuseppe, it being published loudly and known in the ghetto that he had been sodomizing him for a long time, around 4 [o'clock] in the morning, I went into said house.

[Testimony by Angelo di San Lazzaro, no date mentioned in the text:]

As a matter of habit, said Jews engage in strangenesses and live in the house of Stella [daughter of] Leuccio the Jew [in the area of the] Butchers, and said Leone left and returned many times, as did Lazzaro too.

I mean to say this of Lazzaro. In the room where they live they hold a lad named Simone [son of] Giuseppe, a Jew, and they lead him around publicly, and it's said that they even let him sleep in their bed and that they sodomize him, [and] this is said publicly.

[Testimony by Leo di Corneto, no date mentioned in the text:]

Lazzaro and Leone take freedoms, [and though] said Simone observes differently, however, Leone and Lazzaro bring him along to the markets and wherever they go, it seems […] in Rome. Simone is a handsome lad of sixteen and it is said that said Leone and Lazzaro bring him and keep him in the room and that they sodomize and abuse him, and this is well known in the ghetto, though whether or not it is true I don't know.

[Testimony by the defendant Simone, March 24, 1624:]

We used to go throughout the year to the markets and since Lazzaro and I had been in Perugia, about two months ago, [and because] Leone was also travelling, I asked him for the key of this room for said Lazzaro […] and he gave it to me, we then came [back] to Rome, Lazzaro and I, and because said Leone was staying with said Lazzaro here in Rome, we both slept in the same bed, since there is no other bed in said room […] from Friday at 5 P.M. until around three, in the house of Stella where I have a room—that is, it's kept by my [acquaintance] Lazzaro Abbina who, having gone away, left me the room together with another named Leone […] said Leone had stayed with said Lazzaro here in Rome, all sleeping in the same bed, because there isn't another bed in the room […] On some days we slept even four together, the other [person] sleeping with us being another Jew called Sforza who is the brother of Leone, who is 35 or 36 years old […] We had been sleeping together for a month, I on one side, Leone in the middle, and Lazzaro on the other side.

[Testimony by the defendant Simone, April (about a week after the 17th), 1624:]

I say that no evidence will ever be found, that it isn't true what the surgeons say, and their words have no value, they are a bunch of dunces, because I swear on my conscience that I never did such a thing, and moreover I want to say that I saw the copies of the trial and I found information that one is a public surgeon, and the other isn't a surgeon but a barber who doesn't understand these things, and while they want to testify, they are nothing but enemies of the Jews and are extremely deceitful as my defense will demonstrate, and the court will be able to call two capable men and two capable men who can say the truth […] because I stand here in the hands of Justice [and may] truth follow the evidence.

Processo, Tribunale Criminale del Governatore (Archivio di Stato di Roma), Processi r. 189, cc. 1050–1272. As published in Serena Di Nepi, "Che questo è pubblico in ghetto. Se poi sia vero o no io non lo so': Un caso di studio sulla struttura sociale del ghetto di Roma attraverso un processo per sodomia (1624)," in *Storia economica e storia degli ebrei Istituzioni, capitale sociale e stereotipi, secc. XV–XVIII* (FrancoAngeli, 2017). Reprinted by permission of FrancoAngeli. Translated from Italian by Dr. Shira Klein. Copyright © 2019 Print-O-Craft Press. I thank Dr. Serena Di Nepi for sharing her research on this case and clarifying its context.

Further Reading

Ferguson, Gary. *Same-Sex Marriage in Renaissance Rome: Sexuality, Identity, and Community in Early Modern Europe* (Cornell University Press, 2016).

Herzig, Tamar. "The Prosecution of Jews and the Repression of Sodomy in Fifteenth-Century Italy." In *L'inquisizione Romana, i giudici e gli eretici: Studi in onore di John Tedeschi* (ed. Anne Jacobson Schutte and Andrea Del Col, Rome: Viella, 2017), 59–74.

Rocke, Michael. *Forbidden Friendships: Homosexuality and Male Culture in Renaissance Florence* (Oxford University Press, 1996).

46. Poetry of Sarmad Kashani (Delhi, Mid-Seventeenth Century)

Sarmad Kashani (Sarmad of Kashan; also known as Muhammad Sa'id Sarmad) was born into a well-to-do Jewish family of merchants and scholars in Kashan (Iran) around 1590. It seems he studied to become a rabbi and then became a trader of gems and luxury textiles. In 1632, his trade brought him to the Indian port city of Thatta (today in Pakistan), and there he fell in love with a Hindu youth named Abhai Chand. This love was a mystical revelation, inspiring him to devote his life to the pursuit of spiritual unity; he immediately tore off his clothes and abandoned his mercantile pursuits. Abhai became Sarmad's disciple (in his only surviving poem, Abhai writes "I submit to Moses' law; I follow your religion and guard your way / I am at once a rabbi of the Jews, an unbeliever, and a Muslim"), and they travelled across the Indian subcontinent, eventually reaching Delhi, where they were welcomed at the Mughal court of Dara Shikoh. In his time at the Delhi court, Sarmad wrote hundreds of mystical *rubaiyat* (quatrains), and described Judaism for the author of the *Dabistan-i Mazahib*, an encyclopedia of world religions written at the Mughal court around 1655. Sarmad's own religious affiliation is not clear; some claim he converted to Islam, or Hinduism, or both, while his poetry reveals a syncretic mystical faith that strives for the truth of all religions while adhering to the external frameworks of none. Like other mystical poetic traditions, Sarmad's *rubaiyat* use the metaphor of earthly love, including homoerotic love, to describe longing for the Divine. Sarmad was executed by Dara Shikoh's brother, the emperor Aurangzeb, for heresy in 1660. His grave in Delhi is still a site of pilgrimage for Indians of all faiths to this day.

I.

O veiled one, why don't you reveal yourself
How long shall I search for your dwelling?
I yearn to embrace you, hold you by my side,
How long will you stay hidden from me?

II.

My beloved does not even glance at me—what shall I do?
The heart's wail he does not hear, what shall I do?
In my heart he is forever present
But is unaware of its state, what shall I do?

III.

I am crazy for the luster of my beloved who is different
I am amazed by his beautiful form which is different.
The rest are involved in cares and woes which are different,
My fears and grief are about something that is different.

IV.

I have been saddened by that curly ringlet—
I had not planned it; it was my luck.
I am now a prisoner of that curl
As if it was a fetter around my foot.

V.

I am in sorrow, having sowed the seeds of lust
I now pluck flowers discolored a thousandfold.
I must extinguish these flames
Before they become a blazing fire.

Sarmad Kashani, *Rubaiyat Sarmad Mahmud* (ed. Nawab Ali Saulat, Delhi: Shahjahani Press, 1921), as translated in Saleem Kidwai, "Sarmad (Persian)," in *Same-Sex Love in India: Readings from Literature and History* (eds. Saleem Kidwai and Ruth Vanita; Palgrave, 2000), 157–158.

Further Reading

Ezekiel, Isaac A. *Sarmad, The Jewish Saint of India* (Punjab: Radha Soami Satsang, 1966).

Fischel, Walter J. "Jews and Judaism at the Court of the Moghul Emperors in Medieval India." *Proceedings of the American Academy for Jewish Research* 18 (1948), 137–177.

Katz, Nathan. "The Identity of a Mystic: The Case of Sa'id Sarmad, a Jewish-Yogi-Sufi Courtier of the Mughals." *Numen* 47:2 (2000), 142–160.

Prigarina, Natalia. "Sarmad: Life and Death of a Sufi." *Islamic Philosophy Yearbook* 3 (2012), 314–330.

47. Poetry of Salim al-Shabazi (Yemen, Mid-Seventeenth Century)

Salim (or Shalem) al-Shabazi (1619–ca. 1679) is considered one of the greatest and most well-known Yemenite Jewish poets. A rabbi and scholar from the southwestern Yemeni province of Ta'izz, al-Shabazi composed hundreds of poems in Hebrew and Judeo-Arabic; many of his poems are still sung in Yemenite communities to this day, and several of his compositions have been made famous by Yemenite-Israeli folk singers (such as *Im Nin'alu*, as sung by Ofra Haza). His work, which spans a variety of liturgical and non-liturgical genres, draws on Jewish precedents as well as a local poetic form in Yemeni Arabic known as *ḥumayni* poetry. His Arabic poems are often explicitly erotic and sensual, which some Yemenite Jewish thinkers found distressing, and which they attempted to explain away as metaphorical or Kabbalistic imagery. Like his Andalusi predecessors, al-Shabazi wrote love poetry directed at both boys and girls; this poem praises the "prince of the doe-eyed [*sid al-ḥur*]," whose body is luminescent in beauty, and claims that he is as beautiful as the biblical Joseph, a common description not only in al-Shabazi's work but in Arabic *ḥumayni* poetry as well.

Were you to see the prince of the doe-eyed at the summit of Mount Sinai,
You would say: "blessed be the One who created him."
    The light of his face outstrips that of the crescent moon, affixed in the heavens,
All of the young gazelles are enamored of him,
    His nose is as delicate as a sword's cutting edge,
He is a skilled youth—I am astounded by his attributes,
    His eyes are a cup of wine that wash over me,
And mesmerize my recalcitrant heart,
    His lips are like rubies chiseled with the letters *alif, ba,* and *jim,*
His mouth tastes sweet like pomegranates and basil—a cure for every ill,
    His teeth are as lustrous as pearls [text damaged]
His neck is that of a gazelle who has wandered off, alone, a fugitive,
    who disturbs all of the gazelles [with his beauty].
He has amazed all of my brothers and has given me drink,
    I spent the night with him, drunk,
And he said: "O poet from among the forgetful" [i.e., mankind],
    Wake up! Morning has risen! Speak precisely about my religion,
And stir the best of minds from their slumber,

Do not pay attention to the other gazelles, who censure me,
For I am like Joseph in beauty.

Shalom Serri and Yosef Tobi (eds.), *Shirim Ḥadashim Lerabbi Shalom Shabazi* (Jerusalem: Ben Zvi Institute, 1975). As translated in Mark Wagner, *Like Joseph in Beauty: Yemeni Vernacular Poetry and Arab-Jewish Symbiosis* (Leiden: Brill, 2009). I thank Dr. Mark Wagner for sharing some additional context and clarifying my reading of the poem. Copyright 2009 by Koninklijke Brill NV. Reprinted by permission of the author.

Further Reading

Wagner, Mark. "Arabic Influence On Šabazian Poetry in Yemen." Journal of Semitic Studies 51:1 (2006), 117–136.

Wagner, Mark. "Major Themes in the Poetry of R. Salim al-Shabazi." In *Studies in Arabic and Hebrew Letters in Honor of Raymond P. Scheindlin* (eds. Jonathan Decter and Michael Rand, Gorgias Press, 2007), 225–247.

48. A French Traveler Reports on Jewish Dancing Boys (Aleppo, 1664)

The phenomenon of feminine "dancing boys" (known as *köçek* in Turkish, *khawal* in Arabic, and *bacha* in Persian) was widespread across the Levant and Central Asia, from the Middle Ages well into the twentieth century (see sources 30 and 74); the dancers were often ethnic and religious minorities, like Jews, Greeks, Armenians, and Roma. This source comes from Jean de Thévenot (1633–1667), a French Orientalist and botanist, who travelled extensively through the Levant, Central Asia, and India. Here, de Thévenot describes a week-long celebration (*zineh* or *zinah*—literally, "adornment") which took place in Aleppo, June 22–28, 1664, for the birth of a local noble's first son. A Jewish troupe of dancers and musicians staged a performance featuring two Jewish boys dressed in feminine clothing, which de Thévenot found disturbing both for its effeminacy and its implicit invitations to homosexual activity. He acknowledges that this type of "filthiness" exists among Europeans as well, but claims that in Europe "at least they are not so frequent, and are wrapt up in clean Linnen; but these express every thing plainly and down right." Many European travelers were horrified not only by what they saw as flagrant violations of gender norms but by the positive reception these dancers received, as de Thévenot indicates here. The Orientalist associations of the Middle East, and Arabs in particular, as lascivious, hypersexual, and prone to homosexuality continued to shape perceptions of the region well into the twentieth century (see sources 55, 94, and 105). We know little about the dancers themselves; the few accounts we have of their life after "growing out" of dancing indicate that as adults they lived as men, fully accepted in the local community.

The second day of the *Zineh* the Musellem being come to the great Khan, to visit the Scheick Bandar (he is the Judge of the Merchants, and Master of the great Khan;) he was received upon a Divan erected before the Gate, where at first he was regaled with Coffee, Sorbet and Wine. Then about ten of the Clock he was conducted to another Divan prepared against the Wall at the lower end of the Court, to see a Comedy to be acted by Jews. The Court served for a Theatre, there are onely two Cresset-lights of Pine-wood which they took care to keep burning; and that sufficed to light all that great Court; twenty steps from the Divan, four or five Jews sitting on the ground, played on several Instruments and sung to them.

The Ballet began by the entry of a Turk who danced to the sound of Instruments, and shewed a thousand feats of agility of body, but all most infamous and lascivious; next followed two Jewish youths in the Apparrel of the Maids of our Countrey, who acted almost the same postures, from time to time whirling very fast round, and for a pretty long while at a time. Then were several other entrys all different, and amongst the rest, one wherein there was a Jew in the dress of a Franck, which extreamly pleased the People of the Countrey, who look upon our habit to be altogether ridiculous. But all these entrys were performed with abominable Lasciviousness, not onely in gestures but words, acting in presence of all, the most filthy postures imaginable, and at every turn using most obscene and bawdy expressions. Their whole discourse in general was nothing but filthiness, from which if in some places of Christendom the Stage be not altogether free, at least they are not so frequent, and are wrapt up in clean Linnen; but these express every thing plainly and down right, which pleases the Turks best, and I observed that fopperies spoken without sense or coherence were sufficient to make them tear their Throats with laughter, provided the words were filthy and obscene: In short, it is horrid and incredible to see how far the impudence of the Turks transports them to lust and especially to Sodomy.

Besides this ignominious entertainment, several Players upon Instruments, that go about the Town, (every Company consisting of two Hoboys and a little Boy that plays on a Timbrel,) stopt before the gate of the great Khan and played, in expectation of some gratuity from the Scheick Bandar who was still on the Divan opposite to the Gate, and who after they had played for some time, sent some half a Piastre, others a quarter, and to some a whole Piastre.

Jean de Thévenot, *The Travels of Monsieur De Thevenot into the Levant: The Second Part* (trans. Archibald Lovell, London: H. Clark, 1687).

Further Reading

Boone, Joseph. *The Homoerotics of Orientalism: Mappings of Male Desire in Narratives of the Near and Middle East* (Columbia University Press, 2014).

Karayanni, Stavros Stavrou. *Dancing Fear and Desire: Race, Sexuality, and Imperial Politics in Middle Eastern Dance* (Wilfrid Laurier University Press, 2009).

Shay, Anthony. *The Dangerous Lives of Public Performers: Dancing, Sex, and Entertainment in the Islamic World* (Palgrave, 2014).

49. Rumors of Homosexual Activity in a Dutch Sephardi Yeshiva (Amsterdam, 1674)

Intimate relationships between male yeshiva students, based in the prescriptions of rabbinic tradition (see sources 13 and 15) have been documented throughout Jewish history (sources 52, 77, and 116). In this incident, which took place in the famed Sephardi yeshiva of Ets Haim in Amsterdam, two students are accused of having had sexual relations, and are sentenced to expulsion. The subsequent scandal causes an uproar in the local community, and in the end the charges are dropped, for "the activities of young men are meaningless." The two students mentioned here, Isaac Netto (dates unknown) and Eliau Lopez (1648–1713), both left Amsterdam a few years later to enjoy well-respected rabbinic careers with Sephardi communities in the Caribbean: Netto went to Surinam in 1676, while Lopez left in 1678 for Barbados and then Curaçao, where he served from 1693 until his death. The rabbi who made the decision, Ya'aqov Sasportas (1610–1698), was born to a prominent Sephardi family in Oran (Algeria), and served throughout Algeria and Morocco before traveling to Europe, where he held positions as a rabbi and yeshiva head in London, Hamburg, Livorno, and Amsterdam, where he died.

To Rabbi Yehoshua' [Jehosua] da Silva, 19 Adar II [27 March 1674]:

An impure deed, incomprehensible to the human intellect, was done during those painful days [when Sasportas was bedridden from a leg injury some months earlier]. Some of the students in the *beit midrash*, because of their jealousy and rivalry with one another, spread a rumor, "*at which the ears of anyone who heard it would tingle*" (I Samuel 3:11): namely, that two upstanding students, Yitshaq Neto [Isaac Netto] and Eliyahu Lupits [Eliau Lopez], were suspected of homosexual relations, Heaven forbid. These matters were brought before the *mahamad* [the Jewish communal council], and in this punitive court their sentence was delivered: expulsion and exile.

When it was signed, their color fled and they were left white-faced [from embarrassment; cf. *b. Baba Metsia'* 58b] and there arose much "*contempt and anger*" (Esther 1:18). Then their anger was kindled against the shepherds [i.e. leaders; cf. Zachariah 10:3] and they decided to seize the *beit midrash* of Ets Haim. A great panic took hold of the community, while the faces of the students "*grew pale*" [with fear; Joel 2:6], sleeping in shame and covered in embarrassment. When the anger in the house of Torah had grown, and the zealous students did not stop insulting them, they lodged a complaint against the elders of the *mahamad*.

Hearing "*the uproar of the city*" (Isaiah 66:6) and "*the strong fury*" (Proverbs 21:14), in order to quell the fire of rebuke [the *mahamad*] twice sent the cantor of the community to me, [asking me] to gather my strength and lean on my staff to get up from the bed in which I had been lying. But there was no strength in me to stand up, so I was forced to call upon two students who supported me, one on each side. When I came before the *mahamad*, I found the leaders of Ets Haim with them, and before them was a Torah scroll on which the witnesses would swear, to verify their testimony in front of me.

But when I heard their words, the affair exasperated me and I told them that the activities of young men are meaningless [*hevel*], and that there was nothing more for us to do to them than to have them beaten and punished with a rod for bearing false witness. I then proved this to the men of the *mahamad* with calm and gentle language; my words dropped onto them and their mouths opened wide for the rains of my speech (cf. Job 29:22–23), and all the people from every quarter (cf. Genesis 19:4) supported me, and rested on this. Their sentence [of exile] was canceled and my decision was made public.

Ya'aqov Sasportas, letter to Jehosua da Silva, as published in Isaiah Tishbi, "Yedi'ot ḥadashot 'al qehilat ha'anusim belondon 'al pi iggerot Sasportas bishnat 5425 (1664–1665)," in *Galut Aḥar Golah: meḥqarim betoldot 'am yisra'el mugashim liprofesor Haim Beinart limel'ot lo shiv'im shanah* (ed. Avraham Grossman, Jerusalem: Ben Zvi Institute, 1988), 470–496. Translated from Hebrew by Noam Sienna.

Further Reading

Arbell, Mordehay. *The Jewish Nation of the Caribbean: The Spanish-Portuguese Jewish Settlements in the Caribbean and the Guianas.* Jerusalem: Gefen Publishing, 2002.

Ben-Ur, Aviva, and Jessica Vance Roitman. "Adultery Here and There: Crossing Sexual Boundaries in the Dutch Jewish Atlantic." In *Dutch Atlantic Connections, 1680–1800* (ed. Gert Oostindie and Jessica V. Roitman, Leiden: Brill, 2014), 183–223.

Goldish, Matt. "The Amsterdam Portuguese Rabbinate in the Seventeenth Century: A Unique Institution Viewed from Within and Without." In *Dutch Jews As Perceived by Themselves and by Others: Proceedings of the Eighth International Symposium on the History of the Jews in the Netherlands* (eds. Chaya Brasz and Yosef Kaplan, Leiden: Brill, 2001), 9–20.

50. Mussar Exercises for Those Tempted by Sexual Transgressions (Izmir, 1712)

As indicated by the title, *Sheveṭ Mussar* (The Rod of Instruction) belongs to a popular genre of early modern Jewish literature known as *mussar*, or ethical literature: prose works aimed at cultivating particular behaviors, ideals, and attitudes. Alternating between chastisement and exhortation, works of mussar cover all aspects of Jewish life, including education, prayer, business, charity, and sexuality. Here, the author recommends a mental exercise for the (male) reader who might be tempted by sexual activity with a young man: to imagine the shame they would feel if they were to meet in the future, which the author feels certain will prevent him from acting on his desires. He also provides counsel for unwanted sexual desires for a Jewish woman (the solution: contemplate the inherently disgusting nature of the female body) or a non-Jewish woman (the solution: imagine her as the non-kosher animals that she eats). His description of the encounter reveals his assumptions about male-male sexual activity in the context of Sephardi communities in the Ottoman Empire: he describes the reader (presumably older and well-educated) as the penetrator (*rovea '*), and the object of desire as a younger, penetrated partner (*nirva'*). Despite his warnings, it is clear that sexual activity between Sephardi men was not only common in this period, but often ignored or quietly tolerated (see sources 37, 42, 52, and 55). Written by Eliyah HaKohen Haltamari (ca. 1640–1729), a preacher and scholar of Kabbalah from Izmir, *Shevet Mussar* was first printed in 1712, and reprinted in dozens of editions over the next two centuries, including translations into Yiddish, Judeo-Spanish, and Judeo-Arabic.

If his inclination tempts him to lie with a man as with a woman, let him consider that once the beard of his partner [*nirva'*] is full, and especially if they meet when they are both grown old, they will feel so much shame and embarrassment and disgrace and dishonor, as they remember how they had lain with each other. Furthermore, neither of them will be able to take pride in performing *mitsvot* in public in front of the other, even if he has repented—surely it would bring shame to take pride in himself in front of one who has angered his Creator, for he will remember the time of the deed by which he was polluted and he will feel disgraced.

In particular, if the active partner [*rovea'*] is poor and the passive one [*nirva'*] is wealthy—how could [the poor one] go to beg of him and ask him for kindness, for what could he remind [the wealthy one] of, to stir his mercies? He has no grounds to remind him of any merits; indeed, he would actually arouse the memories of their evil deeds [together], and the wealthy one will add to this the anger that such a debased one had defiled him. And if the matter is reversed, and the active partner is wealthy, and the passive one is poor, then his having touched that diseased body will disgust him throughout his life. What's more, when he sees himself dressed lavishly, while his poor partner is wrapped in tattered rags and hiding his face from him, being too embarrassed to look at him—this will send him into great shame.

When a man considers these things, it is practically impossible that his inclination will overpower him to lie with a man. For immediately when this notion occurs to him, his blood will congeal, and certainly also when he thinks of the great ignominy and disgust, and the strangeness of the act itself.

Eliyah HaKohen HaItamari, *Shevet Mussar* (Salonica, 1712). Translated from Hebrew by Noam Sienna.

Further Reading

Ben-Naeh, Yaron. "Mishkav Zakhar Baḥevrah HaYehudit Ha'Othomanit." *Zion* 66 (2001), 171–200.

Ben-Naeh, Yaron. "Moshko the Jew and his Gay Friends: Same-Sex Sexual Relations in Ottoman Jewish Society." *Journal of Early Modern History* 9:1–2 (2005), 79–105.

Lehmann, Matthias. *Ladino Rabbinic Literature and Ottoman Sephardic Culture* (Indiana University Press, 2005).

Ze'evi, Dror. *Producing Desire: Changing Sexual Discourse in the Ottoman Middle East, 1500–1900* (University of California Press, 2006).

51. A Gender-Bending Jewish Runaway Arrives in New France (Quebec, 1738)

The historical phenomenon of people who were raised as women but who live partly or completely as men presents numerous interpretive complexities. In some cases, it seems clear that these individuals understood themselves to be men in every way; in other cases, it seems that their intention was to pursue marriage or partnership with women; and in yet other cases, their life as a man opened new professional, economic, and social opportunities (see source 73 for a twentieth-century case). The life of Esther Brandeau / Jacques La Fargue is one such story of multiple boundary-crossings. Born in southwestern France, to a French branch of the Dutch Sephardi Brandon family, they spent several years working as a young man in various French cities and on ships, eventually reaching the French colony of Québec on the land of the native Huron-Wendat Nation. There, Esther / Jacques was doubly "outed" as both a woman and a Jew. At the time, French law prohibited any non-Catholics from settling in its colonies—Esther/Jacques is the first known Jewish person to have entered what is now Canada. When

Esther/Jacques was asked, "to state for what reason she [sic] had so concealed her sex during five years," they avoided the question, explaining only that they sought "the same liberty as the Christians." But, refusing to convert to Christianity—the superintendent reported that "she is so flippant that at different times she has been both obedient and obstinate with regard to the instruction the ecclesiastic authorities desired to give her"—they were sent back to France, where they disappear from the archival record.

15th September, 1738.

This day, before the undersigned, *Commissaire de Marine, chargé a Québec de la police des gens de mer*, appeared Esther Brandeau, aged about twenty years, who embarked at LaRochelle as a passenger, dressed in boy's clothes, under the name of Jacques La Fargue, on the vessel "St. Michel," Sieur de Salaberry, commander, and declared her name to be Esther Brandeau, daughter of David Brandeau, a Jew, trader, of Saint Esprit, diocese of Daxe, near Bayonne, and that she is of the Jewish religion;

that five years ago her father and mother placed her on a Dutch vessel, Captain Geoffroy, in order to send her to Amsterdam to one of her aunts and to her brother;

that the vessel having been lost on the bar of Bayonne, in the moon of April or May, 1733, she was happily brought safe to shore with one of the crew, that she was received by Catherine Churiau, a widow living at Biaris;

that two weeks thereafter she started dressed as a man for Bordeaux, where she shipped as a boy, under the name of Pierre Mansiette, on a vessel commanded by Captain Bernard, destined for Nantes;

that she returned on the same vessel to Bordeaux and there shipped again in the same capacity on a Spanish vessel, Captain Antonio, for Nantes;

that on reaching Nantes she deserted and went to Rennes where she took service as a boy at the house of one Augustin, a tailor, where she remained six months;

that from Rennes she went to Clissoy where she took service with the Recollets as a servant and to run messages;

that she remained three months in the convent and left without warning for St. Malo, where she found shelter at the house of a baker named Seruanne;

that she next went to Vitré to get a place there and entered the service of Sr. de la Chapelle, an ex-captain of infantry;

that she left the situation because her health rendered her unable to watch the said Sr. la Chapelle who was always sick;

that when returning to Nantes, and when one league from Noisel, she was taken for a thief and confined in the prison of Noisel aforesaid;

that she was set free, after twenty-four hours, because it was found that a mistake had been made;

that she then went to La Rochelle, where assuming the name of Jacques La Fargue, she took shipping as a passenger on the said vessel, "St. Michel."

Upon which declaration we called upon the said Esther Brandeau to state for what reason she had so concealed her sex during five years. Whereupon she said: That when she escaped from shipwreck and reached Bayonne she entered the house of Catharine Churiau, as above stated, that the latter made her eat pork and other meats the use whereof is forbidden among the Jews, and that she thereupon resolved not to return any more to her father and mother in order that she might enjoy the same liberty as the Christians.

Whereof we have indicted these presents as our *procès-verbal*.* And the said Esther Brandeau hath signed with us, on the day and in the year aforesaid.

Collated,

(Signed) VARIN.

"Procès verbal de l'interrogatoire d'Esther Brandeau, 15th September, 1738." Archives nationales de France, Série C11A, Fonds des Colonies, Correspondence générale, Canada, ff. 129–130. As published (in French and English translation) by Joseph Marmette, "Report on French Archives," in *Report on Canadian Archives* (ed. Douglas Brymner, Ottawa: Maclean, Roger, and Co., 1887), xxxi–xxxviii. I thank Dr. Heather Hermant for bringing this source to my attention. Line breaks added for clarity.

*In French, Belgian, and Dutch law, a *procès-verbal* is a detailed certified report written by a magistrate or police officer.

Further Reading

Choquette, Leslie. *Frenchmen into Peasants: Modernity and Tradition in the Peopling of French Canada* (Harvard University Press, 1997).

Hermant, Heather. *Esther Brandeau / Jacques La Fargue: Performing a Reading of an Eighteenth Century Multicrosser*. Ph.D. dissertation, Utrecht University, 2017.

52. A Sephardi Rabbi Decries Homosexual Activity in His Yeshiva (Salonica, 1769)

While homosexual activity was frowned upon by rabbinic authorities in the Ottoman Empire, it was clearly widespread in local society among both Jews and non-Jews and was not treated with any more severity than other transgressions of ritual law (for other examples, see sources 37, 44, and 55). It was seen as a sexual misdemeanor, but not an indicator of any personal identity or permanent orientation; in fact, in this excerpt from *Orḥot Yosher* (Paths of Righteousness), a rabbinic work on the customs of Salonica (today Thessaloniki, Greece), the author sees the temptation to engage in homosexual activity as a danger for any young man. He explains that he and his colleagues in Salonica were so concerned by the prevalence of sexual activity among unmarried men, especially the students of local yeshivot, that they had to establish a *taqqanah* (communal ordinance) establishing curfews and restricting the movement of unmarried men, which was read aloud in Judeo-Spanish in the local community. The writer, Yitsḥaq Molkho (ca. 1721–1781), was a scholar and preacher in Salonica, belonging to a prominent Sephardi family of rabbis and community leaders.

A man should be very careful that he not allow his son to come and go unattended to festive events and celebrations where most of the bachelors transgress against the prohibition of, *"You shall not lie with a man as with a woman"* (Leviticus 18:22)—the responsibility rests on the father's shoulders if he does not go after them when they go to these celebrations, and especially in a group of friends. Of these [groups] it is said, "the gathering of the wicked is bad for them and bad for the world" (*b. Sanhedrin* 71b), for all of their gathering leads to wickedness, even if they did not intend it so. For in every case temptation dances before them, and it is not possible for youth to resist the flame, as it is written, *"Can one hold fire in his bosom, and his clothes not catch fire?"* (Proverbs 6:27). Therefore, any man who fears the word of God should guard his son carefully when he reaches the age of twelve, for [from this age on] he is tempted very easily.

And for this reason there is no similar prohibition for women, whether unmarried or married, widows or divorcées. For unmarried women, [we are not concerned] because they are secluded and confined; for married women, it is not common for a man and a woman to be alone together in a private place; and in any case, a woman is not tempted so easily, since she fears [God] and has the sense to spurn wickedness. Not so with the young men, who are always found [together] in one place, and who are not ashamed to be in seclusion with one another, although [the Talmud teaches that] "Jews are not suspected of homosexuality" (*b. Qiddushin* 82a). Further, they are brash boys and are easily tempted, for they do not have much shame. This is especially true when there are festive events and celebrations, or when they go out for some drinking or traveling; then their inclinations rule over them.

Therefore, the man who fears the word of God must not let his son go here and there, and if it is necessary at some time for him to go to some celebration or festivity, then his father should go with him, or his legal guardian if he is an orphan, or a relative; and [the chaperone] should not move from his spot, for we have already said that boys need more supervision than girls, since girls are not likely to corrupt themselves. Similarly, one who teaches boys, from ten years old until they are married—the teacher should watch them carefully, and not let them go off to a private place.

I am speaking from my own concerns, for since I was 24 years old until now, when I am 45, I have seen many corruptions, and the latest was the most serious. Two or three students went up to the attic of one of them to study halakhah [Jewish law], but it was later revealed to me that this study session was in fact a corruption. And similarly, another rabbi told me that when he went to deal with some matter and had to leave the students [unattended], he would instruct members of his household to watch them. Therefore, the rabbis of our city [Salonica] made an ordinance that no unmarried student may go about at night to the house of study where married men study. Similarly, in the textile workshops which we have here in Salonica, [they decreed] that no bachelor should inherit the right to have his own loom, for if he has his own loom he would need to have apprentices, and it is not appropriate for a craftsman who is still a bachelor to have apprentices, for temptation dances between them, and similarly for all other crafts. Attached to this ordinance, [we added] the teaching of the Rambam of blessed memory:* namely, that a man without a wife should not teach boys, [to prevent temptation] by the mothers who come with their children.

And this is the text of the ordinances:**

No bachelor may go out to sing—neither at a groom's ceremony, nor at the [*yeshiva* of the] Talmud Torah on Shabbat, nor in any community synagogue where there is [a celebration for] a groom, a father of a newborn boy, or a boy to be circumcised, until he has completed one full year of marriage. [Until then] they may not go with the *pizmonjis* [singers of liturgical poetry] to sing at the night of a circumcision, even if it is a relative, and no young man who is unmarried may go to study sessions at night.

Yitsḥaq Molkho, *Orḥot Yosher* (Salonica, 1769). Translated from Hebrew and Judeo-Spanish by Noam Sienna.

Further Reading

Ben-Naeh, Yaron. "Mishkav Zakhar Baḥevrah HaYehudit Ha'Othomanit." *Zion* 66 (2001), 171–200.

Ben-Naeh, Yaron. "Moshko the Jew and his Gay Friends: Same-Sex Sexual Relations in Ottoman Jewish Society." *Journal of Early Modern History* 9:1–2 (2005), 79–105.

Ze'evi, Dror. *Producing Desire: Changing Sexual Discourse in the Ottoman Middle East, 1500–1900* (University of California Press, 2006).

53. The Scandal of a French Sephardi Banker, his Wife, and an Italian Actor (Paris, 1778–1784)

One of the central occupations of French society of the eighteenth century was producing and consuming scandalous news and gossip, the more salacious the better. These excerpts from the anonymous journalistic pamphlets known as *libelles* describe Samuel Peixotto (1741–1805), a Sephardi Jewish banker

---

* *Mishneh Torah*, Talmud Torah 2:4, drawing on *b. Qiddushin* 82a.
** The following paragraph is written in Judeo-Spanish.

from Bordeaux who became well-known for his famous and controversial divorce case of 1778–1781. Peixotto attempted to have his divorce from Sarah Mendès d'Acosta granted by the royal courts of Paris rather than by a rabbinic court, which sparked an explosive and widely-publicized discussion on the legal standing of Jews in France and the control of their marital practices. Almost immediately, speculations began swirling about the reasons for his divorce, focusing especially on his unusual sexual proclivities. Peixotto is described as "the most debauched buggerer in France," and as having "the Italian palate" (*le goût italien*), a common euphemism in this period for homosexual attraction. In particular, Peixotto was partnered with a notorious actor named Louis Michu (1752–1802), tutor to Marie Antoinette, and famed for his ability to impersonate women convincingly, on and off stage. According to one source, Peixotto initially paid him the exorbitant sum of a thousand *louis d'or* for a single night together, but another describes Michu as "attached" to Peixotto "as his mistress." How long they stayed together is unknown.

I. *L'Espion anglais* [The English Spy], Vol. IX, letter IX (23 July, 1778)

Mr. Peixotto has finally pushed depravity to the point of publicizing his [tastes] contrary to nature, and we can see that he quite publicly keeps a very young, very pretty actor from the Italian theatre (1). Without a doubt, it was in the intoxication of his unrestrained passions that Mr. Peixotto finally formed his senseless plan to reduce a virtuous wife, chosen from the very first families of the nation, to the lowest rung of concubines and to bring upon his own children the opprobrium of bastardhood (2).

Whence could he have conceived such an idea so opposed to humanity, to reason, and to nature? That is what is impossible to understand. It couldn't have been the lure of greater freedom since nothing could have disturbed his life in Paris, far from his abandoned wife in Bordeaux, who had given written consent for the arranged separation in exchange for a modest pension.

Whatever was the motive for his demand for justice, he employed such means that his plan was met with a dim response. He accused his virtuous wife of bad conduct, of licentiousness, of libertinage; he pushed the atrocity to the point of insinuating that his life was not safe with her and dared to publish these calumnies to public bulletin. (3) Even if there had been as much truth as falseness in the claims, it would not have brought about the annulment of his marriage. None of these cases could be recognized according to the laws of France (4); and besides, Mr. Peixotto was not French, however naturalized, but rather Jewish.

Note (1): Mr. Michu

Note (2): Mr. Peixotto has two children, one of whom is a boy between the age of 9 and 10.

Note (3): Mr. Peixotto cared more for his fortune than for his life, the wife having left his house in Bordeaux and lived there in known worry; he would go so far as to say that more than once his days had been ruined by this so-called wife. (*Courrier de l'Europe*, 20 Dec. 1777).

Note (4): This has been well established in the "Memoire of Sarah Mendès d'Acosta, wife of Mr. Samuel Peixotto, countering Mr. Samuel Peixotto," as to the request for an annulment of marriage and Jewish divorce.

II. *Mémoires secrets* [Secret Memoirs], Vol. XVI, 30 (1780)

18 October. Mr. Parisot, hitherto director of the children of the opera, actor and author, had a casting call for Italians. As soon as he appeared before the assembled in order to get to know the actors, Mr. Michu demonstrated his character, declaring, "I think you want to inspect us as if we were a bunch of street performers [prostitutes]." Mr. Volange, embarrassed by the implication, retorted, "Mr. Michu, if I could even tell your sex, then you'd have to deal with me," and all the troupe laughed. He [Michu] effectively had the reputation of being a *bardache* [i.e. an effeminate male courtesan] and being attached to the most debauched buggerer [*Bougre*] in France, a very wealthy Jew named Peixotto who kept him as a mistress.

III. *Correspondence de Mme Gourdan* [Correspondence of Madame Gourdan], 30 (1784)

From Mr. Pexioto [*sic*] (1)

This Saturday. I shall come to your place tomorrow at 10 A.M. Don't forget to get the most beautiful peacock feathers.

Note (1): The editor of these letters believes it useless to obscure the name of the banker and leave only the first initial. He would have been recognized immediately, as soon as one would see that he has spoken of peacock feathers on this note. There couldn't be two people with the proclivities of Mr. Pexioto [*sic*], which was to crawl around his room naked on all fours after having stuck peacock feathers up his rear-end. The young lady with him was obliged to strike his back while saying, "Ah, the beautiful peacock!" We are assured, as well, that this banker has the Italian palate, and that in 1781 he gave a thousand *louis* [*d'or*, i.e. gold coins] to Michu, actor of the Italian theatre, to spend the night with him.

L'Espion anglais (1778), *Mémoires secrets* (1780), *Correspondance de Mme Gourdan* (1784), translated from French by Catherine Power. I thank her, and Dr. Géraldine Gudefin, for their additional help in contextualizing this source. Copyright © 2019 Print-O-Craft Press.

Further Reading

Blanc, Olivier. "The 'Italian Taste' in the Time of Louis XVI, 1774–92." *Journal of Homosexuality* 41:3–4 (2002), 69–84.

Cardon, Patrick (ed.). *Les enfans de Sodome à l'Assemblée nationale, 1790* (Paris: Gay-KitschCamp, 2005).

Humbert, Michel. "Un divorce judaïque devant la juridiction royale: l'affaire Samuel Peixotto—Sarah Mendès d'Acosta." In *Mélanges à la mémoire de Marcel-Henri Prévost* (Presses Universitaires de France, 1982), 307–318.

Oliel-Grausz, Evelyne. "Divorce mosaïque et legislation révolutionnaire." In *Les Juifs et la Révolution française: Histoire et Mentalités* (ed. M. Hadas-Lebel and E. Oliel-Grausz, Paris: Peeters, 1992), 71–84.

54. A Maskilic Satire of Homosexual Activity Among Hasidim (Galicia, 1817)

The rise of the Hasidic movement in Eastern Europe in the middle of the eighteenth century quickly garnered detractors, skeptics, and critics, known as *Misnagdim* (or *Mitnaggedim*, "Opponents"). Criticism of Hasidism also came from *maskilim*, people affiliated with the modernizing movement of the *Haskalah* (Jewish Enlightenment), which aimed to create a liberal and secular Jewish culture. These opponents attacked and ridiculed all aspects of Hasidism, including the perceived ignorance and backwardness of the

Hasidim, their disregard for the norms of intellectual scholarship, the strange rituals of their prayer and celebration, and their attachment to their rabbi, the *rebbe* or *tsaddik* ("saint"). This satirical letter, written for Purim by the maskil Shimshon Bloch (1785–1845) to the noted educator and author Josef Perl (1773–1839), describes how two Hasidim in the Galician town of Rawa-Ruska were discovered engaging in same-sex relations with younger boys; he then presents an elaborate parody of Kabbalistic language that justifies their behavior as a means of preventing other sexual sins and even of hurrying the arrival of the Messiah. While we cannot verify this particular event, the claim of homoerotic behavior getting out of hand in Hasidic circles was a common complaint in this period (for a report from within the Hasidic world in the early twentieth century, see source 77).

With God's help, the first of the week of [parashat] Tetsaveh, "*the* CRY *of Sodom and Gomorrah*" [March 2, 1817].* To my beloved friend, the noble rabbi, the renowned sage, the one who stands as a sign for his people, and in the breach of his nation, the dear-spirited man of wisdom, Mr. Yosef [Perl]:

How long, sir, will these lustful thoughts dwell among us? How long will these cursed sciences be a stumbling block for us? Behold, the time has come for us to abandon these foolish pursuits, uproot the foundations of logic, and go worship God like one of these Hasidim in the country. For what blind one could not see, what fool could not know (cf. Psalms 92:7) that we have erred in our views until now, speaking nonsense about great saints [*tsaddikim*]? Mountains will crumble and hills will melt away, and the words of the saint will abide forever (cf. Isaiah 54:10). The saint Reb Feivush Hovniver** was hosted this past month here in Rave [Rawa-Ruska, in Galicia]. Of all the saints who came there to serve him in love, there were only two about whom he prophesied that in days to come they would be like two lights that would illuminate the land and those who dwell on it.

And what can I say? My face is covered in shame, and I am wrapped in a cloak of embarrassment—for all the words of the saint came true, and not one

---

*Bloch indicates the year with a chronogram, a Biblical word or phrase with the same numerical value as the Hebrew year. Here, the word "cry" has the value of [5]577, or 1816–7 CE. The chosen verse (Genesis 18:20) also introduces the letter's subject matter.

**A student of the Seer of Lublin, from the town of Hovniv, or Ugnev, in Ukraine.

word fell to the ground. Two weeks had gone by, when the heavens discovered his righteousness and all the people saw his glory, that the spirit of God had spoken through him, and that God's words were on his tongue. For it was revealed to all the people that not only did these [two Hasidim] enter a public covenant that they would not be tempted by a woman, but [it was revealed] also that for many years they had not even been dirtied by nocturnal emission. Now, let the so-called sages be ashamed! Now let the philosophizers dig, as they always dig, in the depths of the sciences to seek out the mysteries of nature and uncover her secrets! I know they will ask—how could this be? How could the strong movements with which they sway in their prayers, and likewise the intoxicating drinks that the saints imbibe aplenty so that awe burns in them, not also light in them the desire for love and the pleasure of women? Who could place a lock and bar, or have strength to withhold, the power pushing these luxuries? And despite all this, in front of the eyes of those so-called sages, the rebbe lives! For this was, it was, it was!

All the people of this city will testify to this, and leading them the chief rabbi and head of the *beit din* [Jewish court] here—these two saints were caught in the upper story of the *beit midrash* fooling around sexually with young men, and when this deed became known, the saints admitted that they had been doing this for more than five years, and with more than 30 boys. And surely, could anyone without a twisted heart not admit that in these years, those saints have been undoubtedly preserved both from intercourse with women and from nocturnal emissions, even if their strength is the strength of stones and their emission the emission of horses (cf. Job 6:12 and Ezekiel 23:20)?

The opponents [*mitnaggedim*] who see only with their eyes, and who do not have even a shred of knowledge of the wisdom of truth, might "*complain in their tents*" (Deuteronomy 1:27), thinking that [these men] are sinners and that they have done a great abominable act in Israel. But I myself, who through heavenly grace has merited to taste some of the honeycomb of the wisdom of truth, and whose eyes have been enlightened—I stand at the right hand of their righteousness and I answer, "*Please, my brothers! Do not do so wickedly*' (Genesis 19:7), for why should you sin against these two saints? Surely if their intention had been, Heaven forbid, to do an abominable act and satisfy their inclination, then why would they have done this in the upper story of the *beit midrash*, in a holy place?"

The truth of the matter is like what the saintly Reb Elimelekh [of Lizhensk, 1717–1787] explained in his precious book, *No'am Elimelekh*, about the reason for the prohibition of [mixing] meat and dairy [in parashat Mishpatim]: in truth, each one is completely permissible on its own, and it is only in their combination that the Torah created a new prohibition, since not everyone knows the secret of their mystical unification. Therefore, this is only an innovation, and nothing is forbidden except to those who are ignorant of the secret of unification. Thus the angels ate meat and dairy with our father Avraham of blessed memory (Genesis 18:8), since they knew the secret of unification, and in any case it is known to those graced with the certain knowledge of the secret of unification that there is no prohibition in eating [them] at all.

And thus it is also with homosexual intercourse—for each one is male, and even the private seclusion of two males is not forbidden; rather, the Torah only innovated a prohibition on their intercourse, and even that is only for those who do not know the secret of sweetening of the Divine Judgments by means of the male, as sweetening them by means of the female, and make them all completely of mercy, to draw the heavenly dew from the head of the cosmic male [*ze'ir anpin*] in the greatest will and general happiness, like the secret of *"the dew that descends on the mountains of Zion,"* meaning those who are outstanding in law, blessed is the nation whose case is such, *"for there, God has commanded blessing"* (Psalms 133:3), meaning *"the blessings of breasts and womb"* (Genesis 49:25), of which they will never be comforted. Here, too, you have only a new prohibition [in combination], and whoever knows the sweetening in this way, there is no doubt that all kinds of intercourse are permitted to him. Therefore, most of the saints engage in prohibited sexual activity, but there is no sin for them, for they have been graced with knowledge of the ancient ways [...]

They [i.e. the *mitnaggedim*] respond to me [by saying]: we know how powerful the wisdom of truth is and how great its strength. We know that it can sweeten the bitter waters, and that it has the power to move mountains, to straighten generations and twist straightened ones, to bring order to chaos and to make possible two contradictions for one issue. But reveal to us the secret of the matter: who closed the gate for them to prevent them from going after [older] men, such that they chose for themselves only youth? Rascals! Miscreants! I answered them: how long will you pry into the righteousness of the Hasidim, and muddy the pure waters with your incessant scheming? What fool doesn't know that they only did this in order to hurry the arrival of the righteous savior [i.e. the Messiah]? It is known that the Messiah will not come until all the souls in the Heavenly Treasury [*guf*, literally "body"] have been emptied [i.e. by bearing children, see *b. Niddah* 13b]. Therefore, the great ones who long for redemption will struggle with all their might to intentionally force out the souls from their bodies [*gufam*], by means of various strategies, in every corner they turn to [i.e. masturbation].

But these tender children, the young of the flock who have not yet been aroused and who do not know how to bring out the precious from the cheap— how will they be saved, therefore, to bring out the souls from their bodies, if not by some helper besides themselves? Shall all the souls awaiting the full redemption be shattered on their account? Shall they be anchored without being saved, until these youths grow and become educated men? For before they have grown and emptied all the souls in their bodies, new boys will spring up from every corner, and the matter will unfortunately go on without end. When will the Lord of Hosts have mercy, and answer us with great righteousness, to show us the miraculous end? Therefore, these saints were enlightened to bring out the locked-up souls, enclosed like bones in the bellies of these boys, in order to hurry the arrival of the righteous Messiah, and in order to urge [God] to gather all the Jews to that oasis of righteousness, where they will worship God with sacrificed cattle and sheep. Even if in your minds these [saints] sinned and did beastly deeds, my heart is certain and sure that God will repay their actions and reward them in full [...]

SHIMSHON BLOCH HALEVI

I send regards to the honorable friend, the great teacher, the true sage, the pride and glory of his people, the exalted Mendel Lefin (1749–1826), and to all the *maskilim* who visit in his shade, especially to my friend since youth, the wonderful maskil Moses Friehling [a teacher in Perl's school], greetings to his parents and his child.

My lord, may you do me this favor! Instruct one of your companions to copy this letter and send it to our companion, the sage [Jacob Samuel] Bick (1772–1831) who lives in Brody—perhaps he, too, might return from his foolishness and from his bad path, and repent to heal him.

Letter of Shimshon Bloch Halevi to Josef Perl, as published in Simḥa Katz, "Iggerot maskilim bigenutam shel ḥasidim," *Moznaim* 10:2–3 (1939), 266–276. Translated from Hebrew by Noam Sienna.

Further Reading

Biale, David. "The Displacement of Desire in Eighteenth-Century Hasidism." In *ibid.*, *Eros and the Jews* (University of California Press, 1997), 121–148.

Biale, David et al. *Hasidism: A New History* (Princeton University Press, 2018).

Seidman, Naomi. "The Ghost of Queer Loves Past: Ansky's 'Dybbuk' and the Sexual Transformation of Ashkenaz." In *Queer Theory and the Jewish Question* (eds. Daniel Boyarin, Daniel Itzkovitz, and Ann Pellegrini, Columbia University Press, 2004), 228–245."

Wilensky, Mordekhai. *Ḥasidim Umitnaggedim: letoldot hapulmus shebeneihem bashanim 532–535* (Jerusalem: Mossad Bialik, 1970).

55. An Ashkenazi Rabbi is Horrified by the Prevalence of Homosexual Activity in the Balkans (Constantinople, 1829)

As can be seen from other texts (see sources 37, 44, and 52), Jews in the Ottoman Empire were not particularly distressed about the local prevalence of homosexual activity—an attitude that caused great confusion for some visitors. One Ashkenazi rabbi in the Ottoman Empire, Ephraim Chajes (Ḥayyot), was so disturbed by what he saw around him that he devoted over a third of his book *Miqra'ei Qodesh* (Holy Occasions) to addressing the problem of homosexual activity. Chajes was raised in Hungary in a well-known rabbinic family; he left home intending to move to Jerusalem, and spent a decade traveling throughout Europe and the Mediterranean, spending time in Paris, Tunis, Livorno, Trieste, the Balkans, and finally, Constantinople, where he published *Miqra'ei Qodesh*, a book of *mussar* (see source 50) in Hebrew and in an abridged Judeo-Spanish translation. In the book, he claims that the very idea of male-male intercourse was unknown in Christian Europe, and describes how shocked he was when he first encountered the practice in an unnamed Ottoman Balkan city near Sofia (modern-day Bulgaria). Recounting a lengthy story of discovering his attendant embroiled in an affair with a young Jewish man known for selling sexual favors, Chajes castigates the local Jewish community for their apathy towards what he calls "this ugly and terrible matter, this great evil, this deed that is against the Holy Blessed One and against nature." He recommends harsh punishments for those who succumb to it, as well as a number of practices to ward off the inclination to homosexual activity (and the illnesses that he believed it caused). His overwrought tone demonstrates the degree to which norms around sexual behavior differed between Ashkenazi and Ottoman Jewish communities in this period.

Despite [the fact] that Maimonides wrote in *Issurei Bi'ah* 22:2 [see source 27] that "Israel should not be suspected of homosexual activity," these people (may their names and memories be blotted out) make our holy Torah into a fraud (but despite this falsehood, [I assert that] Moses was true and his Torah was true). In all the [Christian] countries of the world—Spain, France, Italy, England, and Poland—even though these nations believe in Jesus of Nazareth, they still refrain from homosexual activity. And certainly how much more so and more so the Jews separate and distance themselves from this abomination [*to'evah*], such that they do not know or recognize any matter relating to this impurity.

Woe to the ears that hear this! Because of our many sins, in the lands of the Ishmaelites [the Ottoman Empire], even the Jews are suspected of homosexual activity. Oh, woe! Woe to that shame, woe to that embarrassment! We are a disgrace to all the nations. Has anyone heard or seen anything like this: that this abomination is done even among Israel? And because of our many sins, there is nobody who notices, even if they all cry out, "What is this, and why have many troubles come to us, and every day brings worse calamity than before!" But their eyes are blocked from seeing this terrible sin, such that they might find relief for their ills.

At first, when I heard of this ugly and terrible matter, that this plague was seen among the houses of Israel, I did not want to believe it. I said to myself that it was an impossible matter; how could the great descendants of Avraham,

Yitshaq, and Ya'aqov profane the holy covenant and spoil it, being suspected of this ugly and terrible matter, this great evil, this deed that is against the Holy Blessed One and against nature? I did not believe it until I came to a great city of sages and scribes, in the land of Rumelo [Rumelia, i.e. the Balkans], and stayed there for six weeks. I had at that time a young man accompanying me as an attendant, from the city of Sofia in that country.

One time I went to visit a great and respected sage in that community. As I was walking in the main square of the city, a young man came and demanded from my attendant that he pay him two *grosh* [i.e. *kuruş*, a small coin]…[Having carried the argument to the house], now this young man was screaming and crying, and they were caught up in a big argument with each other, and I was puzzled: what is the matter, that he is screaming as if tied up, and crying so bitterly?…While all this was happening, a certain sage came who had been there staying in my guest room, and when he heard the argument of these two, the sage said to my attendant, "Why didn't you want to pay him? I know that this young man is right; you owe him."

Immediately my attendant winked his eyes and motioned with his finger to this sage, who went and stood with him on the side, and my attendant whispered into his ear. When he finished speaking, the sage's expression changed and he came and said to this young man who was demanding [the money], "Get out of here immediately!" and pushed him out of the house. I saw this but did not understand the decision this sage had made. I told my attendant to stand outside, and once he had left I asked this sage, "What did you do? What was this change that I saw? At first you said that the young man was right and my attendant had to pay him, but then you switched, releasing the attendant and pushing the young man, and sent him away without any money." The sage answered me by saying, "It's true that he owes him, but even so he doesn't have to pay—may both of their names and memories be blotted out."

I didn't understand any of what he was saying, because it never occurred to me to suspect of anyone that they would do this terrible abomination, and so he told me explicitly that these cursed ones did this great and terrible deed, and that this was the debt that the young man was demanding—it was incomprehensible. This sage then said to me that he, and many others, knew that this young man (may his name be blotted out) offered his unclean body for hire for this abomination. I raised my voice in bitter weeping when I heard this terrible thing and did not want to see the evil face of this attendant until he had repented; as soon as I found another attendant, I released this one and sent him away. From then on, I believed what had been said to me earlier, and I later heard that there were Jews in other places who were suspected of this abomination, and I heard that in some places the Jews, with the power of the Muslim city authorities, imprisoned some Jews who had done this abomination, may the Merciful One preserve us...*

It is clear and agreed-upon by medical experts that most human and animal illnesses are caused by air that is not clean or pure. And these cursed evil ones, who engage in homosexual activity, cause a stench in the air because of this, Heaven forbid, and this is clear and obvious to all who know the natural sciences: they bring all kinds of terrible illnesses, and especially scabs on the head. And from the prevalence of this evil transgression comes plague, Heaven forbid, and experience proves it, since plagues are not as common worldwide as they are in the lands of the Ishmaelites. It is true that there are other things that also cause plague, like the cleanliness in some matters that is lacking in these countries; but nonetheless, both of these things cause plagues. And this uncleanliness of homosexual intercourse is the main cause of harmful [illnesses]...

If a reasonable person is overcome by their desire to sin, and they do something forbidden by the Torah, then a sage can rebuke them for having done this unreasonable thing, and they will accept his words with love and return to correct behavior. But it is not so with a stubborn man, and especially the one who is outside the bounds of humanity, cursed through the sin of homosexual activity...Rather, it is necessary to beat him with disciplinary lashings, a hundred or more, even if his disgusting and abominable body expires...Why should we wring our hands and take pity on an impure soul? Let him cry, "Impure, impure!" His impurity is still in him, and he is liable to be stoned to death. It is necessary to form some strategy to kill him, in order that others might hear and be afraid and not continue to do this terrible thing...How can he lift his head? How can he eat and drink, how is he able to sleep? How can he wear nice clothing, while his dirty clothing is still on him—the filthiness of

*See source 36 for such an occurrence.

his soul and spirit, distanced and separated from the Holy Blessed One. Woe to us until Judgement Day, woe to us! Now, dear reader: whoever sins and does this terrible evil is already excommunicated and exiled from the God of Israel… May his name be blotted out from under the heavens, and may God separate him for his evil, so that all the evils coming from his deeds should return upon his own head…

Therefore, it is appropriate and correct for every Jew to make a barrier and a fence for himself. The first barrier is: he should be very careful not to have two men sleeping in one bed together, and he should close his eyes to avoid seeing the faces of young men and women…And he should avoid looking at his own genitals, and obviously even more so those of others, even of a child—for these things bring a man to evil thoughts and accustom him to indecency. And if he should happen to have some evil thought, Heaven forbid, then he should imagine in his mind that this is the Angel of Death coming to take away his life and the life of his children, Heaven forbid…The second [barrier] is: he should recite the nighttime Shema when going to bed, with full intention, according to what is written in the prayer books, with the confession, wholeheartedly [resolving] to abandon sin…The third [barrier] is: he should recall that because of the sins of wasting seed and homosexual intercourse, he will bury his own children, Heaven forbid. How could he harden his heart and not have pity on his sons and daughters? [How could he] be so cruel to them that he would cause their death?…The fourth [barrier] is: he should guard himself against engaging in idle talk or falsehoods, Heaven forbid, for it is an evil and very horrid habit, and leads to several sins…Related to this, I heard of a terrible custom that they practice: that when there is some happy occasion, like an engagement or a circumcision or some other celebration, entertainers come, causing laughter and amusement with their various actions; there is no evil like this evil…They [pretend] to be husband and wife, having some argument and talking to one another, saying all kinds of profanities and things that are forbidden to hear, and the crowd of ignorant boors laughs and rejoices. In our many sins, a celebration like this causes evil thoughts and brings people closer to sexual transgression, Heaven forbid. Woe to the ears that hear this, and woe to the eyes that see this!

Ephraim Chajes, *Miqra'ei Qodesh* (Ortaköy: Arap Oglu Bogos, 1829). Translated from Hebrew by Noam Sienna.

Further Reading

Ben-Naeh, Yaron. "Mishkav Zakhar Baḥevrah HaYehudit Ha'Othomanit." *Zion* 66 (2001), 171–200.

Ben-Naeh, Yaron. "Moshko the Jew and his Gay Friends: Same-Sex Sexual Relations in Ottoman Jewish Society." *Journal of Early Modern History* 9:1–2 (2005), 79–105.

Ze'evi, Dror. *Producing Desire: Changing Sexual Discourse in the Ottoman Middle East, 1500–1900* (University of California Press, 2006).

56. Two Jewish Boys Are Tried for Sodomy (London, 1845)

This excerpt, published as a Police Report in the *London Evening Times* in 1845, describes a trial whose "revolting infamy" was "utterly unfit for publication." Five people were accused of "an abominable crime," the usual euphemism for sodomy or homosexual activity: two Quakers, named Jacob Gill and Hartley Archer; a brewer named Thomas Young, and two "Jew boys" from East London, both 16 years old, named Henry and John Hart. One of Gill's former assistants had sent a tip to the police station; the investigating sergeant found all five men together and arrested them that evening. At the trial, the two Jewish youths were acquitted and released, but Gill, Archer, and Young were not so lucky. The testimony of the apprentice had such "disgusting details of abominable profligacy," the judge said, that it "exceeded in its revolting grossness all that came under his observation during the 20 years in which he had sat on the bench," and the three older men were jailed to await the jury's decision. Despite the melodramatic horror of these Victorian crime reporters, it should be remembered that a thriving homosexual community had already developed in London by the eighteenth century, including semi-private gathering places for men attracted to men, called "molly houses." While it's not clear whether this group was gathering in a molly house or had simply met each other in the neighborhood, this document shows how working-class Jews in Victorian England participated (if perhaps only occasionally) in a broader homosexual "subculture."

THAMES—The whole of yesterday, at this court, was consumed in hearing a series of cases the evidence to which is utterly unfit for publication, so unparalleled was the revolting infamy it disclosed. In one of the police-sheets from the Denmark-street station-house, St. George's-in-the-East, H division, were charges by which Jacob Gill, 38 years of age, a tailor, residing at No. 6, William-street, Gloucester-street, St. George's-in-the-East, and Hartley Archer, both professing to belong to the society of Friends or Quakers, and also to have taken the teetotal pledge, Thomas Young, a journeyman brewer, and two Jew boys, named Henry and John Hart, cigar makers, who are cousins, and each about 16 years old, the former residing at No. 3, New-street, Mile-end Old-town, and the latter at 16, King-street, St. George's-in-the-East, were accused of an abominable crime. On the previous day Edward Hyatt, a tailor, but at present carrying on business as baker, at 74, Long-alley, Worship-street, made a communication to Inspector Donegan, who instantly sent Sergeant O'Brien, 5 H, to make the necessary inquiries, and the result of an active investigation was, that the whole of the prisoners were in custody on the above charges, before 10 o'clock the same night. Mr. Lewis appeared for the Jew lads, and Young was undefended. It appeared that the boy Hyatt went on trial to Gill as an assistant in the tailoring business, on Thursday last, and from his account of the proceedings these suspicions were excited against Gill. The evidence of this boy, who fainted away several times whilst giving his testimony, was absolutely hideous. The evidence against Hartley Archer was equally conclusive.

At the instance of Mr. Lewis, the case of the two Jew lads, Hart, was taken first, and they were acquitted and discharged.

Young was locked up in default of bail for the misdemeanour, and, on committing the prisoners Gill and Archer on the capital charge.

Mr. Broderif said, charges of so shocking a nature were very easily made, and, at the same time, very difficult to be disapproved. The evidence in the present case depended on the testimony of a lad, who gave it under apparently great mental suffering, as was obvious to all present, and yet he went through the horrible details, which it was his (the worthy magistrate's) most painful duty to hear, with great clearness and precision. It would be for a jury to say what credit they would attach to the lad's evidence; but, whatever might be the result, he could only say that the disgusting details of abominable profligacy, exposed in the odious narrative which had occupied the court during that day, exceeded in its revolting grossness all that came under his observation during the 20 years in which he had sat upon the bench. Gill he would commit as principal on one charge, and accessory to another. Archer should be also committed as a principal, and it would be the province of a jury to say whether they were or were not guilty of the crimes alleged against them.

"Police." *London Evening Mail*, June 11–13, 1845, p. 3.

Further Reading

Norton, Rictor. *Mother Clap's Molly House: The Gay Subculture in England, 1700–1830*, 2nd edition (Chalford Press, 2006).

Trumbach, Randolph. "London." In *Queer Sites: Gay Urban Histories Since 1600* (ed. David Higgs, Routledge, 1999), 89–111.

57. A Trial for Homosexual Activity in the Old Yishuv (Jerusalem, ca. 1853)

This account is another rare description of the enforcement of a punishment for homosexual activity (see also source 36), here administered within the Ashkenazi Jewish community of the Old Yishuv (Jews who settled in Ottoman Palestine before the late nineteenth century). A factory clerk, accused of improper behavior with one of the workers, was temporarily expelled from the community and then forced to perform public acts of shaming and repentance. But the writer, Yehoshua Yellin (1843–1924), suggests that the whole affair may have been fabricated as part of larger intra-communal tensions. Yellin was born in Jerusalem to Polish immigrant parents and was among the founders of Motsa, the first Jewish agricultural settlement in Ottoman Palestine. His book of memoirs, *Zikhronot Leven Yerushalayim 5594–5668* (Memories of a Child of Jerusalem, 1834–1918), finally published in 1924, is an invaluable record of life in Jerusalem of the Old Yishuv.

I regret that I have to record a disgraceful event that happened at that time, and it was about a certain clerk in a factory in Jerusalem. A rumor began to spread that he had fallen into a serious and disgraceful sin with one of the young men working there. The judges assembled in court, and researched and questioned the facts of the discussion and the witnesses. (I myself was a young boy at the time, around ten years old, and of course I could not have known how correct this research and questioning was).

The result was that the clerk was [found guilty and] sentenced by the court's decision, that he must be separated and distinguished from the community for thirty days, and that he must go to the *beit midrash* of Menaḥem Tsiyyon, in the courtyard of the Ḥurva [synagogue] of Rabbi Yehudah HeḤasid, three times—Monday, Thursday, Monday—dressed as a mourner. He must wrap a black shawl around his face, to fulfill [what was written regarding leprosy, Leviticus 13:45], *"he must cover his upper lip."* Then he must ascend onto the *bimah** after the reading of the *parashah* [weekly Torah portion], and read from a sheet of paper that the rabbis prepared, as follows: "I have sinned against the God of Israel, and I hereby regret [my actions] and return in repentance," etc. I saw and heard all this with my own eyes and ears.

One day, during the days of his banishment, this clerk sent a note to my father of blessed memory [David Tuvia Yellin, 1803–1863], who was a good friend of his, and in it begged him to come to the place near the Armenian monastery (which was at the edge of the city) to see him. My father of blessed memory did as requested, and visited with him for about three hours. Obviously I could not know what they spoke about; I only saw that when [my father] returned he was very emotional, and it was clear that he had been crying. Afterwards, when I was recalling this event, this led me to wonder whether in fact this man had been innocent, and that some dissatisfied people had spread this rumor about him because of another event that had happened some time before this one [regarding a conflict between the followers of Rabbi Shmuel Salant, 1816–1909, and his opponents]…

At that time in Jerusalem there were great scandals about this, and it reached the point that one day a great crowd from both sides assembled in the courtyard of the Ḥurva of Rabbi Yehudah HeḤasid (although most of the crowd were supporters of Rabbi Salant), and they began beating each other with sticks and stones. Given that this clerk mentioned above was a close friend of Rabbi Salant's, until his death, he was at the forefront of those quarreling and fighting. It seems to me that those men who spread the rumor about this clerk were reckless men from the dissatisfied group of those opposed to Rabbi Salant, and they were the ones who gave false testimony

---

*Raised central platform of the synagogue.

before the judges and rabbis, only to cause this innocent clerk to suffer all this pain and punishment.

Yehoshua' Yellin, *Zikhronot Leven Yerushalayim 5594–5668* (Jerusalem: Tsiyyon Press, 1924). Translated from Hebrew by Noam Sienna.

Further Reading

Ben-Naeh, Yaron. "Mishkav Zakhar Baḥevrah HaYehudit Ha'Othomanit." *Zion* 66 (2001), 171–200.

Ben-Naeh, Yaron. "Moshko the Jew and his Gay Friends: Same-Sex Sexual Relations in Ottoman Jewish Society." *Journal of Early Modern History* 9:1–2 (2005), 79–105.

Shemesh, Abraham Ofir. "'Ad kamah hayah gadol toqef habadats bayamim hahem: 'onashim 'al ni'uf ve'al mishkav zakhar biyrushalayim bame'ah ha19." *'Et-Mol: 'itton letoldot erets yisra'el ve'am yisra'el* 188 (2006), 8–11.

58. A Victorian Jewish Artist Celebrates the Mystical Power of Love (London, 1871)

Simeon Solomon (1840–1905) was born in London to a newly-prominent Jewish family—his father, a hat merchant, was one of the first Jews to be admitted to the Freedom of the City of London, a privileged status granted only to distinguished citizens. Solomon excelled as an artist and soon entered the Royal Academy of Arts, becoming the youngest artist to have been exhibited there, at the age of 17. Solomon soon joined a circle of Pre-Raphaelite artists, poets, and writers, including Edward Burne-Jones, William Morris, Algernon Charles Swinburne, and Dante Gabriel Rossetti, who questioned Victorian conventions of art and literature, and defied expectations of gender and sexuality. Solomon's art, which portrayed both Jewish and classical subjects and especially the beauty of androgynous youth, was well regarded, and sought out by galleries and collectors (including Oscar Wilde). In 1871 he published his only literary work, *A Vision of Love Revealed in Sleep*, a surreal fantasy which draws on the biblical language of theophany and the erotic poetry of Song of Songs to imagine a mystical journey with his Soul. On this journey he sees the personification of Love, first "dethroned and captive," then "imprisoned in an alien land of oblivion," then finally enthroned again in glory. In a paradise full of "many whom I knew by name, and who were dear to me," Solomon encounters the blinding vision of the Very Heart of Love, "one who seemed of pure snow and of pure fire, the Very Love, the Divine Type of Absolute Beauty, primaeval and eternal, compact of the white flame of youth, burning in ineffable perfection." This revelation entrusts Solomon with the secrets of true love, which cannot exist "until the day break and the shadows flee away." Indeed, Solomon was right to fear that his world was not ready for the revelation of the secrets of "the love that dare not speak its name." Solomon's promising career soon came to an end when he was arrested in 1873 for "indecent exposure" and "attempted buggery" with a man in a public restroom. Abandoned by most of his friends and relatives, he sank into depression, poverty, and alcoholism; he was admitted to St. Giles Workhouse in 1885 and died in 1905.

Until the day break
And the shadows flee away
        Song of Songs

IN MEMORIAM DDD

Upon the waning of the night, at that time when the stars are pale, and when dreams wrap us about more closely, when a brighter radiance is shed upon our spirits, three sayings, of the wise King came unto me. These are they: *I sleep, but my heart waketh*; also, *Many waters cannot quench love*; and again, *Until the day break, and the shadows flee away*;* and I fell to musing and thinking much upon them. Then there came upon me a vision, and behold, I walked in a land that I knew not, filled with a strange light I had not seen before; and I was clad as a traveller. In one hand I carried a staff, and I hid the other in the heavy folds of a colorless garment; I went forward with my eyes cast upon the earth, pondering, and dazed as one who sets forth upon a journey, but who knows not yet its goal. Then I besought my spirit to make itself clearer before me, and to show me, as in a glass, what I sought; then knowledge came upon me, and I looked within my spirit, and I saw my yearning visibly manifested, and great desire was born, and sprang forth and strengthened my feet and quickened my steps. Now I stood among olive-trees, whose boughs and leaves lay still upon the air, and

---

* Song of Songs 5:2, 8:7, and 4:6.

no light was cast upon them. Then the deep silence was broken by the stirring of the spirit within me; my frame appeared to be rent, and a faintness fell upon me, and for a little space I knew nothing, so powerfully the spirit wrought within me. Then afterwards, as when one who works miracle lays his healing fingers upon another who is maimed, and makes him whole, so my strength was renewed, and I lifted up my eyes; and behold, the form of one stood by me, unclothed, save for a fillet binding his head, whereof the ends lay upon either side his neck; also upon his left shoulder hung a narrow vestment; in his right hand he bore a branch of dark foliage, starred with no blossoms; his face had on it the shadow of glad things unattained, as of one who has long sought but not found, upon whom the burden of humanity lies heavy; his eyes, half shaded by their lashes, gave forth no light.

I knew that my Soul stood by me, and he and I went forth together; and I also knew that the visible images of those things which we knew only by name were about to be manifested unto me. When I gazed into the lampless eyes of my Soul, I felt that I saw into the depths of my own spirit, shadow meeting shadow. Then my Soul first spoke, and said unto me, *Thou hast looked upon me, and thou knowest me well, for in me thou but seest thyself, not hidden and obscured by the cruel veil of flesh. I am come forth of thee for thy well-doing, therefore see to it that thou do me no injury. By me shalt thou attain unto the end I know thou seekest, for he whom we go forth to find may only in his fullness be manifested by my aid; for when he appears to those who, with damned eyes, grope in the waking darkness of the world, I am put aside, and he is not fully known. By me alone shalt thou behold him as he absolutely is; but in visions shall he be seen of thee many times before his full light be shed upon thee, and thy spirit shall be chastened and saddened because of them, but it shall not utterly faint. Look upon me, and I will support thee, and in thy need I will bear thee up. Looking upon me thou shalt read thine inmost self, as upon a scroll, and in my aspect shall thy spirit be made clear. Come...*

Then he and I went on gradually ascending a sandy slope, patched here and there with scanty grass; and against the pale blue sky we saw one, for whom, looking upon him, my Soul dissolved in tears, so stricken with unavailing sorrow was he, so wounded beyond the hope of healing, bound hand and foot, languishing under the weight of his humanity, crushed with the burden of his so great tenderness. I looked upon the face of my Soul, and I knew that he, in whose presence we now stood, was Love, dethroned and captive, bound and wounded, bereft of the natural light of his presence; his wings drooping, broken and torn, his hands made fast to the barren and leafless tree; the myrtles upon his brow withered and falling; and upon that heart, from whose living depths should proceed the voice of the revolving spheres, there was a wound flowing with blood, but changing into roses of the divinest odour as it fell. I stood motionless, my eyes refusing to look longer upon my stricken lord, then drawn unto my Soul, from whom I had no comfort; the voice of the shell of Memory yet sounded in my ears, and I knew that the divine captive read my spirit's inmost thoughts; from his lips proceeded inaudibly the words, *Thou hast wounded my heart.*

After a moment of mystical agony, I raised my eyes: and behold, the vision of Love was gone. Yea, and upon my own heart the words of Love became engraven, and ringed it about with flame; and then I knew to the full how my hands had been among those which had bound and wounded Love thus. Albeit my spirit found how unworthy it was to receive the odour of the roses which came forth of his heart, yet it clung about me, and became as it were a crown to my head, and I was even lifted up because of my humiliation. Then I turned unto my Soul, and saw that his gaze was bent upon me with pity, and he spoke these words: *Alas! look well into thy spirit, search thy heart and pluck from it its dead garlands, cast them from thee and make it clean, and prepare it for him who shall hereafter enter therein; thou art even puffed up because the wound thou hast been one of those to deal sends forth divine fragrance; rather lament that thou hast not left whole the temple whence it comes forth: of thee and of thy like is its destruction: let us go upon our way.* Then we set forward, and silence was between us; the burden upon my spirit lay very heavy, and I knew not how to raise up my eyes…

[My Soul] made an end of speaking, and by the pale beams of the sinking stars I saw an image dimly mirrored in his eyes. I removed my gaze from his face, and looked abroad, and beheld, dark against the wan air of the dying night, Love seated upon a throne lowly and poor, and not worthy to bear him,—no longer, indeed, wounded and bleeding, but still bereft of his perfect glory; in his eyes there shone a soft light of suffering not yet past, but on his brow, where poppies were mingled with the myrtles, there lay the shadow which falls upon one not remembered; upon his parted lips hovered the half-formed smile of a child who halts between weeping and laughter; he was fully clothed in raiment of dim and sullied red and gold; in one hand he bore a poppy branch bound about the myrtle, from which the stars had fallen one by one, and in the other a golden globe whose brightness was obscured and shamed by dust; his feet were wholly hidden in the thick growth of weeds and poppies that crowded round his throne; he spoke no word, only the faint sounds in the air about him and the grief-dimmed eyes of my Soul told me he was Love imprisoned in an alien land of oblivion—forgotten, put away.

Again my heart sank, and the flowing of its streams waxed dull, and the words of him bound by the sea burned upon it with a more ardent flame, and the vision we passed from filled my eyes, and came forth of them in bitter tears; yet I forgot not the saying of my Soul, that this should be as the darkly revealed sign of the joy to come, for was not Love enthroned—poorly indeed—and had not the shadow of suffering well-nigh lifted, albeit indeed its seat remained, and looked upon the countenance of him beside me; and behold, upon it, despite the eyelids drooping with foregone grief, I saw the longed-for smile, and I took content upon me.

Our course now lay along an upward slope, whereon the poppies waxed scantier, and the weeds less rank; a soft mossy grass soothed our wayworn feet, and I could see by the light of the dying stars that small golden blossoms lay in a pattern upon the sward. As we neared the brow of the hill, I knew that a yet unseen and mysterious presence was about to be revealed to us; soft breezes bore his light to us upon their wings, and voices from the passing Night spoke to us of him; he was half-seated, half-lying, upon a height beyond which was stretched out the faintly glimmering sea; there lay upon him yet the shadow of Night, but his face had upon it the radiance of an expected glory, the light of glad things to come; his eyes were yet soft with the balm of Sleep, but his lips were parted with desire; his breath was as that of blossoms that awake and lift up their heads and give forth their odours; his dusky limbs were drawn up as if in readiness to depart, and his great and goodly wings softly beat the air; with one hand he cast away his dim and dewy mantle from him, and with the other he put aside the poppies that had clustered thickly about him; as he turned his head to the East, the poppies fell from his hair, and the light rested upon his face: the smile it kindled made the East to glow, and Dawn spread forth his wings to meet the new-born Day. And when the Day was seated on his throne, we passed along a pleasant land that lay beneath the light of a great content; and the radiance yet lingered on the countenance of my Soul, and the sadness that had made the curves of his mouth heavy, and had dimmed his eye, now gradually departed, and there came upon him an aspect of calm, as of one certain of a good thing shortly to befall, although he knows not fully what it may be; and when I looked upon his eyes my spirit took heart, and I girded myself and set forth with my head no more bent; and we were met by many who had been shown me in my former dreams, and who all bore the reflection of a light upon their faces.

Also I saw with great joy many whom I knew by name, and who were dear to me, and they were clad in garments of beauty, so that it joyed my eyes to behold them. And it appeared to me as though I felt beating upon my breast the warmth that came from theirs towards me; and youth was set a crown upon their heads, and they bore branches blossoming from the breath of youth, and its divine essence colored all the air about them; and I discerned one face in that company beloved of me beyond the rest; a northern sun had set a ruddy sweetness upon it, and southern suns had kissed it into perfect bloom; from the depths of the grey eyes welled up and sprang forth the spirit of Love, and, most loath to depart, yet brooded upon them as the dove in early time upon the waters; a sacred light, as of the guileless dreams of childhood, looked out from them and gladdened my own, and the softness of Sleep was bound upon the head. When I looked upon the face, I felt, indeed, that my travail was well-nigh over, and as it passed from me, and was lost to me, my spirit bathed its dusty wings in the warm, glad tears that bubbled from my heart, and was refreshed. And when the throne of day was set wellnigh above our heads, and there was that in the air which moves the heart of nature, we rested ourselves beside a running stream, whose waters brought joyous sounds from afar, as it were the long-forgotten songs and gentle voices of our childhood, yet laden with a heavier and fuller harmony from a source we knew not yet; and as we journeyed on in the dawn of the evening, an awe fell upon me, as when one enters upon a new and unknown way, and all the air about teemed with the echoes of things past and the vague intimations of things to come.

Then my Soul turned towards me and spoke these words: *Lay upon thy spirit a glad humility, and essay to strengthen thine eyes, that they may bear to behold the things which shall shortly be brought before thee to thy comfort and solace. As thou hast hitherto only seen him we see sinking beneath the burdens that have been laid upon him by thee and by the like of thee; as thou hast seen the glory about him shattered and made dull by reason of the wounds and weakness the bitter darkness of the world has inflicted, so shalt thou now behold him gathering his natural power about him, and clothed with light; but not yet shall it be given to thee to see him in the plenitude of his glory. I will support thee. Look up.*

And now I raised my eyes and looked upon the stream, and it seemed to me as though the waters were cleft apart, and there was a hollow in their midst; and lo, the air about it appeared changed, and its pulses stood still, and the sounds I had heard borne on its wave collected themselves and took form; and the form was of the color of the sun-lighted sea, and within it I saw one borne gently upward, naked, and glowing exceedingly; the stars of the living myrtles burned fresh upon his hair, and his countenance was as the supreme excellence of youth transfigured, the wound upon his heart was healed, and on its place I saw burning a ruddy flame, whereof the tongues came forth to me and touched my own, whereon were engraven the words which I heard Love speak when we saw him bound to the tree, and in their stead the flame wrought this saying, letter by letter, *Many waters cannot quench Love, neither can the floods drown it*; and now the radiant mist wherein he was lifted up rose and enfolded him, and hid his aspect from me, and its form was dispersed, and it was changed to gentle sounds in the stream, and all the air about became as it was before...

Now there arose before me the image of him whom we had seen sleeping in the ruined temple; his arms were wound about his head, which lay back upon them; he was naked, but his form was wrapped about with the soft star-lighted air; his lashes were no longer moist with tears, but his face shone as became one through whom the Very Love was to be revealed. And now I felt the heart of the universe beat, and its inner voices were made manifest unto me, the knowledge of the coming presence of the Very Love informed the air, and its waves echoed with the full voices of the revolving spheres. Then my Soul spoke to me and said, *In the beginning of time the universe and all that was therein was grey, and its springs were without life, as a fair body, joyless and lacking beauty, because no spirit stirs it; light had not come upon it; and, as when one is in a trance, the pulses are dead, and await the aid of that which shall enter them and make the dead alive; even so, there sprang forth, of its own power and holy ardour, a light over the face of all things, and the heat of it made them glow, and the grey became green: the golden air sang over all, and an universal hymn arose and went up, and its voice yet gladdens the circling worlds. As the prophet saw in the dark valley the dead bones come together and take life upon them, even so Love, who was the light, smiled upon the uninformed countenance of things, and it was kindled because of it; and there went from him a two-fold essence, whereof the streams have flowed for ever, and cease not to flow; and by them are we upheld, and our spirits replenished; and, as the priest holds the flower-starred crown over the heads of the bridegroom and the bride, so now and again do the streams unite within us, and Love, whence they go forth, is the crown over us and the light about us. But through the thick veil of the darkness of the world this is not seen or known of men, but only through the spirit may it be made clear unto us; and the spirit soars aloft rejoicing, and is girt about with delight because of it.*

And now the image of Sleep filled the orbit of my sight, and through the veil of his form I saw him who bore the mystic saffron raiment wherewith he had covered his hands. My spirit well-nigh fainting, I turned unto my Soul, and knew by the increasing glow upon him that strength was given me yet again to lift my eyes. Well was it for me that what came was revealed to me through the veil of Sleep, else I could not have borne to look upon it.

From out the uplifted hands of him who stood within the Holy Place there sprang forth a radiance of a degree so dazzling that what else of glory there was within the temple was utterly obscured; as one seeing a thin black vapour resting before the face of the mid-day sun, so I saw upon the radiance the brooding cherubim, their wings meeting, their faces hidden; I saw within the glory, one who seemed of pure snow and of pure fire, the Very Love, the Divine Type of Absolute Beauty, primaeval and eternal, compact of the white flame of youth, burning in ineffable perfection.

For a moment's space I shielded my eyes from the blinding glow, then once more raised them upon the Beatific Vision. It seemed to me as though my spirit were drawn forth from its abiding place, and dissolved in unspeakable ardours; anon fiercely whirled round in a sphere of fire, and swiftly borne along a sea of throbbing light into the Very Heart. Ah, how may words shew forth what it was then vouchsafed to me to know? As when the thin, warm tears upon the cheek of the sleeping bride are kissed away by him who knows that she is wholly his, and one with him; as softly as his trembling lips are set upon the face transfigured on his soul, even so fell upon my heart, made one with the Heart of Love, its inmost, secret flame: my spirit was wholly swallowed up, and I knew no more.

Then all this wondrous vision was fulfilled, and looking upon the sky, I saw that the stars had set and the dawn had spread his wings over the world; and again the words of the sage King, *Until the day break and the shadows flee away*, came into my mind.

Simeon Solomon, *A Vision of Love Revealed in Sleep* (London: F.S. Ellis, 1871).

Further Reading

Cruise, Colin and Roberto C. Ferrari. (eds.). *Love revealed: Simeon Solomon and the Pre-Raphaelites* (London: Merrell, 2005).

Dau, Duc. "The Song of Songs for difficult queers: Simeon Solomon, Neil Bartlett, and A Vision of Love Revealed in Sleep." In *Queer Difficulty in Art and Poetry: Rethinking the Sexed Body in Verse and Visual Culture* (eds. Jongwoo Jeremy Kim, Christopher Reed, Routledge, 2017), 34–47.

Morgan, Thaïs. "Perverse Male Bodies: Simeon Solomon and Algernon Charles Swinburne." In *Outlooks: Lesbian and Gay Sexualities and Visual Cultures* (eds. Peter Horne, Reina Lewis, Routledge, 1996), 61–85.

White, Chris (ed.). *Nineteenth-Century Writings on Homosexuality: A Sourcebook* (Routledge, 1999).

59. A Jewish Woman with "Contrary Sexual Feeling" (Würzburg, 1875)

In the mid-nineteenth century, writers and philosophers (particularly in central Europe) began advocating for the civil and social rights of people who were drawn emotionally and erotically to the same sex. They created a new public discourse about this topic, arguing that these kinds of people formed a separate social category, and that their erotic behaviors and feelings were inherent to their identity. The German writer Karl Heinrich Ulrichs (1825–1895) suggested the term *Urnings / Uranians* for them, while the Hungarian journalist Karl-Maria Kertbeny (1824–1882) coined the word *homosexual* in 1869, which was eventually adopted by other writers. At the same time, doctors and medical professionals became increasingly interested in (and in many cases, concerned by) the circumstances of people with this newly-defined orientation. One of the first medical studies of this orientation was an 1870 article by the German psychiatrist Carl Friedrich Otto Westphal (1833–1890), who described patients with what he called "contrary sexual feeling" (*Konträre Sexualempfindung*). In the journal article excerpted here (the second such study to appear), a German doctor presents the case histories of two Jews whom he has diagnosed with Westphal's "contrary sexual feeling:" a young woman named Jette (Yetta), as well as a male schoolteacher named Abraham. The author, Hermann Gock (1848–1910), was an assistant physician in the psychiatric ward of the Juliusspital clinic in Würzburg, central Germany.

An Article on the Study of Contrary Sexual Feeling, from the Würzburg Psychiatric Clinic

On the 24th of May of this year, Jette B, a 28-year-old Jewish maidservant, came of her own free will to the Mental Department of the Julius Hospital/Clinic. She said that she feels so sick and miserable, that she is unhappy and would prefer to die. (It was discovered later that she had tried to drown herself a few days earlier). When asked about the reason she was so unhappy, she said, frankly and calmly, that she was in love with her [female] friend. She has had this passion for a long time and has fought against it, because she recognizes that it is sick, but she can't resist it on her own.

All of her thoughts are taken up with her friend. If only just once she could embrace and kiss her, the way she wants to! But she doesn't dare talk with her friend about it. [In this way] she might still be able to avoid her misfortune.

Frequently she would fly into a true rage, at times when she felt a particular impulse to embrace her friend but couldn't. After that she would become completely apathetic again to whatever is going on around her, couldn't work, and would often stare at nothing, but she just kept thinking about her friend.

Now she just wishes desperately that she'll be helped in the clinic. However, she immediately added that there is no possible help for her, and that she's so deeply caught up with her thoughts of love "that she has forgotten her own self."

The patient was accepted into the department…The patient's father died 10 years ago, supposedly from some kind of heart trouble, and he had never showed signs of mental problems. However, her mother, who was 54 years old when she died of consumption 8 years ago, is supposed to have become weak-minded in her last years. It could not be determined whether any siblings of the father or mother were affected with any relevant conditions.

The patient has a brother and a sister, both of whom are healthy, married for a long time, and have healthy children. During her childhood the patient claims she had no serious illnesses. She says herself that during her time in school learning was hard for her, because she was "flighty" and engaged in many stupid antics. At that time, she spent almost all her time with boys and preferred to take part in their games…

Her menses began at 12 and a half…Around this time her particular preference for young girls began to show—particular for those to whom she felt drawn by how they looked at her. She needed only to look into such a girl's eyes and she was in love, and couldn't rest until she could come closer to her. She would follow her chosen one, step by step; she would become red when speaking with her, and be jealous when others spent time with her. Her greatest happiness was to kiss and press herself against such a girl, and when she did that, she always felt an erotic sensation in her genitals. This drive to kiss and press herself against a beloved girl usually arose shortly before and after the monthly arrival of her period.

Since she began puberty, when she was feeling this way, the patient would also masturbate and fantasize about the beloved girl. At 14 the girl came to work for people she didn't know, as a result of her family's economic situation. She worked in different places as a servant and has been here in Würzburg for four years.

During this time the patient said that she was often exposed to pestering by men. A mentally-disabled son of her employer supposedly tried to rape her. However, she resisted all such efforts and would have absolutely nothing to do with men, as they didn't interest her in the least. Indeed, at times she felt a true horror of men, and would only have anything to do with those who seemed somewhat effeminate...She even rejected actual marriage proposals; she was still so ruled by the thoughts of her friend that she couldn't even contemplate them.

In contrast, during this whole time her preference for girls intensified— not for all of them equally, but just for particular ones, namely those with blue eyes and gentle features who belonged to the better classes. It was no longer enough to kiss and embrace them; now she tried to get them to sleep with her in one bed, at which point she would grab their genitals and become sexually excited. If the girl resisted, the patient would get very upset, which was, in fact, observed in the period of time just before her admission to the clinic.

Three and a half years ago, she had met a girl with whom she had im- mediately fallen in love, upon first seeing her irresistible eyes. She tried to be together with her as much as possible, but didn't trust herself to invite her friend into intimate activities, because such things would have made no sense or been understandable to the one she loved. Though the patient hadn't thought of it previously, she was beginning to realize the wrongness of her feelings. It became clearer to her that others, like her current friend, didn't have similar feelings to hers, and she began to believe that she is sick.

In light of these realizations, she became neglectful of her work, which was not particularly strenuous. She became fully absorbed in her thoughts, and would stare at nothing for long periods of time. She felt horribly unhappy, and believed she would become healthy if only she could, just once, kiss and em- brace her friend. However, she didn't trust herself to express her desires when she was together with the girl.

From repressing her sexual arousal, she often became overexcited. She would undress completely, would scream and cry without stopping, and wouldn't calm down until one of the other serving girls in the same house would let her to sleep together in bed with her. She wanted then to grab that girl by the gen- itals; but she had the best experience when the girl pressed on her, and she'd therefore masturbate and imagine she was "sleeping" with her friend. These times of intense excitement occurred most often just before and just after her period, and in these times, according to the patient, the instinct to embrace her friend was particularly powerful, which then (when she wasn't able to satisfy her desire) brought about a state of mania.

After this, she always felt very flat and indifferent to her surroundings; she accomplished her work, but only when ordered, and then very mechanically and often erroneously. Not only was she bothered because she couldn't embrace her friend and satisfy her sexual instincts, but also, because of her sensitivity and mistrustful jealousy she often misinterpreted comments from her girl-friend, even inoffensive ones or harmless jokes.

In April of this year, her friend said something that particularly upset Jette. At a gathering the conversation turned to age, and Jette's friend said that if she were as old as Jette and not yet married, she would throw herself into the Main [river]. This statement dramatically increased the patient's already-growing discomfort; she already knew that she could not marry, because she only ever had thoughts of "her friend" and could never be happy with a man. The agitation that broke out when she got home again, became, according to her employer, so extreme that they needed help from the family doctor. The patient had often had similar sick feelings in the past, but always got the advice to marry. Therefore, her employers had found for the patient many marriage opportunities, but the patient always rejected every offer. There was only one offer that she even considered, and that was a man who was already old. She thought that at the most one such as him could make her happy; but ultimately she came to the same conclusion, because thoughts of her girl-friend still always got in the way.

From this time onward the sick feeling kept increasing, and with it the feeling that she couldn't fulfill her work duties, and furthermore that she was causing so much grief to her relatives through her passion, which she was no longer able to control. In light of all of this she felt so unhappy and weary of life that she tried to drown herself. Finally, she grasped at the hope that she could be helped in the clinic, and this is why she sought to admit herself here...

In her first days at the facility, the patient was restless, which she blamed on the environment, saying that she is not psychologically ill and is negatively affected by being around sick people. She cries a lot and complains that she has ruined her young life through her passion and weak-mindedness. She said she only wants, just once more, to embrace and kiss her girl-friend, and then preferably die because she has no other purpose in this world. When encouraged to work she did start, but soon gave it up and stayed obsessed with her thoughts. Shortly after being admitted she developed an attachment for a [female] attendant and on another patient, an almost childlike one. She tried to caress them, but they had no patience for her, so she tried to sneak up on them unseen, in order to embrace and kiss them.

In the night she often asked the attendant for the permission to sleep with her, and got very upset when refused and had to be forcibly taken to her room. After a few days, the patient was acting calmly in all interactions. She frequently asked permission to leave, because she believed she would go crazy in the company of so many psychologically ill patients. In contrast, she reacted very coldly to the convulsions of other patients; she herself points this out, and mentions that in the past, she couldn't have seen such a thing without great excitement. She says that now, through the relief of her suffering, she has absolutely no feelings left at all. She wishes desperately to be freed from this sick status and hopes for improvement.

Her menses came twice during her stay at the institution, and was moderately strong and didn't cause her pain. However, as mentioned, the patient became sexually excited just before and just after, as we have already seen, from how she sought after affection from the attendant and the younger patient. Other than that, the patient behaved calmly, worked assiduously, and was therefore, as she wished, allowed to go home on July 22.

At home she was, according to her relatives, quite calm at the beginning, almost listless and apathetic. After a few weeks, however, she again became excited with her "contrary" sexual feelings, followed by a deep depression. In the influence of this depression the patient tried again to drown herself. She recovered soon thereafter, was quite reasonable, and showed more participation in what was going on around her. After a short time, she was again employed as a serving girl.

Hermann Gock, "Beitrag zur Kenntniss der conträren Sexualempfindung aus der Würzburger psychiatrischen Klinik." *Archiv für Psychiatrie und Nervenkrankheiten* 8 (1875), 564–574. Translated from German by Aaron Hodge Greenberg Silver. Copyright © 2019 Print-O-Craft Press.

Further Reading

Foucault, Michel. *The History of Sexuality, Vol. 1: The Will to Knowledge* (London: Penguin, 1976).

Hekma, Gert. "Sodomy, Effeminacy, Identity: Mobilizations for Same-sexual Loves and Practices before the Second World War." In *The Ashgate Research Companion to Lesbian and Gay Activism* (eds. David Paternotte and Manon Tremblay, Ashgate, 2015), 15–30.

Katz, Jonathan Ned. *The Invention of Heterosexuality, 2nd edition* (University of Chicago Press, 2007).

Schwartz, Gudrun. "'Viragos' in Male Theory in Nineteenth-Century Germany." In *Women in Culture and Politics: A Century of Change* (eds. Judith Friedlander, Blanche Wiesen Cook, Alice Kessler-Harris, and Carroll Smith-Rosenberg, Indiana University Press, 1986), 128–143.

60. Binyomin and Senderl, from Mendele Moykher Sforim's "Travels of Benjamin III" (Odessa, 1878)

Sholem Yankev Abramovitsh (1836–1917), better known by his pen name Mendele Moykher Sforim (Mendele the Book Peddler), was one of the foremost Jewish novelists of the nineteenth century, with many celebrated works in both Yiddish and Hebrew. His stories drew initially from the modernizing philosophy of the *Haskalah* (Jewish Enlightenment) but were inspired most of all by the reality of Jewish life in Eastern Europe. Turning to critique the *maskilim* (proponents of the *Haskalah*), he began to address political issues of Jewish powerlessness and passivity, and the yearning for sovereignty, as in his 1878 novel *Kitzer Masoes Binyomin HaShlishi* (The Brief Travels of Benjamin the Third). This complex and biting satire claims to be the travelogue of an explorer, in the model of two famous Jewish travelers named Benjamin: Benjamin of Tudela (Spain, twelfth century) and Israel Joseph Benjamin (Romania, 1818–1864). It also recasts Cervantes' *Don Quixote de la Mancha* in a Jewish idiom: Don Quixote becomes the bumbling Binyomin of Tuneyadevka, in search of the Ten Lost Tribes, and his loyal Sancho Panza is "Senderl the *yidene* [housewife]." The relationship between Binyomin and Senderl is described throughout the text as a marriage; they flee their wives and instead resolve to travel together, "a pair made in heaven." Scholars have read this parody of Jewish sexuality and gender roles in a variety of ways, including a critique of the Jewish failure to live up to European standards of masculinity, and an exposure of the patriarchal system that equates a woman's position with abuse, subjugation, and abandonment.

Chapter Three: How Binyomin Came to Be Associated with Lady Senderl

When he was among little children, Senderl, too, became a child. Often he would chatter and play alongside them, taking great delight from it. Among them, Senderl was truly like a gentle cow in the way that he permitted the children to approach, to ride him and to scratch his mug. Little pranksters would climb up to his head and tug his beard. Folks used to fuss over him and cry out:

"Respect, insolent children, for an elder! For a man with a beard! Where do you get off pulling his beard?!"

"It's no problem, no problem, don't worry," Senderl called to them. "What do I care? Let them bother me a bit."

Senderl didn't lick any honey at home, either. His wife wore the pants and he sure knew it. Bitter fate. Every sentence she uttered instilled fear in him, yet he always received her commands lovingly. The night before a holiday she would begin cleaning the room, and would tie a tichel [headscarf] over his beard. He would peel potatoes, roll and cut noodles, stuff fish, haul wood to the oven, and make a fire, meticulous as a woman. For this, people called him Lady Senderl [*Senderl di yidene*].

And it was to Lady Senderl that our Binyomin chose to open his heart, peeling the egg he needed peeled. But why Senderl of all people?

It's so: because Binyomin had always felt a bit of affection for him. Something about Senderl was very appealing to him. Senderl had helped him come to agreement on many matters, and their conversations simply made him happy. Binyomin learned from this that Senderl was not a stubborn person. He, Senderl, would grab hold of a plan and give everything to it. And if Senderl became stubborn on certain points, Binyomin, with God's help, would strengthen his tongue...

And so it was that Binyomin one day went up to Senderl, and was struck by the sight of him, sitting on a milking stool and peeling potatoes. One of his cheeks was severely inflamed, and under his eye was blue as if it had been scratched by a claw or talon. Senderl sat tormented and gloomy, full of regret.

Senderl's wife was not home.

"Good morning, Senderl! Why do you look so troubled, darling?" said Binyomin, coming around and touching Senderlekh's cheek lightly with his finger. "She's away? Where is she?"

"At the market."

"Excellent!" Binyomin let out a cry for their great good luck. "Put down your potatoes, my soul, and come into this alcove with me. There's not anybody in there, is there? I wish to reveal my heart to you. I can't hold back any longer, it's cooking my blood, oh, quick, darling, quicker, she could return and interrupt us before we're ready!"

"What do we care? You want quick, I'll be quick, what worry do I have?" Senderl replied, entering the alcove.

"Senderl!" Binyomin began, "Tell me, do you know what's on the far side of Tuneyadevka?"…

[Binyomin describes the exotic lands of the Lost Tribes]. "Oh, ho!" said Binyomin, inflamed with a new idea that had befallen him. "Senderl, what if we really made this journey happen? Dear little fool, now you have an excellent opportunity. I'm going anyway, and I want to take you with me. Not to mention that traveling in twos is cozier. Maybe I'll make you a storybook king when we get there. Take my hand! What will you do, little fool, sit and suffer in exile with your poor wife? Look at your cheek, poor dear. Here you have only a bleak and familiar fate. Come on, Senderl! You won't have any regrets."

"If you really want this," Senderl said, "So it will be. Oh, what worry do I have? I really must be a fool, the way you've showed me that I've already lost myself."

"My soul, let me kiss you!" Binyomin exclaimed with great happiness, and for love embraced Lady Senderl. "You have me, my soul. Answering my wooden question with a single word. Now I'll speak as you did: Oh, my dear, my own, what worry do I have? Now another question: How will we pay for it?"

"Expenses? Binyomin, you will dress yourself and turn your *kapote* [coat] inside out. Believe me, we won't need much. Old clothes are all right on the road. No doubt we'll find beautiful new *kapotes* when we get there."

"Yes, true. I know we won't have any problems there. But won't we need money for food on the way?"

"Oh, and what is it that you need to eat, Binyomin? Shall you bring a cake along with you? What for? Are there no taverns or houses along the road?"

"Senderl, I don't understand what you mean," Binyomin wondered aloud.

"I mean," Senderl answered innocently, "If there are houses along the way, we'll do what other Jews do. Whoever answers the door now will need a door to knock on later. It's a Jewish thing, an act of loving-kindness."

"Indeed you're right!" said Binyomin joyfully. "Now that we've got light in our eyes, bless Hashem, let's go—in the morning, before dawn, so that the sleeping world won't see us depart. Lost time is a sin, you know?"

"You want morning, it will be morning. What's it to me?"

"In the morning, very early. Do you hear, Senderl? I will leave the house silently, and meet you by the idle windmill. Don't forget, Senderl—in the morning, very early, you must return here. Don't forget!" said Binyomin again before turning to go.

"Wait a minute, Binyomin, hold on!" said Senderl, fumbling in the breast pocket of his coat, and pulling from it a sweaty piece of leather tied with ribbons and tied with twenty knots. "Do you see, Binyomin, that this bundle holds all the money I've accumulated in the years with my wife, for all the time that I was married to her. What a wonderful beginning for us, huh?"

"Now, darling, you're worth the effort—every one of your limbs should be kissed in turn, and everything between them," said Binyomin in a high-pitched voice, catching Lady Senderl in a lively embrace.

"Oh, I hope you're both caught with the plague! Look at this, I beg you— these two beginning their great love, while in the house the goat is eating the potatoes!" This cry came suddenly.

The cry came from Senderl's shrew of a wife. She was aflame with anger, holding the goat with one hand and grabbing Senderl to her with the other. With a lowered head, Senderl slowly submitted to her and returned to the house like an errant child about to learn a painful lesson.

"Stay strong, my soul, this is the last time before blessed morning," Binyomin whispered softly into Senderl's ear. Then, like a little cat, he tiptoed out of the house.

Chapter Four: How Binyomin with Senderl Left Tuneyadevka Behind

Very early in the morning, even before the shepherd had gathered the cattle and the flock, our Binyomin was already standing, ready, beside the windmill, with a little pack under his arm. Inside the pack was everything necessary for the journey, enough: tallis and tefillin, a copy of the Derech Chaim, a Hückel hat, a copy of Tehillim [Psalms], and all the other books he could not do without, like a craftsman without his tools. His Shabbes *kapote* lay to the side—one must present a good face to the world when fulfilling one's obligations among the gentiles. In his wallet he had fifteen half-grozsy for the journey, which he had hidden from his wife under a cushion…

Meanwhile, a considerable amount of time passed, and Senderl wasn't there. Binyomin started to worry a little, and his happiness was shattered. He looked everywhere, wearing out his eyes in the process, but it was futile. No one had heard anything, and no one had seen anything. Senderl!

Could it be possible that his wicked wife had honored him with some task? Not only was it late, but all of Tuneyadevka was still deliciously asleep. People would not begin peeling their potatoes until later.

Our Binyomin didn't know what to do, and his happiness left him, it left him hard. Should he return home? Feh, that would be shameful. Alexander the Great broke the bridge that connected him to India, because he didn't wish to be able to return. Leave without Senderl? No, that's embarrassing. Really terrible! Senderl is so necessary. Ever since the two of them teamed up, Binyomin's eyes had been full of light. To set out without Senderlekh would be a strange and wild thing. It wouldn't turn out well—like a ship without a rudder, like a government without a minister.

Suddenly, he saw from far away something that looked like a human figure. It was obviously Senderl, and yet—it was not Senderl coming. It was someone wearing a chintz frock, with a *tichel* around their head.

Binyomin's heart throbbed and went dead, he was pale as a sheet. It seemed to him that his wife was walking towards him—no, she didn't walk, she strode, she ran, and soon she was running flat-out, and then she would gather him in a tight embrace, bring her stony, bitter heart to him, and haul him home with a tearful lament.

"Only God knows," said Binyomin, very alone, "How I am at this moment stuck in the same old trouble, wounded all over, that I would prefer meeting a hundred monsters to encountering my own wife. Bless Hashem, I will soon be brave enough to return to the windmill and hide there, watching as a lion does his prey."

A moment later, Binyomin sprang from his hiding place with a fearsome leap and a mad cry: "Ho, Senderl!"

Senderl was approaching, wearing a chintz robe with a greasy tichel tied under his cheeks, blue below his eyes from scratches, a walking stick in each hand, and a substantial pack over his shoulders.

He looked Binyomin in the eyes and put the charm on him, like a beautiful, bedecked bride looking into the eyes of her groom.

Binyomin crowed his delight: "Like a deer who desires gushing waters, like someone parched in the desert who finds a lively, flowing spring that trickles down from a high cliff, did my desiring flesh gladden at the sight of Senderl, my *bashert* [soul mate], my trusted pal…"

Chapter Five: In Which Our Heroes Soon Make Their First Departure

Our heroes departed abruptly, and they traveled quickly, lightly, straight on. They went fast, as if running before a soldier or a whip. Their wide coattails, which were swept up in the wind, held them steady as the sails of a quick-moving ship. Magpies and crows, which were walking about on the ground, moved aside, as is the way of the land, and screamed distractedly from every direction, fearful of the two-legged creatures who ran by with enthusiasm and ardor.

No pen would be able to describe how happy they were then. It gave them rare pleasure, and they were profoundly content—glad for one another, and glad for the world...

"Senderl," Binyomin called at the pause, "Do you know why I'm saying such a thing? Do you know why I'm singing this *niggun* [wordless tune] now?"

"You must be hungry," Senderl answered innocently. "Binyomin, you may sing—sing you, sing. And I'll do something else meanwhile."

As he spoke, Senderl put his hand in his pack and pulled out a bag.

"So you don't know, or on the other hand you forgot that I did this, Senderl," Binyomin said. "Little fool, I will explain to you my reason for it."

But Senderl was occupied with opening the bag very, very slowly. When Binyomin had a look, his whole body became light with pleasure. Everything wonderful was in the bag: bread, pieces of challah, everything left over from Shabbes: cucumbers, radishes, onions, and heads of garlic. Senderl had not forgotten to prepare anything, just like a good *baleboste* [housewife], and this elevated him in Binyomin's eyes, crowning him in higher esteem than any woman. Binyomin's heart was truly glad, for Hashem had brought him a *bashert*, a dear friend for the journey. Senderl was god-sent, like manna in the desert.

Afterwards, when they had refreshed themselves, Senderl wrapped up the bit of food that was left over and put it in the bag, saying, "This bit of food will be useful to us again, and this bag another thousand times, for our whole lives. With that, God willing, we need only go with it from house to house, and God, bless him, will help us!"

"Senderl," cried Binyomin, strengthened by Senderl's words, "We are each other's match from heaven. Together we are like a body and soul. While you worry about material things, like eating and drinking on our journey, I'll worry about spiritual things."

Sholem Yankev Abramovitsh, *Kitzer Masoes Binyomin HaShlishi* (Odessa, 1878). Translated from Yiddish by Diana Clarke. Copyright © 2019 Print-O-Craft Press.

Further Reading

Garrett, Leah. *Journeys beyond the Pale: Yiddish Travel Writing in the Modern World* (University of Wisconsin Press, 2003).

Peleg, Yaron. "Homoeroticism and the Creation of Modern Jewish Masculinities." *Jewish Social Studies* 13:1 (2006), 31–58.

Seidman, Naomi. "Theorizing Jewish Patriarchy *in extremis*." In *Judaism Since Gender* (eds. Miriam Peskowitz and Laura Levitt, Routledge, 1997), 40–48.

Seidman, Naomi. *The Marriage Plot: Or, How Jews Fell in Love with Love, and with Literature* (Stanford University Press, 2016).

61. Poetry of Emma Lazarus (New York, 1876 and 1880)

The poet Emma Lazarus, born in 1849 into a prominent American Spanish-Portuguese family, is well known for her poem, "The New Colossus," written in 1883 and inscribed on the base of the Statue of Liberty in 1903, which describes the statue as "a mighty woman with a torch," who cries, "Give me your tired, your poor / Your huddled masses yearning to breathe free." Lazarus' poetry experimented with the conventions of European poetic forms and Judaic content, and she identified proudly and strongly with secular Jewish culture. In several of her published and unpublished poems, Lazarus openly expressed a yearning for emotional and erotic connection with other women, but nothing is known about her own sexual or romantic life; she died of Hodgkin's disease in 1887, at the age of 38. In "Dolores," she contemplates her sleeping companion, and imagines (impossibly, it seems) uniting with her in marriage. "I dare not call thee aloud, nor cry," she writes, "But I will whisper: Dolores, tis I." In return, Lazarus remembers when "her low voice murmured, Yea, I am thine, / And the large world rang with my happiness." Similarly, in "Assurance"—a poem which was not published in Lazarus' lifetime, and kept in manuscript for decades after her death—Lazarus recalls a fantastical dream of an erotic encounter in a mysterious garden, where "cheek pressed to cheek, the cool, hot night-breeze / mingled our hair, our breath, & came & went." Her interlocutor urges her to believe in the reality of their dream-encounter, leaving Lazarus with the declaration (emphasized in the original manuscript): *"this is the thing that is!"* Lazarus' biographer Esther Schor writes that this poem is "about being chosen by desire—erotic desire, and for the body and soul of a woman...a poem of vocation, about being called by *eros* to a vital, sexual life."

Dolores

A light at her feet and a light at her head,
    How fast asleep my Dolores lies!
Awaken, my love, for to-morrow we wed—
    Uplift the lids of thy beautiful eyes.

Too soon art thou clad in white, my spouse:
    Who placed that garland above thy heart
Which shall wreathe to-morrow thy bridal brows?
    How quiet and mute and strange thou art!

And hearest thou not my voice that speaks?
    And feelest thou not my hot tears flow
As I kiss thine eyes and thy lips and thy cheeks?
    Do they not warm thee, my bride of snow?

Thou knowest no grief, though thy love may weep
    A phantom smile, with a faint, wan beam,
Is fixed on thy features sealed in sleep:
    Oh tell me the secret bliss of thy dream.

Does it lead to fair meadows with flowering trees,
    Where thy sister-angels hail thee their own?
Was not my love to thee dearer than these?
    Thine was my world and my heaven in one.

I dare not call thee aloud, nor cry,
    Thou art so solemn, so rapt in rest,
But I will whisper: Dolores, tis I:
    My heart is breaking within my breast.

Never ere now did I speak thy name,
    Itself a caress, but the lovelight leapt
Into thine eyes with a kindling flame,
    And a ripple of rose o'er thy soft cheek crept.

But now wilt thou stir not for passion or prayer,
　　And makest no sign of the lips or the eyes,
With a nun's strait band o'er thy bright black hair—
　　Blind to mine anguish and deaf to my cries.

I stand no more in the waxen-lit room:
　　I see thee again as I saw thee that day,
In a world of sunshine and springtide bloom,
　　Midst the green and white of the budding May.

Now shadow, now shine, as the branches ope,
　　Flickereth over my love the while:
From her sunny eyes gleams the May-time hope,
　　And her pure lips dawn in a wistful smile.

As one who waiteth I see her stand,
　　Who waits though she knows not what nor whom,
With a lilac spray in her slim soft hand:
　　All the air is sweet with its spicy bloom.

I knew not her secret, though she held mine:
　　In that golden hour did we each confess;
And her low voice murmured, Yea, I am thine,
　　And the large world rang with my happiness.

To-morrow shall be the blessedest day
　　That ever the all-seeing sun espied:
Though thou sleep till the morning's earliest ray,
　　Yet then thou must waken to be my bride.

Yea, waken, my love, for to-morrow we wed:
　　Uplift the lids of thy beautiful eyes.
A light at her feet and a light at her head,
　　How fast asleep my Dolores lies!

Last night I slept, & when I woke her kiss
Still floated on my lips. For we had strayed
Together in my dream, through some dim glade,
Where the shy moonbeams scarce dared light our bliss.
The air was dank with dew, between the trees,
The hidden glow-worms kindled & were spent.
Cheek pressed to cheek, the cool, the hot night-breeze
Mingled our hair, our breath, & came & went,
As sporting with our passion. Low & deep,
Spake in mine ear her voice:
                              "And didst thou dream,
This could be buried? this could be asleep?
And love be thrall to death? Nay, whatso seem,
Have faith, dear heart; *this is the thing that is!*"
Thereon I woke, and on my lips her kiss.

Emma Lazarus, "Dolores," *Lippincott's Monthly Magazine* 17 (June 1876), 666–667. "Assurance," as published in Gregory Eiselein (ed.), *Emma Lazarus: Selected Poems and Other Writings* (Toronto: Broadview Press, 2002).

Further Reading

Schor, Esther. *Emma Lazarus* (Schocken Books, 2006).

Turpin, Zachary. "Yearning to Breathe Free: Emma Lazarus's Queer Innovations." *J19: The Journal of Nineteenth-Century Americanists* 4:2 (2016), 419–424.

62. A Tunisian Rabbi Rebukes his Community for Adultery, Homosexuality, Sabbath Violation, and Other Sins (Tunis, 1886)

Shuvah Yisra'el is a short booklet written by the Tunisian rabbi Yehudah Jarmon (1812–1912) and published in Livorno in 1886. It is part of a new genre of Judeo-Arabic literature that emerged in Tunisia in the second half of the nineteenth century: moralistic pamphlets and essays that attempted to fight the growing trends of assimilation and secularism caused by the French colonial occupation, the educational initiatives of the Franco-Jewish Alliance

Israélite Universelle, and the growing entanglement of North African Jews in European social and cultural developments. While the local rabbinic establishment had generally supported the expansion of French colonial presence and the opening of Alliance schools, they began to fear the loss of Jewish identity, and these pamphlets urged Jews to return to traditional religious observance and castigated them for abandoning Jewish communal affiliation. In this excerpt, Jarmon lists the fourteen sins which he sees as plaguing the Jewish community of Tunis and for which he demanded repentance. Jarmon is especially concerned with public and visible violations, such as Sabbath violation, shaving the beard, and adopting Western fashions. He describes homosexuality here only briefly as "an odious sin, more odious than the others," and its inclusion in this essay suggests that Jarmon was trying to associate homosexuality with foreignness and the European influence that he believed was corrupting the moral values of his community.

These are the stipulations of repentance with the strength and help of God, so that God, of Praiseworthy Name, might forgive us and remove God's scathing anger from us and is merciful to us, forgives us, and grants us life, Amen.

1. The first sin is adultery, [for which] the sinner's judgment is overtaken by Satan in order that he commit this sin…And in this time of the exile, it is [still] a very great sin, one that includes two sins. The first that he committed a transgression with the wife of [another] man. And the second is that he caused a great sin, namely that he caused a man's wife to be divorced from her husband…especially if she had children by this man. This is what has been wrought by the man who committed this sin with the wife of [another] man.

2. The second sin is the violation of the sabbath publicly, in front of people. We will enumerate the types of violation of the sabbath. The first is the one who smokes a cigarette on the sabbath. He opens his shop, selling and buying, either with money or without money. Likewise, the one who opens the tavern on the sabbath, [and] those who open the cafes of the Jews on the sabbath… And traveling on the railroad on the sabbath, either with money or without money, riding the carriage on the sabbath, riding the omnibus on the sabbath, especially if the omnibus is owned by Jews and its animals are owned by Jews

and the workers [operating it] are Jews…And prostitution on the sabbath, the one who has a transgression that he leaves for the sabbath day. He visits his prostitute on the sabbath day. This is a very great sin, entailing two sins in one…

3. The third sin is speaking wickedly of others. It is the sin of the one who speaks foolishly, of which there is no greater sin than this. There is no benefit in it, nor comfort to the soul. The sin of prostitution is still forgivable, because the natural impulses of mankind push one toward it. And however he repents, it is possible for him to be forgiven by God. In turn, this sin of foolish speech is very difficult to excuse, because [the one who commits it] defiles his mouth without any benefit or pleasure to his body…

4. The fourth is the one who goes without praying for months or long stretches of time. No prayer, no tallit, no phylacteries. A Jew who remains characterized by the description "the head of him who puts no phylacteries on" is not considered Jewish. The phylacteries are considered a sign and a marker that we are Jews. And abandoning prayer is considered a rank even lower than [that of] a gentile, because even the gentiles believe in, pray to, and worship God, of Praiseworthy Name.

5. The fifth is the one who leaves his wife [ritually] pure [but] in very shameful clothing. She is a man's wife, yet remaining naked as her husband perceives her, and likewise another man, not of her household, sees and perceives her [in this state] and as such he desires to perform a transgression with her, may the All-Merciful protect us. Her husband is held accountable for this sin…

6. The sixth is the one who insults the religion for no reason. He makes himself angry and brings himself to insult the religion of Moses our dear teacher, who is our strength and our light among the nations. Also, the one who mentions the name of our dear Master one hundred times in vain for no reason. And especially…the one who, after mentioning the name of God, speaks wickedly and foolishly. This is a very strong sin; [in fact] there is no greater sin than this.

7. The seventh sin is those people who sit in the cafes with the intention of looking upon the wives of other men…This sin is considered to be three sins…[First,] he emits seed for naught. This is a very great sin. The flood would

not have come to the world if not for the sin of the emission of seed for naught. Second, by way of this desire he violates one of the ten commandments, in which the dear Torah said do not covet your companion's wife. Third, the one over whom Satan takes power...loses money beyond measure in order to commit a transgression with this woman whom he desired. All of this stems from that accursed desire. He defiles himself, the one who desires the wives of [other] men, may God save us.

8. The eighth sin is homosexual intercourse, [the sin of] the one who follows after young men. That is an odious sin, more odious than all others. His life is cut off in this world and the hereafter, may God save us.

9. The ninth is the one who is not merciful to the poor, especially on the sabbath and the holidays, during which we are obligated to rejoice...

10. The tenth is the one who is mean toward his Jewish cousin, [one] weak and poor. He is mean toward him, insulting him or hitting him and throwing him down. Or he is mean to him, withholding his money from him seeing that that he is poor and does not have a compassionate shoulder and chest [upon which to lean]. Or the one who is mean to his cousin, encroaching upon his property, overreaching into his house or his shop, driving him out from it. This is a very strong sin, for which there is no forgiveness...All of these sins are unforgivable, even if [the one who commits such a sin] seeks forgiveness from his friend and removes the harm that he has done to him.

11. The eleventh believes that he is Jewish [but neglects] these three signs [that] remain with him, by which we are Jewish. The first is acts of loving-kindness. He gives alms as long as he is healthy. And wherever he meets a Jewish cousin...unrightfully imprisoned, he does all he can in accord with his bodily health in order to liberate and see his cousin. The second is that he be reserved, meaning that [he] is humble to the one who is not greater than him...and he does nothing disgraceful in front of people. The third is that he be compassionate, meaning that he has mercy and compassion upon all of his Jewish brothers.

12. The twelfth is the one who defiles himself [by] walking with his wife while she is menstruating, or makes himself disgraceful with her or approaches her; this is a very great sin. He must quarantine her [from himself] until she goes to the bath and immerses. Also, the one who defiles himself [by] walking

with a Christian woman or with a Muslim woman and has intercourse with this girl of the diaspora, may the All-Merciful protect us.

13. The thirteenth: this stipulation refers to shaving, specifically the one who shaves his beard. He who shaves the beard is obligated to take five lashes (of the whip). The religious judges should give him five lashes. And likewise, [this applies to] the man who shaves and goes to the barber so that he shaves his beard for him. He should also be whipped by the religious judges five times. And the one who shaves his beard is called an apostate. His likeness is that of a gentile, may the All-Merciful protect us. And after his death, in the hereafter his punishment is that a pair of plucking cows will lay him on the ground and pluck out his beard. They stand on his heart until they pluck out the hairs of his beard.

14. The fourteenth: this stipulation stands in the place of all others, for it is [very] great: the dear Torah which is the prize of our hearts…and equally great, the sages who study it. No-one should insult any sage, great or small; rather, he should invite the sages into his house…

These are the fourteen stipulations of repentance, if with the help and succor of God we accept upon ourselves these stipulations and we establish them…God, of Praiseworthy Name, will forgive us, grant us (long) life, and not hold us accountable for past sins…Speedily and soon, amen!

Yehudah Jarmon, *Shuvah Yisra'el* (Livorno: Eliyahu Benamozegh, 1886). Translated from Judeo-Arabic by Joshua Picard. Reprinted by permission of Joshua Picard.

Further Reading

Picard, Joshua. *Tunisian Judaeo-Arabic Essays on Religion and Ideology in the Late-Nineteenth Century* (MA thesis, Brandeis University, 2016).

Tobi, Yosef, and Tsivia Tobi. *Judeo-Arabic Literature in Tunisia, 1850–1950* (Wayne State University Press, 2014).

63. Poetry of Amy Levy (London, 1889)

Amy Levy (1861–1889) was born in London to an acculturated, upper middle class Anglo-Jewish family. She received an excellent education, and was the first Jewish woman to be admitted to Newnham College of

Cambridge University. Her first volume of poetry, *Xantippe and Other Verse*, was published in 1881, and over the next decade she published two more poetry collections, three novels, and many articles. She traveled throughout Europe and in Florence met and fell in (unrequited) love with Vernon Lee (Violet Paget), a British lesbian writer and essayist, to whom she dedicated several love poems. Levy's works deals critically with Anglo-Jewish identity and community, especially her controversial second novel, *Reuben Sachs* (1888), which takes up the theme of Sephardi intellectual and racial superiority. Her work also expresses the importance of a female presence in urban public space, walking the streets and riding the omnibus. She struggled all her life with depression, and with alienation as a woman and a Jew; she committed suicide in 1889, just before her 28th birthday. Oscar Wilde eulogized her, saying of her 1888 novels *Reuben Sachs* and *The Romance of a Shop*, "to write thus at six-and-twenty is given to very few...The world must forego the full fruition of her power." These poems are taken from her final poetry collection, published just after her death; they speak of female presence, encounter, and relationship. In "A Wall Flower," she describes her emotions watching a woman dance with men (a situation reminiscent of Sappho's poem in source 1), and imagines "some other where, not here," where they could dance together. Carolyn Lake argues that "dancing, a cultural activity of heterosexual courtship, is used here as a stand-in for what the speaker is unable to intelligibly do—love a woman." In her sonnet to Vernon Lee, she writes of loving exchange: "You broke a branch and gave it to me there / I found for you a scarlet blossom rare" but concludes with pessimism that "of the gifts the gods had given to each / Hope unto you, and unto me Despair." In the poem "At a Dinner Party" she hints of the potential for connection, the hidden meanings of glances exchanged across a room and unnoticed by the "dull" and "blind" world: "It is our secret, only ours."

A Wall Flower

I lounge in the doorway and languish in vain
While Tom, Dick and Harry are dancing with Jane.

My spirit rises to the music's beat;
There is a leaden fiend lurks in my feet!

To move unto your motion, Love, were sweet.
Somewhere, I think, some other where, not here,
In other ages, on another sphere,
I danced with you, and you with me, my dear.

In perfect motion did our bodies sway,
To perfect music that was heard alway;
Woe's me, that am so dull of foot to-day!

To move unto your motion, Love, were sweet;
My spirit rises to the music's beat —
But, ah, the leaden demon in my feet!

Borderland

Am I waking, am I sleeping?
As the first faint dawn comes creeping
Thro' the pane, I am aware
Of an unseen presence hovering,
Round, above, in the dusky air :
A downy bird, with an odorous wing,
That fans my forehead, and sheds perfume,
As sweet as love, as soft as death,
Drowsy-slow through the summer-gloom.
My heart in some dream-rapture saith,
It is she. Half in a swoon,
I spread my arms in slow delight.—
O prolong, prolong the night,
For the nights are short in June !

London in July

What ails my senses thus to cheat ?
What is it ails the place,
That all the people in the street,
Should wear one woman's face?
The London trees are dusty-brown

Beneath the summer sky ;
My love, she dwells in London town,
Nor leaves it in July.
O various and intricate maze,
Wide waste of square and street ;

Where, missing through unnumbered days,
We twain at last may meet!

And who cries out on crowd and mart?
Who prates of stream and sea?
The summer in the city's heart—
That is enough for me.

To Vernon Lee

On Bellosguardo, when the year was young,
We wandered, seeking for the daffodil
And dark anemone, whose purples fill
The peasant's plot, between the corn-shoots sprung

Over the grey, low wall the olive flung
Her deeper greyness; far off, hill on hill
Sloped to the sky, which, pearly-pale and still
Above the large and luminous landscape hung.

A snowy blackthorn flowered beyond my reach;
You broke a branch and gave it to me there;
I found for you a scarlet blossom rare.

Thereby ran on of Art and Life our speech;
And of the gifts the gods had given to each
Hope unto you, and unto me Despair.

At a Dinner Party

With fruit and flowers the board is deckt,
The wine and laughter flow;

I'll not complain—could one expect
So dull a world to know?

You look across the fruit and flowers,
My glance your glances find.—
It is our secret, only ours,
Since all the world is blind.

Amy Levy, *A London Plane-Tree and Other Verse* (London: T. Fisher Unwin, 1889).

Further Reading

Beckman, Linda Hunt. *Amy Levy: Her Life and Letters* (Ohio University Press, 2000).

Hetherington, Naomi, and Nadia Valman (eds.). *Amy Levy: Critical Essays* (Ohio University Press, 2010).

Lake, Carolyn. "'All the World is Blind': unveiling same-sex desire in the poetry of Amy Levy." In *Changing the Victorian Subject* (ed. Maggie Tonkin et al.), University of Adelaide Press, 2014, 241–258.

Scheinberg, Cynthia. *Women's Poetry and Religion in Victorian England: Jewish Identity and Christian Culture* (Cambridge University Press, 2002).

64. A Russian Jewish Thinker Studies "Unisexuality" (London, 1895)

Marc-Andre Raffalovich (1864–1934) was born in Paris to a family of wealthy Russian Jewish bankers originally from Odessa. At the age of 18, Raffalovich moved to London, where he established a salon, published several books of poetry, and involved himself (despite facing antisemitism and xenophobia) in the circle of artists and writers surrounding Oscar Wilde. At one of his salons he met the young poet John Gray (1866–1934), reputed to be Wilde's inspiration for the eponymous protagonist of *The Picture of Dorian Gray* (1890); Raffalovich and Gray soon became lifelong companions. In 1894 Raffalovich entered the field of sexology and began contributing articles on what he called "unisexuality" to medical journals, culminating in 1896 with the publication of *Uranisme et unisexualité: étude sur différentes manifestations de l'instinct sexuel* (Uranism and Unisexuality: A Study of Different Manifestations of the Sexual Instinct). That same year, Raffalovich converted to Roman Catholicism. For many Victorian homosexuals, including Wilde, Catholicism held deep aesthetic attraction, through its reverence for the beautiful male body of Christ and saints like St. Sebastian (the name that Raffalovich took at his conversion), and its emphasis on the Platonic love of beauty. For other Jewish homosexuals, it seems that the homosocial male communities of Hasidism had a similar pull (for example, in sources 77 and 79). Gray was ordained as a priest in 1905, and the two of them moved to Edinburgh, where Raffalovich financed the building of Gray's parish church; they died four months apart, in 1934. In this 1895 article (later incorporated into his book), Raffalovich explains his understanding of "unisexuality" as simply a variant form of sexuality, which he believed to be "congenital," or inherent from birth—it is not perverted or degenerate. He sees no immorality in homosexuality; in fact, he claims, there is an inherent link between "inverts" or "uranists" and a kind of mystical or religious potential, which he argues should be nurtured through education and celibacy—something which his own relationship with Gray seemingly modelled.

Introduction

I have neither desire nor time to write an encyclopedia of inversion, still less to review the discoveries, the opinions and the assertions of other writers and their followers or adversaries. I have wished primarily to submit to my readers certain observations as new and as exact as possible. I have criticized with all possible respect my predecessors, masters or followers; and I have decided to make an appeal to all those who have at heart the diminution of suffering and debauchery among the children of the present or the coming generations.

The education of congenital inverts (or uranists, to employ the word invented by a famous invert) has not yet been under taken. We are strangely ignorant of the indices of homosexuality in children. Homosexuality is increasing and will increase. We can hardly cure the inverts. Hypnotism is not satisfactory and marriage is the worst of remedies, sacrificing the peace and health of the children to the improbable cure of the father and his doubtful restoration. There are already too many inverts and perverts who are married and who are fathers and hypocrites for marriage to save the honor of a homosexual.

The education of the uranist is a desideratum; it will be ere long a necessity. If we apply ourselves to the discovery of the uranistic child, to his development and the amelioration of his condition, if we encourage in him continence, chastity, soberness, duty, we shall find ourselves in the presence of a new class adapted for celibacy, for study, for religion (since the realization of their desires is not of this world.) Like the ideal physician of Plato, the best of them will be of sufficiently weak character to understand the sins of their fellows, and of sufficient strength of will to make themselves useful.

Meanwhile (and this is meant for those who think that every Utopian scheme is vain, and they would not be wrong if such uranists had not always existed) the chastity of certain great men (whatever be the cause of it) has contributed greatly to civilization. The study and the furtherance of the education of uranists would have immediate results. Not only could many little beings now already begotten or wailing in their cradles be benefitted, but many new facts would be learned.

The causes of uranism (I speak of first causes) are probably as mysterious as those of the difference of sex; they probably do not lie within the province of our science, but we may be able to attain a knowledge of their mechanism, their ascendency, their heredity.

In the following pages I shall not attempt to study the prenatal causes of uranism, that I may not be embarrassed by hypotheses. After some observations which have appeared in the *Archives d'anthropologie criminelle* and which have been received with an interest very gratifying to me…then I shall indicate my theory of sexuality; and I shall conclude by urging scholars, teachers and parents to attend to the moral education of uranistic children.

Some Observations upon Inversion

In my capacity as an observer and living much in the world, I have known many inverts and noted others. Their confessions serious, sad, trifling, shameless—their lies and their reticence, have taught me many things either generally unknown or neglected.

These are some of the observations.

The inverts are not at all content with the old explanation of the feminine soul in the masculine body. Some of them are more masculine than other men and are attracted to their own sex in proportion to the resemblance. They say that they despise women too much to be effeminate. Others think that similarity is a passion comparable to that excited by sexual dissimilarity. As men, they love men; but they affirm that if they were women, they would love women. These are the unisexuals par excellence. They are also the superior and the most interesting ones, they are perhaps the only ones who do not deceive either for the pleasure of deceiving or unconsciously. It might be admitted (and this would be a pretty general rule) that the more moral value a unisexual has the less effeminate he is.

It is an error to suppose that the unisexuals, the inverts, recognize each other. This is one of their boasts which has been often repeated; but one of their subjects of conversation is the very question whether this or that one shares their tastes, habits or proclivities. The effeminate of course recognize each other, but one may recognize them quite as easily without being himself effeminate. But prudence, self-love, pride, self respect, a deep affection, a thousand sentiments, prevent a unisexual from betraying himself thus unless he is debauched or very effeminate. I think that the congenital inverts are less vicious and debauched, more honorable and estimable than most perverts. One may without much inconvenience (or even without any) be united by the ties of friendship with a congenital invert; but I have never found a pervert whose perversion was simply sexual. It is, however, possible that exceptional circumstances—isolation, or the influence of a remarkable and superior invert—should act upon an individual and invert him without great injury to the rest of his character. In this case one would not be aware of the inversion, for it would be limited to the relations with a single person, the superior invert, and it might be at length refined to such a degree as to be unrecognizable and as for the inversion produced by isolation, it would disappear with this isolation; or if it persisted, it would remain absolutely sexual. It is with the congenital invert that the inversion is most often absolutely sexual. The born invert is accustomed to his character, his inversion is not acquired from vice or weakness or vanity or the love of gain or imitation or cowardice or fear or from the desire to win over someone who is necessary or useful, which are all causes of perversion.

The physicians who try to cure inverts have not sufficiently noted the dangers to which they expose their patients. They may transform their invert into a pervert. I do not think much of permanent cures of the sexual sense. Every imperfect cure may make of an invert a pervert; and if the invert is dangerous and contagious, the pervert is much more so. He has more points of contact with the normal young man; he startles him less, he takes less complete, though easier, possession of him than does the invert. The men who have seduced, corrupted and defiled the souls and lives of their younger companions are usually perverts. They have not always been unisexual. They have more power. They are more vicious. The unisexual who attempts bisexuality is as corrupt as the normal sexual man who attempts unisexuality; they have all vices, both those natural to them and others. Let the medical healer remember this before undertaking a congenital invert. Rather than to add the vices of the normal man to the abnormality which he has, the superior invert (it is he alone who would have a strong desire to change his condition; the inferior inverts find adequate satisfaction all too easily) should try—under proper direction—to lift himself above himself and his vice. The tendencies of our time, particularly the prevalent contempt for religion, make chastity more difficult for every one, and the invert suffers more from this than others. Instead of debasing the honorable invert by making him run after prostitutes and subsequently to become the unfortunate husband of a less fortunate wife and the father of children who will suffer as much as he or more, the attempt should be made to occupy and interest him and to show him the horizons which he can attain by dint of effort and of will...

So I protest that we should not make a practice of pitying the inverts as inverts. The enthusiastic uranists do not wish to change. With whom should they? The true homosexuals, those who have the passion of similarity, if they were women would love women; so also the true homosexual if he were a man would love a man. Let us pity humanity as a whole if we wish; let us pity it bitterly if we have no religion; but let us not pick out the inverts for our utmost pity. I cannot repeat this admonition too often. The abject or enthusiastic inverts do not think that they are by any means to be pitied. The superior inverts are no more to be pitied than superior heterosexuals. As for the inverts who moan and lament and who beset writers with their stories, they are usually persons who would have moaned and lamented if they had been heterosexual. No one finds easily a person of the opposite sex who satisfies at the same time sex, the soul and society and the family. Why should the invert have that which the heterosexual finds with so great difficulty? How many heterosexuals are unhappy by reason of their sexual life? Syphilis, nervous disorders, disrepute, the dissolution of many bonds, as well as many other things, pursue the heterosexual who is unfortunate or devoid of character.

The individual who is neither chaste nor sober nor vigorous nor reasonable nor very courageous nor very enlightened nor very pious is always to be pitied whether he be invert or heterosexual. The inversion of the great inverts may always be pardoned; it does not hinder them from being themselves, from accomplishing their work in the world. Do we believe that Plato, Walt Whitman, Michael Angelo, the Great Condé, Winckelmann and the host of others deserve or desire pity for their homosexuality?

Great men are great by reason of what they are, in spite of all the infirmities and the accidents of this life. Men of genius, whether homosexual, heterosexual or indifferent, make it very plain that men are not to be classified according to their sexual bent, but for other considerations of a different order. If great men and men of large heart and lofty spirit find them selves outside the pale of the pity which people like to organize for the aid of inverts, ordinary men who are uranists and who are sick, degenerate, unbalanced, weakly, unfortunate, hypocrites, ought to be judged like the sick, the unfortunate, the feeble or the craven—but why excite our sympathy for them? Read carefully their autobiographies and tell me frankly and honestly, would they have been worth any more, would they have been more happy, more virtuous, if they had been heterosexual and as prone to sexuality?

As for prostitutes, extortioners of hush-money, adventurers, let us be just; but not indulgent! I speak of prostitutes of all degrees of the social hierarchy. Even those who gladly sell themselves and who love their business and their keeper are given over to the extortion of hush-money and theft. The man of the world who resorts to one of them knows what threatens him and hardly deserves the pity that would gladly be given him if one considered the consequences only of his folly. The hypocrites or the cynical debauchees who try to deprave or who do deprave children, young boys or very young men are treated by public opinion with commendable justice and contempt. This severity and this contempt ought not to be diminished. The inverts often share this contempt and some of them avoid each other and criticize each other and spurn each other. This is less from sexual inappetence, I think, than because they understand each other and despise each other too much…

Uranists are precocious and precocity ought always to be guarded and given the food of which it has need. Love of pretty things, of dress and of objects of art should make us watchful without leading us to discourage them. On the contrary the predilection for the artistic has aided more than one uranist to lead a possible or respectable existence; only this predilection should receive this most serious possible attention that it may not become a bent for mere amateurism.

The uranists are often very superficial; amateurs of all kinds are recruited from them.

Many of the arguments used in favour of women may be employed in favour of the inverts. If one speaks to a defender of women of their intellectual inferiority and lack of loyalty, he will say, they have never had a chance, they have never been taught any of these things.

Well! since the invert is not burdened with maternity nor by all the vexations of the female sex, why not try to make him serve humanity? He has many defects and many vices inborn, but our civilization and our education do not and cannot improve his condition. The bees and the ants have workers who do not reproduce. Is it possible, barely possible, to make some use of the uranists?

Marc-André Raffalovich, "Uranism: Congenital Sexual Inversion." *Journal of Comparative Neurology* 5 (1895), 33–65 (trans. C. Judson Herrick).

Further Reading

Erber, Nancy, et al. (eds. and trans.). *Marc-André Raffalovich's* Uranism and Unisexuality: A Study of Different Manifestations of the Sexual Instinct (Palgrave, 2016).

Roden, Frederick. *Same-Sex Desire in Victorian Religious Culture* (Palgrave, 2002).

Roden, Frederick. "Marc-André Raffalovich: A Russian-French-Jewish-Catholic Homosexual in Oscar Wilde's London." In *Jewish/Christian/Queer: Crossroads and Identities* (ed. Frederick Roden), Routledge, 2016.

65. An Ottoman Sephardi Rabbi Rules on Gender Transition (Izmir, 1896)

The question of how to accommodate the fluidity of bodies and genders within the system of Jewish law has engaged rabbinic thinkers since antiquity (see source 5). In this responsum, an Ottoman rabbi, Yosef Pallache, deals with the question of whether a married woman who has been "changed" into a man must still obtain a *get* (divorce certificate) from his former husband. Ruling that this person is now a man in every respect, and supporting his claim with an appeal to early modern scientific knowledge, Pallache rules that there is no need for a *get*, since the "woman" of the original contract no longer exists. Pallache then points out that this man cannot reasonably recite the morning blessing that thanks God for not having created him a woman, since he was in fact initially created so; therefore, the rabbi suggests a new blessing, thanking God "who has transformed me into a man"(!). Rabbi Yosef Pallache (1815–1896) was a member of a renowned and widespread Mediterranean Sephardi family of rabbinic scholars; his father Ḥayyim, and brother Avraham, each served as Chief Rabbi (*haham-başı*) of Izmir. Pallache's opinion was quoted by Rabbi Eliezer Waldenberg (1915–2006) in his important 1970 responsum on sex affirmation surgery, in *Tsits Eli'ezer* (Vol. X, 25.26.6).

QUESTION: Is a proper *get* [divorce certificate] necessary in the following circumstance: a certain man married a young Jewish woman, and was with her in the manner of men and women, but after some many years an event occurred to her and she was changed from female to male in every respect. What is the law in this case, for one who had been a woman and married to a man, and then became a man? If he wishes to marry another woman, does [this husband] need to give a proper *get* to divorce her according to the laws of Moshe and Israel? Or rather, does he not need to give a *get* for now, or at all, since she is not a woman [any longer] but a man? Do not be surprised by this question, since all things are possible and there is nothing new under the sun, as you can see in the book *Yad Ne'eman, Liqqutim* 62b,* where he brought several examples like this,

---

*Ḥayyim Avraham Miranda (ca. 1723–ca. 1802), *Yad Ne'eman* (Salonica, 1804).

and additionally wrote that one young woman was transformed into a man at the very hour that they were leading her under the wedding canopy.

RESPONSE Regarding the case discussed by the [author of the] *Yad Ne'eman*...[he wrote that] a holy one from among the sages of Jerusalem (may it be rebuilt and resettled) was wondering whether this woman was obligated in circumcision or exempt—but it is obvious that she is exempt, since Scripture says, *"every male's foreskin"* (Genesis 17:14), meaning one whose essence [*'iqqar*] was male is obligated in circumcision, but not for one who was female in essence but was made male.

Regarding our question, it seems that a *get* is not needed, since he is a man now and not a woman; for the format of the *get* is that a man gives it to his wife and writes "you were my wife," but [in this case] there is no "wife," but a man...** And regarding this event, that an adult woman should be transformed into a man—how could it happen in a natural way, that this inverted world could be grasped by human intellect? Do not be surprised by this, for it was already explained in the book *Yad Ne'eman*, which wrote, "You should know that scholars of anatomy have not found any difference between the forms of the organs of males and those of females except that hers are internal and his are external, meaning the genitals, for a woman has within her a member and testicles, as is known. And in a case where there is excess heat and additional blood, perhaps the female genitals expand and thus the internal member can be turned out, and from female they will be turned male. And in reverse: if there is insufficient blood, and excess cold, the male genitals could shrink and return into the body, and thus from the male form they would become female, etc..."

And so it seems logical that since this woman has many visible signs that he is a man, as can be seen by everyone, he does not need a *get*, since he is not a woman but a full man, even as we have said, for this man who was a woman first and then changed into a man. Thus it seems to me that when [this man] says the morning blessings he should not say, "Blessed are You, Lord our God, Ruler of the universe, who has not made me a woman," since he had been made a woman at first, in his mother's womb, and was brought into the world in the

---

** The translation follows the shifting pronouns used by Pallache; he initially refers to the individual in question as "she" but switches here to "he."

form of a woman; rather, he should say, "Blessed are You, Lord our God, Ruler of the universe, who has transformed me into a man [*shehafkhani le'ish*]…"

Yosef Pallache, *Yosef Et Eḥav* (Izmir, 1896), Even Ha'ezer, §5. Translated from Hebrew by Noam Sienna.

Further Reading

Gray, Hillel. "Not Judging by Appearances: The Role of Genotype in Jewish Law on Intersex Conditions." *Shofar: An Interdisciplinary Journal of Jewish Studies* 30:4 (2012), 126–148.

King, Helen. *The One-Sex Body on Trial: The Classical and Early Modern Evidence* (Farnham: Ashgate, 2013).

Lewental, D. Gershon. "Pallache Family (Turkish Branch)." *Encyclopedia of Jews in the Islamic World* (ed. Norman Stillman, Leiden: Brill, 2012).

Ze'evi, Dror. *Producing Desire: Changing Sexual Discourse in the Ottoman Middle East, 1500–1900* (University of California Press, 2006).

The Sources:
Modern Voices
(1900-1969)

66. The Ben Ish Ḥai Prescribes a Remedy for Homosexual Activity (Baghdad, 1901)

The sixteenth-century Kabbalistic prescriptions of Yitsḥaq Luria for sexual misconduct (see source 41) continued to resonate in Jewish communities over the following centuries. In this responsum from nineteenth-century Baghdad, Luria's stringent rituals of atonement are converted into more practical and lenient solutions. The writer was one of the great rabbinic scholars of the Iraqi Jewish community in the nineteenth century: Yosef Ḥayyim al-Ḥakham (1835–1909), also known as the Ben Ish Ḥai, after the title of his most popular book. Elsewhere in his responsa the author also recommends other possibilities for atoning for homosexual activity, including: performing the ritual of *tashlikh* (throwing breadcrumbs into flowing water, normally done between Rosh Hashanah and Yom Kippur), donating money to charity, wearing sackcloth, and additional prayers and recitations of biblical and Kabbalistic texts.

QUESTION: I was asked by the holy saint Abba David Eliyahu [d. 1876] of blessed memory...regarding the *tiqqun* [remedy] for homosexual activity. The rabbi, the holy Ari of blessed memory [Yitsḥaq Luria], had written that one should fast for 233 [days], and roll in the snow [see source 41]. If one had fasted for 233 [days] in the winter, but there was no snow at all, would it be effective to do the rolling in snow afterwards when it was available, or is it necessary that the rolling in snow should happen during the days of fasting? And if you believe that the rolling in snow is effective at any time, then if he did not have access to any snow, would the *tiqqun* of fasting still be effective for him if he did not roll in the snow, but gathered snow in one place and let it [melt] into water and immersed in it—would that be sufficient, or not?

RESPONSE: Regarding this question we will answer that this matter is explained in the writings of our master the Ari of blessed memory, in *Sha'ar Ruaḥ HaQodesh*: "And it is necessary regarding this *tiqqun* that these fasts be performed during the winter, when the snow falls, and he should bathe in it. It does not matter, regarding the matter of snow, whether it is at the beginning of the fasts, or at their end; only that it happens on some day out of [the second stage, which comprises] 161 fasts, and not on another day." Thus we have it:

the *tiqqun* of the snow must be during those days of fasting. Be that as it may, it is certain that if he did not perform the *tiqqun* of the snow during the days of fasting, but during a later period without fasting, this is also a *tiqqun* for that sin, except that he has not attained a full and complete *tiqqun*, since it is this *tiqqun* of the snow that belongs to this particular matter...So where one cannot find snow, and performs only the fasting, he is certainly [in the category of] one who is coerced, and "the Merciful desires the heart" (*b. Sanhedrin* 106b), since he is [already] bearing the weight of this great fast, and the world can witness that if he had snow available to him, he would roll or immerse in it, and therefore the Holy Blessed One will certainly consider him as if he had done the full and complete *tiqqun*.

In any case, it seems to me that he should try at the very least to find some piece of snow during his days of fasting, large enough that he can roll his hands in it from his fingertips up to his shoulders, front and back, nine times. A piece of snow [or ice] like this can be obtained in the wintertime, if he places some water in a bowl on the rooftop overnight; in the early morning, there will be a piece of snow [or ice] in that bowl. Before [the ritual], he should say this prayer: "For the unification of the Holy Blessed One and Divine Presence, etc., I hereby declare myself ready to roll my hands right and left in snow nine times. May it be Your will, my God and God of my ancestors, that You consider and accept and desire this rolling of my hands in snow nine times as if I had rolled my whole body in snow nine times, and may it ascend to You as if I had performed all the proper intentions of rolling in snow. '*Purge me with hyssop, and I will be purified; wash me, and I shall become whiter than snow*' (Psalms 51:9)." He should recite this verse three times, and then recite the following verses: "*And Benayahu the son of Yehoyadah was the son of a valiant man etc.*" until "*and David set him over his guard*" (II Samuel 23:20–23), and "*May God's pleasantness be with us etc.*" (Psalms 90:17) twice. Then he should roll his hands in the snow, right and left, nine times, from his fingertips up to the shoulder; and he should be careful to perform *neṭilat yadayyim* [ritual handwashing] first, so that his hands are cleansed before rolling them in the snow...

And regarding the question of spreading out the snow to immerse in it, this matter is already explained in the writings of our master the Ari of blessed memory, as he wrote, "Also, if there is a *miqveh* [ritual bath] into which snow falls, and you immerse in it nine times, that is sufficient." Nonetheless, you should know that you must immerse in it while it is still very cold, and not after it warms up and is no longer in its coldest state. For the secret of this *tiqqun* depends on his immersing in the snow while it is very cold, so that by means of this he cools down his body, and this will prevent him from warming up his body later [in forbidden sexual activity].

Yosef Hayyim, *Rav Pe'alim* (Jerusalem, 1901), Yore De'a, §44. Translated from Hebrew by Noam Sienna.

Further Reading

Greenberg, Steven. *Wrestling with God and Men: Homosexuality in the Jewish Tradition* (University of Wisconsin Press, 2004).

Hirschkowitz, Isaac. "Rabbi Yosef Hayyim's Halakhically and Kabbalistically Based Approaches to Homosexuality: A Spatial-Traditional Study." *Jewish Studies Quarterly* 20:3 (2013), 257–271.

67. An Algerian Jew in France Runs a Gay Bar (Paris, 1908)

By the nineteenth century, Paris already had a reputation as a highly-charged sexual space for both homosexual and heterosexual pursuits (and for both men and women). There were many spaces in the city where men and women interested in same-sex romance (and more) congregated: public gardens and bathhouses, the quays of the Seine, the Palais-Royal, and the cafés of the Montmartre neighborhood. One such café was run by an Algerian Jew named Moïse (Maurice) Zekri, who was born in Algiers in 1879 and came to Paris around the turn of the century, part of a large wave of migrant Jewish and Muslim Algerian men looking for work in the metropole. Zekri's café, called Maurice's Bar, soon became known as a hotspot for gay men, and because of this it was subject to constant harassment, surveillance, and police raids. The records here describe a raid that occurred in April 1908, in which three men "found in indecent positions" were arrested. A later report adds that these men were female impersonators or drag queens, known as Otero, Bobette, and Suzanne; the report explains that "the names of these regulars explains well enough why the tribunal was forced to pronounce the session closed." Zekri's identity as an Algerian Jew meant that French anxieties around sexuality were combined with both antisemitism and anti-Arab/anti-Algerian sentiment (note that he is misidentified in one source as "Mohammed"). Zekri went on to open another gay café in Montmartre, called La Perle, and then tried his luck abroad, with stints in Belgium, Italy, and Argentina. After the First World War, he returned to Paris and opened a fur store. Like Eve Adams (see source 82), Zekri was detained by the Nazis after the invasion of France and deported to Auschwitz, where he was killed in 1942.

Le Messidor, April 19, 1908
JUST LIKE BERLIN—A MORAL SCANDAL
The aftermath of a police raid—Under investigation—The indicted

We reported yesterday that Mr. Valette, chief of the mobile brigade, led a police raid on an establishment of Duperré St. where certain individuals of ambiguous morals regularly meet. It was Mr. Leydet, investigating judge, who was charged by the Public Prosecutor to open a judicial investigation into this affair.

The magistrate gathered this afternoon in the cabinet. At 2 P.M., under the direction of municipal guards, three of the indicted parties were led in and the judge began the first interrogation of their identity. We were found to be in the presence of a true moral scandal, which brought to mind the one which had unfolded, some years ago, on Dunkerque St., in a café with the symbol of a golden scarab [Le Scarabée, the first gay bar in Paris, raided and closed in 1900]. Genuine orgies have been happening on Duperré St., for many months now, in an ultra-chic bar. The clients of the establishment, which are exclusively men, are recruited from all classes of society.

Every evening, from 10 P.M. to 2 A.M., at the mercy of the least desirable affinities, a very mixed group would assemble, composed mostly of beardless and rouged young men, and old gentlemen in search of special sensations. After receiving many complaints addressed to the Police Prefecture, Mr. Lépine gave the order to Mr. Valette to act. The chief of the mobile brigade, who had already known of this bar's existence from the reports of several of his inspectors, took measures to ensure a successful roundup. When he appeared on Duperré St., accompanied by six security agents, the establishment was overflowing with people. The attitude of most of the people present could have left no doubt about the kind of distractions they were in search of.

Mr. Valette proceeded to a summary examination of the [bar's] clients, and arrested seven individuals found in indecent positions. Of this number, only three arrests were maintained. All the other people were invited to give proof of their identity. We will add that we have no desire for the Public Prosecutor to provide more detailed circumstances regarding this scandal.

Le Messidor, April 20, 1908

A NEW MORAL SCANDAL

The complaints—About the arrests—Disgusting bacchanalia—Interesting statements

In the two previous issues, *Messidor* published documented information about the police raid, carried out by the mobile brigade on a nighttime establishment on Duperré St., close to Pigalle Square. The establishment is well known by thousands of Parisians, and there is not a single inhabitant of the neighborhood who has not complained about its regulars. One person close enough to the situation to be well-informed made the following interesting statements to us regarding this affair:

An Odd Café

In the nighttime café that carries the sign "At Maurice's Bar," they meet up: all the pimps, all the prostitutes, and all the inverts* [*invertis*] who feel the need to waste whatever money they had been able to obtain, while making a great fuss. At midnight, the champagne flows freely. Leaning against their lords and masters, prostitutes and inverts play mandolins and guitars, and perform all the tunes in their repertoires, without worrying about the neighbors. The night owl, up late, who ventures into this place, might encounter strange scenes; but no-one will start any quarrels to make him degenerate himself. Sometimes, disgusting orgies will conclude these meetings.

---

*A common early twentieth-century term for homosexuals.

The Complaints

On repeated occasions, the residents of neighboring buildings have filed complaints against the owner, known in the underworld by the name Maurice the Algerian, but hidden in the civil registers, as in the police books, under his real name, Mohammed Ben Sekri [*sic*—Moïse Zekri]. Serious incidents have occurred on many occasions, sometimes in the establishment itself, and sometimes in the street. Last year, around this time, gunshots were exchanged between a number of clients; Mohammed, who inserted himself, was seriously injured. The establishment stayed open, however, since Mr. Hamard, who knew the owner more than anyone else, saw good reason to prevent its closure, for reasons of service, no doubt.

The Arrests

Everything leads one to believe, then, that he had a definite plan. The incidents which followed would seem, essentially, to support this assertion. Three arrests were made. "So few?" one might ask; but if we refer ourselves to the information that we have gathered, these three arrests permit the security agents to compile an interesting file, to establish numerous records, and then proceed ultimately to make numerous sensational captures.

The affair, moreover, is infinitely more important than anyone could have supposed. Some people of very enviable positions are already mixed up in this scandal. Their names will soon be revealed. And the hearings, which promise to be long and exciting, will throw a new light onto the activities of a category of individuals, living on the margins of society, prepared for the most infamous tasks, and who move with equal ease, painted and rouged, to the Palais[-Royal].

Newspaper reports in *Le Messidor*, April 19 and 20, 1908. Translated from French by Noam Sienna. I am grateful to Dr. Régis Revenin and Dr. Leslie Choquette for sharing their research on Zekri and confirming his biographical details. I also thank Ben Ratskoff and Adam Amir for helping with additional archival research on Zekri.

Further Reading

Choquette, Leslie. "Gay Paree: the origins of lesbian and gay commercial culture in the French Third Republic." *Contemporary French Civilization* 41:1 (2016), 1–24.

Guedj, Jérémy. "Variations identitaires: homosexualités juives dans la France de l'Entre-Deux-Guerres." *Archives Juives* 44:2 (2011), 86–101.

Katz, Ethan. *The Burdens of Brotherhood: Jews and Muslims from North Africa to France* (Harvard University Press, 2015).

Revenin, Régis. *Homosexualité et prostitution masculines à Paris 1870–1918* (Paris: L'Harmattan, 2005).

Sibalis, Michael. "Paris." In *Queer Sites: Gay Urban Histories Since 1600* (ed. David Higgs, Routledge, 1999), 10–37.

Sibalis, Michael. "The Palais-Royal and the Homosexual Subculture of Nineteenth-Century Paris." *Journal of Homosexuality* 41:3–4 (2002), 117–129.

68. "Memoirs of a Man's Maiden Years:" A German Jew's Transition (Berlin, 1907)

When Karl M. Baer was born in the small German town of Arolsen in 1885 (not 1884, as his text states), the attending doctor was unable to determine the newborn's sex, but since the genitalia appeared female "on superficial inspection," he declared the child to be a girl (the precise details of Baer's intersex nature remain unknown today). Baer grew up as a German Jewish girl named Martha, went on to study social work, and became a well-respected journalist. Baer fought against the problem of sex trafficking and was active in local B'nai Brith lodges and Zionist organizations. While on a speaking tour in Ukraine, he met a young Jewish woman from Bukovina (Czernovitz, today Chernivtsi), named Beila Hanna Heilpern, with whom he fell in love. But Baer was deeply dissatisfied with his life as a woman, and had always felt himself to be a man. In 1906, at the age of 21, Baer began consulting with Magnus Hirschfeld (see source 72) to begin the process of transition; a year later, he completed the process, and had all official records (including his birth certificate) amended. That same year he published a memoir (with the help of Hirschfeld, who also contributed an epilogue) under the pseudonym "N.O. Body," which was enthusiastically received. In the memoir, Baer disguises his Jewishness, substituting one foreignness for another (claiming his family were French Catholics rather than German Jews) and Christian references for Jewish ones (e.g. placing his birth on Whitsunday rather than its true date, Shavu'ot). But it is nonetheless a compelling and personal account of his journey to claim his true gender. His identity as the author was an open secret among his friends and acquaintances, and Baer continued to participate in the same social circles after his transition. He married his love Hanna in 1907, and later served as director of the B'nai Brith Lodges of Berlin. He immigrated to Palestine in 1938 with his second wife Elza, and died in 1956; he is buried in the Kiryat Shaul cemetery in Tel Aviv.

This book tells a true story. In it, what was probably the strangest youth [who] ever lived, shall speak with its own voice. This life needs to be believed, as strange as it may seem. But strangeness need not be equated with lies. In this book, I wish to speak of a life that lay like a burden on an obscure human being until a woman's soft white hands lifted the weight from him and transformed his sorrow into joie de vivre. It is the story of the confusion and conflicts that arose for me from my very own nature.

I was born a boy, raised as a girl. The fabric of my life was twisted from tangled threads until, with a mighty blow, the inner nature of my masculinity tore apart the veil of half-truths that upbringing, habit, and vital necessity had spun about me. One may raise a healthy boy in as womanish a manner as one wishes, and a female creature in as mannish; never will this cause their senses to remain forever reversed. But customs and habits bind so tightly that it needed an impulse from without, which was, however, also felt strongly from within, before I resolved to undertake the decisive outer transformation.

And the decision fell when a woman entered my life. I also wish to speak here of the love of this woman, who cleared the thorns from my path and transformed my life which had been nothing but dark torment into a joyous blessing.

My entire life was a path filled with thorns, until, finally, I reached her...

I was born on Whitsunday in 1884. A Sunday child. My parents were well educated and, at that time, well-off. I am the youngest child. When they were very young, three siblings fell victim to an epidemic children's disease. My mother, who at that time was a month from giving birth to my brother, had to part with three hitherto healthy children in a single week. She was twenty-two years old on the day of her marriage, and forty when I was born; my father was six years older. I resemble neither of them, but generally favor my paternal family: fine limbs, long slender feet, and a longish, oval face.

I know nothing of the time before my birth, but of my birth, I have been told that it proceeded normally. The midwife congratulated my mother on the birth of a splendid little girl and then called my father, to whom she said that the physical properties of the newborn were so strange that she was unable to decide to which sex the child belonged. She assumed it was a girl.

My father, too, inclined toward this view, whereas my mother wished to raise her child as a boy. They decided to consult a doctor. The family doctor we had then was an excellent man, however, anything but a doctor. "On superficial inspection, the shape has a feminine appearance; ergo we have a girl before us," he summarily decreed.

My mother raised several objections and wished to consult a leading medical authority; however, she was overridden, and my sanguine father put her off until some time in the future. His main worry had been to make sure that the doctor (by means of a handshake) and the midwife (by means of a large sum of money) would keep silent, so that this dreadfully disagreeable thing should not become known in wider circles. With that in his interest was exhausted; the unhappy child would have to get through life as best it could…

[As a young adult, N.O. Body goes to work in a shop.] Gradually, I was losing the feeling that I was a boy altogether. I had read in a pseudoscientific book that in anemic and poorly developed girls, menstruation did not begin before the twenties. Thus, I came to believe sometimes that I was an abnormal girl. The fact that I was more attracted by female bodies than by men I attributed to an artistic taste.

This auto-suggestion favorably influenced my relations with my companions. I was more relaxed, which resulted in their being friendlier toward me. I still remember some of the scandals we talked about. One day, it leaked out that one of the [unmarried] salesmen was going to be a father. We were very indignant about the degenerate girl and viewed the young man with lascivious curiosity. We continued to speak of it and about how the young man might have managed it, after we had gone to bed.

Although we knew a little about the nature of the relations between the sexes, the little we knew was so muddled that we could not picture it. In any case, we feared men, as they all seemed to us to be brutes, each one of them a Bluebeard, even the husband, who surely raped his wife anew daily. Every woman seemed a saint, forced to submit to such a greedy monster.

I also remember when a prostitute who was known all over town made a purchase in our shop. We were divided into two parties then; the one despised her; the other, to which I belonged, pitied the unfortunate creature, who was so poor that she had to suffer the torture of daily debauchery. Of course the girls did not use that expression, but a much coarser one that I cannot repeat here. We were of the opinion then that women had to bear all the pain and suffering. This was in agreement with my dreams, in which women served me, and I was their severe master.

I also remember that one young girl had a tumor on her breast. The doctor prescribed massages, and as I was particularly clever with my hands, I had to do it. This always greatly aroused me. Those amorous dreams became more and more frequent, and that girl an ever greater role among the figures in my dreams. I kissed and caressed her, naturally only in my dreams. I did have a desire to kiss her during the massages, but I was fearful and controlled myself. The impulse to kiss came over me often during this time. My dreams, which had formerly been of a more brutal character, now contained a tender premonition of a true love life.

We were also surprised to hear about lesbian love then. We admired this love, which we thought was more delicate and without pain, but we hardly believed in it. It occurred to me that I alone perhaps felt like a lesbian. Then again, I pushed the idea firmly aside…

[N.O. Body falls in love with Hanna. A leg injury forces him to see a doctor.] I stared at him. Could I trust this man? His calm, finely featured face, which was turned toward me in friendly sympathy, and his entire manner gave me confidence in him. I recalled my desire to confess. A doctor was bound to silence by his professional duty, and I had to speak. I no longer had the strength to bear my suffering in silence. So I took his hands and told him what gave us such joy and was, at the same time, so ill-fated and made us so unhappy. His face remained calm and friendly. Then he asked me a number of questions. I told him the story of my childhood, the secret of my body, and spoke to him of the countless sorrows and humiliations of bygone days. A heavy burden was gradually lifted from my soul as I at last spoke openly of what had depressed me for so long.

The doctor listened in silence and then said I would have to allow him to examine me thoroughly. When he finished, he spoke to me encouragingly. There was no reason to be sad. My love for my lady friend was no vice, and, by the way, as far as love was concerned, there was no vice, perhaps only in sensuousness, it was a natural feeling. "If you wish to be close to your friend and you can secure a future for her, then go ahead and marry her! You are as much a man as I am!" Only a minor operation, which he explained to me, was needed. The doctor in Bergheim who had examined me at birth was an ass. Moreover, my body seemed to have developed in a decidedly masculine way only during the last few years. I should take courage; the authorities could not deny permission for my transformation, and then I could marry my lady friend with a clear conscience.

It was as though dark veils had been torn from my eyes. The doctor was right. Physically, I was a man. And I had often been told that I had the spirit of a man.

A frenzy of joy and delight overcame me. I no longer heard what the kind old gentleman was saying. I lay there with my eyes shut, dreaming. For years, I had been unable to find the words for prayer; now I was overcome by an ecstatic, fervent thankfulness to God. I forgot where I was, saw Hanna's face, radiant with joy.

The doctor stood beside me and, with a friendly nod, shook my hand. I lay still for many hours. The new state of affairs was so overwhelming that I could not yet seriously grasp it. Now a bright light lay on our dark path…

During this period, shortly before the final decision, I still had to overcome many inner struggles. I considered the enormity of the step. Would I become accustomed to this new life? Would Hanna grow accustomed to the altered circumstances? And would I be able to provide her with an adequate livelihood? But all those considerations disappeared at the blissful thought of a future at Hanna's side…

We discussed the legal aspects of the matter and decided that it was necessary to obtain scientific certificates from renowned medical authorities, which were needed to justify my petition.

With copies of these certificates, I applied to the Minister of the Interior, who replied that he was not the proper addressee. Although my lawyer had immediately pointed out the futility of this step, I still had hoped to spare myself going through all the official channels, as my case was so unusual. My lawyer then sent the petition to the proper place. The senior civil servants responsible proved to be very obliging. At the end of December 1906, after correspondence, and after I had been personally interviewed repeatedly, we received the news that my petition had been granted.

I had already begun to change outward appearance before official permission had been granted. As a first step, my hair had to be cut. When I had this done, I was still wearing women's clothing. The barber thought it was a sin to sacrifice such beautiful hair to a whim.

After my hair had been cut, the shape of my head was more visible; I was told that the masculinity of my expression now came into its own, and I thus looked quite odd in women's clothing. Some days later, I had myself measured for my first frock coat.

The first time I walked across the road in men's clothing. I felt such a great of uneasiness that I would have liked to turn back. Men's clothing is quite a bit lighter than ladies'; the wind had free access to my body, and, at first it seemed improper to be going out in trousers without skirts on top. I imagined that everyone on the street was staring at me. This insecure feeling lasted for several days, until at last I grew accustomed to it. Another thing however to which I grew accustomed only with great difficulty, was greeting people. I repeatedly forgot to raise my hat, and nodded like a lady. Once when I asked directions of a gentleman in the street, his answer was so unfriendly that it surprised me, until it occurred to me that I had forgotten to raise my hat.

Altogether, social niceties caused me many a difficulty at first. For example, I had to greet the older gentlemen among my acquaintances before they greeted me now, which I regularly forgot to do, and had to be on my guard when conversing with ladies not to touch on subjects that a gentleman does not usually discuss with them. So as not to offend anyone, I was at first very taciturn; but I soon returned to my original uninhibited manner.

At this time, I first had myself photographed again and sent Hanna my picture. In general people were of the opinion that I had changed for the better. She thought so too, and I was very pleased that she did.

A gentleman whom I had known for years before my change had to be told of my secret. Later he assured me that I seemed more familiar to him in the first half hour of our new acquaintance than I had during all the years before.

Recently, I made my first long journey wearing men's clothing. Whereas formerly I had always spent the night in the ladies' compartment, I was now forced to make do with the non-smokers' compartment. It was a strange feeling to spend the entire night together with so many men at such close quarters for the first time. So it seems that education and habit are able to produce strong inhibitions.

My body, which was no longer constricted by bodices and other tight articles of clothing, developed freely and became stronger. I now do gymnastics and other kinds of exercise to compensate for the forced prevention of a healthy development. These efforts have been rewarded by success. I have become stronger and broader, my posture is freer, and physically nothing is likely to remain of my girlhood years other than a slight furrow left behind from tight lacing.

Sorrow and grief had made me old; now I look happy and young—alas, far too young.

The greater freedom that I now enjoy has not really changed my outlook, because my attitudes and opinions were always masculine. Some new aspects have, however been revealed to me.

These small freedoms are extremely pleasant. I can return home late at night without having to fear that every stupid lad may molest me; I am now at liberty to smoke in the street undisturbed and enjoy all the other little privileges that the lords of creation have reserved for themselves.

Some girlish tenderness of feeling remains to me. I do not enjoy listening to obscene stories and humorous magazines and pictures "for gentlemen only" nauseate me. Seldom have so many women unveiled their souls to a man as have to me. I feel sympathy and brotherly love for all women.

We met again, Hanna and I. My transformation did nothing to change the feeling of joy that flows through us as soon as we see each other. We feel an overpowering sense of belonging together and have decided to unite forever as soon as possible…

At the end of my book, I should like to say a word to all mothers. All the pain and confusion that I suffered and that made my life bitter came from a false sense of shame that seeks to veil all things sexual as being unclean…

If you lack courage to speak openly to your children, see to it that it becomes the duty of schools to do so. Think of the dark hours and confusion that you once met with in your own youth. How much suffering and how many battles would I have been spared if, either at home or at school, one single person had spoken earnestly and honestly to me about my sex. My youth would not have been so dark and devoid of joy.

Honest knowledge never drags one down, but rather liberates and elevates one! Where is the mother who does not wish to see her child pure and free? Therefore, let us show our children the paths that lead to purity and freedom! With joyous eyes, I look to the future that lies before me like an endless landscape, filled with sunlight. May life around us rage and thunder, I shall at last enter the battle of life as a person with equal rights, a strong will, and a glad heart.

This book tells a true story, the story of a pitiful life that had to pass through much confusion before the lonely wanderer found the right path. I did not want to write to write this book, but others convinced me that I owed it to mankind as contribution to modern psychology and that I should write it in the interest of science and truth.

Karl M Baer, *Aus eines Mannes Mädchenjahren* (Berlin: Gustav Rieckes Buchhandlung, 1907), as translated in Deborah Simon (ed. and trans.), *Memoirs of a Man's Maiden Years by N.O. Body* (University of Pennsylvania Press, 2006), 7–10, 64–65, and 98–108. Copyright © 2006 University of Pennsylvania Press. Reprinted with permission of the University of Pennsylvania Press.

Further Reading

Funke, Jana. "The Case of Karl M.[artha] Baer: Narrating 'Uncertain' Sex." In *Sex, Gender and Time in Fiction and Culture* (ed. Ben Davies and Jana Funke, Palgrave, 2011), 132–153.

Gilman, Sander. "Whose Body Is It, Anyway? Hermaphrodites, Gays, and Jews in N.O. Body's Germany." In *Jewish Masculinities* (ed. Benjamin Maria Baader, Sharon Gillerman, and Paul Lerner, Indiana University Press, 2012), 131–151.

Koch, Michaela. *Discursive Intersexions: Daring Bodies between Myth, Medicine, and Memoir* (Berlin: Transcript Verlag, 2017).

Sabran, Adi, and Iris Rachamimov. "Bein qiflei hahatsa'it: ḥayyav hashonim shel Karl M. Baer." *Zmanim* 131 (2015), 22–33.

Wallach, Kerry. *Passing Illusions: Jewish Visibility in Weimar Germany* (University of Michigan Press, 2017).

69. A Yiddish Play Presents a Lesbian Romance Onstage (Berlin, 1907)

The remarkable play *Got fun Nekome* (God of Vengeance) was written in Switzerland in 1906 by the Yiddish novelist and playwright Sholem Asch (1880–1957), and premiered at the Deutsches Theater in Berlin in 1907. Performed over the next two decades throughout Europe and North America, in Yiddish as well as several other European languages, the play follows Yankl Tsaptshovitsh, the owner of a brothel in an unnamed Polish town, who is attempting to find a good match for his beloved daughter Rivkele. Unbeknownst to Yankl, who has forbidden Rivkele from going "downstairs" to the brothel, she develops a relationship with the prostitutes working there, especially one named Manke. Rivkele and Manke share tender declarations of love, kissing and embracing each other on stage, and they decide to run away together, where "we'll be together, all day long, all night long. There'll be no father, there'll be no mother...We'll be alone all day long." At the last minute, they are discovered by Yankl; he angrily rejects his daughter, casting her into the brothel, and discards the Torah scroll he had commissioned for her in hopes of attracting a suitor. The play wrestles with questions of boundaries: who is in, and who is out? What is kept "downstairs" and what can travel? Questions of knowledge are also central: what do the characters (and the audience) know about their sexuality, and that of others? When Yankl confronts his daughter, he asks her, "Are you still a chaste Jewish girl? Tell me—right here and now!" But Rivkele can only answer, "I don't know..." For the original audience of *God of Vengeance*, it seems that some configurations of sexuality were unknowable, or at least, ineffable; at the same time, their presentation on stage renders those same experiences visible and knowable in a new way. The play initially received criticism for its unflinching portrayal of the Jewish underworld, and for the shocking treatment of a Torah scroll; however, when the play premiered in English in New York, in 1922, it immediately drew a new level of controversy for the lesbian relationship presented onstage, culminating in the cast's arrest for obscenity in March 1923 (see source 78).

[Act One]

SORRE: (*Starts quickly straightening the room, setting the table. Calls to RIVKELE in the next room:*) Rivkele, Rivkele, come and help me. They'll be here any minute with the Torah scroll.

RIVKELE: (*Appears in the door, unsure of herself.*) Is Papa still here?

SORRE: No, darling, he's gone to the synagogue with Eli and the scribe to bring back some people. The rabbi will also be coming.

RIVKELE: (*Holds up the scroll vestment.*) See how nicely I've embroidered it?

SORRE: (*Busy:*) I see, I see. Comb your hair, get dressed. The minyan's on its way. The rabbi…

RIVKELE: I'll call Manke to come up and do my hair. I love it when she combs my hair. She does it so beautifully, my hair gets so straight. Her hands are so cool. (*She takes an object and taps on the floor, calling:*) Manke, Manke!

SORRE: (*Frightened:*) What are you doing, Rivkele? Don't! Papa's gonna holler. It's not proper for you to be friendly with Manke. You're the daughter of respectable parents and you're gonna get married soon. You're being offered matches, fine matches with Talmudic scholars.

RIVKELE: I love Manke so much.

SORRE: It's scandalous for you to be friendly with Manke. You're a respectable child and you ought to make friends with respectable children. You're being offered matches, fine matches. Papa is having a look at a possible bridegroom for you. Eli said. (*Goes into the other room.*) You've gotta wash up and get dressed. The guests will be here any moment.

RIVKELE: A bridegroom? What's he like, Mommy?

SORRE: (*From the other room:*) A darling boy, a treasure. And a marvelous scholar, from a wonderful family.

(*MANKE appears in the opposite doorway, first poking her head in, her finger coquettishly beckoning to RIVKELE. RIVKELE steals over to MANKE winking at her. The room starts growing dark.*)

RIVKELE: (*Hugs MANKE, while talking to SORRE in the next room.*) Is he good looking, Mommy?

(*MANKE kisses RIVKELE passionately.*)

SORRE: (*From the other room:*) Yes, dearest, a good-looking bridegroom, with black ear locks, and he's got a satin coat and a velvet cap, he dresses like a rabbi. In fact, Eli said that his father is a rabbi.

RIVKELE: (*in MANKE's arms, stroking MANKE's cheeks.*) Where is he going to live, Mommy?

SORRE: (*From the other room:*) In your room, where we'll keep the Torah scroll. The two of you will live there and he'll be studying the holy Torah.

RIVKELE: (*In MANKE's arms:*) Will he love me, Mommy?

SORRE: (*From the other room:*) Very much, my dearest darling, very much. The two of you will have respectable children, decent children…

(*While they're talking, the curtain slowly descends, with RIVKELE in MANKE's arms.*)

[Act Two]

RIVKELE: (*Sticks her head with its black hair through the small window. She's wearing a nightgown and a flimsy shawl. She calls softly:*) Manke, Manke, did you call me?

MANKE: (*Takes a chair, puts it under the window, climbs on the chair, and takes hold of* RIVKELE'S *hands.*) Yes, Rivkele, I called you. C'mon, let's go out and stand in the May shower and pour water on each other and grow taller.

RIVKELE: (*From the window:*) Shhh, speak more softly. I sneaked out of bed so Papa wouldn't hear me…I'm scared he'll beat me.

MANKE: Don't be scared of your father, he won't wake up that soon. C'mon, let's stand out in the rain. I'll loosen your hair. (*She undoes* RIVKELE'S *black braids.*) There, and now I'll wash your hair in the rain.

RIVKELE: I'm only wearing a nightgown. I've been lying awake all night waiting for Papa to fall asleep, so I can sneak down to see you. I heard you tapping and I slipped out of bed. I tiptoed very softly, on my bare feet, so Papa wouldn't hear me.

MANKE: (*Hugs her passionately.*) C'mon, Rivkele. I'm gonna wash your eyes in rainwater. The night is so sweet, the rain is so warm, and everything is so fragrant in this air. C'mon.

RIVKELE: Shush…Shush…I'm scared of my father. He beat me…He locked the door and he hid the key near the Torah scroll. I've been lying awake all night. I heard you calling me. You called me so softly. I was so anxious to see you. So I stole the key from the Ark of the scroll. My heart kept pounding so loudly…pounding so loudly…

MANKE: Wait, Rivkele…Wait…I'll come out to you. (*jumps down from the chair, leaves the basement.*) I'm coming out to you…I'm coming to you. (*She exits.* RIVKELE *vanishes from the window…*)

(*A long pause, the stage remains empty. Then* MANKE *enters, snuggling with* RIVKELE. *They are both wrapped in a wet shawl. Their hair, washed in the rain, is disheveled. Water drips to the floor from their soaked clothing. They are both barefoot.* HINDL *stands behind her cubicle curtain, eavesdropping on them.*)

MANKE: (*Speaks with restrained love and passion, her voice is soft, but deep and resonant.*) Are you cold, Rivkele? Snuggle with me…Snuggle up close to me. Warm up against me, that's so nice…C'mon, let's sit down here on the sofa. (*Leads her over to a sofa, they sit down.*) That's right, that's right…Press your face against my breasts…That's right, that's right…And caress me with your body…It's so cool, like water running between us…(*Pause.*) I uncovered your breasts and I washed them in rainwater that ran over my hands… Your breasts are so white and firm…And the blood in your breasts becomes cool under my hand, like white snow…like frozen water…And they smell like grass in the meadows…And I loosened your hair…Like this…(*Runs her fingers through* RIVKELE's *hair.*) I held your hair like this in the rain and I washed it…And your hair smells so good…like the rain. (*She buries her face in* RIVKELE's *hair.*) It smells so sweetly of May showers…so light, so soft… and so fresh…like the grass in the meadow…like apples on a tree…Cool me like this with your hair…(*She washes her face in* RIVKELE's *hair.*) Cool me like this…No, wait…Let me comb your hair like a bride's hair, parted down the middle with two long black braids. (*Combs* RIVKELE's *hair.*) Do you want to, Rivkele? Yes? Do you want to?

RIVKELE: (*Nods:*) Yes, yes.

MANKE: You'll be the bride. A beautiful bride. Friday evening, you're sitting at the *Shabbes* table with your papa and your mama. I'm the bridegroom, your bridegroom visiting you…Do you want me to, Rivkele? Do you want me to? No?

RIVKELE: (*Nods:*) Yes, Manke.

MANKE: Wait, wait. Your parents have gone to bed…The bride and groom have met here at the table, we're embarrassed…Do you want to? No?

RIVKELE: (*Nods:*) Yes, Manke.

MANKE: Then we huddle together: You're my bride after all, and I'm your bridegroom. We hug (*hugs her*) very tight and we kiss very quietly, we kiss like this…(*They kiss.*) We blush so deeply, we're so embarrassed…Isn't it good, Rivkele, isn't it good?

RIVKELE: Yes, Manke. Yes.

MANKE (*Lowers her face, whispers into* RIVKELE'*s ear:*) And then we lie down in one bed, nobody knows about it, only you and I, like this. (*Hugs her tight.*) Would you like to sleep with me all night, like this, in one bed? Would you like to?

RIVKELE: (*Hugging her:*) I do…I do….

MANKE: (*Embracing her:*) Come to me, come to me.

RIVKELE: (*Very softly:*) I'm scared of Papa…He's going to wake up.

MANKE: Wait, Rivkele, wait. (*Thinks for a while.*) Do you want to come away with me? We'll be together, all day long, all night long. There'll be no father, there'll be no mother. No one will yell or hit. We'll be alone all day long. It'll be so much fun—would you like that, Rivkele? Would you like that?

RIVKELE: (*Closes her eyes.*) Papa won't know?

MANKE: No, we'll run away together, this very night, to Hindl's place. She's got a room in Shloyme's apartment. She told me so. You'll see how good it'll be. Young men will visit us, officers. We'll be alone all day. We'll dress up like the officers and ride around on horses. C'mon, Rivkele, would you like to? Would you like to?

RIVKELE (*Her heart pounding:*) Papa won't hear us?

MANKE: No, no. He won't hear us, he's dead to the world. Listen, you can hear him snorin'. (*Hurries into* HINDL'*s cubicle, grabs her hand.*) Do you have a place? Quick, take us there!

HINDL: (*Jumping up:*) Yes, yes, quickly, to Shloyme. (*She grabs a dress, tosses it over to* RIVKELE.) He'll take care of us.

MANKE: (*Quickly dresses* RIVKELE.) You'll see, it's gonna be so good, it's gonna be so much fun.

(*They get dressed, putting on anything they happen to grab—a shawl, a coat. Then they slowly go up the stairs…*)

[Act Three]

[Yankl and Sorre have found Rivkele with Manke, and confront her.]

YANKL: (*Hastily:*) I want to ask her just one question. Just one question. Tell me the truth. I won't hit you, I won't touch you, it's not your fault…(*Unable to pronounce the words:*) Tell me straight out, the…The…Tell me the whole truth. The truth.

SORRE: What sort of truth is she supposed to tell you? What do you want from her?

YANKL: I'm not asking you. (*Stands up, grabs Rivkele's hand.*) Don't be embarrassed in front of me. I'm a father, a father. You can tell me anything. Tell me plainly. Are you still…Are you still as pure as you were when you left here? Are you still a chaste Jewish girl?

SORRE: (*Pulls Rivkele from her father's grasp.*) What do you want from her? The girl's done nothing wrong, leave her alone.

YANKL: (*Clutches Rivkele's hand, tries to peer into her eyes.*) Tell me the truth, I *will* believe you! Look into my eyes…Right into my eyes…Are you still a chaste Jewish girl? Look into my eyes, right into my eyes! (*Tries to look into her eyes. Rivkele still hides her face in her shawl.*)

SORRE: Why won't you pull down your shawl? Why are you wearing it indoors? (*Yanks down her shawl. Rivkele resists, hides her face in her coat.*)

YANKL: (Hollers:) Tell me now! Don't be ashamed! I won't do anything to you. (*Clutches her hand, draws her over, and peers into her eyes.*) Are you still a chaste Jewish girl? Tell me—right here and now!

RIVKELE: (*Still trying to hide her face in her coat.*) I don't know…

YANKL: (*Hollers:*) You don't know…You don't know? Then who *should* know? What do you mean, you don't know? Tell me the truth. Tell me, are you still—

RIVKELE: Oh, but it was all right for Mama? And it was all right for Papa? I know everything. (*Buries her face in her hands.*) Hit me, hit me! (*Sorre runs over to her with raised hands, ready to hit* RIVKELE. YANKL *shoves his wife away with one blow. Pale, he sits down on his chair, breathing heavily.* RIVKELE *sits down on the floor, weeping loudly. A long, silent pause.* SORRE *wanders about the room, visibly at a loss as to what to do next. After a long pause she takes the broom and begins sweeping silently, almost stealthily. Then she goes over to* RIVKELE, *takes her hand, helps her to her feet, and leads her into* RIVKELE's *room, remaining silent all the while.* YANKL *remains immobile.* RIVKELE *exits…)*

[*A* STRANGER *has come with the matchmaker to ask for* RIVKELE's *hand for his son.*]

YANKL: (*Goes into* RIVKELE's *room and violently drags her out by her hand, she is disheveled and only half dressed. He points to her.*) A chaste Jewish maiden will marry your son. She will have chaste Jewish children like any other Jewish wife. (*To* SORRE:) Don't you agree? (*Laughs wildly to* STRANGER.) Yes, yes, my friend, she'll be a chaste Jewish wife. My wife will lead her to the wedding canopy… Down to the whorehouse! Down there! (*Points to the basement.*) To the whorehouse! (*Drags* RIVKELE *by her hair to the door.*) To the whorehouse!

SORRE: (*Dashes over to them wildly.*) Help, everybody, he's gone crazy! (*She tries to pull* RIVKELE *away from him.* YANKL *shoves her away, drags* RIVKELE *out by her hair.*)

YANKL: Down to the whorehouse! (*Exits with* RIVKELE. *We can still hear her weeping.*)

STRANGER: (*Amazed and alarmed:*) What's going on here?

(ELI *winks at him. Tugs at his sleeve and nods toward the door.* STRANGER *stands there, dumbfounded.* ELI *pulls him toward the door, they leave. Pause.*)

YANKL: (*Grabs* ELI *by the door and pulls him back in.*) Take along the Torah scroll. I don't need it anymore.

CURTAIN

Sholem Asch, *Got fun Nekome* (1907), as translated in Joachim Neugroschel, "God of Vengeance," *Pakn-Treger: the journal of the National Yiddish Book Center* 23 (1996), pp. 16–39.

Further Reading

Hoffman, Warren. *The Passing Game: Queering Jewish American Culture* (Syracuse University Press, 2009).

Seidman, Naomi. "Staging Tradition: Piety and Scandal in God of Vengeance." In *Sholem Asch Reconsidered* (ed. Nanette Stahl, Beinecke Rare Book and Manuscript Library, 2004), 51–61.

Warnke, Nina. "God of Vengeance: the 1907 Controversy Over Art and Morality." In *Sholem Asch Reconsidered* (ed. Nanette Stahl, Beinecke Rare Book and Manuscript Library, 2004), 63–77.

70. A Russian Scholar Describes the "Maiden of Ludmir" (Saint Petersburg, 1909)

Throughout the history of Hasidism (see source 54), there have been women who took on the role of a *rebbe* with followers. The most famous of these is Khane-Rokhl Verbermakher (born ca. 1805), known as the Maiden of Ludmir (or Ludomir, today Volodymyr-Volynskyi, Ukraine). The adoption of a leadership role traditionally reserved for men, according to the stories told about these figures, went along with other gender-transgressive practices like wearing the ritual prayer garments of *tallit* and *tefillin*; in other ways, their behavior resembles other female figures in the shtetl, like the *firzogerin* (women's prayer leader) or *opshprekherke* (folk healer). This 1909 article, by the Russian Jewish historian and folklorist Samuel Abba Horodezky (1871–1957), is the first published account of the Maiden of Ludmir, and Horodezky returned to the topic several other times over the following decades. Here, he portrays her not only as praying "three times a day like a man" and wearing *tallit* and *tefillin*, but also as possessing the soul of an unknown male *tsaddik* (saint). But with almost no direct evidence from these "female rebbes" themselves, it is impossible to say anything about their own self-conceptions of gender. Did they see themselves as masculine women? As men? Possessed by the soul of a deceased *tsaddik*? Beyond the binary systems of gender? How they understood their communal role—as rebbes, pious maidens, folk healers, "holy virgins," or something else entirely—is equally unknowable.

The Maiden of Ludmir (Die Ludmirer Moid)*

Within Hasidism the woman is generally assigned a modest, passive role: she can, from time to time, passively approach the "tzadik," pour her soul out to him, and receive from him the principles of blessedness. Very rarely in the history of Hasidism do we encounter active womanly natures which have an influence on their surroundings. To the number of such holy women approaching the level of "tzadik" belongs an enigmatic personage, appearing in the second quarter of the nineteenth century and memorialized in folk tales by the name of "the Maiden of Ludmir."

She was born in the city of Ludmir or Ludomir (Vladimir-Volynskii) around 1815. Her name was Khana-Rokhel'. She was the only daughter of her father Monesh Verbermakher, a prosperous and somewhat bookish man; her mother was also adept in religiously-edifying women's literature. As a girl, from an early age, she drew attention to herself with the beauty of her face and her rare intellectual abilities. Even as a child, she studied the Bible in the original and learned to write in ancient Hebrew; then she imbibed much from the Haggadah, the midrash, and morally-edifying books. The young girl prayed three times a day like a man, and prayed with ecstasy that caused astonishment in all those around her. The locals said that the daughter of Rabbi Monesh was worthy of being made a tzadik.

The extraordinary merits of the young girl, on one hand, were the good fortune of her father—on the other hand, they made Khana-Rokhel', just as soon as she had left childhood behind, an object of heightened attention of "shadkhens" [matchmakers]: parents looking for a daughter-in-law. She was approached with brilliant marriage proposals from other cities, but old Monesh declined all of them because he didn't want to offer a large dowry. Before long, Khana-Rokhel' was paired with a youth from her own native city. These events caused an upheaval in her spiritual life. Knowing her fiancé from childhood, the young woman fell in love with him with all the passion of her ardent soul; she felt the impulse to meet with him, to speak one-on-one with him, to pour out her soul to him; but according to the customs of that time, this was considered impossible: rendezvous between bride-to-be

---

*Footnote in text: "Stories of old Volyn locals who personally knew and remembered the Maiden of Ludmir have served as the materials for this article."

and groom-to-be were strictly forbidden. The young girl fell ill as a result of her longing for her beloved. Nobody paid attention to this. Her father was constantly busy, and her mother, who loved her very much, had died before then. Then the young woman began to isolate herself from people. She spent entire days in her room, leaving home only to visit the grave of her mother and cry out her grief there.

One day—as the legends tell—when Khana-Rokhel' sat at the grave of her mother, she fell into unconsciousness. When she awoke, it was already evening, and around her in the cemetery was not a single person. It was eerie to the young woman in this kingdom of the dead; very frightened, she set home running home across the old cemetery, where the holy men of old were buried. Along the way she stumbled and fell upon one of these holy graves. She cried out and fainted. The guard of the old cemetery heard her scream and went up to the young woman, and when she came to, took her to her parents' house. In the weeks after this, she was dangerously ill; she didn't say a single word. The doctors had given up on any cure of the patient. But one day, she suddenly called to her father to her and told him: "I was just now in heaven, present at the proceeding of the heavenly "beitdin" (court) and there they gave me a new, very elevated soul." After a few days she recovered.

From that time onward, she began to behave as a man: she wore the "tallis-koton" with "tzitzis" (a short four-cornered breastplate with "filaments of vision"), clothed herself in the prayer robe ("tallis") and phylactery ("tefillin"), and abandoned herself all day to prayer and the Torah. She replaced her fiancé with the act of prayer ("tnoim"): she decided not to get married, because she had risen above the world of the flesh.

In the meantime, the father of the holy "virgin" had died and left her a large estate. She built a new "bes-gamedrash" [*beis hamedrash*, i.e. House of Study] with a separate room.* In this room she sat constantly praying and studying Torah.

The glory of the "Maiden of Ludmir" spread throughout all the nearby shtetls and settlements, and many people, women and men, went to her on

---

*Footnote in text: "This tabernacle still exists in Vladimir, and is known under the name "Grünstübel" [*sic*; actually *gornshtibl*, 'little second-story room']. Hasids of the Rotmistr congregation pray there."

pilgrimage as to a holy person; even scholars and rabbis went to see her. But she wouldn't let anyone close to her. The majority of the time she sat alone in her room, in front of the open doors, and the people, gathering in the neighboring hall of the "bes-gamedrash," listened to her speak through the open doors.

She was known as a miracle worker. It was said that she knew the secrets of heaven and could heal the sick. She indeed healed the patients who came to her with various herbs.

Little by little around her formed a particular group of hasids, which were called the "hasids of the Maiden of Ludmir." She prayed in her "bes-game-drash," and on Saturdays, during the "third meal," they gathered to hear her preaching: the words of the preacher wafted to the listeners sitting in the tab-ernacle from the neighboring room, where the holy maiden isolated herself.

The famous tzadiks of the time expressed astonishment at the matter of a new colleague in woman's dress. Some traveled to her to see this phenom-enon; she called every one of her visitors by name, even the most obscure of them. But in the end many tzadiks began to doubt: perhaps an "unclean force" was speaking from the lips of this young woman? They began to try to convince her to change her way of life and get married; but she didn't even want to hear of this. Only after some time, when the well-known tzadik Mo-tel' Chernobyl'skii [Mordekhai of Chernobyl, 1770–1837, and Horodezky's own great-grandfather] began to persuade her, did she acquiesce and marry a rabbi.

Rabbi Motel'—as the legends say—said of the Maiden of Ludmir: "The soul of we-know-not-which tzadik has been reborn in this woman, but in any case it is hard for the soul of a tzadik to find peace in the body of a woman." He wanted to recast the soul of this woman into a lower, normal state by way of marriage, the arousal of womanly feelings and relations. But he did not succeed in this. The husband of the maiden was frightened to have relations with such a holy woman, and soon divorced her. She married a second time—and again it ended in divorce. Thus the Maiden of Ludmir remained a virgin until her death.

However, after her second "marriage," although it was fictitious, her al-lure began to lessen. People no longer traveled to her for "miracles," but rather considered her only a holy woman ("tzadikes"), gifted in some measure with the "holy spirit" ("ruach ga-kodesh" [*ruaḥ haqodesh*]), as reported by one of her personal acquaintances.

In the last years of her life, the Maiden of Ludmir departed to live in the Holy Land.

Samuel Abba Horodezky, "Ludmirskaya Dyeva (Die Ludmirer Moid)," *Evreiskaia Starina* 1:2 (1909), 219–222. Translated from Russian by Jamie Parsons. Copyright © 2019 Print-O-Craft Press.

Further Reading

Deutsch, Nathaniel. *The Maiden of Ludomir: A Jewish Holy Woman and Her World* (University of California Press, 2003).

Kauffman, Tsippi. "'Outside the Natural Order': Temerl, the Female Hasid." *Studia Judaica* 19:1 (2016), 87–109.

Lewis, Justin Jaron. "Eydele, the Rebbe: Shifting Perspectives on a Jewish Gender Transgressor." *Journal of Modern Jewish Studies* 6:1 (2007), 21–40.

Rapoport-Albert, Ada. "On Women in Hasidism: S. A. Horodecky and the Maid of Ludmir Tradition." In *Jewish History: Essays in Honour of Chimen Abramsky* (eds. Ada Rapoport-Albert and Steven J. Zipperstein, London: Halban, 1988), 495–525.

71. An Anglo-Baghdadi Poet Writes in Gratitude to a Homosexual Activist (Kent, 1911)

Siegfried Sassoon (1886–1967) was an Anglo-Jewish poet, a scion of the wealthy Sassoon family of Baghdadi origin. Siegfried's Indian-born grandparents, Sassoon David Sassoon and Farha (Flora) Reuben, were prominent philanthropists in the Anglo-Jewish community, but when their son (Siegfried's father), Alfred Ezra Sassoon, married a non-Jewish woman, Theresa Thornycroft, they broke off contact with him. In his writing and his personal life, Siegfried Sassoon wrestled with the meaning of his Jewish heritage, a conflict made only more complex after his father's early death. Another struggle for Sassoon was coming to terms with his homosexuality, something which was not uncommon in the upper-class British society of his time but was forbidden to discuss or acknowledge. In this letter, he pours out his inner feelings to Edward Carpenter (1844–1929), a British socialist and activist for homosexual rights.

In his magnum opus, *The Intermediate Sex: A Study of Some Transitional Types of Men and Women* (1908), Carpenter argues that "Uranians" represent a separate class of people with special qualities, who deserve to be valued and given distinctive place in society (as did Raffalovich before him; see source 64). In this letter, Sassoon explains to Carpenter that reading *The Intermediate Sex* has "opened up the new life" for him, and allowed him to accept his own sexual inclinations as healthy and natural. He evens adds that his brother, Hamo Watts Sassoon is "exactly the same," and speculates that his father "had a strong vein of the homosexual nature in him." During the First World War, Sassoon went on to serve with distinction, and his war poetry is regarded as one of the finest articulations of anti-jingoist sentiment and the horrors of war, alongside the work of his friends Robert Graves and Wilfred Owen.

WEIRLEIGH, PADDOCK WOOD—KENT

Dear Edward Carpenter,

I am sending you a few sonnets; not for what is <u>in them</u>, but <u>to thank you</u> for all that I reverence and am grateful for in you & your writings. It was not until October last year, when I was just 24, that, by an accident, I read your "Intermediate Sex," & have since read "Towards Democracy," & "Who Shall Command the Heart." I am afraid I have not studied socialism sufficiently to be in sympathy with what I know of it; but your words have shown me all that I was blind to before, & have opened up the new life for me, after a time of great perplexity and unhappiness. Until I read the "Intermediate Sex," I knew absolutely nothing of that subject, (& was entirely <u>unspotted</u>, as I am now), but life was an empty thing, & what ideas I had about homosexuality were absolutely prejudiced, & I was in such a groove that I couldn't allow myself to be what I wished to be, & the intense attraction I felt for my own sex was almost a subconscious thing, & my antipathy for women a mystery to me. It was only by chance that (when I had read y[ou]r book) I found my brother (a year younger) was exactly the same. I cannot say what it has done for me. I am a different being, & have a definite aim in life & something to lean on, though, of course the misunderstanding & injustice is a bitter agony sometimes. But having found out all about it, I am old enough to realise the better or nobler way, & to avoid the mire which might have snared me, had I known 5 years ago. I write to you as the leader & the prophet.

I am afraid my life is occupied a good deal with things that you may not approve. I live here mostly, in the country with my mother, cricket in summer, & riding & hunting in winter; & I am thankful to say, I am as good as those others in their sports, & have some of their strength & courage. My other life is all taken up with poetry & an intense passion for music (though I am <u>not a brilliant</u> player). Anyhow I am not mixed up with smartness & luxurious social doings, as my name might lead you to think. I am a nephew of Hamo Thornycroft, the sculptor. I send a photograph, as I know you are interested in our cases, which is the reason why I have written you so much in the egotistic strain. The only other work I have read is Symond's "Problem in Greek Ethics." My father died in 1894 aged 35. He was a nephew of Sir Albert Sassoon, & those other plutocrats; he was intensely musical, & I think had a strong vein of the homosexual nature in him.

I hope you are well and I am sure you are happy & at peace with this bitter world. May your reward be in the generations to come, as I pray mine may be. I am not religious, but I try to believe that our immortality is <u>to be</u> (in those immortals whom our better lives may lead to, & whose immortal ways are marred and kept back by the grossness of unworthy souls). I take as my watchword those words of yours —

Strength to perform, & pride to suffer without sign —

From

SIEGFRIED SASSOON

The most recent photo was taken at Oxford, by Nevill Forbes, who has spoken to me about you a great deal.

Siegfried Sassoon to Edward Carpenter, July 27, 1911. Sheffield City Archives, Edward Carpenter Collection, MSS 386-179. My thanks to Alison Darby for retrieving this document.

Further Reading

Caesar, Adrian. *Taking it Like a Man: Suffering, Sexuality, and the War Poets* (Manchester University Press, 1993).

Lawson, Peter. "Siegfried Sassoon: The Great War, poetry, and Jewishness." *Jewish Quarterly* 47:1 (2000), 59–64.

Moorcroft, Jean. *Siegfried Sassoon: The Making of a War Poet: A Biography, 1886–1918* (Duckworth, 1998) and *Siegfried Sassoon: The Journey from the Trenches: A Biography, 1918–1967* (Routledge, 2003).

Rowbotham, Sheila. *Edward Carpenter: A Life of Liberty and Love* (London: Verso Books, 2009).

72. Magnus Hirschfeld Records Life Story of Jewish Lesbian (Berlin, 1914)

Magnus Hirschfeld (1868–1935) was a German Jewish physician and sexologist, and one of the earliest modern activists to advocate for the civil and legal rights of homosexual and transgender people. In 1897 he founded the *Wissenschaftlich-humanitäres Komitee* (Scientific-Humanitarian Committee) to attempt to repeal Paragraph 175, the section of the German Penal Code that criminalized homosexuality (although it was not repealed until 1987 in East Germany, and 1994 for Germany as a whole—see source 109). This text is an excerpt from his 1914 book *Die Homosexualität des Mannes und des Weibes* (The Homosexuality of Men and Women), which was based on the responses to his "Psycho-biological questionnaire" that he collected between 1900 and 1913; he claims to have received 10,000 answers! Here he presents an example of the 127-question form, with the answers of a young Jewish lesbian named Agnes (whether this is a pseudonym or not is impossible to tell). Agnes, from an assimilated Berlin Jewish family (she writes that she "believes in God in Goethe's sense"), describes how she struggled with depression and suicidal thoughts, and a poor relationship with her family, but that she now considers herself "innocent, totally healthy, and natural," and has no desire to change her sexual orientation. Hirschfeld wrote numerous articles and pamphlets, managed a journal for the study of sexuality, and in 1919 founded the *Institut für Sexualwissenschaft* (Institute for the Science of Sexuality). In that year, Hirschfeld also wrote and starred in an educational film, *Anders als die Andern* (Different from the Others), which showed the negative effects of discrimination against homosexuals; this is often described as the first film to portray homosexuality on screen. In addition to his advocacy work, Hirschfeld also pioneered treatment for transgender and intersex people (see source 68), providing counselling and legal assistance, and working with doctors to develop the first hormonal therapies and surgical interventions. Hirschfeld was one of the early targets of Nazi propaganda, which linked antisemitism and homophobia to argue that "Jewish perversion" was destroying the Aryan nation. In May 1933, while Hirschfeld was on a worldwide speaking tour, student members of the National Socialist Student League attacked the *Institut für Sexualwissenschaft* and burned its library in a public bonfire. Hirschfeld died of a heart attack in Nice in 1935, leaving his books and papers to his former partner Karl Giese (1898–1938), and his personal effects to his last partner, Hong Kong sexology student Li Shiu Tong (Tao Li, 1907–1993).

Psychobiological Questionnaire

(*We ask that you please answer the questions on the sheets of paper provided and number each answer to correspond with the number of the question.*)

PRELIMINARY REMARK. *In your own interest and in the interest of scientific research, we ask you please to take the time and make the effort to answer the following questions as precisely and as truthfully as possible.*

You may rely on strict confidentiality. If you have doubts about signing your full name on the questionnaire, which guarantees secrecy under medical and professional confidentiality codes, please provide a number or any initials you choose. In the case of a few questions, for example those referring to parentage and childhood, we recommend you consult older relatives prior to answering the questions. If you do not know the answer to a question, or if you need more time to answer it, please simply leave the space blank. Furthermore, please use the margin to answer questions requiring short answers; otherwise, as much as possible outline your answers in the format of the questionnaire. Finally, it is requested but in no way required that you include photographs of yourself (preferably at different ages), as well as one that approximates the type of person who attracts you.

(I) PERSONAL PARTICULARS

A) NAME, AGE, SEX, RACE, OCCUPATION, ADDRESS, RELIGION.

Agnes W, 18, female, music student, Berlin, Jewish.

(B) MARRIED OR SINGLE?

Single

[...]

(17) DO ANY OF YOUR MALE FAMILY MEMBERS HAVE A FEMININE APPEARANCE?
DO ANY OF YOUR FEMALE FAMILY MEMBERS HAVE A MASCULINE APPEARANCE?

My brother is somewhat of the feminine type, but only a practiced observer would notice it. For example, when he was small, we often used to dress him in girls' clothing and put jewelry on him. Even now he still has the nickname "Gretchen with the pearl necklace," even though he definitely hates the name. The boy takes after my mother: small mouth, thin nose, and a fairer complexion than mine.

(18) DO YOU KNOW OF CASES OF ABNORMAL SEXUAL ORIENTATIONS IN YOUR FAMILY (PARENTS, SIBLINGS, DISTANT RELATIVES)?

A cousin, son of one of my mother's sisters, 30 years of age, is homosexual. As for my father, in spite of his Don Juan nature, I have often observed features that would make you think he was homosexual, but he is totally unaware of the fact. For example, he once got very excited in a restaurant when he saw a young man with a fabulous figure. Totally beside himself, he said, "I could go for a man like that." Another time, he lost his appetite because he saw a young man, whom we had met as a gentleman in a nightclub, now playing second violin in an orchestra. His disappointment made him forget everything else.

[...]

(37) AT WHAT AGE DID YOU FIRST ATTEMPT TO HAVE SEXUAL INTERCOURSE AND UNDER WHAT CIRCUMSTANCES DID THIS OCCUR?

At age 14. In our shop I fell in love with a prostitute. At first I hoped to attract her with mere enthusiasm. Then, only on my part I touched and caressed her. I did not know myself what I wanted from her. Only when I kissed her (her hands, arms, neck, lips, and face) and the like did I get the desire for something more. And suddenly I did find a way to get it. One time we were sitting, pressed close to each other on the stairs, and I suddenly touched her breast with my hand. Of course, she removed my hand. But up until recently we had a relationship with each other that was sometimes very exciting and at other times less so. As far as I can remember, that was the first thing that brought me into the realm of sexual matters.

[...]

(70) HOW RELIGIOUS ARE YOU (PIOUS, INDIFFERENT, SKEPTICAL, BELONG TO A SECT)? WHAT IS YOUR POSITION ON METAPHYSICS, MIRACLES, SUPERSTITIONS, SPIRITUALISM, GHOSTS, PREMONITIONS, MYSTICISM? DO YOU HAVE ANY EX-PERIENCES TO SUPPORT YOUR VIEWS? WHAT ARE THEY? HAVE YOU CHANGED YOUR RELIGION?

> Believe in God in Goethe's sense. I don't pray or go to church. At age 10 I gave up the religion I had as a child, after hearing a discussion at school about the Reformation. I think spiritualism is nonsense. On the other hand, up until just a few years ago I looked for fairies under every stone and rock in the woods. I liked little people. For a long time, I feared and looked for goblins. I was especially attracted to the idea of the existence of elves. One of the fairy tales about them was and continues to be my favorite. Today, except for one's own power, I don't believe in anything.

[...]

(123) HAVE YOU STRUGGLED HARD AGAINST YOUR NATURE? BY WHAT MEANS AND WITH WHAT RESULTS? WERE YOU TREATED BY A PHYSICIAN, WHAT TREATMENT, AND WITH WHAT RESULTS?

> Yes, by separation from the loved one, by forcing myself to date young men, etc. Without success, because afterward, I seized the opportunity all the more vigorously and in any way possible to act on the relentless feelings I had for women. I underwent psychoanalysis, which completely released the suppressed feelings of guilt I had up to that time of my natural tendency.

(124) HAVE YOU FELT VERY UNHAPPY? ARE YOU EVER SICK OF LIFE? DID YOU ATTEMPT SUICIDE? HAVE YOU HAD CONFLICTS (UNPLEASANTNESS) WITH YOUR FAMILY, THE AUTHORITIES, OR WITH OTHER KINDS OF PEOPLE, FOR EXAMPLE, BLACKMAILERS? DID YOUR DRIVE BRING YOU INTO CONFLICT WITH YOUR RE-LIGIOUS OR SOCIAL VALUES?

Knowing that in most people's opinion and even in my own circle I'm considered a "criminal" against natural law, the joy of life and of work is not exactly great. For these reasons, a few times I was suicidal, but at the last moment stopped myself, because I would think about my responsibility to my parents. I took this step repeatedly not out of spite or anything like that, but because I was driven by despair. As a consequence of the lack of means for any kind of expression or understanding and enlightenment about my situation, I looked at my entire life, especially my future, as a failure, as unfulfilled, and as unhappy. By means of psychoanalytic treatment, I took the opposite view. Today, the thought of doing violence to myself never enters my mind. As far as my family is concerned, my mother characterizes my contrary natural tendency as her greatest unhappiness. Consequently, there has been no understanding on her part, and our relationship has suffered for years. I have had no unpleasantness with the authorities; on the other hand, I have been turned away by friends. I never had religious conflicts, but social ones, in so far as people demand and desire a tendency that is not in my nature, and that I should play the role of a young woman, while I am a man. In that way, I continue to come into conflict with the truth and the interpretation of the world.

(125) What do you yourself think about your sexual condition? Do you feel guilty or innocent, diseased or healthy, natural or unnatural? If it were possible, would you wish your nature were different or are you satisfied with your present natural, sexual tendency?

I consider myself innocent, totally healthy, and natural, because it precisely corresponds to my nature. I am satisfied with my natural, sexual tendency and do not think any change is worthwhile or in my case even possible.

(126) With regard to sexual deviations, what experiences have you had with others, such as bisexuality. homosexuality, masochism, etc.? Do you socialize with others who have similar feelings or do you keep to yourself? Do you know people who feel as you do and approximately how many? How many do you think there are and based on what reasons? Have you observed them more frequently in members of certain ranks, classes, or peoples?

With regard to bisexuality, I am convinced that it is more common than normal people think. In the case of women and young women, it occurs because before marriage, especially in the so-called good circles, they have no opportunity at all to provide themselves with a release for their drives. In my opinion, of the few women I knew who were helped by auto-eroticism, most of them followed the bisexual principle and were not in the least hurt by it, at least not those who believed the role of same-sex intercourse was one of last resort. Moreover, I do not consider it to be seduction whenever one or the other goes entirely over to homosexuality. They are not "seduced ones"—nature breaks a path and finds its way, even if a person has at first taken a thousand wrong turns. After a longer or shorter period of time, the "seduced persons" at the right moment return to their familiar element that was perhaps misguided. Or, they were homosexual from the very beginning and sooner or later, perhaps after unhappy experiences, were guided all by themselves to their own natural tendency. I stand alone with my feelings. The idea of a homosexual community does not appeal to me. I cannot sanction the orientation which, solely because of a similar natural tendency, pretends also to create equality in society; normal people also do not form a closed phalanx, and it would never occur to normal people, as it were, to gather some kind of interest from Mr. X or Mr. Y because they loved women! But the conduct of homosexuals themselves, as far as I understand it, has its core in this unity of a common cause and I find that this kind of equality contradicts the foregone conclusion with which they usually are wont to depict their situation. From a matter of course, you just don't become interested in the sameness of a third party. Perhaps you will interject, "birds of a feather flock together" or "artists and others off the beaten track also find themselves joining together." But here, I think, it has to do with an intellectual community, and it is a more accepted bond than that of sexuality!

(127) Have you formed an opinion about the natural goal of your own sexual feelings and what it is?

Up to this day, I cannot base my natural tendency on any kind of intentional influence, unless it is the possibility of a more concentrated influence in areas denied to normal women. People gradually will have to come to realize that intellectual children who pursue an education can have equal value for the world and society as, according to popular logic, women's occupations as wife and mother, a foregone conclusion and natural. You should not criticize contrarysexual women, even if it's only because of the struggle they have in order to have what their normal sisters get handed to them on a silver platter, and because only after thousands of adversities can they make a place for themselves and find the benefits and nature they had from the very beginning.

Magnus Hirschfeld, *Die Homosexualität des Mannes und des Weibes* (Berlin: Louis Marcus Verlagsbuchhandlung, 1914), as translated in *The Homosexuality of Men and Women* (ed. and trans. Michael A. Lombardi-Nash, Prometheus Books, 2000), 290–315.

Further Reading

Bauer, Heike. *The Hirschfeld Archives: Violence, Death, and Modern Queer Culture* (Temple University Press, 2017).

Beachy, Robert. *Gay Berlin: Birthplace of a Modern Identity* (New York: Alfred A. Knopf, 2014).

Dose, Ralf. *Magnus Hirschfeld: The Origins of the Gay Liberation Movement* (trans. Edward Willis, New York Monthly Review Press, 2014).

Mancini, Elena. *Magnus Hirschfeld and the Quest for Sexual Freedom: A History of the First International Sexual Freedom Movement* (Palgrave, 2010).

Plant, Richard. *The Pink Triangle: The Nazi War Against Homosexuals* (Henry Holt, 1988).

73. A Jewish Immigrant's Gender Transition is Revealed After Death (Chicago, 1915)

Like other cases of people who were raised as women but who lived as men (see source 51), it is difficult to know exactly how to interpret the story of Ben Rosenstein; based on the surviving records, it seems most appropriate to use his chosen name and pronouns. Born Ida Weinstein in Poland in 1889, he came to the United States in 1908 and landed in New York, where he joined the thousands of other young Jewish immigrants working low-paying factory jobs. After meeting his partner Pauline Rosenstein, he transitioned to living as a man, apparently inspired in part by the socialist atmosphere of the Jewish labor movement (this article describes him reading Marx and Tolstoy; another article claims that he attended Yiddish socialist lectures on the Lower

East Side). The couple moved to Cleveland, then Detroit, where they are recorded in the 1910 census as the newly-married couple "Bennie [sic] and Pauline Rosenstein." Shortly afterwards, Ben Rosenstein contracted tuberculosis and they moved to Chicago, where despite support from the Hebrew Immigrant Aid Society (HIAS) he died in 1915. The sensationalist Tribune reporter claims that Rosenstein was a "girl husband" whose "industrial marriage" was simply one of economic convenience; but his own testimony—such as his refusal of a women's sanitarium, and his wish to be buried in his suit—suggests that he was sincere and serious about his masculine identity (and his commitment to Pauline). At the same time, some aspects of Ben's identity are paralleled by the presence of masculine women in lesbian communities of the early twentieth century, and Ben and Pauline's relationship might also be understood as an early forerunner of the "butch/femme" culture of working-class lesbians that was common in industrial American cities like Chicago, New York, and Buffalo, in the 1920s–1950s and beyond.

Chicago Daily Tribune, February 8, 1915

DEATH REVEALS GIRL 'WED' GIRL TO FIGHT WANT

"Husband" Got Man's Wage With Mallet After "Industrial Union"—Then Phthisis* Came

Three persons yesterday morning crowded the small bedroom in the rear of the second floor of 2146 Ogden Avenue. They were Mr. and Mrs. Ben Rosenstein and Mrs. Rosenstein's mother. Ben Rosenstein was dying—of tuberculosis at the age of 26.

"Pauline, I am sorry,"—the effort brought coughs. "Please bury me in my first black suit—you know." The young wife at the bedside buried her face in a pillow. The mother at the end of the bed prayed aloud in Hebrew. The dying victim continued between short labored breaths: "We've been happy. I think I have done right. I wish it was true that 'dead men tell no tales.'"

Doctor Reveals Grim Joke

A few hours later Ben Rosenstein died. The undertaker and the doctor revealed the grimness of the dying joke. Ben Rosenstein was a woman.

---

*Tuberculosis.

Seven years ago Ida Weinstein landed at Ellis Island, a flaxen haired, full cheeked Jewish immigrant from Russian Poland. She brought with her to Pittsburgh the two children of her brother-in-law, Sam Cohen. Sam had paid her passage.

Ida Weinstein at 19 years old found that the wage for a girl supply worker in a cigar factory was not one that she could live on. In domestic service she was handicapped by her inexperience and the position did not coincide with her ideas of American liberty.

Read Marx and Tolstoi

She had been reading Marx and Tolstoi. At the Jewish Shelter house in New York she met Pauline Rosenstein, 19 years old, very frail, and out of work. The girls roomed together to cut expense. In their hall bedroom one night they worked out the new idea. Ida, the strong one, could earn a better wage as a man than the two could as women. Ergo, Ida should be a man. They would get married. An "industrial wedding," they called it. So they went to Cleveland and took a room as Mr. and Mrs. Ben Cohen.

The girl husband had clipped her hair and dressed herself in a black suit of clothes. She found factory work and was able to obtain a salary much higher than she had received as a woman. The work was harder—but then, Ida told Pauline she was strong and by extra exertion could work right along with the men in the factory or the workshop.

Bigger Pay Envelope

The extra exertion was forgotten in the joy of the bigger pay envelope. The girls were able to live in better quarters, eat better food, and go to the theater once a week. Pauline worked at such odd jobs as she could get. "Ben Rosenstein and his wife" never owed the room rent and their credit was always good at the delicatessen. They always went out together in the morning. The girl husband donned overalls and swung a mallet in a furniture factory. She was in the packing department. Aside from a high pitched voice, which the other workmen joked about, "Ben Rosenstein" was considered a good employé and a willing worker.

In the course of time they moved to Detroit. Again in the packing department of a furniture factory Ida found wages more satisfactory than those received by the women workers. She was even able at times to leave Pauline at home and adventure into the smoke hazy poolrooms or behind the mystic screens of saloons.

BEGINS TO LOSE WEIGHT

Then the industrial husband began to lose weight. She returned home at night exhausted, and arose in the morning tired. She noticed that the fringe of cropped blonde hair was frequently damp on her forehead. She began to lag at her work. One night she came home with her arms aching and pains running through her back. Her face was damp with perspiration and her hand were cold.

The next morning the boss put another workman in the place of the absent "Ben Rosenstein." The industrial husband had broken down under the burden of a man's work. She lost weight—a severe cold—and she found herself too weak to even search for a new job, much less fill it. Unable to make out on the "woman" salary of Pauline, who was working in a hospital, the two young women invested the remainder of their money in a railroad ticket and came to Chicago. For three or four years the name of "Ben Rosenstein" has been carried on the books of the Jewish Aid society. The charity investigators reported that "Ben Rosenstein had tuberculosis, that he was too weak to do any work, that he was in need of medical attention."

Physicians from the society examined the patient, according to Pauline Rosenstein, and discovered the secret of her hidden sex. They offered to place her in a sanitarium in the country where she might recover. But they insisted she would have to put in the woman's ward. The young woman would not consent.

In the meantime Pauline's mother, who did not know until yesterday that her daughter's "husband" was not a man, was trying to get Pauline to separate from her husband. "He is a sick man, my daughter," she said. "He can't live long. You must get a '*get.*'" A "get" is a ritualistic divorce under the orthodox Hebrew church which a childless wife must receive from her dying husband if she wishes to marry again without the consent of her husband's brothers.

Ida Weinstein's first dress in six years will be a shroud. She will be buried tomorrow. Sam Cohen went out in the backyard last night and burned "Ben Rosenstein's first black suit."

Pauline Rosenstein, 26 years old, sat on a stool next to the stove in the kitchen of her home and told her side of the "economic marriage." Sometimes she referred to her dead companion as "him" and sometimes as "her." "I have been working awful hard while she has been sick," she said, "sometimes eighteen hours a day, just to keep things going along with the money from the society."

"Many times I wished that I had dressed up like a man like Ida. I would have been willing to do it during this last sickness, but I was afraid. Ida was not afraid. I feel I have lost my best friend in the world."

Chicago Daily Tribune, February 9, 1915

DRESS, NOT SUIT, WILL BE SHROUD

Girl "Husband" to Be Buried Today in Woman's Garments

Ida Weinstein will wear today the first dress she has worn in seven years. It will be a burial dress. When the rabbi reads the Hebrew burial service he will say nothing about "Ben Rosenstein"—the name Ida Weinstein assumed to help support her girl "wife," Pauline Rosenstein. The black suit which Ida Weinstein wore when she started the "industrial union" with Pauline Rosenstein will not be the funeral garb of the "girl husband," as she requested while dying in the Ogden avenue flat. An order from the physician caused the suit to be burned.

In the flat where "little Bennie," as the girl furniture worker was known among her friends on the west side, lived Pauline cried and cried yesterday. She sat during most of the day at the head of a black bundle which lay on the floor. Two candles burned at one end of it.

Terrible Fight for Food

"I wish I could bring her back," she said. "What does it matter now, though. She's dead. If I could only tell how much she was to me. I wish I could tell the terrible fights for food that we have made together. Seven years ago 'little Bennie' and I started out to make our way. It was for me that she died." Pauline Rosenstein's mother was in the room. It was cold. Occasionally the mother turned over the few coals in the stove with an iron poker. The stove gave little heat.

"Won't you eat something—just a bite?" the mother asked. "I don't want to be bothered," came back the answer from the girl. "I can't eat. I only want to think of 'little Bennie.'" Relatives of the girl will look after the burial, which will take place this morning.

PHYSICIAN TELLS OF CASE

Dr. Isadore M. Trace of 924 South Ashland avenue, connected with the Jewish Aid Society, said the case was one of the strangest he ever encountered or heard of. Dr Trace was one of the physicians who examined "Ben Rosenstein" when the "girl husband" was seized with tuberculosis and discovered his patient's real sex, although he did not expose the stricken young woman.

"The fact that the girl masqueraded as a man in order that she earn a man's wage to enable herself and Pauline to live," said Dr. Trace, "offers much for economists and social workers to think about. All other considerations set aside, it certainly showed heroic courage."

"Death Reveals Girl 'Wed' Girl to Fight Want," *Chicago Daily Tribune*, February 8, 1915, 1 and 7. "Dress, Not Suit, Will Be Shroud," *Chicago Daily Tribune*, February 9, 1915, p. 13. I thank Jacqueline McCoy at the Cook County Clerk Bureau of Vital Records for her persistence in retrieving Ben/Ida's records.

Further Reading

Cleves, Rachel Hope. "Six Ways of Looking at a Trans Man?: The Life of Frank Shimer (1826–1901)." *Journal of the History of Sexuality* 27.1 (2018): 32–62.

Feinberg, Leslie. *Stone Butch Blues* (Ithaca: Firebrand Books, 1993).

Kennedy, Elizabeth Lapovsky and Madeleine Davis. *Boots of Leather, Slippers of Gold: The History of a Lesbian Community* (Routledge, 1993).

Kosak, Hadassa. *Cultures of Opposition: Jewish Immigrant Workers, New York City, 1881–1905* (SUNY Press, 2000).

Nestle, Joan (ed.). *The Persistent Desire: A Femme-Butch Reader* (New York: Alyson Publications, 1992).

Skidmore, Emily. *True Sex: The Lives of Trans Men at the Turn of the Twentieth Century* (New York University Press, 2017).

74. An Account of Persian Jewish Dancing Boys (Iran, 1916)

Despite rabbinic censure, "dancing boys" remained sources of entertainment throughout Jewish communities in the Levant and Central Asia from the Middle Ages until the twentieth century (see sources 30 and 49). In

Iran, Jews were particularly prominent as musicians and entertainers during the Safavid, Afsharid, and Qajar dynasties (1501–1925). The figure of the "boy dancer" who performed in feminine attire, known as *bacha* (boy) or *zanpush* (woman-dressed), was popular in Jewish and non-Jewish circles in Iran until the mid-twentieth century, when changing social perceptions of gender and sexuality discouraged this practice. The Franco-Jewish philanthropic organization Alliance Israélite Universelle (AIU), in particular, made considerable efforts to "save" these dancers from what they saw as a debauched life of homosexual prostitution. As with the Ottoman *köçeks*, it is difficult to characterize this phenomenon, since it seems to blur the boundaries of sexuality, gender, performance, and identity. While the performers were identified as male, and seem to have lived mostly as men outside of their professional performances, they also occupy similar social roles to other communities of transgender women and non-binary genders, such as the *hijra* of South Asia, and so might be considered as part of a transgender continuum of shared practice. This account of Jewish *zanpush* was published (with an accompanying photograph!) in an American travel magazine by Alfred Heinicke, a writer and photographer from Waldheim (in eastern Germany), who traveled throughout Iran in the first decades of the twentieth century.

Exhibitions of dancing are another very popular form of after-dinner entertainment. This trade prospers among the Jewish families in the country; all the members as a rule taking part in it, the elder ones providing the music and the younger the dancing. Like all Oriental sights, when seen for the first time it is entertaining; but once is quite enough. There is little grace or good taste in the performance, and it is only tolerable after a good dinner and in congenial company.

The warm Eastern nights, the many flickering lights and an animated assembly all laughing and talking merrily give the whole scene an Oriental touch and fascination which recalls the Arabian Nights. The *tamtam*, a three-stringed guitar, and a fiddle are the instruments which accompany the chanting boys.

With fingers pressed into their ears and flushed faces, they begin to chant a love song at the top of their voices. Sadly and slowly it soars higher and higher until it breaks off with a quivering squeak like the snapping of a violin string. These dancing boys wear fancy dresses which look very smart and gay in the lamplight; their hair is worn long, in locks falling down their necks, giving them a girlish appearance.

On their fingers are castanets, and while all the muscles of the lower part of their bodies quiver and shake, the outstretched hands with clicking-castanets keep time to the dance. The dancers are also good acrobats, and now and then a somersault made with a burning candle in each hand arouses a thunder of applause from the excited onlookers. Scene after scene is enacted before the highly interested and very much excited guests. Presently the dancers are treated to smokes, sherbet, sweetmeats, also to arrack; and they begin to mingle freely with the guests, who clap their hands partly in applause, partly to keep time with the shrill music till things culminate in pandemonium.

Moslems, at other times very strict, fraternize with the dancers, embrace them, and even exchange kisses—very Eastern indeed!

Heinicke, Alfred. "The Day of a Well-To-Do Persian." *Travel* 27 (August 1916), 30–33.

Further Reading

Loeb, Lawrence. "Jewish Musicians and the Music of Fars." *Asian Music* 4:1 (1972), 3–13.

Meftahi, Ida. "Dancing Angels and Princesses: the Invention of an Ideal Female National Dancer in Twentieth-Century Iran." In *The Oxford Handbook of Dance and Ethnicity* (ed. Anthony Shay and Barbara Sellers-Young, Oxford University Press, 2016).

Najmabadi, Afsaneh. *Women with Mustaches and Men Without Beards: Gender and Sexual Anxieties of Iranian Modernity* (University of California Press, 2005).

75. Marcel Proust Compares Jews and Inverts (Paris, 1921)

Marcel Proust (1871–1922), one of the foremost French novelists of the early twentieth century, was born to a French Catholic father and an Alsatian Jewish mother (the grand-niece of Adolphe Crémieux, French Minister of Justice and founder of the Alliance Israelite Universelle). Proust was raised as a Catholic, but he was close to his mother's Jewish family and became an active defender of Alfred Dreyfus, the Jewish captain falsely accused of treason in 1894. While Proust was romantically and sexually involved with men, his ambivalence about his sexuality (and his Jewishness) are central themes in his work, especially his magnum opus *À la recherche du temps perdu* (In Search of Lost Time), published in seven volumes between 1913 and 1927. In this excerpt from the fourth volume, *Sodom et Gomorrhe* (Sodom and Gomorrah), Proust characterizes homosexuality not just as an identity but as a kind of ethnic minority, which he explicitly compares to Judaism, painting a complex and effusive picture (with the longest sentence of Proust's writing) of a community with its own gestures, languages, and ways of recognizing each other. He even goes so far as to imagine, with some incredulity, a "Sodomist movement" modeled on Zionism. The book goes on to document the various love affairs, both homosexual and heterosexual, of the men and women in the Narrator's social circles.

[These inverts are] without honor except precariously, without liberty except provisionally until their arrest, without any position but an unstable one—not unlike that of the poet celebrated yesterday in all the salons, applauded in all the theatres of London, but chased the next day from all lodgings without being able to find even a pillow to rest his head, who turns the grindstone like Samson and says: "The two sexes will die, each on their own side" [from Alfred de Vigny, "La Colère de Samson"]; [they are] excluded even (excepting days of great misfortune where the largest number rallies around the victim, like the Jews around Dreyfus), from the sympathy—sometimes from the society—of their fellow kind, who give them the disgust of seeing that which they are, depicted in such a mirror that (unflattering to say the least) accuses them of having all those defects which they would prefer go unremarked in themselves, and which makes them understand that what they call their love (and to which, through wordplay, they annex all of that which poetry, painting, music, chivalry, and asceticism have aggregated under the banner of love) follows not an ideal of beauty that they have chosen—but instead refers to an incurable disease, again like the Jews (except for those that frequent only their own race and, as such, have only in their mouths ritualistic prayers and sacred pleasantries), who flee from each other, searching instead for their opposites, those who do not want anything to do with them, pardoning their rejections and intoxicated by their kindnesses; but they are also brought together with their peers by the ostracizing which affects them and the scorn into which they have stumbled, having ended up acquiring, as if by a persecution not unlike that of the Israelites, the physical and moral characteristics of a single race, sometimes beautiful, often frightful, finding (despite all the mockeries that some who are more mixed and better assimilated to the adverse race, and so relatively less inverted, heap up onto those who remain) a relief in visiting their peers, and even validation in their existence, so that, while denying that they are indeed a race (in which name lies the greatest injury), they voluntarily unveil anyone who succeeds in hiding that they are in fact one of them, not so much to harm, which they don't mind, but to excuse themselves; and they go in search, not unlike a physician for appendicitis, of finding this inversion into history, taking pleasure in recalling that Socrates too was one of them, like the Israelites who say that Jesus too was Jewish, not realizing that there were no abnormal ones when homosexuality was normal, just as there were no anti-Christians before Christ, not realizing that it is scorn alone that makes the crime, precisely because it does not let anything survive that is not resistant to all sermons, all examples, all punishments, by virtue of an innate disposition so very special that it repels other men (even though it can accompany itself with higher moral qualities), more than certain vices that contradict it, like theft, cruelty, and bad faith, which are better understood and so are more often excused by the common man...

These descendants of the Sodomites, so numerous in fact that we can apply that other verse in Genesis to them: "If anyone can count the grains of dust of the earth, so too your descendants shall be numbered," are thus planted across the earth, and they have access to all the professions, and are similarly invited to all of the most exclusive clubs such that, when a Sodomite is excluded, the black balls [that exclude him] are mostly sodomites, but those who take care to condemn sodomy, having inherited the lie which permitted their ancestors to leave such an accursed city. It is possible that they will indeed return one day. Certainly, in all sorts of countries they form an oriental colony, cultured, musical, malicious, which has such charming qualities and nonetheless has unbearable defaults. We will see this unfold in the following pages; but I would like to provisionally prevent the disastrous mistake, running parallel to that which encourages the Zionist movement, of seeking to create a Sodomite movement and to even rebuild Sodom. But the Sodomites will leave these cities having hardly arrived so as not to appear to be from it, will take a wife, will maintain mistresses in other cities where they would find all the suitable distractions. They will go to Sodom only on days of extreme necessity, when their own cities would be empty, like those times when famine brings wolves out of the woods. That is to say, all in all, this would happen as it does in London, in Berlin, in Rome, in Petrograd, and even Paris.

Marcel Proust, *Sodom et Gomorrhe* (Paris: Galimard, 1921), translated from French by Jesus Leyva. Copyright © 2019 Print-O-Craft Press.

Further Reading

Carlston, Erin. "Secret Dossiers: Sexuality, Race, and Treason in Proust and the Dreyfus Affair." *Modern Fiction Studies* 48:4 (2002), 937–968.

Freedman, Jonathan. "Coming out of the Jewish Closet with Marcel Proust." In *Queer Theory and the Jewish Question* (eds. Daniel Boyarin, Daniel Itzkovitz, and Ann Pellegrini, Columbia University Press, 2003), 334–364.

Guedj, Jérémy. "La figure du juif efféminé: Genre, homophobie et antisémitisme dans la france des années 1930 à travers les discours d'extrême droite." In *Hommes et masculinités de 1789 à nos jours* (ed. Régis Revenin, Paris: Autrement, 2007), 220–235.

76. A Member of Hashomer Hatsa'ir Describes the Importance of Male-Male Erotic Feeling (Bitania, 1921)

Hashomer Hatsa'ir, a nationalist-Zionist youth movement that began in Galicia in 1913, drew on German youth movements like the Wandervogel, which celebrated the power of Eros within the *Männerbund* (male group); even though these ideas were often linked to antisemitic notions of Aryan masculinity (as in the work of Hans Blüher), the leaders of Hashomer Hatsa'ir attempted nonetheless to incorporate them into their Jewish movement. Meir Yaari, one of the most prominent thinkers in the movement, wrote, "Let us consecrate the erotic experience which ennobles us and fuses us as a brotherhood and an *Eda* (Bund)." The erotic drive of the Eda was part of the power that thinkers like Yaari believed was necessary to create a new kind of Jewish community, one which was freed from the repression and neuroticism of the European Jewish diaspora. This excerpt is from a report of Benjamin Dror (1900–1988), who was born in a religious family in Lwów (Lviv/Lemberg), but as a teenager left the Orthodox world to join Hashomer Hatsa'ir, and became a member of Bitania, a short-lived settlement of Hqshomer Hatsa'ir in the Galilee from August 1920 to April 1921. Here Dror emphasizes how "erotic feeling between men" is constructive, creative, and necessary for the "spiritual heart of the nation." In their quest to combat the stereotypes of Jewish weakness and effeminacy, members of Hashomer Hatsa'ir idealized (at least in theory) the generative potential of male-male erotic connection. This was critiqued by many — one reviewer of Kehilyatenu, the book of essays on Bitania in which Dror's report appeared, wrote that the collection's allusions to "Eastern mysteries" left him wondering if they were those of Socrates and Alcibiades, or those of Oscar Wilde — and by the 1930s, the tone of Hashomer Hatsa'ir had turned more toward Marxist views of class struggle and revolutionary education. Nonetheless, even though the period of the Bitania project folded within a year, it left a considerable impact on the growing kibbutz movement and on Zionist mythology in general.

Erotic feeling between men engages them into a community and endows that community and the individuals in it with a firm position in the universe. Erotic feeling between males and females gives the individuals their entire lives, being a part in the unfolding of humankind and the chain of future generations. The first kind of Eros appeared both among the ancient Greeks and the Jews. An association of men [ḥever gevarim, i.e. Männerbund] formed erotic bonds and thereby became a cultural nucleus, a spiritual heart of the nation, a font from which the people drew their creative powers for generations. The Hasidim found in the male society the House of God. This is to say that an abstract idea found its expression in drinking, dancing, singing, in a circle of men who are joined together at the moment of excitement.

Benjamin Dror, "Qevutsatenu harishonah," in Kehilyatenu (1921), as translated in Ofer Nur, Eros and Tragedy: Jewish Male Fantasies and the Masculine Revolution of Zionism (Academic Studies Press, 2014), p. 158. Reprinted by permission of Academic Studies Press.

Further Reading

Geller, Jay. "Freud, Blüher, and the Secessio Inversa: Männerbünde, Homosexuality and Freud's Theory of Cultural Formation." In Queer Theory and the Jewish Question (eds. Daniel Boyarin, Daniel Itzkovitz, and Ann Pellegrini, Columbia University Press, 2003), 90–120.

Peleg, Yaron. "Heroic Conduct: Homoeroticism and the Creation of Modern, Jewish Masculinities," *Jewish Social Studies* 13:1 (2006): 31–58.

77. Mordechai Jiří Langer Writes History of Homosexuality in Judaism (Prague, 1923)

Mordechai Jiří Langer (1894–1943) was a Czech Jewish writer and poet, described by Shaun Halper as "the first intellectual in Jewish history to seriously engage with homosexuality as a Jewish issue." As Halper demonstrates, Langer was the first Jewish writer to articulate a homosexual identity using an internal Jewish vocabulary, and to see homosexuality as a concrete and continuous element of Jewish history and culture. Raised in a suburb of Prague in a secular Jewish family, he became attracted to Hasidism in his teen years, and at the age of 19 joined the Belzer Hasidim—an experience which he later describes as intensely homoerotic. During the First World War, Langer became involved in Zionist activism, and left the Hasidic world (although he remained an observant Jew) to study psychology and philosophy, becoming active in the Jewish literary scene of Prague (including a friendship with Franz Kafka). Around 1920, Langer began to think and write explicitly about Jewish homosexuality in both prose and poetry (see source 87). The title of his 1923 book, *Die Erotik der Kabbala* (The Eroticism of Kabbalah), is misleading—it is not restricted to Kabbalah, but in fact attempts to trace the role of Eros, and in particular homoeroticism, in Jewish history from antiquity to Langer's own time. Langer's book was a response to contemporary antisemitic German theories of homosexuality, such as those of Hans Blüher, that portrayed the "manliness" of male-male Eros as central to Western civilization and antithetical to Judaism. Instead, Langer argues that Eros was a central force in Judaism as well, drawing on a wide-ranging set of examples from Jewish history, including Rabbi Yoḥanan and Resh Laqish (see source 13), homoerotic medieval poetry (see sources 18–20 and 22–25), the male circles of sixteenth-century Kabbalists in Safed (see source 41), and the homoeroticism of the Hasidic yeshiva (see source 54), as in the excerpt presented here. The impulse to create a "gay canon" or comprehensive listing of "great homosexuals in history" was a common aspect of homosexual writing throughout the nineteenth and early twentieth centuries, but Langer's innovation was to incorporate it into a Jewish framework encompassing history, theology, sociology, and politics. Here he describes the circle of the *yoshvim* (yeshiva students) as an ideal all-male society, or *Männerbund*, held together by Eros (for a similar concept of Zionist pioneers as an erotic *Männerbund*, see source 76). When it came to the actual expression of homosexual desire, however, Langer could only say that the "official position" required those people to suppress their sexual energy for the benefit of society—a heroic tragedy that echoes other homosexual literature of the period (see source 64).

To understand what kind of love [*Liebe*]* dwelled between the "*yoshvim*," one only has to step into the *beis ha-midrash*, where they are enveloped with their studies [*wo sie sich mit ihrem Studium beschäftigen*]. Here sit two young men, with beards just beginning to cover their chins, "studying" assiduously over thick Talmud-folios. The one holds the other by his beard, looks deep into his eyes, and in this manner explains a complicated Talmud passage. And there, two friends pace around the hall deep in conversation, while embracing one another [*sie halten einander umschlungen*]. (During meals one can see that they always dine out of the same bowl). In the dark corner stand a pair. The younger of the two rests his back against the wall, the elder has the entire frontal part of his body literally pressed against him [*der ältere liegt förmlich mit der ganzen Vorderseite seines Körpers an ihn gedrückt*]; they look lovingly in each other's eyes, but keep still. What could be playing out within their pure souls? They themselves don't even know...

The boy's soul, suddenly taken by an inexplicable yearning [*Sehnsucht*; alternatively: "lust"] for the rabbi, finds no peace at home. Not only in his nightly dreams, but also—and this is for the Hasidim a sign of grace [*Gnade*]—while awake the shining form of the rabbi appears before his eyes. Finally, he decides: He leaves a comfortable home—often against his father's will and his mother's tears—and travels to the city of the rabbi, in order to "cleave" [*anschmiegen*; alternatively, "to nestle up to"] to him (to be *dovek*) forever. As soon as he arrives and it is determined that he is serious, he is greeted with open arms by the "*Chevre*" [social group]. Soon he finds himself in the middle of a circle

---

* All bracketed and parenthetical comments in Halper's translation.

of friends [*Freundeskreis*], who "draw near" [*annähert*] to him through various tenderness [*Zärtlichkeiten*] and it doesn't take long to find an older student who has "the same soul" to study with, which he accepts with great joy. How blessed he feels.

Mordechai Jiří Langer, *Die Erotik der Kabbala* (Prague: Josef Flesch, 1923), 108–109, and 116, as translated in Shaun Jacob Halper, *Mordechai Langer (1894–1943) and the Birth of the Modern Jewish Homosexual* (Ph.D. dissertation, UC Berkeley, 2013), 34–35. Reprinted by permission of Shaun Jacob Halper.

Further Reading

Halper, Shaun. "Coming Out of the Hasidic Closet: Jiří Mordechai Langer (1894–1943) and the Fashioning of Homosexual-Jewish Identity." *The Jewish Quarterly Review*, 101:2 (2011), 189–231.

Ilany, Ofri. "Homo-Semitism: Jewish Men, Greek Love and the Rise of Homosexual Identity." In *Internal Outsiders—Imagined Orientals? Antisemitism, Colonialism and Modern Constructions of Jewish Identity* (eds. Ulrike Brunotte, Jürgen Mohn, and Christina Späti, Würzburg: Ergon-Verlag GmbH, 2017), 131–142.

78. Sholem Asch Defends God of Vengeance Against "Wrong Interpretation" (New York, 1923)

When Sholem Asch's controversial 1906 play *God of Vengeance* (see source 69) was first performed in Yiddish, audiences were mainly worried that the violent and abusive underworld that it portrays would reflect badly on the Jewish community. By 1922, when it premiered in English—first at the Provincetown Playhouse, in Greenwich Village, and then, in 1923, at the Apollo Theatre under Harry Weinberger—a new issue had emerged: how Jews and non-Jews alike would understand the lesbian relationship that it portrayed. Within a month of the play's opening at the Apollo, the entire cast, as well as the play's manager and the theatre's director, were arrested on obscenity charges; the initial complaint was actually lodged by the noted Reform Rabbi Joseph Silverman of Temple Emanu-El. While fighting the case in court, Weinberger published a booklet in support of the play with essays from "prominent Men and Women," including Abraham Cahan (editor of the *Forward*), glowing reviews from theatre critics, and an "Open Letter" from Sholem Asch himself. Asch explains that he is compelled to write this letter "because of the wrong interpretation of my play, *The God of Vengeance*." He emphasizes that his goal is to present a universal story, which presents Jews as they are, neither entirely good nor bad. He also explains specifically that the scenes between Manke and Rivkele "were the most poetic of all" when performed on European stages; but somehow, they had a different character in English, on an American stage in New York. "The love between the two girls," he writes, "is not only an erotic one. It is the unconscious mother love of which they are deprived...rather than the sensuous, inverted love of one woman for another." The word "invert" was a common term in the first decades of the twentieth century for homosexuality (the lesbian has a male soul, and the gay man has a female soul, and thus they are "inverted"), and Asch's use of it here indicates that Asch understood (and rejected) this model of same-sex desire; it seems he was concerned about how new American understandings of sexuality would lead viewers to misinterpret his work. Weinberger eventually won an appeal in the New York State Court of Appeals, but the play continued to garner controversy, and in 1946 Asch prohibited the further production of *God of Vengeance* in any language.

OPEN LETTER BY SHOLOM ASCH

Because of the wrong interpretation of my play, *The God of Vengeance*, now running at the Apollo Theatre, I wish to make the following statement:

I wrote this play when I was twenty-one years of age. I was not concerned whether I wrote a moral or immoral play. What I wanted to write was an artistic play and a true one. In the seventeen years it has been before the public, this is the first time I have had to defend it.

When the play was first produced, the critics in Germany, Russia, and other countries, said that it was too artistically moral. They said that for a man like "Yekel Shepshovitch," keeper of a brothel, to idealize his daughter, to accept no compromise with her respectability, and for girls like Basha and Raizel, filles de joie, to dream about their dead mother, their home, and to revel in the spring rain, was unnatural. About two years ago I was approached by New York producers for permission to present the play in English. I refused, since I did not believe the American public was either sufficiently interested or adequately instructed to accept *The God of Vengeance*.

I don't know whether I can explain the real feeling I wanted to put into this play. It is difficult for an author to comment on his own work. As to the scenes between Manka and Rifkele, on every European stage, especially the Russian, they were the most poetic of all, and the critics of those countries appreciated this poetic view. This love between the two girls is not only an erotic one. It is the unconscious mother love of which they are deprived. The action portrays the love of the woman-mother, who is Manka, for the woman-child, who is Rifkele, rather than the sensuous, inverted love of one woman for another. In this particular scene, I also wanted to bring out the innocent, longing for sin, and the sinful, dreaming of purity. Manka, overweighed with sin, loves the clean soul of Rifkele, and Rifkele, the innocent young girl, longs to stay near the door of such a woman as Manka, and listen within.

As to the comment that the play is a reflection on the Jewish race, I want to say that I resent the statement that *The God of Vengeance* is a play against the Jews. No Jew until now has considered it harmful to the Jew. It is included in the repertoire of every Jewish stage in the world and has been presented more frequently than any other play. *The God of Vengeance* is not a typical "Jewish play." A "Jewish play" is a play where Jews are specially characterized for the benefit of the Gentiles. I am not such a "Jewish" writer. I write, and incidentally my types are Jewish for of all peoples they are the ones I know best. *The God of Vengeance* is not a milieu play—it is a play with an idea. Call "Yekel" John, and instead of the Holy Scroll place in his hand the crucifix, and the play will be then as much Christian, as it is now Jewish. The fact that it has been played in countries where there are few Jews, Italy for instance, and that there the Gentiles understood it for what it is, proves that it is not local in character, but universal. The most marked Jewish reaction in the play is the longing of "Yekel Shepshovitch" for a cleaner and purer life. This is characteristically Jewish. I don't believe a man of any other race placed in "Yekel's" position would have acted as he did in the tragedy that has befallen his daughter.

Jews do not need to clear themselves before any one. They are as good and as bad as any race. I see no reason why a Jewish writer should not bring out the bad or good traits. I think that the apologetic writer, who tries to place Jews in a false, even though white light, does them more harm than good in the eyes of the Gentiles. I have written so many Jewish characters who are good and noble, that I can not now, when writing of a "bad" one, make an exception and say that he is a Gentile.

Sholom Asch.

Sholem Asch, "Open Letter." In *The God of Vengeance: Is the Play Immoral?—Is It a Great Drama?* (ed. Harry Weinberger, New York, 1923). Reprinted by permission of David Mazower on behalf of the Sholem Asch estate.

Further Reading

Friedman, Andrea. *Prurient Interests: Gender, Democracy, and Obscenity in New York City, 1909–1945* (Columbia University Press, 2000).

Friedman, Jonathan. "Jews, Homosexuality, and the Performing Arts in the United States: Sensibilities and Tensions, 1890–1969." In *ibid., Rainbow Jews: Jewish and Gay Identity in the Performing Arts* (Lexington Books, 2007), 31–58.

Hoffman, Warren. *The Passing Game: Queering Jewish American Culture* (Syracuse University Press, 2009).

79. Poetry of Jacob Israël De Haan (Amsterdam, 1917 and 1924)

Jacob Israël De Haan (1881–1924) was a Dutch Jewish poet, activist, author, and journalist. The open depiction of gay love in his first novel, *Pijpelijntjes* (Pipelines), provoked a scandal when it was first published in 1904, and De Haan was fired from his jobs as a children's columnist and schoolteacher. At the end of the First World War, De Haan became involved in the Zionist movement, and moved to Mandate Palestine in 1919. He was disappointed, however, by what he perceived to be an unwillingness on the Zionist side to integrate into Arab society, and he began to spend time both with local Arabs and with the Hasidic communities opposed to Zionism, in particular the Eda Ḥaredit (Orthodox Council of Jerusalem) and its leader, Rabbi Yosef Ḥayyim Sonnenfeld (1848–1932). In 1924, a month after publishing his second book of poems, De Haan was murdered by an agent of the Haganah, a Jewish paramilitary organization in Mandatory Palestine (1921–1948), which attempted to frame his death as caused by a jealous

Arab lover or an angered Arab father; this is considered the first political assassination in Israeli history. S. Y. Agnon once recalled in a letter meeting "an Arab who spoke fine Yiddish...He was the well-known companion of De Haan, may his name be erased, i.e. his 'wife.'" De Haan's homoerotic poetry demonstrates his attempts to integrate his Jewish identity with his erotic attractions. His legacy is equally complex; his memory is still venerated by the anti-Zionist segments of the ultra-Orthodox world, who annually pay their respects to his grave on the Mount of Olives, while a line of his poetry (*naar friendschap zulk een mateloos ferlangen*, "for friendship such a boundless longing") is engraved on the Homomonument in Amsterdam, the Dutch memorial for gay men and lesbians killed in the Holocaust.

To a Young Fisherman

Your naked feet more tender than a tulip,
A rose less handsome than your ruddy cheeks,
In no other's eyes did I read more replete
Such a boundless hankering for friendship.

Behind us the eternity of the sea,
Above paled grey the everlasting sky,
Drifting on the lonely beach just we
Alone, no other than the sea to pry.
I went to my City, our last day ended.
You sail and fish content, I drift and brood
and find no city refuge nor stiller field.
I am so tired, yet much I have loved,
Forgive me much, ask not what I withstood
And pray I never to your beauty yield.

To a Friend

I always recognize spring's earliest sign,
Not in the brightening of murky days
Nor in the tempering of winter's ways
And not because dark night retreat does chime.

And not because the first bright blossoms bloom
In sun-drenched field, beside the dike, the dell,
In hedgerows, by the water, on the swell
Of the dune, whereby its creatures' play resume.

But because in your deep blue eyes I chart
Spring's dawn more beautiful each passing day,
With spring's softness your young smile I survey,
And something stirs profoundly in my heart.

Blest be every hour that Day wins back from Night,
Morning and evening, blessed sunshine,
But not without you, would that I be blind
With you, than in others find my delight.

Blest the song, but for you alone, my Mate,
Sing out my song or dwell in reverie
And let cruel fate strike dumb my melody
Should this my song to someone else relate.

The Young Shepherd

Your land is beautiful. The gold-sheaved wheat
Dries sturdy grain slender in soft sunlight,
Meadows merge with horizons beyond sight...
But lovelier still than this, your young face sweet.

The gentle laugh of your gladdening mouth
Opens your lips, and tenderly they rise,
And laughter lights within your clear blue eyes,
Your cheeks are roses, red and round.

Young lad, who guard the flocks with such delight,
Who live a wanderer's life with birdsong, breeze,
And kind sunlight, return pensive when you see
The Wide West blush and blanch its waning light,

The city beckons you. And its shrill life
Shall spoil your splendor, sorrowful defile,
But in my Songs' clear cadences the While
Your Beauty I'll preserve from further strife.

Uncertainty

What does this late hour hold for me,
The City stalked by sleep,
I rest my legs by the Temple wall;
God or the youthful Moroccan lad?

Sleeping Lad

You're not a scholar, nor are you a poet.
You're just a youthful Yemenite lad.
But whose feet tread the earth lighter?
Who gives God more satisfying sleep?

Little Chaim

Love of life, it surely is to name
A little Lad as this Chaim or Life.
His Mother gave her milk to him
And God a share of His celestial sleep.

"To a Young Fisherman," "To a Friend," and "The Young Shepherd" from *Liederen* (Amsterdam: van Kampen & Zoon, 1917); "Uncertainty," "Sleeping Lad," and "Little Chaim," from *Kwatrijnen* (Amsterdam: van Kampen & Zoon, 1924). Translated from Dutch by Dr. Brian Doyle, with the poems from *Liederen* first appearing in "The Love Songs of Jacob Israël de Haan," *The Gay and Lesbian Review*, September 1, 2006 (http://www.glreview.org/article/article-964/).

Further Reading

Berkowitz, Michael. "Rejecting Zion, Embracing the Orient: the life and death of Jacob Israel De Haan." In *Orientalism and the Jews* (ed. Ivan Kalmar and Derek Penslar, Brandeis University Press, 2005) 109–124.

Boone, Joseph. "Modernist Re-Orientations: Imagining Homoerotic Desire in the 'Nearly' Middle East." *Modernism/modernity* 17:3 (2010), 561–605.

Giebels, Ludy. "Jacob Israel de Haan in Mandate Palestine: was the victim of the first Zionist political assassination a 'Jewish Lawrence of Arabia'?" *Jewish Historical Studies* 46 (2014), 107–129.

Hekma, Gert. "Homosexuality and the Left in the Netherlands." *Journal of Homosexuality* 29:2–3 (1995), 97–116.

80. Poetry of Sophia Parnok (Saint Petersburg, 1905–1924)

Sophia Parnok (1885–1933) has been called "the Sappho of Russia" for her lyrics of female love, inspired by the classical poetry of Sappho (see source 1). Born Sonya Yakovlevna Parnokh to a middle-class Jewish family in Taganrog (southwestern Russia), she began writing poetry in her adolescence, expressing her early awareness of her attraction to other women. Her complex sense of herself as different from others was also informed by her chronic illness and fatigue (probably caused by Graves' disease), and by her Jewishness, although she was attracted to Russian Orthodoxy (like other members of the assimilated Russian-Jewish intelligentsia), and converted shortly before the Russian Revolution of 1917. She was briefly married to her fellow poet Vladimir Volkenshtein, but she divorced him in 1909, writing to her friend Mikhail Gnessin that "I have never, unfortunately, been in love with a man." Over the course of her life she passionately pursued a series of female partners, including the poet Marina Tsvetaeva (1892–1941), the actress Lyudmila Erarskaya (1890–1964), and the mathematician Olga Tsuberbiller (1885–1975). Her earliest poetry (preserved in two handwritten notebooks) already expresses her erotic orientations to women; after encountering Russian translations of Sappho's poetry around 1914, she began writing Sapphic-inspired verse (collected in *Poems*, 1916, and *Roses of Pieria*, 1922), which linked her own romantic life with a lesbian community across time. Her poems "Cain" and "Hagar" suggest that she remained invested in Judaism after her conversion, and identified in particular with outsiders and those on the margins, calling Cain "our tribe's forefather / of madmen—poets." In "Kitchen-Garden," Parnok develops her voice as a mature poet, describing her struggles to grow food in the Crimean town of Sudak; her garden, which resists cultivation, also suggests an erotic struggle with a woman (perhaps her lover at the time, Lyudmila Erarskaya, who was recovering from tuberculosis), which Parnok hopes will yield fruit. Parnok faced heavy censorship from Russian authorities, especially for the religious themes of her work, and after her 1928 collection *Vpolgolosa* (Half-Voiced), she was forbidden from publishing poetry; with little support, and failing health, she died a few years later.

I Know (1905)

To Nadezhda Poliakova

I know profoundly well—you've shown me everything,
The breathing of the skies, the mighty breaker's murmur,
And twinkling of the stars inside the depths of air,
And lightning's vivid laugh in gloomy quietude
By giving me yourself in brilliant harmony.

Like a Small Girl (ca. 1914/1915)

To Marina Tsvetaeva

Like a small girl you appeared in my presence ungracefully.
- Sappho

"Like a small girl you appeared in my presence ungracefully"—
Ah, Sappho's single-line shaft pierced to my very core!
During the night I leaned over your curly head pensively,
Motherly tenderness stilling my heartbeat's mad rush—
"Like a small girl you appeared in my presence ungracefully."

I recalled your avoiding my kiss with some subterfuge,
I remembered those eyes, their pupils incredibly wide...
You entered my house, delighted with me as a novelty:
Colorful slippers, a sash, or maybe a handful of beads—
"Like a small girl you appeared in my presence ungracefully."

But under the mallet of love you are gold—and so malleable!
Leaning, I cradled your face, pale in the passionate shade,
Where it appeared death had passed like a snowy-white powder-puff...

I'm grateful to you as well, my sweetness, because in those days
"Like a small girl you appeared in my presence ungracefully."

That Evening (1915)

To Marina Tsvetaeva

That evening was dimly-smoldering—
But for me a tempestuous one.
On that evening, as you had desired,
We went out to the "Union."*

I remember your hands, weak from happiness,
The veins—networks of navy blue.
And my touching your hand was impossible,
Ensheathed in its glove by you.

Ah, again you had moved so close to me,
And again you turned to the side!
And I realized: you were untouchable,
Regardless of how I tried.

Then I said: "In the dark your alien
Dark-brown eyes look so remote…"
To a waltz they showed scenes of Switzerland—
In the mountains a tourist and goat.

I smiled—you didn't respond to me…
Each of us thinks she's the aggrieved!
And lightly, so you wouldn't notice it,
I leaned over and smoothed your sleeve.

Cain (ca. 1920)

"I have gotten a man from the Lord,"
And a first maternal smile

---

*The Union Theater, located at Nikitsky Gates, in Moscow.

At the world's first firstborn
Eve smiled.

"Why has your face fallen?"—
—How brightly burns my brother's sacrifice!
And brighter than the rival's offering
Was jealousy ignited.

That's him, the first lover, and accursed,
But was it not said to Cain:
"On whoever kills you, sevenfold
Shall vengeance be taken."

More pleasing than the lyre's rumble
Are those words. Its heart celebrates.
Cain, our tribe's forefather
Of madmen—poets.

Hagar (ca. 1920)

So Hagar sits in obloquy
And gushing forth in streams
The spring pours out a threnody
*Beerlachai-royi.***

Those lands belong to Abraham,
But this expanse—to none.
Around her, only wilderness
To Shur itself does run.

Despair, despair instinctual!
In her Egyptian eyes,
Disconsolate, elongated,
A nascent teardrop cries.
The frigid torrent's shimmering,
A dagger's cutting edge—

** *Be'er-laḥai-ro'i*, "The Well of the Living One Who Sees Me," the name Hagar gives to the well in the desert (Genesis 16:14).

O, terrifying, childless,
O, dread proprietress!

"Hagar!"—And then her countenance
Dark-skinned is drained of blood.
She looks—her eyebrows lifted at
An angel of the Lord...

Kitchen-Garden (ca. 1924)

The greedy saline soil had eaten everything.
I rooted out the twisted writhen roots of
The vines that curled here once upon a time—
The earth was nubbly, desiccated, scabby,
Like a feverish sick woman's lips...
Beneath its lacerated sole my foot
Grew calloused from leaning on the shovel,
My hands were swelling with a painful fire,
As iron would collide with buried skulls.
She put up quite a fight against me with
A kind of atavistic vengefulness, but I
Went at her with my pick—like so, like so,
I will outstubborn your stubbornness!
Here sprightly peas will soon begin to curl,
The corn will raise its thick stalks skyward,
An elephantine pumpkin, big with child,
Will loose her serpent tresses like the Gorgon.
Ah! Neither crocuses nor snowdrops smell
In spring so satisfyingly of spring as
The garden bed's first-blooming cucumber!...
The sharp fang of my pick shone in the sun,
Around me, clumps of earth bobbed up and crumbled,
A sea breeze blew, the sweat ran down my back
And cooled, congealing as a cold slender snake—
And never had the rapture of possession

Burned through me with such cloudless
Completeness and such piercing pride…

And in the valley there, the almonds fade
And in their place the peach trees start to bloom.

As published in Sophia Parnok, *Stikhotvoreniya* (Moscow, 1916), *Rozy Pierii* (1922), and *Sobranie stikhotvorenii* (ed. Sofia Poliakova, St. Petersburg: Inapress, 1998). Translated from Russian by Dr. Diana L. Burgin; I thank her for sharing her research on Parnok and confirming her biographical details.

Further Reading

Burgin, Diana L. *Sophia Parnok: The Life and Work of Russia's Sappho* (New York University Press, 1994).

Burgin, Diana L. "Laid Out in Lavender: Perceptions of Lesbian Love in Russian Literature and Criticism of the Silver Age, 1893–1917." In *Sexuality and the Body in Russian Culture* (eds. Jane T. Costlow, Stephanie Sandler, and Judith Vowles, Stanford University Press, 1993), 177–203.

Engelstein, Laura. "Lesbian Vignettes: A Russian Triptych from the 1890s." *Signs* 15:4 (1990), 813–831.

Healey, Dan. *Homosexual Desire in Revolutionary Russia: The Regulation of Sexual and Gender Dissent* (University of Chicago Press, 2001).

Shrayer, Maxim. "Sophia Parnok." In *An Anthology of Jewish-Russian Literature: 1801–1953* (ed. Maxim Shrayer, Armonk, NY: M.E. Sharpe, 2007), 199–202.

81. An American Zionist Writes of Her Erotic Connection to Women (Reḥovot, ca. 1925)

Jessie Sampter (1883–1938) was born in New York City to an assimilated, middle-class German-Jewish family. At the age of 12 she contracted polio and lived for the rest of her life with chronic pain, muscle weakness, and limited mobility. Sampter developed her own sense of Jewish peoplehood through literature and poetry, inspired by her friendships and discussions with Mary Antin, Mordechai Kaplan, Henrietta Szold, and Josephine Lazarus (Emma Lazarus' sister). Increasingly drawn to Zionism, Sampter moved to Mandate Palestine in 1919, living in Reḥovot and then the kibbutz of Giv'at Brenner, publishing dozens of books, essays, and educational materials about Zionism.

Soon after her arrival she met a Russian immigrant named Leah Berlin, and the two of them lived together, along with a Yemenite orphan that Sampter adopted, for almost all the remainder of her life. This excerpt from Sampter's unpublished autobiography, *Speaking Heart* (written and revised over the course of the early 1920s) describes Sampter's adolescence and her friend Nora, whose intense relationship she calls "one of the great things of life." Her recollections connect her disability and her own erotic desires through the complexity of her embodied experience. In another unpublished essay, titled "Validity," Sampter reflects, "It was always only half: a child that was not born to me, love without domesticity, walks from which one had to drive home, and independence with strings on it. And yet, as I figure up the account, it seems to have been all valid. Every kind of life is life if one lives it."

I loved beautiful persons. Physical beauty seemed a virtue to me, a service, that made it possible to forgive its owners even stupidity and graver failings. Yet ~~compassion~~* suffering drew me ~~even~~ more than beauty. At Christmastime—or rather Hanukkah—one of the great things of life happened to me: I met my friend, Nora. She, though a year younger than I, was taller and beautifully built, and the first thing I noticed was that her skirts were too short. Perhaps because I did not wish to look at her face. Already she had the ample build that later developed into the Venus de Milo or Winged Victory type; her golden brown hair fell in heavy braids almost to her knees. The right side of her face was beautiful, fair, a gracious profile; on the left side she was blind, an eyelid missing from birth; and the side of the nose was scarred by operations, the mouth drawn awry. I took her hand; it was muscular, vibrant, electric. We talked. We did not say much: school, poetry, novels, trifles. We resolved to meet again.

In three weeks we knew that we were intimate friends. Misery loves company. Nora had a father and mother and sister and brothers, high school to go to, a chum and some friends. I met them; I did not chum with them; I was too shy and suffering. She invited me to go with her to a Sunday school class at the Reform Synagogue, or Temple. I told her I was an atheist. "Never mind, we'll ask the teacher." The teacher attracted me; she said I should come. I enjoyed it…

I said [to Nora]: "I like you very much."

---

*Crossouts as in the manuscript.

"I don't like anyone," she answered.

"Yes you do, you know you like me."

She couldn't deny it.

"Of course, I'm extreme," she admitted, "but it's those social qualms. It's being afraid people won't like you, or that they only pity you. You know. We'll never get over it, so we might as well grin and bear it…"

My exceeding modesty was in part due to the defects of my body which I shrank from exposing even to women. I hid my heavy steel brace when I was not wearing it…When I began to surmise what marriage meant, I marveled, though without fear, how anyone could endure it. Biological abnormalities of some sorts, of which I read in scientific books, thrilled me with horror. Especially the conception of the Hermaphrodite, man and woman at once. Suppose I were that? Would I know? Did I perhaps secretly and horribly long for it, as an escape from dependence on the love of others?…

Incomprehensible yearnings! I used to wish Nora were a man, then—who knows?—we might marry. She drew me with a physical attraction that also repelled or frightened or troubled me. The touch of her electric hand on my heart would send a thrill through me, would heal or soothe the pain that still so often centered there. She was big and strong. Sometimes she would draw me down to sit on her lap, sometimes in a wild, desperate mood she would grab my throat and pretend she was going to strangle me. I liked it. I found consolation in our mutual sorrows, and to her alone I could speak without shame of the longing for death but I did not understand what was the force that drew us together, the deep, dark connection that sometimes made me suspect I had known her in some prenatal world, in a cavern of the pregnant earth.**

Jessie Sampter, *Speaking Heart* (Reḥovot, ca. 1925), unpublished manuscript in Jessie Sampter Papers, Central Zionist Archives, A219\11, 57–60, 68, and 80 (insert). I thank Dr. Sarah Imhoff for directing me to this source, and for generously sharing her own research on Jessie Sampter with me.

Further Reading

Imhoff, Sarah. "Incomprehensible Yearnings: Zionism and the Queer Kinship of Jessie Sampter." In *Queer Loves in Jewish History: From Ancient Israel to Europe before the Shoah* (eds. Corinne Blackmer and Shaun Halper, forthcoming).

** This paragraph was typed on a separate piece of paper and stapled into Sampter's manuscript.

Wolf, Rebecca Boim. "Jessie Sampter and the Hadassah School of Zionism (1883–1938)." In *The Women Who Reconstructed American Jewish Education, 1910–1965*, (ed. Carol K. Ingall, Brandeis University Press, 2010), 46–62.

82. A Polish Jewish Lesbian is Deported for Obscenity (New York, 1927)

Eve Adams was the name adopted by a Jewish woman born Khave (Ewa) Zloczewer, in Mława, Poland, in 1891. Immigrating to the United States in 1912, she spent a few years traveling the country selling radical magazines. In the early 1920s, she ran a bohemian tearoom in Chicago called the Grey Cottage, which catered to gay men and lesbians, anarchists, socialists, and labor organizers. Moving to New York, she opened another tearoom in Greenwich Village at 129 MacDougal Street, referred to as Eve's Hangout— it was described in a homophobic local paper as a place "where ladies prefer each other. Not very healthy for the she-adolescents nor comfortable for he-men." Her cafe hosted poetry readings, musical performances, and perhaps also intellectual discussions with radical activists in Adams's circle, including American Jewish anarchists (and advocates of free love) Emma Goldman and Ben Reitman. As described in the following articles from the entertainment magazine *Variety*, her tearoom was raided in 1926, and an undercover female police officer confiscated a pioneering book Adams wrote (under the name Evelyn Addams) titled *Lesbian Love*. *Variety*'s reports are full of unsubstantiated rumors and homophobic references to "temper-amentals" (gay men) and "man-haters" (lesbians), and they reinforced the common fear of the time that older, predatory butch lesbians would corrupt younger innocent girls. The alleged sign at the entrance reading "Men are admitted but not welcome," may also be a homophobic fabrication. This antagonism to Adam's cafe can be understood as a backlash against the permissive culture of urban American entertainment culture in the 1920s— many other gay and lesbian clubs at this time also found themselves subject to surveillance and police raids. For publishing an "obscene" book and for allegedly flirting with the policewoman, Adams served a year and a half in prison. Since Adams was not an American citizen, she was then deported back to Europe. She settled in Paris, where she befriended (and sold the books of) a number of local and visiting literati, including Henry Miller and Anaïs Nin. After the Nazi invasion of France, Adams fled to Nice, but was deported to Auschwitz on December 17, 1943, and murdered there.

Variety, July 7, 1926

EVELYN ADDAMS, 1 YR. AND DEPORTATION

Boss of Eve's in Village Sold "Dirty" Book—Man-Hater Besides

Evelyn Addams, 35, of 38 Washington Square West, proprietor of "Eve's" tea room at 129 Macdougal Street, Greenwich Village, found guilty in the Court of Special Sessions of possessing and distributing an indecent book, was sentenced to serve a year in the penitentiary in Special Sessions. It was also ordered that the immigration authorities be notified to deport her to Poland at the expiration of her sentence on the ground that she is not a citizen.

Miss Addams was previously convicted to disorderly conduct in the Tombs Court and the sentence covered the two charges.

Miss Addams, who assumes mannish clothes and is a self-confessed "man-hater," was arrested June 17 by Policewoman Margret Leonard at the "tea room." The police officer told the court she was ordered to investigate the place as a result of complaints received concerning the actions of young girls.

Mrs. Leonard said Miss Addams immediately started to "flirt" with her and produced a book entitled "Lesbian Love," which the defendant claimed to be the author of. Miss Addams, according to the officer, advised the latter to read it. Mrs. Leonard did and caused Miss Addams' arrest. To make it harder the officer added an additional charge of disorderly conduct basing this on the general attitude and actions of Miss Addams.

Variety, July 28, 1926

EVE ADDAMS' RING OF RICH CULTISTS

Investigation Into Surrounding Circumstances and Companions in Village

Arrest and conviction of Evelyn Addams, former proprietress of Eve's Tea Room, Greenwich Village, may lead to a further investigation by District

Attorney Joab Banton in ferreting out a supposed ring of wealthy women cult-ists known to be operating in that section.

Banton and the police believe the Addams woman was being financed as a procuress for this ring and will make a concerted effort to land the higher-ups. The assumption is based on report of the probation officer which investigated the convicted woman's record after conviction.

The report revealed that Miss Addams' living apartment on Washington Square cost $250 a month in addition to the $200 monthly rental for the Tea Room. The latter was a soft-drink place with no cover charge and 50c a throw for beverages. A check-up on receipts during the several months the place was in operation showed a gross weekly intake of from $60 to $75 dollars, hardly adequate to meet rental expenses of both places.

It was ascertained that Miss Addams had no other recorded income than that from the tea room. Prior to that she had been selling "The Quill" and other magazines in various tea rooms of the Village and had been so financially low often proprietors of other places staked her to small sums.

RESORTS FOR "TEMPERAMENTALS"

Miss Addams had been around the Village for two years as a magazine vendor. Shortly before launching the tea room venture she had affected mascu-line attire and became a regular at the various resorts catering to "temperamen-tals" until a police drive chased most out of the district. Eve then opened her own place on Macdougall street and practically gave the tip-off on what kind of joint it was through placarding the main entrance with a sign which read "Men are admitted but not welcome."

Simultaneously with the opening of Eve's place the big parade of close-cropped women in mannish attire was on again in the Village. In most cases the mannish ladies were accompanied by girls of tender years and some not so tender. When things were dull Eve would occasionally grab an armful of mag-azines and make a round of other places, rounding up unattached females and inviting them over to her tea room. With a good crowd in the door would be locked promptly at 1 A.M. but the mob in was allowed to remain.

Policewoman Margaret Leonard of the "Flapper Squad," assigned to in-vestigate, made the arrest in the Addams case. At the trial in Special Sessions,

New York, Miss Addams was sentenced on a disorderly conduct charge to six months in the workhouse and a similar term for distributing the book, with both running concurrently, and a recommendation that she be deported back to Poland as an undesirable when liberated.

REFUSES TO TALK

After conviction Miss Addams is reported as having been questioned by members of District Attorney Banton's staff as to who was financing her, but she refused to volunteer information. Several other attempts have been made to question her since commitment to the workhouse, but she has refused to talk.

Reports around the Village are to the effect that she has stood pat throughout the proceedings upon promise to be taken care of liberally by the others involved.

On the day of sentencing some one had seemingly assured a coterie of her disciples that she would be liberated on a reasonable doubt certificate. A gala celebration had been set at the tea room to welcome back their "martyr." Evelyn did not show. She dined at Blackwell's Island instead.

A detailed cop was on hand to see that the celebration to the absent honor guest was kept within bounds of decency and he had been ever since at the Macdougall street tea room for the same purpose.

Variety, July 7, 1926, p. 33, and July 28, 1926, p. 37. I thank Barbara Kahn for first introducing me to the story of Eve Adams and sharing her research with me; I am also deeply grateful to Jonathan Ned Katz for his assistance in contextualizing these sources, and for generously sharing his own insights and research on Eve.

Further Reading

Chauncey, George. *Gay New York: Gender, Urban Culture, and the Making of the Gay Male World 1890–1940* (Basic Books, 1994).

Kahn, Barbara. "The Spring and Fall of Eve Adams" (New York: Theater for the New City, 2010) and "Unreachable Eden" (New York: Theater for the New City, 2012).

Katz, Jonathan Ned. *Eve Adams Living* (University of Wisconsin Press, forthcoming).

Lambert, Josh. *Unclean Lips: Obscenity, Jews, and American Culture* (New York University, 2014).

Reis, Martha Lynn. *Hidden Histories: Ben Reitman and the 'Outcast' Women Behind 'Sister of the Road: The Autobiography of Box-Car Bertha'* (Ph.D. dissertation, University of Minnesota, 2000).

83. A Young Jew Joins a Homosexual Gang (Warsaw, 1927)

The *khronik* (crime blotter) was a digest of scandalous and titillating events supplied by local journalists and police reports, which formed a regular feature of several Yiddish papers during the first half of the twentieth century. The short snippets of news open a window into an area of Ashkenazi Jewish life often ignored: the raucous, violent, sexually-charged lives of gangs, prostitutes, thieves, gamblers, and other members of the Jewish underworld. In this blurb, published in the Warsaw paper *Der Moment* in 1927, local Jewish mother Khaye Anter engaged the police to locate her missing 19-year-old son Aren (Aharon). He was found in the company of a gang of homosexuals (the Yiddish uses the new term *homoseksualisten*), having "befriended" (*gekhavert*) a certain Adam Mikhalak. The police discovered that Aren had already been arrested under a false name, and that in fact this group maintained their own "workshop," where they forged documents "for their cohorts who did not want their real names to be known in case they were arrested." This was a regular problem (as demonstrated by sources 67 and 82), and we might even consider this workshop an early form of homosexual activism. Despite police harassment of this type, Warsaw had a thriving gay and lesbian scene in the inter-war period. While this particular group seems to be only men, items of lesbian interest appeared in the Yiddish press as well; the short story "Der Shidekh in Partshev" (The Betrothal in Parczew) by Alter Kacyzne (1881–1941), published in the Warsaw literary journal *Literarishe Bleter* in 1928, describes an erotic relationship between two women, referencing "the enchanted blooms of ancient Lesbos." With this news item in *Der Moment*, as is typical for the *khronik*, there is no follow-up; what happened to Aren, Adam, and the rest of this gang of *homoseksualisten* is not known.

THE HOMOSEXUALS USED FALSE DOCUMENTS

Mrs. Khaye Anter informed the police that her 19-year-old son Aren left home and disappeared for two weeks. Because he took his mother's jewelry, an investigation was initiated. The police arrived at the conclusion that the missing young man had befriended one Adam Mikhalak who was arrested last week with a large group of homosexuals. It also appears that Anter had also been arrested with the homosexuals, but had given the police a document with a fake name.

Anter had already been released and was on his way home when he was re-arrested as a result of the new investigation in order to determine who gave him the falsified documents. It became apparent that the unmasked band of degenerates maintained their own "workshop" for forging documents for their cohorts who did not want their real names to be made known in case they were arrested. The "workshop" also produced false documents for those who were transported as merchandise outside the country.

Moment, December 9 1927, as translated in Eddy Portnoy, *Bad Rabbi: And Other Strange but True Stories from the Yiddish Press* (Stanford University Press, 2018), 228–229. I thank Dr. Eddy Portnoy for bringing this source to my attention.

Further Reading

Cohen, Natan. "Shund and the Tabloids: Jewish Popular Reading in Inter-War Poland." *Polin: Studies in Polish Jewry* 16 (2003), 189–211.

Kellman, Ellen. "Dos yidishe bukh alarmirt! Toward a History of Yiddish Reading in Inter-War Poland." *Polin: Studies in Polish Jewry* 16 (2003), 213–241.

Portnoy, Eddy. "You Think You've Got Troubles? Stories from Warsaw's Yiddish Crime Blotter." In ibid., *Bad Rabbi: And Other Strange but True Stories from the Yiddish Press* (Stanford University Press, 2018), 228–229.

Stanley, John. "Constructing a Narrative: The History of Homosexuality in Poland." In *New Social Movements and Sexuality* (ed. Melinda Chateauvert, Sofia: Bilitis Resource Center, 2006), 32–50.

84. A Gay Cabaret Song from Weimar Germany (Berlin, 1927)

The Weimar Republic—the democratic state of Germany between the World Wars—is often mythologized as a liberal and decadent paradise. While the truth of gay life in Weimar Germany was far more complex, there were certainly arenas of cultural life that allowed for fluidity of gender and sexuality. One such area was the cabaret, an important avenue for singers, dancers, and other performers to celebrate innuendo and playful transgression. The chorus of this cabaret song, written in 1927 by the Jewish librettists Fritz Löhner-Beda and Richard Fall, asks a certain Moritz whether his feelings are *kühle oder schwüle*—literally, "cool or humid," but also referencing the slang meaning of *schwüle* as homosexual (translated here as "straight or sideways"). Performed by the popular cabaret artist Paul O'Montis (1894–1940), himself an openly gay Jewish singer, the witty double-entendre would have been clear. In 1933, O'Montis fled Nazi Berlin to Vienna, and then Prague, but he was arrested there and deported to the concentration camp of Sachsenhausen. Like other gay Jewish prisoners, he received exceptionally harsh treatment (see source 95), and he was found dead in his cell in 1940; the official report is that he committed suicide by hanging, but it is more likely that he was beaten and tortured to death.

What feelings do you have, Moritz?
From films, you surely know
The handsome Valentino
And been amazed repeatedly
By Harold Lloyd's dexterity.
The mixing of these two
I have seen, it's true
And testify thereto
That is he.
He arrives at five for tea, I note
In spats, cravat and morning coat.
In short, that look from shoes to throat
Such is Moritz Weiss.
The gait, the look, the quiet tread
The trousers of the finest thread
As all hearts' rhythms upward sped
And in a whispered voice:

What are your feelings these days, Moritz Moritz Moritz?
Are they straight or sideways, Moritz Moritz Moritz?
You don't affirm, without denyin'
You seem patrician yet so plebeian
You have a heart for many, Moritz Moritz Moritz
But too pretty, so not true to anyone.

The pretty Mrs. Camilla
Received him in her Villa.
She oft said she would thank him
To visit in her sanctum.
Like a steady flame
This somewhat older dame
Just a bra around her frame
She sits there.
But not using her, he chose
To sit in a Buddha pose
And blow smoke out of his nose.
It caused her stress.
She laid all out as best she might
A squeeze, a feel, without the light
She waits and waits
No response in sight.
What could be amiss?

What are your feelings these days, Moritz Moritz Moritz?
Are they straight or sideways? Moritz Moritz Moritz
You don't deny, you don't attest
Something's clearly wrong at best
You have a heart for many, Moritz Moritz Moritz
But too thick for faith or trust.

Fritz Löhner-Beda and Richard Fall, "Was hast Du fur Gefuhle, Moriz?" (Vienna: Wiener Boheme, 1927). Translated from German by Dr. David A. Greenberg. Copyright © 2019 Print-O-Craft Press.

Further Reading

Beachy, Robert. *Gay Berlin: Birthplace of a Modern Identity* (New York: Alfred A. Knopf, 2014).

Hájková, Anna. "Den Holocaust queer erzählen." In *Jahrbuch Sexualitäten*, Vol. 3 (eds. Janin Afken, Jan Feddersen, Benno Gammerl, Rainer Nicolaysen, and Benedikt Wolf, Göttingen: Wallstein, 2018), 86–110.

Lareau, Alan. "Lavender Songs: Undermining Gender in Weimar Cabaret and Beyond." *Popular Music and Society* 28:1 (2005), 15–33.

Mungen, Anno. "'*Anders als die Anderen*,' or Queering the Song: Construction and Representation of Homosexuality in German Cabaret Song Recordings Before 1933." In *Queering the Popular Pitch* (eds. Sheila Whiteley and Jennifer Rycenga, Routledge, 2006), 67–82.

Wallach, Kerry. *Passing Illusions: Jewish Visibility in Weimar Germany* (University of Michigan Press, 2017).

85. Poetry of Dina Lipkis (Kiev, 1928)

While many Ashkenazi women published poetry, short stories, novels, and other literary works in Yiddish in the late nineteenth and early twentieth centuries, it is rare to find any direct expression of homoeroticism between women. Hinde Ena Burstin suggested the term "lesbo-sensuous" for poems like this one, by Dina Lipkis (born 1900), which speaks of longings and sensual desires without explicit eroticism. In "On the Other Side of the Wall," Lipkis attempts to describe her feelings for the young woman sleeping "on the other side of the wall" from her, but her ellipses and dashes leave her thoughts unfinished and unsaid. She detests the "stony cold" of the wall separating them and she dreams of the wall sliding away to reveal naked warmth and the touch of her hand. Dina Lipkis (or Libkes) was the pen name of Dina Kipnis-Shapiro, born in the Ukrainian shtetl of Slovechno in 1900; her brother, Itsik Kipnis (1896–1974) was also a Yiddish writer. Lipkis moved to Kiev as a young woman and published a number of stories, poems, and translations there; the poem presented here was republished in Ezra Korman's anthology of Yiddish women's poetry, *Yidishe Dikhterins Antologye* (Chicago, 1928). Lipkis apparently survived the Second World War in Central Asia, and returned to Kiev after the war.

On The Other Side Of The Wall

Dedicated to L.R.

On the other side of my bedroom wall,
A young woman sleeps beside me, enthralled.
I know, she knows,
That on the other side of the wall!…

Sometimes, in my dream,
The wall slides away and
I can feel her naked warmth—
Her hand—

My youth bubbles up in me,
I wake up and see—
A wall!
Deathly-detestable is this walled oldness,
This stony cold…

On the other side of my wall,
A young woman sleeps beside me, enthralled.
I know, she knows,
That on the other side of the wall…

Dina Lipkis (Dina Kipnis-Shapiro), "Fun Yener Zayt Vant," in *Yidishe Dikhterins Antologye* (ed. Ezra Korman, Chicago: L.M. Stein, 1928), 307–308. Translated from Yiddish by Hinde Ena Burstin; I thank her and Ri J Turner for bringing this source to my attention.

Further Reading

Burstin, Hinde Ena. "Female Fantasies from the Other Side of the Wall: Twentieth Century Lesbo-Sensuous Yiddish Poetry." In *Jews & Sex* (ed. Nathan Abrams, Nottingham: Five Leaves Publication, 2008), 38–51.

Fuks, Khayim Leyb. "Dine Libkis." In *ibid.*, *Leksikon fun der nayer yidisher literatur* (Congress for Jewish Culture, 1956–1981), translated by Joshua Fogel, yleksikon.blogspot.ca.

Hellerstein, Kathryn. *A Question of Tradition: Women Poets in Yiddish, 1586–1987* (Stanford University Press, 2014).

86. Poetry of Anna Margolin (New York, 1929)

Like the poems of Dina Lipkis (see source 85), these poems, by Anna Margolin (1887–1952), might also be termed "lesbo-sensuous." They speak of female desire, separated from male presence—in "On a Balcony," two women touch their hands "in longing (*benkshaft*)" but are interrupted by a man "like a grand and superfluous decoration." In "My Venus Wears Silk Slippers," Margolin describes the sensual and erotic beauty of a woman's body, at once material ("from her bronze hair / pearls stream") and ethereal ("lightning, fog, smoke"). And in "Her Smile," she portrays the internal struggle of a woman torn between the daytime world of her husband and children, and her nightly dreams of love: "her rosepainted fingernails touch / her girlfriend's small, pointed breast / and fall away, remain still / and happy until they pass." The smile with which the poem ends leaves us wondering: is it a smile of resignation, or of determination to change? Anna Margolin was the pen name of Rosa Lebensboim, born in Brist (today Brest, Belarus). She came to America at the age of 19, and quickly became enmeshed in the Yiddish literary circles of New York. She returned briefly to Europe, and then Palestine (where she had her only child, Naaman, with Yiddish writer Moshe Stavski), and then back to New York. Her work is widely lauded as some of the finest twentieth-century Yiddish poetry, expressing her quest for self-fashioning and the creation of a visual language.

On A Balcony

From a distant summer hot laughter floats toward me
from two small and dainty women
leafing through a picture book.
Their hands meet in longing.
Soft shoulders searching, quivering.
Over a thirsty, orange-red landscape
the bright bodies leap in confusion.

A man towers powerfully over them
with heavy grace,
like a grand and superfluous decoration.

My Venus Wears Silk Slippers

My Venus wears silk slippers
on her glamorous bare feet.
Her lap is a crimson iris.
Her hips are broad and defined.
From her bronze hair
pearls stream and quiver

in a whispering chorus
kissing her oblong breasts.
On her pale, lyrical lips—
melancholy and ardor.
And in her eyes,
lightning, fog, smoke,
softly shadowed
by a broad, black-feathered hat.

Her Smile

Her smile is autumnal over her world—
cool, weary and withdrawn,
the toil of the house, the years in harness,
and with husband and child
the eternal, naive dialogue.

That is daytime.

But at night, locked in sleep,
her face is alien. In a thick linen nightshirt
she dances in the tavern now with soldiers and sailors,
tossed to and fro by turbulent hands.
Lurking eyes suck her in,
ox-like heads, stiffly bent,
heels stomping, shoulders, elbows
whirling around her menacing, closer, teeth flashing
greedy, teeth biting into lips.
Here blood strives to spill itself
here, love is like a slaughter.

And love is a toxic flame that makes
the roads weird and bloody. It conjures up
a barbarous city of night, a street, a house,
girls in a circle,
she in the centre, tanned and jaunty.
Slowly, her rosepainted fingernails touch

her girlfriend's small, pointed breast
and fall away, remain still
and happy until they pass.
And joy, song, lamentation
are in the devotion of hot fingers.
And eyelashes painfully flutter
on a face made stony as a god's.
She saw her life as
a wild and pretty story one has read
but not finished and in the middle became distracted
about a steely, solemn night,
which holds the last mystery in the lap,
where all stories end—
Like a lofty flame,
frozen stiffly in the golden dance, a dead flame.
Grey wind and grey sea,
and out of the red evening rolled the sad gold,
liberated from joy, she goes
to the last frosty solitude,
not knowing that nearby, someone is watching.

Her face is a locked door for him,
behind which fear lurks. He looks and suffers.
He suffers.
His lips rouse her soul from darkened roads,
her lips quiver in dream.
Slowly, she opens her eyes,
slowly, she smiles at her husband
and returns from a great distance.

Anna Margolin, "Oyf a Balkon," "Mayn Venus Trogt Zaydene Shikhlekh," and "Ir Shmaykhl," as translated in Shirley Kumove, *Drunk from the Bitter Truth: The Poems of Anna Margolin* (SUNY Press, 2005).

Further Reading

Hellerstein, Kathryn. *A Question of Tradition: Women Poets in Yiddish, 1586–1987* (Stanford University Press, 2014).

Weiman-Kelman, Zohar. *'So the Kids Won't Understand': Inherited Futures of Jewish Women Writers* (Ph.D. dissertation, UC Berkeley, 2012).

87. Mordechai Jiří Langer Writes and Publishes Homoerotic Hebrew Poetry (Prague, 1921 and 1929)

Around 1920, Mordechai Jiří Langer (see source 77) began thinking and writing about his understanding of the place of homosexuality in Judaism. In this letter, sent to the Zionist essayist and literary editor Ya'aqov Rabinovich (then living in Petaḥ Tiqva), Langer pleads with Rabinovich to help him publish his homoerotic Hebrew poetry. Bemoaning the rejections he has received, Langer defends the content of his poetry, which deals with "comrade-love" (*ahavat rea'*) like that of David and Jonathan; he emphasizes that his goal is "to awaken (*le'orrer*) this feeling again, this comrade-love in these, our enlightened days." He did eventually publish his historical study of Jewish homoeroticism, *Die Erotik der Kabbala*, in 1923, and his first volume of Hebrew poetry in Prague in 1929. Langer fled the Nazis in 1939, but fell ill during the winter, and after being held in the British Mandate detainment camp in Atlit, died in Tel Aviv at the age of 49. As Halper has demonstrated, while Langer modeled his poetry on historical Jewish precedents, there was a core difference: Langer understood himself as a homosexual poet—a term and concept foreign to earlier periods. At the same time, his use of medieval poetry was essential for his sense of lineage, and for his argument that he was merely reviving a tradition already present in every strand of Jewish history. In his poetry, Langer uses literary techniques shared with other homosexual European poets of the time, like Arthur Rimbaud and Federico Garcia Lorca: metaphors of secrets and dreams, coded allusions, and a claim to a lineage of glorious history. In "Meeting," he speaks—using the biblical language of Song of Songs—of a beloved who "beckoned to my heart." But the poet turns away, declaring that he "will embark alone" on his tragic path, bearing only the secret that "perhaps in the heart of my darkness a light is hidden." Similarly, in "To My Comrade" (*El Re'i*), the poet describes his "limber, perfect" beloved as carrying "the interminable sorrow of [the] sweet secret" of *Ein Sof*, the Kabbalistic vision of an infinite and indefinable God. Recalling "that hour of bliss" when he and his companion walked together, the poet invokes "an ancient legend" of two men who loved one another with great yearning, and who ascended to heavenly gardens of eternal light and love.

I.

Prague, 26 Adar II 5681 [March 31, 1921]*

Honorable sir!

As I express my hope that you still remember your servant, I hope you will allow me to trouble you with my following request:

You sir were the first that I showed my poems to when you were in Prague due to the congress of Ha-Poel ha-Tzair, and if I am not mistaken, you were interested in my poems; for you said the following to your servant: "your poems are poetry" and you advised me as follows: "send your poems to Klausner or Frishman because only these two understand new things that have not yet been said in our narrow literature." This was the content of your words. And now know my lord what happened to my poems after I did as you commanded: I sent the two poems you read then to Mr. Klausner in Jerusalem in the hands of Dr. H. Bergmann, and then after several months, I received a reply from Klausner informing me that though my poems are beautiful and original in their content, "as well as their execution," their meter is no meter (they are indeed made according to the Sephardic meter!), "and a poem without meter is not a complete creation" (?) [Langer's question mark]. This answer of his upset me slightly and I did not send him my poems again.

After this I sent select poems in the hands of a designated emissary to Berlin to Klatzhkin. Dr. Max Brod wrote a recommendation to Martin Buber and asked him to publish them (Max Brod likes my poems and he told me to rewrite them in *Ashkenazit* when they are set to be published) but Buber replied in the name of Klatzhkin that "although..." etc., but they have linguistic defects (and therefore he contradicts Klausner's reasoning) and what's more, they only publish famous authors in "Avar" on principle [*davka*] (!). After this I sent a booklet of my poems to D. Frishman in the hands of Eliezer Shteinman who I consulted upon his journey to America through Prague and who

---

* All bracketed and parenthetical comments in Halper's translation.

also took much interest in my poems. From him I received a postcard in which he informed me that he showed them to Frishman but he "didn't sing their praises" and added to console me that "though our author is elderly and has no understanding of the yearnings of the young."

And now I beseech you sir to try and publish my poems in one of our many newspapers that Eretz Israel has been graced with…And especially perhaps some young editor free of all literary conservatism and predetermined judgments will be able to accept them! Because it is clear to me that it is not because of their external form, i.e. since they were composed either in a totally free style like the poetry of the most modern poets of Europe or they are bound in the ancient rhymed furniture like the poetry of Yehudah Halevi and his friends (for bottom line even the return to this form is current, I believe, among the new poets here in the West)—rather it is their content, it and only it, which caused my poetry to not be willingly accepted by our "great ones."

Does it make sense in our present generation, which is all hate and all rage and animosity, that a man shall appear and sings songs of companion-love, songs like that sung by courtiers for their true loves?! Has this abomination not been done in Israel since the days of David who eulogized his friend Jonathan: "I grieve for you, my brother, Jonathan. Very dear you were to me. More wondrous your love to me than the love of women!" How strange this elegy rings in our cold age, an elegy of sublime and exalted human feeling that has been extinguished from Hebrew heart in the tragedy of their bitter exile, may it be swift…And now here I come and my soul to arouse this feeling again, this companion-love, in these, our enlightened days—does it make sense? And not only this but especially in the Sephardic meter and in the *nusakh* of "*Selikhot*" and "*Yotzrot*…"

With your generous staff, my honorable sir, try to publish my poems in the Land [of Israel]'s newspapers and I will be eternally grateful to you. For if I cannot at this moment make aliyah to you all [join you], at least my poems, the children of my soul, will see the light of the Land of Israel's sun and my soul shall rejoice.

With feelings of respect and affection,

Mordechai Dov Langer

Respond promptly!

To My Comrade

Like clouds that disperse at once to reveal
star's eternal white gaze over earth,
you too appeared before your lonely slave
and unknowingly stirred his desperate heart.

When I saw your stature, limber, perfect,
shooting flares of enchanting youth;
when I stared, parched, into your devoted eyes,
in which Yah, the Eyn-Sof, submerged his limitless depths
and the interminable sorrow of his sweet secret.

Then I moaned and my spirit shakes
like a taut harp cord stroked by hand, and
my intensity in waves of song sweep toward you
because the sea of my everlasting frost
you kindled with the rippling heat of your touch.

And when my heart recalls that hour of bliss, that night's beauty;
the two of us walking the streets,
you placed your arm gently around my back
and recall as I recalled (as if concealed by fog)
the ancient legend, that pulls at the heart:

Of the love of two comrades, who with great yearning
embraced one another;
and drunk in their embrace they rose silently
to higher worlds; to tranquil gardens
where endless light and love exist always.

Meeting

My being was bereft of peace on a night of murk, a night of cold,
and a current of life brought you to me—and passed.

Join me
you beckoned to my heart, and your lips dripped with myrrh.
And I upon my path will embark alone,
far far away.
Since I told myself: perhaps in the heart of my darkness a light is hidden.

Mordechai Jiří Langer, letter of 26 Adar II 5681, and *Piyyutim Veshirei Yedidot* (Prague: Josef Flesch, 1929), as translated in Shaun Jacob Halper, *Mordechai Langer (1894–1943) and the Birth of the Modern Jewish Homosexual* (Ph.D. dissertation, UC Berkeley, 2013), 213–215 and 245–246. Reprinted by permission of Shaun Jacob Halper.

Further Reading

Halper, Shaun. "Coming Out of the Hasidic Closet: Jiří Mordechai Langer (1894–1943) and the Fashioning of Homosexual-Jewish Identity." *The Jewish Quarterly Review*, 101:2 (2011), 189–231.

Ilany, Ofri. "Homo-Semitism: Jewish Men, Greek Love and the Rise of Homosexual Identity." In *Internal Outsiders—Imagined Orientals? Antisemitism, Colonialism and Modern Constructions of Jewish Identity* (eds. Ulrike Brunotte, Jürgen Mohn, and Christina Späti, Würzburg: Ergon-Verlag GmbH, 2017), 131–142.

88. Poetry of Yokheved Bat-Miriam (Tel Aviv, 1930)

In both Yiddish and Hebrew modernist poetry, Jewish women declared their affiliation in a community of intellectual and social companions. In this poem, first published in 1930, Yokheved Bat-Miriam speaks to another unnamed woman whose presence is an "enthused annunciation" and an "unexpected encounter;" the poet speaks of "a certainty which dreams to be." While she calls out to this other presence, in the end she cannot close the distance between them, writing that it is better "in secret distance / to wait for you in vain." The famous Hebrew poet Raḥel (Rachel Bluwstein Sela, 1890–1931) responded to this poem, dedicating her poem 'Ivriyyah (published in November 1930) to Bat-Miriam, with the epigraph "I am black and beautiful" (sheḥorah ani venavah; Song of Songs 1:5). Bat-Miriam, in return, rededicated this poem to Raḥel when she published it again in 1932, after Raḥel's death. Born in the small Belorussian village of Keplits in 1901, Yokheved Bat-Miriam studied in Moscow and Odessa, and was part of a collective of modernist Hebrew poets known as the Hebrew Octoberists. Immigrating to Palestine in 1928, she changed her patronymic family name (Zhelezniak) to the matronymic Bat-Miriam, and continued to write Hebrew poetry that celebrated women's voices and experiences. She ceased writing poetry after the loss of her beloved son Nahum (Zuzik) Hazaz in the War of Independence in 1948; she received the Israel Prize in 1972 and died in 1980.

To Me You Are An Annunciation

To me you are enthused annunciation, commanding
Another essence to keep.
To me you are un-expected encounter, rejoicing
Ere still the light it did see.

To me you are a discovery's distant vanishing verge
Of a certainty dreaming to be,
Of a yearning delusion, enwrapped
By that which cannot be.

You call, repeat un-seen
And answering you is me.
Good for me your vanishing from me
Good for me your enwrapping silently.

Good for me in secrets-distance
To wait for you in vain.
You are my heart's blood sent hope
For that which will no more come to me.

Yokheved Bat-Miriam, "Lenokhah," *Moznayim* 16 (August 1930), 3–4. Translated from Hebrew by Zohar Weiman-Kelman; I thank her for bringing this source to my attention, granting permission to republish her translation, and providing additional background. Copyright © 2019 Print-O-Craft Press.

Further Reading

Finkin, Jordan. "Enclosed in Distances: The Poetic Experiments of Yokheved Bat-Miriam." In ibid., *An Inch or Two of Time: Time and Space in Jewish Modernisms* (Pennsylvania State University Press, 2015), 156–180.

Pardes, Ilana. "Yocheved Bat Miriam: The Poetic Strength of a Matronym." In *Gender and Text in Modern Hebrew and Yiddish Literature* (eds. Naomi B. Sokoloff, Anne Lapidus Lerner, and Anita Norich, Jewish Theological Seminary of America, 1992), 39–63.

Weiman-Kelman, Zohar. *Queer Expectations: A Genealogy of Jewish Women's Poetry* (SUNY Press, 2018).

Zierler, Wendy. *And Rachel Stole the Idols: The Emergence of Modern Hebrew Women's Writing* (Wayne State University Press, 2004).

89. A Jewish Woman is Arrested for Practicing "Sapphic Love" (Salonica, 1931)

The new scientific vocabulary around sexuality that emerged in the late nineteenth century soon expanded beyond the French, German, and English contexts. This article, which appeared in the Salonican journal *Makedonia* in 1931, describes "an unprecedented case of homosexuality [*omofilofilia*]," which it also labels "Sapphic love [*Sapfikous erotas*]." In Greece, the first decades of the twentieth century had seen the emergence of explicit gay and lesbian literature, due in some part to a new interest in the work of Sappho (for example, the poetry of Konstantin Cavafy [1863–1933], and Dora Rosetti's lesbian novel *The Two Lovers*, 1929); whether this had any effect on public perception of lesbian relationships, as in this case, is difficult to say. The event documented here concerned a Sephardi Jewish woman from Salonica, Gilda Pelosoff, who had engaged in "Sapphic love" both with another Jewish woman, as well as a younger Greek Orthodox woman, whose neighbors alerted the authorities. The sensationalist and antisemitic tone of the article is in keeping with the journal *Makedonia*, whose editor, Nikos Fardis, was affiliated with the nationalist extremist organization National Union of Greece, and who had published a Greek translation of the *Protocols of the Elders of Zion* in the paper in 1928.

AN UNPRECEDENTED CASE OF HOMOSEXUALITY IN THESSALONIKI

The Role Of A Degenerate Jewess— The Victim—A Young Schoolgirl

Under the auspices of the policeman of the Third Precinct, interrogations are currently being carried out on an unprecedented case of homosexuality, the victim of which was a graduate of the School for Girls. Months ago, the 18-year-old graduate of the School, Christodouli Varvaridou, resident of Navarinou Street, was lured by the degenerate Israelite Gilda Pelosoff into orgiastic pleasures of Sapphic love, during which the first was deflowered by the other.

It is noteworthy that the degenerate Israelite so insistently lusted after Varvaridou, that she was jealous to an insufferable degree and threatened continuously that she would murder her, if she caught her with another woman or even a man. These relations between the two women were perceived by the neighbors, who, with indignation, expelled from Varvaridou's home her lover and denounced the events to the policeman of the Third Precinct.

Mr. Vardoulakis, conducting the interrogations, ascertained that the denounced events took place, furthermore, he extracted from Gilda Pelosoff the confession that, before Varvaridou, she had Sapphic love with an Israelite prostitute. The assembled case file was sent to the Prosecutor.

"Mia protakoustos ipothesis omofilofilias en Thessaloniki." *Makedonia*, 23 October 1931, p. 6. Translated from Greek by Dr. Krinis Kafiris. I am very grateful to Dr. Paris Papamichos Chronakis and Rita Spathi for uncovering this document and sharing it with me. Copyright © 2019 Print-O-Craft Press.

Further Reading

Antonopoulos, Panagiotis. "From Marietta Mpetsou to Rita Mpoumi: Sappho, lesbian literature and feminism in Greece from the late 19th century to the interwar years." In *Speaking To/Against Certainties: Genders, representations, subjectivities* (ed. Demitra Vassiliadou et al., Athens: OMIK, 2013), 11–44.

Naar, Devin. *Jewish Salonica: Between the Ottoman Empire and Modern Greece* (Stanford University Press, 2016).

Rosetti, Dora. *The Two Lovers* (ed. Christina Dounia, Athens: ETP Books, 2017).

90. Jews Join the Crowd at a Drag Ball (Chicago, ca. 1932)

While perhaps made famous by Jennie Livingston's 1990 documentary film *Paris Is Burning*, the practice of performing gender transgression known as "drag" has been a central institution in European and North American queer and trans culture since the early twentieth century (see source 67). Originating as masquerade balls, "drag balls" thrived in American urban centers like New York and Chicago and drew vast and diverse crowds of participants and spectators. Often held on Halloween or New Year's, they provided safe places for gender play, flamboyance, and community celebration, free from harassment and scrutiny; they were also spaces for racial and ethnic integration, where White, Black, Latino, and Jewish participants were able to mingle freely. In this account, a divinity student from the University of Chicago, Myles Vollmer (1905–1968), reports his experience at a drag ball held in the Bronzeville neighborhood on Chicago's South Side. Vollmer describes a diverse crowd, both in terms of gender and race, writing that "there is a preponderance of Jews and Latin nationalities, although homosexuality is no respecter of races. Many of the men are of Polish blood. Negros mingle freely with whites. There seemingly is no race distinction between them." While Vollmer does not specify if the Jews are there as spectators or participants, there were Jewish drag queens and kings who performed in nightclubs and balls in this period, such as Buddy Kent (Malvina Schwartz), who performed across New York from the 1940s into the 1960s.

Twice a year, with the knowledge and protection of Chicago's officialdom, do the homosexuals of the city gather in great numbers for their semi-annual costume ball, at which conventions and repressions are flung to the winds. New Year's Eve, and Halloween mark the occasions for the celebrations of the "shadow world."

Picking our way carefully down South Wabash Avenue late New Year's Eve, through the grey area extending from Van Buren Street south, we arrived at the Coliseum Annex. The sidewalks and entrance to the hall were crowded with men hanging around. joking at the arrival of each newcomer in costume, overly eager to enter into conversation with you. Our guides told us that they were all "wise" and curious, some just looking on, others there for a possible pick up with some homosexual at the Drag, some there to prey on the less experienced boys who were inside cavorting to the music. We were soon to discover that where homosexuals congregate, there also are the racketeers, blackmailers, jackrollers, and all their ilk who prey on another's misfortune-made possible because a hypocritical society insists on calling homosexuality a "crime"—as though the poor unfortunates could help themselves!

Entering the hall, one recognized at once the uniformed guards from the Chicago Stadium, very much in evidence, and also noted that they were selected for their size and by numerous uniformed policemen, and several plain-clothes men—for this was one occasion when official Chicago put its approval on the public appearance of its intermediate sex.

Despite the rundown appearance of the Annex, it was an unusual and colorful sight—to see five hundred persons dancing standing about, swaying to the music of a colored jazz orchestra. It was a strange and unconventional sight, however because here we see two young men in street clothes dancing together, holding one another in close embrace, as any girl and boy would at any dance, save, perhaps that the two youths were much more intense in their forbidden roles.

Here are two persons, both dressed in gorgeous evening gowns one with a tiara, both in slim high French heeled satin slippers and heavily jeweled, dancing together gracefully, without any suggestive movements. And both are men! Heavily powdered, with brows penciled and rouged lips and cheeks, their arms and hands making effeminate gestures, it is difficult to discern their true sex. One is clothed in what must have been a costly white evening satin gown, of the newest mode, form clinging at the hips, and falling in folds to the floor. The other is more colorful in a slim green gown with complementary accessories. One wears a titian colored wig, carefully arranged, to simulate his feminine role; the other is content to dance with only his gown and made up face. We learn that the "girl" in green is one of the theatrical world's best known female impersonators; but in the shadow world, "she" is just another "belle." The picture is repeated over and over—colorful evening gowns, satin slippers, French heels, silken hose gracefully displayed, tiaras, feathered fans, flashing jewelry—all gliding about the hall. Gliding is the only name for it: no women could be more graceful. Trains are carefully held up by curled and manicured fingers. Couples dance together, swaying to every type of step, from the more restrained and dignified postures, to dancing of the most suggestive types. One sees two "girls" bowing courteously to one another, and a moment later, another couple—both young men, dancing cheek to cheek, bodies glued to one another in the most suggestive way. The "girls" (men homosexuals in female costume) move about swaying their shoulders, rolling their hips and the only clue to their masculinity is their heavier skeletal frames, or occasionally a more masculine featured face.

Here is something else. Two young men, very slender, in sack suits well tailored, with ties and shirts well matched are dancing. But they seem different from the other men in street clothes who are dancing together. This couple is too graceful for masculine movements. Then we see that they are two girls—both lesbians, finely featured, with boyish bobbed haircuts, playing the role of young manhood. We begin to see many other similar couples together, lesbian girls with their lovers…

Around the edges of the hall are a fringe of on-lookers like ourselves remaining in the semi shadows. Some curious, others homosexual, but not daring to come out publicly and dance for fear of recognition; others occasionally slipping out for a dance when the urge became too strong; others who are waiting for their lovers and finally those waiting for a pick up, to prey on the gullible homosexuals. All types are there, pimps, panderers, blackmailers, "trade," the oversexed lower classes with no high moral code, ready for fling, be it man or woman; prize-fighters, the so-called "meat" for homosexuals—and athletes are strangely susceptible to the advances of an effeminate youth, who will make love to them passionately.

There are harlots there; not plying their trade, of course, for competition is too keen, but attending with their own parties. For there is a strange bond that links homosexuals and harlots together. Possibly it is because both are social pariahs.

Falsetto voices sound in our ears. We hear expressions such as "Maude"; "Dearie"; "Fannie"; there are shrill exclamations of glee and merriment as the men in women's clothing frequent the toilets marked plainly Women. The men's toilets seem to be used only by those in masculine attire. It is not long before a real woman ventures into her proper restroom, and emerges to call a guard to dispossess the "girls" in there. A scuffle follows while a burly stadium guard attempts to expel the "girls" who shrilly protest that they belong in that particular restroom—the guard all the while trying to keep a serious face.

Physically, all types are there. Homosexuals thin and wasted, others slender and with womanish curves: others overfed and lustfully fat. Most of the younger homosexuals have pallid complexions with rather thin hair, due, perhaps to overindulgence. There is a preponderance of Jews and Latin nationalities, although homosexuality is no respecter of races. Many of the men are of Polish blood. Negros mingle freely with whites. There seemingly is no race distinction between them.

It is a garish affair, with a hollow, mocking, ring about it all. Many homosexuals of better class, who have succeeded in making some adjustment to society by bluffing the public, looked in, to leave at once in disgust. The group of onlookers are too dangerous to be seen with, blackmail is a common racket: and the homosexuals participating are going to the limit too freely in careless abandon. Discretion is flung to the winds, as they "let themselves go" on one of the two nights of the year when they can openly "be themselves," reveal their true natures, and be with others of their without fear of arrest or public censure. All the pent up longings and desires of months are being given free rein on this rare occasion—and there no question in our minds that the release will lead to excesses later.

Vollmer, Myles. "The New Year's Eve Drag." Manuscript report, Ernest W. Burgess Papers, Box 140, Folder 2, Special Collections Research Center, University of Chicago Library.

Further Reading

De la Croix, St. Sukie. *Chicago Whispers: A History of LGBT Chicago before Stonewall* (University of Wisconsin Press, 2012).

Drexel, Allen. "Before Paris Burned: Race, Class, and Male Homosexuality on the Chicago South Side, 1935–1960." In *Creating a Place For Ourselves: Lesbian, Gay, and Bisexual Community Histories* (ed. Brett Beemyn, Routledge, 1997), 119–144.

Heap, Chad. *Slumming: Sexual and Racial Encounters in American Nightlife, 1885–1940* (University of Chicago Press, 2009).

Ryan, Hugh. "The Three Lives of Malvina Schwartz—Butches, Femmes, and Mobsters: Inside the world of America's early drag superstars." *Hazlitt*, Oct. 12, 2016 (https://hazlitt.net/longreads/three-lives-malvina-schwartz).

91. A Baghdadi Escort Boy Confesses His Sins as a Spirit (Baghdad, 1933)

Although belief in demons and spirits has been a part of Judaism since antiquity, a new idea emerged in the Kabbalistic circles of the sixteenth century:

the reincarnation of souls (see source 41), and thus also the possibility of possession by a deceased spirit, known as a *dibbuq* (literally "cleaving,"often spelled *dybbuk*) or simply as a *ruah* (spirit). In many cases, during the interrogation or exorcism, the spirit reveals secrets of the community of the possessed (see source 44) or confesses their own sins committed while alive. The following description of exorcisms come from the work of Yehudah Ftayya (1859–1942, also spelled Fattiyeh or Petaya), a Baghdadi rabbi and Kabbalist, and a student of the Ben Ish Hai (see source 66). In several of Ftayya's stories, homosexual activity is presented as one of the many possible sins which can damage a spirit and thus cause a *gilgul* or *dibbuq*. In this account, the *ruah* of a young Baghdadi Jew named Yehudah ben Yonah, who had died in an airplane accident during the First World War, confesses to his dalliances with Ottoman army officers. In a disturbing end to the story, Ftayya rejoices that Yehudah's soul is reincarnated in a child who is blinded and scarred by smallpox, so that he would not fall prey to the same temptations as his previous incarnation.

[One *ruah* told me:] you should know that *ruhot* can only recognize the same sins in living people that those *ruhot* themselves had done while they were alive. Since they know the blemishes in their own souls, they can recognize the blemishes in the living souls that are similar to their own blemishes. It is also known [to them] how many times they transgressed with that sin; i.e. if that *ruah* was an adulterer while alive, then now they can look at a man and see if he is an adulterer or not, and with whom he committed adultery—a virgin or not, a widow or a divorcée, betrothed or married, whether it was natural [i.e. vaginal] or unnatural [anal] sex, Jewish or non-Jewish, and how many times he did it. Similarly, one who had sex with another man—[the *ruah* can see] whether he was active or passive, and how many times he sinned in this particular sin. For each and every sin creates a defect in his soul... And because of our many sins, in this time, half our women go whoring away from their husbands, and virgins too, and homosexual activity too, which I shall not even discuss. If only the Merciful One would look to the righteous of the generation who live in this city, of which there are maybe 50 righteous ones who are now past middle age and have never committed sins of a sexual nature...

In the year 1918, during the week of Pesaḥ, a woman named Khatun bat Yonah Yosef came to me. She said to me that for two years now, every so often she feels a stabbing pain in her heart, and sometimes she falls helplessly to the earth, and a severe illness grips her, and she rolls on the ground, front and back, for four cubits or more; frequently, she comes and goes in this rolling so severely that her limbs break...I checked her, and I found a *ruaḥ* in her. After some focused Kabbalistic meditations [*yiḥḥudim*] it spoke with me and told me that it was Yehudah ben Yonah, the brother of this woman Khatun, and the other woman with them was his mother.

At the time of the war of the Allied powers, which began on the 10th of Av [August 2], 1914, the Ottomans took young Jewish men from all areas to the army, but [Yehudah] was not taken with them, because he was *"beautiful in build and appearance"* (cf. Genesis 29:17 and 39:6), and loved by all the army officers. Only in 1916 was he finally required to go to war, and he left in the month of Shvat [February]...And he was 24 years old—small in years, but great in sins and transgressions as if he were a hundred years old. For he was beautiful in build and appearance, and so all the army officers loved him—he would fulfill their desires, and those of their wives, and he accepted payment from both sides, and from other licentious women, too. Everyone loved him and would bribe him to make their desires his desires, from whatever angle he desired, and at any time he desired—even during menstruation. Other prohibitions accompanied them, for he considered all the prohibitions of the Torah like permissions to him. In a very short time, prohibitions and transgressions and sins had clustered, as numerable as dust, until he was completely caught up in his many sins and transgressions, and he died in that terrible death [in an airplane accident], may the Merciful protect us...

After [four years of work, and splitting Yehudah's soul into whole and damaged parts], I said to Yehudah, "Come here so that I can perform *yiḥḥudim* for you," and he came forward. I began to perform *yiḥḥudim* to repair the remaining part of his soul that was damaged, and I treated him through *yiḥḥudim* for about a year. During this time, one night someone knocked on my door; they told me that a child had been born and would be circumcised tomorrow. The father of the child had quarreled with the mother, for he wanted to invite non-Jewish women to dance and sing at the celebration, while his wife refused this disgraceful thing, so he swore that he would not sit on the Chair of Eliyahu [to hold the child during the circumcision], and angrily went to his room and closed the door. [The stranger said,] we came to invite you to sit on the Chair of Eliyahu instead of his father. I went the next day to the house of the mother, where they were circumcising the child, and I spoke gently to the child's father, [asking him] to undo his vow and sit on the Chair, but he covered his face with his robe and refused to see me or notice my words. So I sat on the Chair and was the child's *sandeq* [who holds the child during circumcision], and during the circumcision I prayed to the Holy Blessed One that this child would not damage his covenant [*yifgom brito*, i.e. engage in improper sexual behavior], and would not have sex with a man, neither as the penetrator or the penetrated, as Yehudah ben Yonah did.

Just then, it occurred to me that this child must be [the reincarnation of] the good portion that was separated from Yehudah ben Yonah's soul. And thus a quarrel had arisen between the child's father and his wife, in order to allow me to become the *sandeq* on the day of his circumcision. And "*who is like the wise man, and who knows a matter's interpretation*" (Ecclesiastes 8:1) like the Holy Blessed One? God afflicted this child with smallpox, and the beauty of his face was marred, for it was all pitted [with scars], and his two beautiful eyes were blinded, and one of his pupils lost almost its light, so that he could barely recognize the letters; in order that he should not succeed [in being tempted to] have sex with men or to commit adultery. And he is still alive, and now, in the year 1933, he is ten years old.

Yehudah Ftayya, *Minḥat Yehudah* (Baghdad: Elisha Shoḥet, 1933), 51a and 54a–59b, translated from Hebrew by Noam Sienna. I thank Dr. Bryan Roby for bringing this source to my attention.

Further Reading

Ben-Naeh, Yaron. "Qaton bashanim vegadol bafsha'im: sippuro shel na'ar livvui yehudi mibagdad." *Et-Mol: 'itton letoldot erets yisra'el ve'am yisra'el* 166 (2002), 25–27.

Bilu, Yoram. "The Taming of the Deviants and Beyond: an analysis of 'dybbuk' possession and exorcism in Judaism." In *Spirit Possession in Judaism: Cases and Contexts from the Middle Ages to the Present* (ed. Matt Goldish, Wayne State University Press, 2003), 41–72.

Giller, Pinchas. "Ftayya (Petaya), Judah." *Encyclopedia of Jews in the Islamic World* (ed. Norman Stillman, Leiden: Brill, 2012).

92. An Underground Gay Club in Mandate Palestine (Tel Aviv, 1934)

This story was part of a sensationalist column that ran in the weekly gossip paper 'Itton Meyuḥad in January 1934, describing the seedy "underworld"—cocaine dens, brothels, and criminal gangs—that was already thriving in the newly-established city of Tel Aviv, which was only 25 years old at the time. In this section, the anonymous reporter describes the "ABC," the *Algemeiner Buseranten Club* (General Buggers' Club) as an institution catering to homosexual men where they could meet, dance, and enjoy themselves freely. While the beginning of the article associates this type of club with the urban European experience, as indeed the German name of the ABC might indicate, the reporter goes on to attribute the prevalence of "these types" to Jaffa, the Arab periphery of the "First Hebrew City."

IN THE UNDERWORLD OF TEL AVIV

A.B.C.

In almost all the cities of Europe, there are these sorts of establishments, called "clubs," as it were. The meaning of the initials [A.B.C.] is "*Algemeiner Buseranten Club*" [General Buggers' Club], namely "a general establishment for homosexuals [*homoseqsualistim*]." "Masculine" men and "feminine" men meet each other in these "clubs," and hold orgies.

In the East these types are more common, and it is well known that in our country you don't have to go hunting for them with candles. It is enough to take a short trip down the alleys of Yafo [Jaffa] and the cafés there. And whoever has open-enough eyes will see the "rascals" making out lustily in front of all passers-by.

These pairs are not satisfied only with Yafo, but they want to have enjoyable outings as well, and to that end they come to Tel Aviv. Apparently even in the Hebrew City, or more accurately in its suburbs, there are residents who have this diseased orientation. Indeed, because of them a kind of "A.B.C." has been established here—an establishment for meetings, and intentionally in the center of the city, in one of the well-known cafés. There, in the deep dimness that prevails in a sort of side room, these men gather to enjoy themselves.

Around the tables they all sit in pairs, drinking and eating; from time to time someone puts on the Pathéphone [record player], and men embrace each other and go to dance. These dances are lustful, arousing the inclinations of the dancers and stirring up disgust in whoever looks on from the side. In the late hours of the night, the pairs begin to disperse. Trolley after trolley goes by, dispersing the pairs and scattering them to all corners of the First Hebrew City...

"Baʻolam hataḥton betel aviv." *Itton Meyuḥad*, January 31, 1934, as published in Ofri Ilany, "'Negaʻ nafos bamizraḥ': teʻurim shel homoseqsualiyyut baʻittonut haʻivrit shel tequfat hamandat," *Zmanim* 131 (2015), 8–21. Translated from Hebrew by Noam Sienna. I thank Dr. Ofri Ilany for generously sharing this source with me and helping contextualize it.

Further Reading

Fink, Amir Sumakaʼi, and Jacob Press. *Independence Park: The Lives of Gay Men in Israel* (Stanford University Press, 1999).

Ilany, Ofri. "'An Oriental Vice': Representations of sodomy in early Zionist discourse." In *National Politics and Sexuality in Transregional Perspective: The Homophobic Argument* (eds. Achim Rohde, Christina von Braun, and Stefanie Schüler-Springorum, Routledge, 2018), 107–120.

93. Poetry of Édouard Roditi (Paris, 1935)

Édouard Roditi (1910–1992) was born in Paris to a Jewish family with roots around the Mediterranean (his father, born in Constantinople, was of Romaniote and Sephardi descent; his mother, born in France, was of Ashkenazi and Flemish Catholic descent). As a young man, he studied in England, and became involved with modernist writers and poets, including encounters with James Joyce and a friendship with T.S. Eliot. Returning to Paris, he joined the Surrealist circles of André Breton; it was there that he published his first book of poetry, *Poems for F.* (printed in 250 copies). Inspired by a two-year affair with an older married man, the poems describe the tragic beauty of love, and the power of art to preserve that fleeting moment. To the end of his life, Roditi kept the identity of F. a secret, saying only that he was an Austrian painter, twenty years older than Roditi. In 1937, Roditi came to the United States to study at the University of Chicago, where he became close friends with his fellow gay Jewish writer, Paul Goodman. After the war he served as a translator and interpreter for the U.S. Army and the U.N., including at the Nuremberg trials, but he was fired in 1950 during the "Lavender Scare" led by Senator Joseph McCarthy (see source 112). He settled in Paris (although he returned often to the United States to teach in the 1970s), publishing dozens of essays, novels, art criticism, and books of poetry; he also produced important translations from French, German, Portuguese, Spanish, and Turkish, including the work of Albert Memmi, Paul Celan, Yaşar Kemal, C.P. Cavafy, and Fernando Pessoa. Roditi was particularly affected by the rise in European antisemitism in the 1930s, which inspired his collection of poems, "Three Hebrew Elegies" (1941), which explore the meaning of Judaism through the characters of Judah Leon Abravanel, Glückl of Hameln, and the prophet Ḥabbaquq. Roditi continued to write poetry on Jewish themes, many of which were collected in his anthology *Thrice Chosen* (1981); he also saw his epilepsy as a kind of chosen identity, parallel to his Jewishness (and homosexuality) in shaping his sense of self. In a 1975 interview, he reflected that "every day I thank God for having made me a homosexual and a Jew...I certainly wouldn't want to be anything but what I am."

To love is not only to touch the loved hands
lips limbs warm loins or the loved one's breast,
but to enter and to enter where the loved one stands
to stand with loved feet for loved feet are best

to live and to move within the loved skin
to love the loved one till one loves oneself
to eat the loved one to be the loved one in
the depths of one's own loved self

which is too difficult and never can be done
because time and place have fixed each face
and the earth cannot be stars moon or sun
and I cannot live in the loved one's place

[...]

Seeing you disappear round this corner
is no new pain, is seeing another
drown while we were swimming together
or a third leave with a new lover.

Knowing that I have been a new lover
and that an end must come to our love
makes my love an argument against
Time whose stroke of judgement must cut short

all quibbling of love's laws and precedents.
While we are yet walking here together
between the street-corner where I first
met you and that other where we part,

while our brief love yet lasts, let us
forget all other streets and other lovers,
each one forgetting that he has been another
lover in another love and in another street

[...]

Whether in exile my home-sick eyes
turn inward towards remembered scapes,
or, in despair, compare, or recognize
in wild-foreign features your friendly shapes,

You are my fatherland: familiar hills,
mimicked by clouds in every sky,
your shoulders that shut my world where, folded
in your arms and rounded by their streams, I lie.

Kisses, more countless and more bright
than stars, yet light my nights; you lie
beside me still, more close, more real,
though you are gone and I left alone.

You cannot cheat me, dear, nor death.
Entombed within my heart, await
what trumpet-calls to liberate
you from my love love, me from your loss?

[...]

Writing letters in spring-time and expecting
answers in autumn, with half the year,
half the world to cross, all days and ways
to unravel, lest we meet.

Forgetting my questions before your answers
reach me from where you sit and wonder
what my words now mean, that miles and whiles
leave meaningless, lest they hurt.

All words we write ever lose their meaning;
so many walls must steal the echoes
of my reproaches! Whose speech can reach
those who have fled, lest they love?

Distance and days are stronger than death
and never yield their prisoners.
All time and place are foes. Who knows?
We may meet, both strangers.

Édouard Roditi, *Poems for F*. Paris: Editions du Sagittaire, 1935. Reprinted by permission of Garrett White, on behalf of Five Ties Publishing. I am grateful to Michael and Mason Bondi (Édouard Roditi's nephew and grand-nephew) for granting permission to include Roditi in this project and confirming his biographical details.

Further Reading

Cándida-Smith, Richard. *Inventions and Imitations: tradition and the advanced guard in the work of Edouard Roditi*. Interview with Roditi, Oral History Center, University of California, Los Angeles, 1986.

Endres, Clifford. "Edouard Roditi and the Istanbul Avant-Garde." *Texas Studies in Literature and Language* 54:4 (2012), 471–493.

Koskovich, Gerard. "Edouard Roditi: Tales from Two Cities." *The Advocate* (April 17, 1984), 59–61.

Leyland, Winston. "Interview: Edouard Roditi." *Gay Sunshine* 29/30 (1976), 10–16.

Roditi, Édouard. *De L'homosexualité*. Paris: Sedimo, 1962.

Roditi, Édouard. *Thrice Chosen*. Santa Rosa, California: Black Sparrow Press, 1981.

Simon, Sherry. "Edouard Roditi: A Polyglot in the Twentieth Century." In *In Translation: Honouring Sheila Fischman* (ed. Sherry Simon, McGill-Queen's University Press, 2013), 98–112.

94. A Newspaper Report on Sexual Deviancy Among Youth (Tel Aviv, 1936)

During the period of the British Mandate of Palestine (1918–1948), colonial authorities introduced legislation that criminalized consensual sexual relations between men, not only in Palestine but across all British colonies. The Orientalist perception of the "East" as overly sensual and prone to homosexual activity reinforced the imagined hierarchy between European superiority and local degeneracy. Discussions of "sodomy" and other types of sexual behavior between men, whether in medical, legal, or popular literature, repeatedly blamed deviant cultural norms; in particular, the burgeoning Zionist Jewish community worried that this kind of "unnatural" behavior would undermine the success of their nationalist project. Like the earlier report in *'Itton Meyuḥad* (see source 92), this article connects male-male sexual relations to the fluid interactions between Ashkenazim, Sephardim, and non-Jewish Arabs. Part of a larger report on youth delinquency, it was published in the labor movement Histadrut's journal *Davar* in July 1936 by the pioneering journalist Brakha Ḥabas (1900–1968), a Lithuanian-born writer whose family immigrated to Ottoman Palestine in 1908, and who devoted her life to education and children's welfare.

There is yet another type [of delinquency]—a fine inheritance from our neighbors, and it is not known how we will free ourselves of this trouble: primitive and distorted sexual relations. Masturbation and sodomy [*ma'asei Sedom*] in different forms—both minor and serious. This is encountered also in summer camps, but it was clearly revealed in its most serious form in the sentencing of a young man, which took place recently in Tel Aviv:

There was a family that had a boy and girl. The father—Ashkenazi, a baker, in a good financial position, a member of the Histadrut [trade union]—was on the edge of abnormality. After many years of family life, he separated from his wife, married a second woman, then had a child (today four years old), a complete idiot—doesn't speak, doesn't answer to anything. The girl, 18 years old, has been a prostitute for two and half years now, lives among Arabs, disappears from the house, and nobody knows where she is. The boy, 14 years old—beautiful, talented, intelligent—worked in an office. He was going to be sent to an educational institution in the Emek [in northern Israel]. About two or three years ago, he met a young Sephardi bachelor in the public bathhouse who gave him money and coerced him into sodomy.

Last year, he became connected to a young Arab, the son of a wealthy orchard owner, and he would service him. That one opened a *konto* [credit account] for him in an Arab café in Neve Shalom [a Jewish neighborhood between Jaffa and Tel Aviv], and the young man lived in luxury. They would also meet each other in this café. In this neighborhood there was an upright family from Salonica, with two twin children, and one of them (the "untalented" one stayed at home, having lost a finger in a work accident) was gradually brought into this "business"—he was sought after by the young Arab to work in his father's orchard, which provided the cover for where their abominable activities were done. One evening, around the time of the Events [*hame'oraot*, i.e. the Arab Revolt of 1936–1939], the young men were invited as always to the orchard. There they abused them all night. They even granted them, in reward for this, gifts of money, a broken pistol, and two daggers. In the morning, the young men had finished. They were told to flee; they wanted to travel from there to Haifa and decided to open a brothel there. But in the Egged [bus] station, they aroused suspicion because of the large sum of money they were carrying, and because of the bicycle that they wanted to load on the top of the car. They were reported to the police—and the matter was discovered.

And where was the bicycle from? A story inside a story. The Ashkenazi youth—after being convinced that this was good "business"—had meanwhile become connected to an Arab shoemaker, and this one gave him money and shoes, and even bought him a bicycle. When this aroused suspicion in the youth's father, the shoemaker appeared and explained that the youth was working for him, was a good worker, and he had bought the bicycle with his wages. Now the father has kicked his son out. He has rented a room on the edges of Jaffa and says that he would like to study detective work.

All these events detailed here are, of course, in the category of "out of the ordinary." But they are an established fact, as well as a warning sign of where we will be, if we do not take preventative measures against this evil.

B.Ḥ.

Brakha Ḥabas, "Bein yeladim ʻazuvim." *Davar*, July 21, 1936, as published in Ofri Ilany, "ʻNegaʻ nafots bamizraḥ': teʻurim shel homoseqsualiyyut baʻittonut haʻivrit shel tequfat hamandat," *Zmanim* 131 (2015), 8–21. Reprinted by permission of the Lavon Institute for Labour Movement Research, Israel. Translated from Hebrew by Noam Sienna. I thank Dr. Ofri Ilany for generously sharing this source with me and helping contextualize it.

Further Reading

Darr, Orna Alyagon. "Narratives of 'Sodomy' and 'Unnatural Offenses' in the Courts of Mandate Palestine (1918–48)." *Law and History Review* 35:1 (2017), 235–260.

Ilany, Ofri. "'An Oriental Vice': Representations of sodomy in early Zionist discourse." In *National Politics and Sexuality in Transregional Perspective: The Homophobic Argument* (eds. Achim Rohde, Christina von Braun, and Stefanie Schüler-Springorum, Routledge, 2018), 107–120.

Sofer, Jehoeda. "Testimonies from the Holy Land: Israeli and Palestinian Men Talk about Their Sexual Encounters." In *Sexuality and Eroticism Among Males in Moslem Societies* (eds. Arno Schmitt and Jehoeda Sofer, Binghamton: Harrington Park Press, 1992), 105–120.

95. A Swiss Jew is Sent to Dachau for Homosexuality (Germany, 1936)

When the Nazi regime of the Third Reich came to power in 1933, it immediately began implementing its vision of purging German society of the groups it deemed racially and culturally impure and inferior—Jews in particular, but including also Roma, Communists, political dissidents, trans people, and gay men and lesbians. The first "concentration camps" were established in 1933 to detain those accused of being "enemies of the state." Jewish homosexuals, doubly stigmatized, received some of the harshest treatment in the camps. When Leopold Obermayer (1892–1943), a Swiss Jewish wine merchant, complained in 1934 to the police chief of Würzburg that his mail was being monitored, the Gestapo searched his home and discovered a safe deposit box with photographs of naked men; Obermayer was arrested, subjected to beatings and interrogations, and sent to the Dachau camp. Because of his Swiss nationality, he was allowed to appear at trial, and Obermayer filed this complaint describing the insults he had suffered as a Jew and a homosexual, emphasizing that his homosexuality had "not harmed public welfare in any way." Meanwhile, the Nazi officials involved in this case publicized it heavily, as a smear campaign against the perverted and disgusting nature of Jews. Obermayer was sentenced to ten years of penitentiary and sent back to Dachau; in 1942, he was transferred to Mauthausen, where he was killed in 1943.

To the Chief Prosecutor!

We had a conversation this morning concerning my spiritual welfare, and unfortunately I could see that you view me—unjustifiably—with mistrust and you're treating me more or less as a political prisoner, not a regular one.

All other prisoners are given access to a clergyman of their faith without first undergoing a torturous and embarrassing religious inquisition. You subjected me to the "Gretchen" question: "What's your take on religion?" I reluctantly conclude that my faith is being insulted.

Fortunately, I was able to reassure you with my answers; otherwise, I might have had to suffer the same fate as Renate Singerin of Würzburg-Oberzell: Würzburg has the "distinction" that it was there, in 1743, that the last "witch" was burned alive in Germany.

Mr. Prosecutor, I hope you now realize from our discussions that the worst mistake you could make would be to treat me with extreme mistrust. After all, I am a Swiss citizen whose mother tongue is German, and German culture and community are mine as much as yours. The more decently you treat me, the less cause I'll have to say hateful things about Germany, as the political police claim I've done. I have personally experienced negative discrimination from your political police, judges, district attorneys, court officials, etc. I don't deny, and neither will you, that there are all kinds of miscreants among my fellow Jews as well as my fellow citizens, just as there are among your people. But it would be unworthy of an educated person to ascribe the crime of an individual to a whole people.

When it comes to protecting my rights I remain uncompromising, and I unconditionally reject slander of Judaism and of me as a Jew—even at the risk of endangering myself in the short run. I also reject any and every compromise when it comes to issues of equality before the law. And I categorically deny have harmed public welfare in any way. I hope the day will come when people in Germany will regard the persecution of homosexuality in the same light as they view the burning of witches in Oberzell. Are you aware that until around 1862, in Bavaria homosexual activity wasn't even punishable at all?

In particular, I must regretfully report that Prosecutor Steeger treated me very prejudicially. In the interest of an objective hearing I would be grateful if another expert would represent the prosecution, since for the past two years Herr Steeger has belonged to the "circle of the accursed." That is why I'm requesting a "new man" in this position; please also refer to the complaint I filed and that you have seen.

Shortly I will give you documentation about how I have been insulted and mistreated by the justice system.

Further Reading

Grau, Günter, and Claudia Shoppman (eds.). *The Hidden Holocaust?: Gay and Lesbian Persecution in Germany 1933–45* (Routledge, 2012).

Giles, Geoffrey. "Why Bother About Homosexuals? Homophobia and Sexual Politics in Nazi Germany" (United States Holocaust Memorial Museum, 2002).

Hájková, Anna. "Den Holocaust queer erzählen." In *Jahrbuch Sexualitäten*, Vol. 3 (eds. Janin Afken, Jan Feddersen, Benno Gammerl, Rainer Nicolaysen, and Benedikt Wolf, Göttingen: Wallstein, 2018), 86–110.

Plant, Richard. *The Pink Triangle: The Nazi War Against Homosexuals* (Henry Holt, 1988).

Wünschmann, Kim. *Before Auschwitz: Jewish Prisoners in the Prewar Concentration Camps* (Harvard University Press, 2015).

96. A Reader of the Yiddish Forward Tells of Gender Transition in the Shtetl (New York, 1936)

In this remarkable letter to the editor of the *Forverts* (Jewish Daily Forward), a reader writes in response to stories of female athletes in Europe and the United States transitioning to men, a phenomenon widely covered in the Jewish and non-Jewish press during the 1936 Summer Olympics in Berlin. The writer of this piece, Samuel (Yeshaye) Kotofsky, was a 60-year-old grocer living in Brooklyn, who had immigrated to the United States in 1902. Kotofsky claims that gender transition is nothing new, telling the *Forverts* a story from his hometown of Krivozer (Kryve Ozero), a small shtetl in southern Ukraine. He describes how a young Jew from their town, raised as a girl named Beyle, had always felt uncomfortable with gender, "not quite a woman, but also not quite a man." Beyle's father had even consulted important Hasidic rabbis, the First Tolner Rebbe, David Twersky of Talne (1808–1876) and Avraham Yaakov Friedman of Sadigura (1820–1883), to no avail. At the age of 23, Beyle left for Odessa, where "an important professor" helped Beyle transition to the man he knew himself to be. Returning to the shtetl, he was welcomed with open arms and renamed Berel-Beyle. He married, "learned to *daven* [pray]," and was generally regarded "as a fine, upstanding Jew." How precisely this unnamed professor assisted Berel-Beyle, and the exact nature of Berel-Beyle's transition, is unclear. If Kotofsky's timing is to be trusted, Berel-Beyle's transition would have happened in the last decade of the nineteenth century, some ten to fifteen years before German doctors pioneered the basics of medical gender transition with clients such as Karl M. Baer (see source 68). It is likely that Berel-Beyle was intersex and treated with a combination of therapy and surgery like other cases of intersex people in the late nineteenth century, although it is not clear from this text how or with what specifically. Although this text raises more questions than it answers, it is still an invaluable account of the acceptance of gender transition among Ashkenazi Jews around the turn of the twentieth century.

AT THE AGE OF 23, THE GIRL BECAME A BOY

A Reader Tells an Interesting Event
from their Shtetl in Ukraine

Worthy Editor of the *Forward*: Not long ago I read a story in the *Forward* that took place in America, about how a girl became a man. But that's not news to the people in the town where I'm from. Permit me to tell the story in your paper.

In our shtetl of Krivozer, Ukraine, everyone knew Beyle, the girl who sold herring, geese and other foodstuffs. She was a tall redhead and sturdily built. She also spoke with a deep bass voice and walked about with hard and heavy steps. The way she carried herself always brought forth an uncertain feeling: something like, she's not quite a woman, but also not quite a man. When she was still a child, her father would often take her to see the Tolner Rebbe, Reb Dovidl, and sometimes to the Sadigura Rebbe, to ask for help. The only answer he ever got was "God will help, God will help." The father would return home anguished and unhappy.

In the meantime, the years flew by and Beyle grew, too, until she reached the age of 23. One fine morning, Beyle left for Odessa, where she was introduced to an important professor. She spent a long time under his care, under which Beyle eventually became a man. The story was well known and was in all the papers—all Russia talked of it.

In the shtetl, we waited impatiently for her return. And on the day when Beyle was to arrive, half the shtetl ran to the bridge to greet her, or better said, to greet *him*. And she wasn't called Beyle anymore: now she was Berel. And when we saw "her," it was as if we were stunned: Before our eyes was a handsome, healthy, redheaded man. Anyone who didn't know Beyle previously would never have known that he had been a girl.

From then on in the shtetl, "she" was called Berel-Beyle. With the help of the professor, the government freed him from military service. Berel-Beyle soon learned to daven and was in synagogue every day. Later on, he got married to an old girlfriend, Black Rachel, who was a nice girl. In our shtetl, Berel-Beyle always had a good name as a fine, upstanding Jew.

Yeshaye Kotofsky, 2817 W 32nd St., Brooklyn, New York.

"Tsu 23 yohr iz di meydl gevoren a bakhur." *Forverts*, November 19, 1936. Translated from Yiddish by Dr. Eddy Portnoy; I thank him for bringing this source to my attention and permitting his translation to be reprinted. I am also grateful to Dr. Laurie Marhoefer, Dr. Dan Healey, Dr. Katie Sutton, Dr. Rainer Hernn, and Adrian Kane for their generous input regarding the context of this source.

Further Reading

Healey, Dan. *Bolshevik Sexual Forensics: Diagnosing Disorder in the Clinic and Courtroom, 1917–1939* (Northern Illinois University Press, 2009).

Hernn, Rainer. *Schnittmuster des Geschlechts: Transvestitsmus und Transsexualität in der frühen Sexualwissenschaft* (Gießen: Psychosozial-Verlag, 2005).

Mak, Geertjie. "Conflicting Heterosexualities: Hermaphroditism and the Emergence of Surgery around 1900." *Journal of the History of Sexuality* 24:3 (2015), 402–427.

Marhoefer, Laurie. *Sex and the Weimar Republic: German Homosexual Emancipation and the Rise of the Nazis* (University of Toronto Press, 2015).

Portnoy, Eddy. "Transgender Jews May Be Nothing New." *Forward*, October 11, 2011 (https://forward.com/articles/144546/transgender-jews-may-be-nothing-new/).

97. A Sexologist Explains Homosexuality in Mandate Palestine (Tel Aviv, 1940)

By the 1930s, the pioneering science of "sexology" that had developed in Europe around the turn of the century (primarily in Germany, and to a lesser extent France, Russia, and England—see sources 64, 68, 72, and 96) had been translated and adapted to many new environments, including the New Yishuv, the Zionist Jewish settlement in the British Mandate of Palestine. One prominent sexologist was the Odessa-born physician Avraham Matmon (1900–1974), who immigrated to Palestine with his family in 1904. After receiving his medical degree in Berne, and working in Vienna and Cairo, Matmon then opened an Institute of Sexual Science in his home in Tel Aviv, modelled after Hirschfeld's *Institut für Sexualwissenschaft* in Berlin, which hosted classes and public lectures, published a medical journal, and offered private sexual consultation sessions. Matmon was particularly interested in the Zionist promise of Jewish regeneration, not just politically but physically as well; in his lectures and publications he advocated for marital counseling to avoid inheritable ailments, as informed by the race science and eugenics of his day. In this interview, he distinguishes between "sodomy" (*mishkav zakhar*) as a behavior (which he sees as depraved, perverse, and decidedly "Oriental" in origin), and "pure homosexuality" (for which he uses the Hebrew neologism *homoseqsualizm*), which he associates with the European intellectual upper class, and which he believes has concrete physiological causes. Unlike Hirschfeld's *Institut für Sexualwissenschaft*, Matmon does not advocate for equal rights for homosexuals, but rather urges the public to prevent the spread of this "psycho-pathological degeneration."

Homosexualists In Tel Aviv

WHAT IS THE OPINION OF THE SEXOLOGIST DR. MATMON ON THIS DISEASED PHENOMENON?

In connection with the discovery of a nest of depravity by the police of Tel Aviv, we turned to Dr. Avraham Matmon, the well-known sexologist, and we asked him to supply us with a scientific explanation for the disease beginning to establish itself in our land.

Dr. Matmon received our representatives in his waiting room on Ha-Shaḥar St., and gently agreed to our request. He gave the single condition that in order to provide the clearest explanation, the response take the form of questions and answers.

Our first question was: *Is homosexuality* [homoseqsualizm] *the same as the sodomy* [mishkav zakhar] *mentioned in the Torah?*

From a scientific standpoint, there is a difference between homosexuality and sodomy. Homosexuality is a deviation from the normal human sexual orientation. This deviation is a constitutional deviation in the natural functioning of a person's sexual glands. Because of this deviation, the normal human sexual orientation, which is towards someone not of their own sex (a man for a woman, and vice versa), is transformed into an orientation towards someone of their own sex (a man for a man, a woman for a woman). Sodomy or pederasty [*pederastiyyah*] is a depravity (perversion) of sexual orientation and drive, which is expressed in the intimate relations between two men.

How does the homosexual [homoseqsualistan] *respond to one who is not of their own sex?*

Homosexuals do not have any attraction to the opposite side. The reverse is true: intimate relations, or even thinking about intimacy, with someone who is not of their own sex brings up disgust and total rejection. The pederast can bring himself to have sexual relations with women as well as men. For pure homosexuals, their romantic life is not necessarily expressed in intimate relations.

Is homosexuality found among women?

Homosexuality can be found among both men and women, and according to the professor Magnus Hirschfeld, in almost equal quantities. (Homosexuality among women is called *lesbism* [*sic*] from the name of the island of Lesbos, where in ancient Greece there were sanctuaries of lesbian women, called *mesollelot* in the Talmud).

Is it a crime, or a flaw?

Over the course of generations, and in our own days, people have considered homosexuality to be sexual perversity and an abomination. Only at the end of the last century have many researchers begun to deal with this question from a purely scientific perspective. Much has been done by Dr. Magnus Hirschfeld, the world-famous sexologist, who was the first to openly defend homosexuals, since according to him this is no crime, but a physical flaw that must be taken into consideration. This teaching of Hirschfeld strengthened the hands of the homosexuals, especially in Germany, who gathered together to defend their "rights" to a sexual life in keeping with their natural orientation and construction. They have sought to have marriage legalized between men, and for this purpose also abolish the well-known Paragraph 175 of the German civil code which criminalizes sodomy [*mishkav zakhar*].

Where is homosexuality common?

Homosexuality and sodomy are reasonably common not only in the East, but also in Europe and especially Germany. Now the leaders of German youth want to introduce this ritual of love between men as one of the principles of the Nazi state. In the East, this affliction is very common, but mostly sodomy. Cases of pure homosexuality are very rare, in my opinion, in the East. Most of the cases are cases of depravity and lust for sodomy, especially among young men. In the cities of the Far East (Indochina, China, India), and also in Egypt, one can see men sitting in public places with their "youths" just like men sit with their women in Western countries. In most of the cases of pederasts in the East, they also have wives, and many of them stop their perversity after starting family lives.

In general, scholars believe that homosexuality and pederasty are phenomena of psycho-pathological degeneration, and those that are entrenched in it are mostly degenerate men, both in a physical and a psychological sense. Because of this, we might explain why the majority of homosexuals are actually found in the more intellectual [social] levels (while sodomy is more common in the lower levels). Perhaps it appears more common in these levels because for them it is accompanied by an exaggerated visibility, because of the cynical approach of cultured homosexuals who want to make from their flaw a sort of special sign of a more elevated personality.

What is the situation in the Land of Israel?

Until a few years ago, this affliction was not common at all among Jews. Among Ashkenazim, I saw a few isolated cases, but they were mostly from clearly degenerative families (families of psychopaths) and they were mostly cases of pure homosexuality. Most of the cases were among men and youths of low intellect, the children of drunkards, families afflicted with syphilis, etc. In recent years, the number of homosexuals in this land has increased, and most of the men afflicted with this are educated men, although degenerate emotionally and spiritually, almost in the full literal meaning of the word.

It seems to me that among the cases in this land, only a small portion of them are of pure homosexuals. Most of them are characteristically depraved. It is up to the public to be concerned about this—concluded Dr. Matmon—that these diseased men do not cause public moral harm by the continuous tempting of young men of weak intellect and lacking character into these sorts of shameful activities.

"Homoseqsualistim betel aviv." *'Itton Meyuḥad*, July 5, 1940, as published in Ofri Ilany, "'Nega' nafots bamizraḥ': te'urim shel homoseqsualiyyut ba'ittonut ha'ivrit shel tequfat hamandat," *Zmanim* 131 (2015), 8–21. Translated from Hebrew by Noam Sienna. I thank Dr. Ofri Ilany for generously sharing this source with me and helping contextualize it.

Further Reading

Hirsch, Dafna. "'We are Here to Bring the West, Not Only to Ourselves': Zionist Occidentalism and the Discourse of Hygiene in Mandate Palestine." *International Journal of Middle East Studies* 41:4 (2009), 577–594.

Ilany, Ofri. "'An Oriental Vice': Representations of sodomy in early Zionist discourse." In *National Politics and Sexuality in Transregional Perspective: The Homophobic Argument* (eds. Achim Rohde, Christina von Braun, and Stefanie Schüler-Springorum, Routledge, 2018), 107–120.

Kozma, Liat. "Sexology in the Yishuv: The Rise and Decline of Sexual Consultation in Tel Aviv, 1930–39." *International Journal of Middle East Studies* 42:2 (2010), 231–249.

Kozma, Liat. "Translating Sexology, Writing the Nation: Sexual Discourse and Practice in Hebrew and Arabic in the Late 1930s." In *Sexology and Translation: Culture and Scientific Encounters Across the Modern World, 1880–1930* (ed. Heike Bauer, Temple University Press, 2015), 135–152.

98. A Gay Jewish G.I. Writes a Defense of Homosexuality (Boston, 1940)

Between 1942 and 1946, thousands of American soldiers were issued Section 8 discharges from the American military for homosexuality, known as "blue" discharges because of their blue paper. One such soldier was Allen Bernstein (1913–2008), an American Jew born in Nashua, New Hampshire, to Ashkenazi immigrant parents. Bernstein had enlisted voluntarily in 1940, but was arrested and jailed for expressing interest in another male soldier; after admitting that he was gay, Bernstein was discharged in

1944 (following decades of appeals, this was finally overturned in 1981, and Bernstein was granted an honorable discharge and veteran status). In 1940, just before entering the Army, Bernstein typed an extraordinary 149-page manifesto, titled *Millions Of Queers (Our Homo America)*. In it, he argues that homosexuals (whom he calls *queers, homoes* [sic], and *gays*, some of the earliest testimony for these terms) should have the freedom to love and live as they wish. While Bernstein fights against some stereotypes of his time—such as the myth that gay men were all effeminate "fairies" and all lesbians were masculine "dikes"—he also internalized many negative beliefs about homosexuality, including that long-term homosexual relationships were impossible. Above all, he emphasizes that homosexuals are part of American society, and should not be criminalized or subjected to social pressure. After his discharge, Bernstein married a woman (telling her that he was gay) and had two children; he spent most of his post-Army life in Maine, where he was active in the Maine Lesbian/ Gay Political Alliance, American Veterans for Equal Rights, The AIDS Project, Am Chofshi (a group for LGBTQ Jews in Maine), and a men's group called Mainely Men. His manuscript sat for decades in the archives of the National Library of Medicine, where Dr. Randall Sell uncovered it in 2010 and identified the author.

What

Two and a half to three million American adults are made criminals by outdated laws forbidding them from expressing their natural affection for someone of their same sex. Similar laws have been on statute books constantly, from Solon's Athens to the present, the same way that prostitution, the world's oldest profession, has existed underground for a large share of its life. The laws have never worked. There always have been man-loving men or woman-loving women. There always will be. They have always managed to obtain their craved sensual satisfaction, despite the efforts of Moses or the Manhattan police force to the contrary. Everybody knows, in a vague sort of general way, that queers exist. No educational campaign, like Parran's for syphilis, is needed to open eyes to sexual aberrations. There may not be more of us numerically these last two or three decades, but we are more in the open. We are seen around more. We are the third sex; the urners; the lesbians, dikes, tribades; the inverts, perverts; the pansies, fairies, transvestists; the aunties, wolves, fags; the pederasts; the homosexuals...

Queers certainly deserve compliments on their successful conspiracy of silence—a truthful word, exposure, and personal economic and social catastrophe. Of course, most of those in small towns manage to have their fun outside and go to the nearest metropolis to be themselves. Among the people they know well, they live a clean, sexless, celibate life. The same as music-lovers on the frontier in pre-phonograph and pre-radio days, they say "no" to and completely shut up one side of their nature. They don't hurt you at all, so why should you poke into their business. There's no point, mother, in your being a completely ridiculous ostrich, and saying queers are found only in cities of 269,000 population and over, to select an arbitrary pointless figure, when there are some right here. At the same time, nothing would be gained by making homosexuals the newest scapegoat for the world's evils, changing from the Republicans or Democrats, Germans or Russians. Just be content to know that there are millions of them here in America, and some even here in Peoria, but let them be and let them live their own lives.

For these three or four or five million American voters, their sexual adjustment is just one additional hurdle to be jumped in an impersonal, indifferent world. It may become an ingrained habit like the half-forgotten limp of a war-veteran. After a generation, one gets used to it. It becomes a part of himself, a phase of his personality. As such, it is much more than whether a man or woman kisses, fondles, or sincerely loves another man or woman, respectively, instead of the more usual sexual crossing. It permeates a whole philosophy of life, and enters into a way of looking at the world. As a change from *The Doctor Looks at Love and Marriage*, consider *The Homosexual Looks at God and the Universe*, equally worth-while because expressing an out of the ordinary vantage point, and equally the result of a lifetime in one, field...

How

How do America's homoes live? You may as well ask how America's redheads or book-readers or people over five feet ten inches tall live. They get up at 7 or 8 to report to work an hour later. They quit work at 4 or 5 or 6 with a half-hour or an hour off for lunch. They sit home, go calling, or pass time wisely or unwisely, if jobless, or on evenings and weekends. How do they live in shared metropolitan cobbyholes, honestly, openly, with people whom they like, with whom they can be themselves? How do they live when their friends know they are Queer, or their whole social set is that way? The answer is the same. It holds true for forty million employed and ten million unemployed Americans; for stinkelectuals passing hours in libraries, and for glamour girls getting their faces in the roto sections, for schoolboy in his teens and grandmother in her eighties. Each day holds, say, eight hours of sleep, eight hours of labor-duties-regular-pattern, eight hours of dressing, eating and leisure. American homosexuals are not a caset [*sic*] or tribe apart. they live in the same cities and ~~houses~~* villages as normal; they work in the same offices and stores. "They infest the same houses, streets, farms, trolley cars, gymnasiums as other Americans; bear the same names; tip coke bttles [*sic*] at the same angle; copulate in the same postures [yes!]; make the same errors in grammar. Yet at the same point theirs does become a different world…"**

Why

Since homosexuality has existed as long as mankind, in every age and country, examining the reason for it brings one directly up to an evolutionary or religious poser. Why are there two eyes, rather than one? Why did the tail disappear in the long line of development from pithecanthropus erectus and the java and cro-magnon man to humanity, as we know it? Why do humans have two hands and five fingers? Why does hay-fever plague millions, and why did typhoid kill whole populations? From Abraham to Darwin, the long line of similar questions that could be asked were mere rhetoric or blasphemy. God the father created mankind in his image as he willed. To question the perfection of his handiwork would mean death from theocratic rulers. In the last century, the answer has changed. Pseudo-scientists say "evolution" where theologies would say "divine purpose". Pressed for explanations, their reasons boil down to descriptions; they tell how but not why…

There is no chief, sole reason for homosexuals. "God made them, as part of his universe" is still the best and blindest answer to "why". Don't call on an

---

* Crossed out in the manuscript.
** Note from text: Fortune; v. 21, no. 2 (Feb '40) p. 95; about the unemployed.

M.D.; knock at Heaven's Gate for enlightenment…Why is there homosexuality? Because there is pleasure in it. Because it is natural. Because it always was and always will be, as part of the universe. Because God so wills…

What To Do About It

Before curing, the cause has to be known. Is it economics or style; hormones or habit; personal weakness or delight in being contradictory. How does an infantile hangover become an old man's tragedy? Is an adult fondness for the same sex an unimportant personal idiosyncracy like being six feet tall or having blue eyes? Is it a lifelong badge of shame for flunking social education during puberty? If so, are all later fumbling attempts to lift the stain doomed to failure, or can people at 37 learn for the first time what they should have picked up at 15? Is homosexuality a social vice like mass addiction to opium, an epidemic in each generation, that can be successfully eradicated for once and for all?

Until those who are supposed to study it decide to interest themselves in all queers, the selected guinea pigs going to them can only be subjected to test and trial, new hopeful guess after old/failed guess, on and on, ever and ever. Until the psychiatrists decide whether the goal is to be a happy homo or happily married human, we may as well knock on Heaven's gate, instead of visiting them. Religion gives only a temporary answer. "God" is no one-word blind panacea. Typhoid was eliminated by doctors peering through microscopes, without clerical vestments. Until our doctors start peering at all of us, coldly and objectively, thru impersonal microscopes that take in all of our lives, we may turn with advantage to priestly robes. Some persons wearing them, followers of Plato, will combine ~~paiderastia~~ pederasty and philosophy to reach the peak of human existence, will minister both to our spiritual solace and sensual pleasure.

Until the psychiatrists decide whether we are sick or well, criminally spreading disease or hypochondriacs without real illness, we can only submit aching hearts to God. He is just and wise and merciful in all his ways, though no man can comprehend his ways. In the divine order of nature, both joy and sorrow serve beneficent ends. In the fullness of time, we shall know why we are tried, and our love brings us sorrow as well as happiness.

Allen Bernstein, *Millions Of Queers* (*Our Homo America*) (Boston, 1940), manuscript held in the National Library of Medicine, HMD MS B 198, as published on OutHistory.org. I thank Dr.

Randall Sell for permission to republish these excerpts, and for sharing his research on Allen Bernstein with me. I also thank Jonathan Ned Katz for providing additional assistance and context.

Further Reading

Bérubé, Allan. *Coming Out Under Fire: The History of Gay Men and Women in World War II, 20ᵗʰ Anniversary Edition* (University of North Carolina Press, 2010).

Katz, Jonathan Ned, and Randall Sell. "'Millions of Queers': A View from 1940." *Gay and Lesbian Review*, Jan–Feb 2015, 23–26 (http://www.glreview.org/article/millions-of-queers-a-view-from-1940/).

Katz, Jonathan Ned. "Analyzing Allen Bernstein's 'MILLIONS OF QUEERS (Our Homo America).'" *OutHistory*, 2014 (http://outhistory.org/exhibits/show/1940-defense/katz-bernstein).

99. Case Histories of Jewish-American "Sex Variants" (New York, 1941)

The last decades of the nineteenth century and the first decades of the twentieth century saw a flourishing of literature devoted to the study of sexuality, and homosexuality in particular; most of these studies were aimed at combining personal testimony with scientific and psychological analysis, to spur broader public acceptance of homosexuality. The book *Sex Variants: A Study of Homosexual Patterns*, first published in 1941, is a remarkable example of collaboration between lesbians and gay men with the medical and scientific establishment with this aim in mind. It was sponsored by the Committee for the Study of Sexual Variants, an organization established in 1935 by the gynecologist Robert L. Dickinson at the request of Jan Gay, a lesbian activist-researcher who had already been collecting lesbian case histories for the past decade in Europe and America. Gay (1902–1960) was born Helen Reitman, the daughter of noted American Jewish anarchist Ben Reitman (although she was raised by her Protestant grandparents). Along with Thomas Painter, a 29-year-old gay man who was also researching sexuality, she formed the Committee for the Study of Sexual Variants with Dr. Dickinson, Dr. George Henry (a psychiatrist at New York Hospital), and several other doctors and academics. Gay and Painter recruited over 200 subjects—lesbians, gay men, bisexuals, "transvestites," and male prostitutes—in New York and interviewed them; from this pool, Henry selected 80 cases for further in-depth studies, and follow-up interviews two years later, which were published as *Sex Variants*. Interestingly, a significant number (comprising 15%) of the subjects were Jewish. While the interviews were edited (and commented on extensively) by Henry, comparisons of the biographies of the few subjects that can be definitively identified with their reported histories in *Sex Variants* suggests that the portrayals are fairly accurate. Henry, however, makes no note of Gay or Painter's contributions to the work, and it is only through extensive research in the last decades that their roles have been identified. These excerpts offer examples of the life-stories of Jews involved in the study: "Moses," whom Henry classifies as a "neurotic schizophrenic homosexual" but who clearly and tragically articulates her desire to be a (heterosexual) woman; "Charlotte," who left her husband to live with her butch lesbian lover; and "Rose," who is very candid about her sexual experiences in the United States and Europe, declaring that "I'm counting on the next fifteen years for something rich and lovely."

Moses I.

GENERAL IMPRESSION.

Moses is a rather heavy-set man of thirty-eight, whose rounded face with high forehead, large nose and mouth and heavy jowls disclose distinct Semitic features. He sits uneasily on the edge of his chair, bent forward in the appealing attitude of an insecure person who apologizes for his intrusion. He appears timid and cringing, expresses gratitude for any attention he receives, and at the same time slyly studies the physician and tenaciously pursues his quest for help.

His voice and manner of speech support this impression. He speaks slowly, scarcely above a whisper, and his mushy articulation makes it difficult to grasp what he is saying. He stands and walks with stooped shoulders and slightly bent forward at the hips, uncertain in his stride and about two feet behind the physician.

As far as his outer garments are concerned Moses is modestly conventional but underneath his suit he wears a corselet, pink panties, and long silk stockings. He derives pleasure from wearing women's clothes and whenever possible his attire is completely female. In public he has a desire to pull up his trousers to show his stockings and he had no hesitation in displaying his undergarments to the physician.

FAMILY BACKGROUND

My father's parents were Rumanian Jews and my mother's were German Jews. On both sides of my family my grandparents had high standards of culture, education, and industry. They were descended from nobility. My father's father was a rather strict and very pious rabbi and my mother's father was a very gracious count, religious and generous to a fault…

Also as a child I used to look at courtly ladies with some sort of exotic or erotic feeling. Mother always asked me to help her button her dress in the back. Why she didn't pick on my sister I don't know. In the closets there were plenty of women's clothes which I would put on and while thus dressed I masturbated myself with my hand or with some part of the clothing. I used to say to myself, "I don't want these genitals." The feeling seemed to be that I wanted woman genitals. I had seen them in picture books and had read about them. I was in a happier frame of mind thinking I was a woman and I was envious of my sister's being a girl…

PERSONAL HISTORY

In high school one of the boys tried to initiate me into masturbation but I told him I knew more about it than he did. He left me alone after that. I had begun masturbating when I was seven and I think I had my first emission when I was nine. It was a very strange sensation but I was not especially frightened.

At ten or eleven I saw the program of Julian Eltinge, the female impersonator. He made an awful impression. I decided to go see him. When I came home I tried it. Seeing him in his act dressed up in feminine clothes gave me a peculiar sensation. It made me feel I was sinking into something, that I was giving up something. I used to feel it in my ear drums.

After seeing Eltinge I used to watch similar performances. Secretly I put on my mother's or my sister's clothing. I would put on everything and walk around and admire myself and try to see whether I had a feminine form. I wondered if I could get one.

I wrote articles for magazines—masquerade ideas. I was always imagining myself in feminine form. I used to imagine myself the central lady in the story. I wanted to be treated as a woman. I wanted a man to kiss me as though I was a woman, and yet I never thought much about sex.

Mother never knew about my interest in women's clothes but I think one of my sisters did. Whenever I saw an opportunity I put on her garments, especially the things next to the skin—her corset, panties, and stockings. She used to ask me about it and I would deny it...

There have been times in the past six years that my wife has urged me to enjoy intercourse with her and while I am in sympathy with her desires I cannot overcome the physical revulsion that overwhelms me. I used to get hold of her left breast and by sucking on it I could induce a passionate frenzy in my wife. At first I thought this was interesting but it has become rather repulsive and I haven't done it in six months.

A few weeks ago she went to a doctor to be stretched. He told her to stop worrying. She wants me to do it now if I can. She tries to touch my genitals but I can't stand it any more. It seems to be a revolting gesture.

I've told my wife about some of my ideas—that I desire to turn into a woman—but I haven't told her everything. She knows about my feminine attire. I voluntarily discussed it with her a year ago. It was the most shocking discovery she ever came across. She was speechless.

My wife deserves better than I am and she shouldn't waste precious time about it. I have suggested annulment. I've tried every possible means to urge her to separate. Once in a moment of insane rage I threatened her with publicity. I had in mind the severing of our relations and giving the reason.

Two years ago I told my wife, through a friend that I was afraid of what I might do—commit suicide by jumping from the fourteenth floor. Thoughts of suicide are always prevalent. During the war I tried to enlist and was turned down. I then got into an open street car and took poison. I woke up in a hospital.

Since my marriage I've made two futile attempts at suicide with poison powders. The last of these attempts was the result of a nervous breakdown. I had been working in a cosmetic store where I played around with perfumes, rouge, face powder and lipstick, together with tweezing my eyebrows and using mascara. I practically ran amok with my excesses, purchasing and wearing such articles of feminine apparel as slips, panties, stockings, corsets and brassieres. It was with the view of either "kill or cure" that I then voluntarily told my wife of my secret. We decided that it was best for me to get away from such work.

My attempts at relations with my wife have always resulted in miserable failure and I have resorted to masturbation. I've been masturbating since I was seven years old but now when I resort to the practice I hope against hope for the impossible, that perhaps in time my genitals will become so useless that I must be castrated. They could operate on my pituitary gland and give me ovarian extract. In time I could assume the role of woman and follow inclinations I have bottled up for so long in my heart of hearts—to do nursing, looking after children. I've had plenty of experience through my sisters' families. I took care of all of their children when they were little tots, much better than their mothers did.

Female nursing has long been an idea I've toyed with, almost all my adult life. If I could only direct the way of life of my sisters and fellow women—how to make their lives happier and healthier—how much happier I would be. I am so positive that I have the necessary vision and foresight, and sufficient human understanding. There are times when the strength of this desire brings tears to my eyes.

I have the ability to imagine myself being changed into a woman and arrayed in female clothing from head to foot, but when I look at my body I am driven to masturbation in order to secure surcease from myself. During this imagining process I place each piece of female clothing on my body with a steady, slow motion that helps to bring on still further the desire to masturbate; I feel completely rested and satisfied with the wearing apparel of a woman, a satisfaction that conveys to me the only peace of mind I have had throughout my life.

Sometimes I dream about being a woman and enjoying myself as a woman. As a child I used to dream I was a heroine, characterized by pureness and goodness. Sometimes I dreamed I was a female cat and that another cat was having relations with me. Recently I dreamed that five or attractive young women were handling me. One was a nurse and another was a doctor operating on my testicles and penis. Then one of them began inserting ovarian extract. Slowly I was falling into an abyss of gratification and satisfaction, a deep sense of sensuality and voluptuousness. Lo and behold, I turned into a lovely young woman—feminine, dainty, rounded shoulders, full bosom, narrow waist, beautiful tresses, well-formed feet and ankles, clear complexion, everything feminine to the minutest detail—a complete transformation. Another young woman was dressing my body with exquisite clothes, my hair was being coiffured and my fingernails polished. Every timbre and fiber in my being, my movements as I walked, my sensations, and my thoughts were expressing themselves in a feminine way.

Sometimes I have attacks of desire to mutilate myself. I would prefer to have my penis removed and a vagina made surgically but sometimes at night I get the idea of doing it myself...

Several times I've been asked if I like men. I don't particularly, unless if I were a woman. I desire to have a child but not as a man. There is so much literature extant on the subject of pederasty that I often question whether or not a complete change of sex could not be established when the psychological aspects of a case are entirely feminine.

Recently while sexually aroused I've had some sort of voluptuous sucking in the rectum. I've had a desire to be a woman with a man. While masturbating I put a towel between my thighs and then have a sexual desire for a man in the rectum. It seems as though I'm going into an abyss and trying to reach for a foothold, as though my body was taking on feminine form. My body becomes tense. This lasts for an hour or so. Recently in a dream a man proposed marriage to me. He was fondling and caressing me. I imagined I could feel his penis pressing against me.

I don't seem to have any shame going around this way garbed in female attire. I'm now wearing women's stockings, a corset and silk underwear. Naturally I very frequently shave my entire body and I also use depilatories. My wife knows this. She seems to want to do everything to help me. Once in a while she tries to get me aroused sexually but I don't like it. I tell her it's no use.

During the past year I've had spasms of hysterical crying. I seem to be very petulant and have to dissemble in a womanish fashion. My mind is in a quandary. I've lost all initiative to get work. Everything overwhelms me and I succumb to a feeling of lassitude, of being immersed and gradually sucked up. What is the way out for me? I wish I knew.

[Henry's note: Since the above was written it was learned that Moses has made two unsuccessful attempts at suicide. His adjustment to his wife has not improved and most of the time he is dependent upon her for support.]

Charlotte N.

GENERAL IMPRESSION

Charlotte is a petite brunette of twenty-seven. Her black hair is worn in a long bob and her eyebrows are plucked. Dark eyes, a thin, shapely nose and full lips are distinguishing features of her oval face. Her good looks are marred somewhat when she smiles and shows uneven teeth. She speaks with the soft, appealing voice of an immature girl but her body in its general form is that of an adult female. In her dress, attitude, and bearing there is a strong feminine allure. She is attentive, frank, and cooperative…

FAMILY BACKGROUND

I know nothing about my father's parents except that they were Russian Jews and that they belonged to a family of small tradesman who were religious and conservative. They had four daughters and two sons. All of them except my father are still in Russia, all are married and all have children…

Mother's parents were Russian Jews also. Grandfather was a shrewd man but not very successful in business. He was twice married and had three children by his first wife and six by his second. Grandmother was more aggressive than he was. She was a little distant toward others but they got along well together…

PERSONAL HISTORY

Marriage was not very successful. My husband was an Italian and I married him against my parents' wishes. I had been twice engaged to one of my own race and religion. One of these I spurned because of his jealousy and the other because I found I cared more for the man I married.

My husband just took me for granted. After the first year his attentions to me were infrequent and of the most casual. Frequently I was alone all day all night. I was depressed by this and by the arguments over it. I was very lonesome. I wanted children but he was too selfish and didn't want to be bothered with the responsibility.

Through my husband's family I met some girls and I used to stop to see them quite often to occupy my evenings. I would stay out as late as I could in order not to be home alone. One of them, a masculine girl [of Irish background named Nora], invited me to her house. She had a girl sweetheart living with her. Both of them were masculine. I was invited to join them. I went every night. I preferred to be there to being at home.

We were very friendly. One night last summer she was drinking and she put her arms around me and told me she loved me. I pushed her away and told her she had been drinking and didn't know what she was saying. I resented it but I didn't want to hurt her feelings. I enjoyed being with her. She asked me to stay all night and I refused.

Finally I stayed. She waited for me to come in. I had been drinking a bit. I didn't know she was a Lesbian. She kissed me and hugged me and used her hand. She got me very passionate. I told her to stop. She knew I hadn't had much relation with my husband. For several weeks I hadn't been intimate with him. Finally she used her mouth. It didn't bother me. It was rather surprising but I didn't realize what it was at a particular moment. She just slipped down in bed. I had an orgasm and it seemed to be greater than any I had with my husband.

We have been living together for the last three months and we have sex every other night. I am always passive. Sometimes she is on top of me and vice versa. I have an orgasm and go to sleep. She is considerate of me. If I want to sleep she just lets me sleep. She's terribly fond of me. She feels she wants me to live with her the rest of her life.

I never thought I would have so much desire. It seems an outlet and I feel I could continue this way but I can't expect it to last. I know people change and from what I have heard they are quite fickle. That's the only reason I've been quite worried about it. She has changed my point of view on a lot of things. I wanted to have a child but since I've known this girl it doesn't seem to make much difference. I've centered all my affection on her.

My feeling toward men has changed. I admire them but physically I don't think I have much desire. Alcohol used to make me passionate for men but now it does for this girl. It makes me lively at times and sometimes I feel like sleeping.

I began drinking about eight years ago with several girls in the Village. I got partially intoxicated several times a week. In the past few years it's been less frequent. I stopped because of the stomach trouble and my eyes were looking very bad, sort of dissipated.

I left my husband when I went to live with this girl. I told him about it. He dismissed it as a whim and seemed confident that I would return to him. As a bribe to get me to return to him he has agreed to let me have a child. He has been trying to make amends but my affection is not with him. I still have a certain amount of regard for him…

If I were in love with my husband I think I would prefer being with him. It's more exciting with this woman and it lasts two or three times as long. She is so tender, affectionate and attentive. It's a longing I have had and she seems to fulfill that greatly.

I feel more protected with her than with my husband. She is very aggressive. My husband is masculine but he's happy-go-lucky. He doesn't seem to take things seriously. He feels it is just a lark and that I will get over it in time. He is very patient with me.

At times I get annoyed by this girl's actions. She is a bit domineering and I have been accustomed to having my own way. She drinks quite a bit and I disapprove of that. If I could depend upon her I would stay. It's just a longing for devotion. I'm really quite normal but she certainly has a strong hold on me. Wanting a child is probably the only thing that will make me change.

When I first heard of homosexuality I condemned it. I never thought I would drift into it myself but I have no regrets.

My husband has been covering me up and my family don't know that we are separated. I haven't seen them very much lately. They know nothing of the homosexual affair.

If I could be sure that this girl would remain faithful I would be willing to end my marriage in spite of the wishes of my family. I'm a bit worried about the future however. I know what the habits and dispositions of these people are. She tells me it isn't so but I have my doubts.

[Henry's note: A year after the preceding was written Charlotte returned for advice about prenatal care. She had returned to her husband and had become pregnant. She was looking forward to having a child.

Later it was learned that a healthy child was born; also that Charlotte's husband had a background of being a wild fellow, that during a period when he was out of work Nora took both Charlotte and her husband into her home, that the husband was discovered attempting to forge Nora's name and that he was arrested for robbery; friends of Nora wanted her to prosecute him but she refused to press charges.]

Rose S.

GENERAL IMPRESSION

Rose has been well described as a statuesque blonde with delicately molded features and white, translucent skin. An aura of long, wavy blonde hair and the voluptuous curves of her body make her seem a woman Rubens might have chosen to paint.

In the capacity of a business woman her dreamy blue eyes become shrewd and penetrating and her low, modulated voice takes on a bargaining tone. She then reveals the masculine, aggressive aspects of her personality.

Rose is now thirty-five years old, somewhat embittered by her experiences and keenly sensitive to any discrimination against Jews. She is still self-conscious because of her large breasts and she is probably aware of her heavy wrists and straight, sturdy legs…

FAMILY BACKGROUND

The information which I can give you regarding my father's family is very scanty. I have been told that the men were scholars and that they were shrewd in business. My grandfather, a Russian Jew, died when my father was seven and my grandmother, an Austrian Jewess, died when my father was born…My father was born in Russia and came to the United States at fifteen. Being an orphan he had to work his way through everything...

[My maternal grandfather] was known as a learned and distinguished man, a student of the Talmud and of other rabbinical writings. He was greatly interested in the emancipation of the Jews in Russia and was instrumental in bringing many of them to America. Although he was married three or four times he had all his children by his first wife. She died young. She was a very sweet, gentle soul, a lovely, lovely person. Both of my grandparents were Russian Jews...

PERSONAL HISTORY

At eighteen I came back to New York to put myself through dramatic school and a two-year university course. I was always studying something and I just took the subjects that interested me. I didn't try for credits.

Soon I met a divorced man, forty-five years old. He fascinated me intellectually. He had traveled everywhere and had a lot of ideas. I've never been able to explain it but I couldn't stand him kissing me. I always fought desperately against him and pretended I didn't enjoy sex with him, even though I did when it finally happened. I grew to hate him but even when I hated him we were mated physically.

A year after I met him we were married...When [our] baby was two years old I met a married woman who was not living with her husband and I fell madly in love with her. That was the beginning. She had two children but she had had a number of affairs with women and was a drunkard. As soon as I met her and looked into her eyes something happened. After that I couldn't stand my husband and I began to lose interest in my child. She invited me to come to hear the radio. I dressed as though I were going to my wedding.

We got so we couldn't leave each other and I left my husband and my child and went to live with her. This was my first homosexual experience. It was so new and so strange that I couldn't respond. She tried everything but it was of no avail. After several weeks my body responded and I was so excited by her that I didn't care. She rubbed her clitoris against mine. She was usually on top making the sexual movements. I think she had a large clitoris. At first I didn't do anything except use my hand. I couldn't bring myself to the french way but toward the end I think I did once and didn't like it.

My husband wanted to know what was happening but I didn't tell him. There were long telephone conversations with him. I never expressed my feeling for this woman in words but he was very jealous of her. I hope it never dawned on him.

This woman drank so much that after six months I felt I had to leave her or she would wreck me. She said she would commit suicide if I left her but I got on a boat and went to Europe just to get away from her.

Something terrible happened to me on the boat. It was a long trip and I missed my child. The night before we landed something snapped in my mind. I suddenly went dumb. I couldn't answer anyone and I walked through the corridors with my eyes closed. I felt I was dying. They called the doctor and then I became hysterical. After I had cried awhile I seemed to be all right.

In four or five months I came back to the United States and found that this woman had had a nervous breakdown and was in a sanitarium. I dashed off to see her. Our feelings for each other then seemed very spiritual. It seemed that nothing physical could happen. We exchanged rings and it seemed that in the eyes of God we were married.

Then I left her to get my baby and I discovered that while I was away my husband had met another woman who wanted to marry him. He agreed to let me take the child back to New York. I waited all day for him but there was not a word until just before my train left. Then his aunt told me that he had taken the child with him to Canada. That stung me so much spiritually that I have never since been able to write to him even though I wanted to find out about my child.

The first thing I did after my child was stolen was to cut off my hair and put on a tie. I got into tailored clothes and tried to talk and walk like a man. I became a very aggressive, masculine person. I became very antisocial and wanted to smash my way through the world. I wouldn't talk to a woman and didn't look at a man. I decided I was going to be a very great success in business. I did nothing but work. I just wasted years.

Two years after I met the first woman, I fell in love with another who was also quite masculine. I was then twenty-six and she was about the same age, a very aggressive business woman but the best looking thing. It was a very violent love affair. She took me into her home and she said she wanted to live with me forever. We couldn't part for a minute. Her mother seemed to understand. In eight months she was untrue to me and I made up my mind it couldn't be anything constructive so I broke it up. It was very hard.

I am very natural about sex. I don't think anything is wrong if you enjoy the person. Physically I don't think homosexual relations are bad. I would have liked to have a child by this last woman if she hadn't played around so much. It's all so cheap. Women are not honest enough. They play around to make you jealous. It's a lovely thing if you don't cheapen it.

In my relations with these women I pretended I was a man and that I had a penis which penetrated the other woman. She pretended that also. With her body against mine and the clitoris against the clitoris the feeling that we were men was much more exciting than just using the finger. We talked about having babies and giving a woman a baby. That's a very common fantasy. A woman who takes the part of a man and uses her body as a man is called "dyke."

Some of the women wanted me to bring an artificial penis back from Europe. There is mad desire to penetrate a woman, especially when you are not able to. They use anything they can find, anything that resembles a man's organ...

Just now I feel I would like to be more like a man and have normal sex. You just feel grand and go out and accomplish things. I do and I don't want children. There are moments when I do but I think the time has passed now for me to have children. I'm counting on the next fifteen years for something rich and lovely.

George Henry (ed.), *Sex Variants: A study of homosexual patterns*, 2nd ed. (New York: Paul Hoebner, 1948), 534–542, 583–588, 927–932. I am grateful to Dr. Jennifer Terry for providing additional information and context for this source.

Further Reading

Meyerowitz, Joanne. *How Sex Changed: A History of Transsexuality in the United States* (Harvard University Press, 2002).

Minton, Henry. *Departing from Deviance: A History of Homosexual Rights and Emancipatory Science in America* (University of Chicago Press, 2002).

Reis, Martha Lynn. *Hidden Histories: Ben Reitman and the 'Outcast' Women Behind 'Sister of the Road: The Autobiography of Box-Car Bertha'* (Ph.D. dissertation, University of Minnesota, 2000).

Terry, Jennifer. *An American Obsession: Science, Medicine, and Homosexuality in Modern Society* (University of Chicago Press, 1999).

100. A Young German Jew Writes his Boyfriend a Love Letter (Berlin, 1942)

This love letter, written in the form of an illustrated booklet, was created in the summer of 1942 by Meir (Manfred) Lewin (1922–1942) as a gift for his boyfriend, Gad (Gerhard) Beck (1923–2012). Lewin and Beck met that year in the Zionist youth movement HeḤalutz, which was one of the few institutions of Jewish life still operating in Nazi Berlin. Inspired by their reading of Schiller's eighteenth-century romantic play *Don Carlos*, Lewin made this gift for Beck to celebrate their relationship. Deportations had already begun, and the remaining Jews in Berlin were divided in their responses: co-operate? Flee? Resist? In the fall of 1942, Lewin and his family were ordered to assemble on Grosse Hamburger Strasse for deportation; Beck was exempt from deportation, since Beck's mother had converted to Judaism, and he was thus classified as a *Mischling*, "mixed-blood." Beck attempted to save his boyfriend, dressing as a Hitler Youth and escorting Lewin out of the assembly camp, but Lewin would not leave his family, and returned to accompany them; the entire Lewin family was murdered in Auschwitz. Beck joined the underground resistance, and survived the war; he emigrated to Palestine in 1947. Returning to Germany in 1979, he devoted the rest of his life to education and activism. Beck published his memoir, *An Underground Life: Memoirs of a Gay Jew in Nazi Berlin*, in 1995 in German, and in English translation in 2000. He donated this fragile booklet to the United States Holocaust Memorial Museum in 1999.

Do You Remember, When?

Dear, kind Gad, I owe you a present, no, I want to give you one, not just so that you get something from me that you can glance through and then lay aside forever, but something that will make you happy whenever you pick it up.

[A drawing of Gad in profile]
How could anyone bring us someone like this?
We asked ourselves in fits of laughter.

[A drawing of Gad tied to a tree]
Oh, we made fun of him when he was hanging there tied to that tree, but
I felt differently…

[A drawing of a book with the cover Don Carlos]
And our group was drawn closer, when Karlos was enjoyed by everyone…

[A drawing of a bed]
Night exists for more than sleep which is why, my love, we stayed awake
so often.

[A drawing of people around a table with a falling bomb]
We lived through many exploding bombs.

[A drawing of people holding hands]
But five minutes later we knew peace again.

Lothar Herrmann only paints rooms, which is why I don't have much
idea how to draw cartoons. Nor am I a mighty poet, but I did it as well as
I could.

Sometimes it looks like this in Meir [i.e. in me]:

A void opens within me
Spirit and body suddenly are lame
The time that follows is torture
In which I seek out the strength to go
on living!
    Often I see myself standing at the
edge of an abyss
Felt my utter abandonment
And the dizziness when I left my eyes
look down

And the sudden draining of blood
from my cheeks!

But suddenly from the blackest depths
A gentle voice came echoing
Looking down I wondered who might
be calling out to me
Although the voice was one I knew at once!
  It was the voice of a sacred power
It was the sound of souls in harmony
It was the essence of our humanity
The quality we must never lose!

When in a single move Destiny
unleashes its terrible game
And sweeps you away to some far
distant land
When our exile stretches ever further
Will the last bonds of our community
be torn apart!?

Then don't lament
Even though the fire torments your
heart
For there is one sure support
a voice that we call friendship!

  [In Hebrew:] *Shavu'ot*
  May 21, 1942
  Forever my best wishes are with you.
  [In Hebrew:] *Be strong and courageous. Your Meir.*

Meir (Manfred) Lewin, "Do You Remember When" (May 1942), as translated by Carol Brown Janeway; online exhibit by the United States Holocaust Memorial Museum, curated by Klaus Mueller (https://www.ushmm.org/collections/the-museums-collections/collections-highlights/do-you-remember-when/). Reprinted by permission of the United States Holocaust Memorial Museum.

Further Reading

Beck, Gad. *An Underground Life: Memoirs of a Gay Jew in Nazi Berlin* (written with Frank Heibert, University of Wisconsin Press, 1999).

Hájková, Anna. "Den Holocaust queer erzählen." In *Jahrbuch Sexualitäten*, Vol. 3 (eds. Janin Afken, Jan Feddersen, Benno Gammerl, Rainer Nicolaysen, and Benedikt Wolf, Göttingen: Wallstein, 2018), 86–110.

Meyer, Beate, Hermann Simon, and Chana Schütz (eds.). *Jews in Nazi Berlin: From Kristallnacht to Liberation* (University of Chicago Press, 2009).

Paragraph 175. Directed by Rob Epstein and Jeffrey Friedman (Telling Pictures, 2000).

Plant, Richard. *The Pink Triangle: The Nazi War Against Homosexuals* (Henry Holt, 1988).

101. *Wasteland*, A Lesbian American Jewish Novel (New York, 1946)

First published in 1946, Jo Sinclair's *Wasteland* is a landmark both of Jewish-American literature and LGBTQ literature. The novel focuses on Jake Braunowitz (who also goes by John Brown), an American Jew struggling with his Jewish identity, and his sister Debby, who is both a committed Jew and a lesbian, although she never uses that word for herself—Jake's psychiatrist describes Debby as a homosexual, a lesbian, and even a degenerate, while the closest Debby comes to naming herself is when when she tells Jake, "the odd ones, the queer and different ones. They were people. I was people...I was them." Through watching his sister, and her conviction in the worthiness of her own identity (as well as her solidarity with other oppressed minorities, especially African-Americans), Jake eventually learns to accept the complexities of his own identity. Jonathan Ned Katz described Debby as "probably the most complex, human, and affirmative portrait of a homosexual (male or female) to appear in American fiction," until the 1960s. The research of Monica Bachmann has demonstrated that *Wasteland* was widely read by lesbians and gay men, who wrote to the author to express their gratitude for a character with whom they could identity. Jo Sinclair was the pen name of Ruth Seid (1913–1995), born in Brooklyn to parents who had fled pogroms in Russia. Seid grew up in Cleveland and began writing while working in a local factory. Like Debby, Seid's social circle was racially diverse, and heavily leftist. Her work was well received: *Wasteland*, her first novel, won the Harper Novel Prize for fiction in 1946; her second novel, *The Changelings* (1955) won the Jewish Book Council of America's 1956 award for the best novel. *The Changelings* deals with the emotional relationship between two teenage girls (one Jewish and one Black); as Elly Bulkin has shown, the first draft—written in 1942 and originally titled *The Long Moment*—is even more explicit in its homoeroticism. Seid herself was generally quiet about her lesbian identity, although she did discuss it more freely in letters from the 1980s and 1990s. She published a memoir in 1993, *The Seasons*, and spent her last years with her partner, Joan Sofer, in Pennsylvania.

If anybody was the big shot, the one to whom Ma looked for whom she prepared meals, it was, of all people—Debby!

His sister Deborah. Well, she went with the house, too. But in an entirely different way. If he could explain how he felt about her! She was different, entirely different from any of them. Look at Roz. Makeup, high heels, divorced, a night club waitress. Look at Sig, a guy who could cry like a woman. Look at Sarah and her awful family. And he, Jack, ashamed, eyes down wherever he went. And then look at Deborah. As if she didn't belong to any of them. As if she had been put into that house by accident. Yes, she looked a lot like all of them, except she was more blond, her eyes much more blue. Yes, she resembled him, especially. They had the same shape face, kind of the same sort of jaw. But what resemblance was there between her brain and theirs? Her—all right, soul! None, absolutely none. Everything she did was different, and the way it. She was the youngest in the family; you know, the baby.

His sister Deborah. She was a book person, a music person. He had always thought of her as a scholar; well, she wasn't really, but she was always monkeying with books and magazines. She was always sitting there in the living room, with a pencil in her hand.

He didn't know a lot about her, no. She had always made him feel funny. She was so damn odd. Smart. My God, you know that girl was the valedictorian of her class in high school. No, not college, nobody in the family had gone to college. Sig went to night college for a little while. He quit after a while.

Oh hell, a person like Debby didn't really have to go to college. Yes, he'd always felt funny about her. He thought that was a feeling of shame, too. The way she looked like a boy, her hair cut short that way. He used to look at her and keep out of her way. He used to think, My God, if the fellows at the office saw her they'd laugh like hell. They'd look at me and say, "Jesus, Brown, what kind of a thing is that? You mean that's your sister?"

Now, he wondered if it was shame. See, she was special. She wrote stories. She was—well it was hard to explain about Debby. When you looked at her you got a feeling strong she was how—clean. See, she was the one clean thing in the house. Everything about her was different. The kind of things she read, the kind of music she liked, the way she talked.

She talked Yiddish to Ma and Pa, sure, and she liked those Hebrew things the old man sang on holidays. But she looked just like a gentile boy. Sure, even in a dress. Around the house she always wore slacks. She'd always worn pants around the house. He could remember when she was a kid; she wore a funny, little pair of shabby knickers, and her hair was cut Buster Brown in those days. She'd looked like a little, tough Dutch boy. Milk-white hair, just like now, only now it was cut like a boy's.

Well, he didn't know, maybe he was still ashamed of her. Would he take her up to the newspaper, introduce her as his sister, to the editor, to Pete, to Wally and Katherine? My God, no! See, she wasn't like other people. She was too different. And there was another example! The whole bunch of them; they were different, not like other people. That's what makes a fellow ashamed. When a fellow is scared to death anybody he knows will ever catch sight of his parents, his sisters. O.K., Sig was nothing to be ashamed about, in his clothes or his speech. But look at his insides! That was something, wasn't it? To be ashamed of your older brother because he's all beat up inside…

It was around that time that I began to watch my sister Deborah as much as I could. Watched her, what she did, how she did it. It was around that time that I began to feel as if there was a secret in the house, in the family. I thought maybe if I could figure Deborah out, then maybe I could figure out that secret.

But I couldn't. How could I figure her out? She was like that music she tuned in on the radio, strong and far away from me, sounds I couldn't understand inside of me. She was a secret, half like a man and half like a woman. Yeah, I began to see in her face and her eyes a lot of what women have there. A softness, a kind of a tender business. The way she talked to Ma sometimes, as if she were the older and stronger, and Ma could lean on her if she wanted to. The way she had nothing to do with the old man, but would bring home candy for Ma sometimes, or a shopping basket, or an umbrella—you know, little presents.

Sometimes, when I turned the key and let myself into the house, at eleven or so, she wouldn't be sitting there under the lamplight. The radio would be playing very softly, her kind of music, and when I'd walk into the other part of the house I'd see a light in the bathroom, the door open. There she was, with a rag and scouring powder, scrubbing the washbowl. Or she'd be on her knees, scrubbing the toilet. I'd see such things often, and to me it was a secret that she did them.

Yeah, and her friends were a secret I couldn't figure out. I would see them in the house on Saturday nights sometimes, and when I'd let myself in, Debby would say, "John, I want you to meet a friend of mine."

I'd say, "How do you do," and walk quick into the dining room, take off my coat, beat it into my bedroom.

Her friends. They were as peculiar as she was. They made me feel funny, sitting there in the living room, smoking and talking, or drinking the coffee Debby had made in the kitchen and carried in.

There was that colored girl. There was this girl, Fran. Jewish. She ran her father's pawnshop. Ma told me she wrote things. Not stories, but *lieder*, Ma said. I finally figured it out, poetry. She was Debby's best friend, Ma said. A thin girl who looked dark and Jewish and sort of afraid. I never saw her smile. I think she was afraid, because sometimes I felt inside the way her eyes looked.

There was a girl they called Toby. Short red hair, a plump girl. She looked kind of like a happy, smiling boy. There was a good-looking woman they called Barbara. Debby had met her in WPA days; she'd been Debby's boss. She was the one who brought a portable victrola with her sometimes, and books of records.

Then that same kind of music that Debby got from the radio would go all through the house, for hours. I could hear it in my bedroom.

I didn't dislike that music. It was really a hell of a lot like Debby. Some of it sounded strong, some sweet and tender, so that it made me feel funny. Music that was a secret to me, like she was, and behind her the house. You can't figure out a secret by watching it. I couldn't understand those people she had over to the house on Saturdays. All I knew was, they were different, too, and she was their friend. It all made me feel twice as hard how different she was. What if I were to meet her downtown some day, right smack on Main Street, and what if I were walking with Wally or Bill when I met her? Or anybody from the paper. "This is my sister Deborah. She's a secret to me, fellows. If you know what the secret of her is, why by God you'll have the secret of that house of mine! And maybe of me, fellows."

Debby. Yeah, and wasn't it a secret how he could feel so mixed up about her? Ashamed, sure, but what about the feeling he always had about her strength and cleanliness, her story writing, her intelligence? You know what? Part of that secret was that she was like Friday night in his mind. When he came home every Friday night to eat supper, he was always glad Debby would be there. She was a part of that night, a part of the small section of his life that was regular, that was there, that was for sure. Like the *cholah* Ma baked every Friday afternoon, like the peppery fish, the golden-colored, thin noodles in the chicken soup…

His head came down, and now they were looking at one another, talking in low tones, nodding their heads. "I guess," [Debby] said, "I had to go to them so that I could. Feel stronger. By feeling not so alone. My doctor helped me figure that out. In those days, I thought of myself as part of any group that was persecuted or looked down on. Any group of people wounded by the world. Jews, Negroes, cripples of any sort. I pitied them, wanted to help them, I wanted to protect them and push them up to where the rest of the world was living."

She smiled. "It was myself I was pitying. It was my own crippled look I was protecting. That was how it started. After a while. I knew I was part of these people because they were part of the world. But not of a special world, you understand. The ordinary world, the whole world. Just as I was part of that world. Nobody had any right to keep that world from me."

"Jews, too," he said very softly.

She nodded. "You too."

He winced, and she smiled gently. "And Ma. Roz. The old man, whom I hated so and did not even want to understand. Jews. But besides the Jews, there were all the others who were hated and laughed at. The world belonged to all of them, as well as to me. All the odd ones, the queer and different ones. They were people. I was people. After a while, I knew I had to hang out with them. I was them."

"Why?" he asked, watching her intently. "You mean, your hair? The way you look?"

He saw her flush, her mouth twist for a second, but she did not look away. "The way I am," she said. Her voice shook for just a moment, then deepened and steadied. "The way I am inside. It's the way I've got to be. I'm a person in the world. There's got to be room for me, too."

Jo Sinclair, *Wasteland* (New York: Lancer Books, 1946), 28–29, 33–34, 139. Reprinted from *Wasteland* by Jo Sinclair by permission of the University of Nebraska Press. Copyright 1987 by Ruth Seid. Published by The Jewish Publication Society, Philadelphia.

Further Reading

Bachmann, Monica. "'Someone Like Debby': (De)Constructing a Lesbian Community of Readers." *GLQ* 6:3 (2000), 377–388.

Bulkin, Elly. "Jews, Blacks, and Lesbian Teens in the 1940s: Jo Sinclair's *The Changelings* and 'The Long Moment.'" *OutHistory*, 2016 (http://outhistory.org/exhibits/show/bulkin).

Hoffman, Warren. *The Passing Game: Queering Jewish American Culture* (Syracuse University Press, 2009).

102. Poetry of Umberto Saba (Trieste, 1924–1947)

Umberto Saba (1883–1957) is celebrated as one of the great lyrical poets of twentieth-century Italy. He was raised in Trieste by his Jewish mother, Felicita Rachele Coen, niece of the great Italian Jewish scholar Samuel David Luzzatto; his Catholic father, who had converted to Judaism to marry Saba's mother, abandoned both his new faith and his new wife just before Saba was born. Saba's poetry and prose express erotic desires both for men, especially his younger family friend Federico Almansi, and for women, especially his wife Carolina (Lina) Wölfler, whom he married in 1909. In 1940 Saba sold his bookshop in Trieste, and spent the war in hiding in various sites around northern Italy; after the war, Saba spent most of his remaining years in Rome, where he died in 1957. He published his poetry as volumes of an ever-expanding collection, the *Canzoniere* (Songbook), between 1921 and 1961; in 1953 he also drafted a semi-autobiographical novel about the coming-of-age of a bisexual teenager in Trieste, *Ernesto*, which was not published until 1975. These poems, which were published in the volumes *Autobiografia* (1924), *Ultima Cose* (1944), and *Mediterranee* (1947), recall the power of youthful homoerotic love with bittersweet memory.

I Had a Friend

I had a friend back then; I wrote to him
long letters like love letters to a wife.
Through these I learned I had a certain grace,
and hidden still, to all except us two.
I gave to him advices sweet and wise,
and many gifts of friendship and of love.
Upon his boyish cheeks I used to see
the rosy blush of dawn across the sky.
Upon those darling locks I would have liked
to place my own two hands some evening then,
some glorious evening, say: This is my friend.
But Fate alas did not believe in him,
or maybe he was not quite as he seemed.
He was as lithe and lovely as a god.

An Old Man Loved a Boy

An old man loved a boy. And he, the child
—a cat in the forest—feared he'd be found out
and castigated for his darkest thoughts.
Now two things leave an imprint in your heart:
the woman who first matched her step to yours,

and the boy who, so that you could rescue him,
has put his trusting little hand in yours.

The youthful tyrant with his sky-blue eyes
open to an abyss, he'd beg and beg
his friend to sing his favorite lullaby.
The old song told a story, and it moved
the boy in a rare and uncommon way;
it seeped into his greedy teenaged years:
now good, now bad. "Enough of that," he'd say,
quite suddenly. "Let's turn off now, let's sleep."
And turned toward the wall, said "I love you"—
after a lengthy silence—"you'd be good
with me forever, with your boy." At once
he fell into a restless sleep. The elder,
with open eyes, no longer slept at all.

Indifferent, oblivious, and still
looking just like an angel. Don't accuse
him in your haste, dear heart. Think: he's alone;
he has a tricky task. He has his life
before him still and not behind. You'll hurry
your death along. Or think of it no more.

A Friend

To find,
when life is in decline, the first ray of light
that shone upon it: a friend. This is the goodness
that I have been given.

Like me and unlike me, rebellious
and docile. I keep him
near me to breathe like
a child born hopeless—
a tender mother.

Soon he will go off on his way
he will go, with doubt and difficulty. He will leave me
to the anguish of my downhill years
with the chaste sweetness of a kiss.

But, if time shall bring its terrors,
then towards peaceful joy I'll turn my mind
for him today.

When The Thought of You

When the thought of you follows me
in the woods, where from time to time
I shelter from my horrors for the day, sweetness
strikes me still as a statue.

Then I arise, resuming my life.

Everything is distant from me, youth,
glory; others with their other care turn me strange.

But that thought of you, that you are alive,
makes me all right. Oh immense
and almost inhuman tenderness!

In Your Father's House

In your father's house you wandered
quietly as a cat. You knew the name,
but not the nature, of pain.

Divided from your friends, the roses
upon your high-boned cheeks faded to white.

Born again from my soul, flowers
of life, my boy, my friend. This is for you,
the last thing that still remains,
tears you cannot see.

From The Solitary Slope

From the solitary slope that drops
into the ocean—which, green today and foamy, is smashing

the city sidelong—the white vista
of Trieste can be seen.

You knew it already—you say—these
streets of mine, where one might meet, at most, a woman—
let the long-mounted anxiety, a boy—
let the North Wind inspire you, take wing
to everything: it flies for you. Then return
to oneself; another passes beside you.

All a world that I loved, to which I gave
myself, that for you alone comes back to life today.

Angel

O you who awake beside old me
in the flower of your youth, eyes that burn
with anger brighter than stars
mouth that renders words harmonious
with kisses given and received, could perhaps my
recklessly loving you be a sin? Now that
is between me and God.

High Heaven! My beautiful shining love!

"I Had a Friend" from *Autobiografia* (Collana di Lugano, 1924). "An Old Man Loved a Boy," "A Friend," "When the Thought of You," "In Your Father's House" and "From The Solitary Slope," from *Ultima Cose* (Collana di Lugano, 1944). "Angel" from *Mediterranee* (Collana di Lugano, 1947). All republished in Umberto Saba, *Tutte le poesie* (Milan: Mondadori, 1998). Translated from Italian by Emmett Ruth. Copyright © 2019 Print-O-Craft Press.

Further Reading

Baldoni, Luca. "'Un Vecchio Amava un Ragazzo': Homoeroticism in Umberto Saba's Late Poetry (1935–48)." *Italian Studies* 60:2 (2005), 221–239.

Hochfield, George, and Leonard Nathan (trans. and eds.). *Songbook: The Selected Poems of Umberto Saba* (Yale University Press, 2009).

Parussa, Sergio. "Reluctantly Queer: In Search of the Homoerotic Novel in Twentieth-Century Italian Fiction." In *Queer Italia: Same-Sex Desire in Italian Literature and Film* (ed. Gary Cestaro, Palgrave, 2004), 173–186.

Van Watson, William. "Adapting to Heterocentricity: The Film Versions of Umberto Saba's *Ernesto* and Giorgio Bassani's *The Gold-Rimmed Spectacles*." In *Queer Italia: Same-Sex Desire in Italian Literature and Film* (ed. Gary Cestaro, Palgrave, 2004), 153–172.

103. Rina Natan Advocates for First Sex Confirmation Surgery in Israel (Tiberias, 1953)

Rina Natan was the first transgender woman known to have undergone medical transition in Israel. Born in 1923 in Siegen, Germany, she immigrated to Israel (then the British Mandate of Palestine) in 1946 and fought in the 1948 War of Independence. In 1953, Natan was arrested in Tiberias while dressed as a woman and she explained to the police that she was a woman "in my soul and in my feelings, but through a physiological mistake I was born as a boy." Inspired by the news of Christine Jorgensen, the American trans woman who had made international headlines in 1952 after her sex affirmation surgery in Denmark, Rina Natan began advocating for surgical intervention for her own case. This article appeared in 1953 in the leftist magazine *Ha'olam Hazeh*, which also published some of the first articles on gay men and lesbians in Israel; its editor, Uri Avnery (1923–2018), became a member of the Knesset in 1965 and introduced the first attempt to decriminalize homosexuality in 1971. Despite this article's sensationalist tone (and consistent use of male pronouns), the profile nonetheless demonstrates a real attempt to generate interest in Natan's struggle, including Natan's own self-advocacy, and stands out among other coverage of Natan in the press for its sympathetic portrayal. In 1954 Natan tried to convince doctors at Assaf Harofeh Medical Center that she had been born intersex (as she claims in this article), but failed to receive medical confirmation. In 1956, taking matters into her own hands, she again attempted surgery on herself; she then arrived at the hospital and explained to the doctors that now they had no choice but to finish the job and "remove these useless organs," which they did. She successfully received a new *te'udat zehut* (identity card) affirming her name and gender, but the media continued to treat her with suspicion and derision, and she struggled to find work and stable housing. In 1958 she left Israel for Switzerland, and eventually returned to Germany, living in Mannheim; she married a German businessman in 1961, and died in Saarbrücken in 1979.

A TWO-SEXED TRAGEDY

When the young woman, tall in stature and wearing a black skirt, entered the café in Tiberias, she did not attract any suspicion from the red-headed waitress. She served her a *kaffeh hafukh* [Israeli cappuccino] without casting so much as an additional glance.

But not Officer Glick. He was sitting opposite the young woman, and looked at her face with extreme attention. Something struck him as out of the ordinary, but what it was he could not say to himself. His focused look at the young woman brought a light blush to her face, and she smiled at him with an extended and enchanting smile.

This smile did not alleviate the police officer's suspicion, and he decided to reach out to his superior officer. This officer appeared in the café, and sat next to the young woman. She was slightly puzzled. When the officer asked for her *te'udat zehut* [identity card], a low, masculine, voice answered him. The young woman acknowledged to the stunned police officer that it was not she, but he.

A False Declaration

Just when the door of the jail cell closed behind the counterfeit woman, the sensation exploded in national newspapers. The newspapers, which had not had a fair news item like this since Operation Satan,* competed to provide malleable descriptions of the woman shaving in prison.

A newspaper appearing in this country in French reported that the arrested man had gone about in the streets, his pants rolled up to his knees, revealing his nylon stockings, while shouting at the top of his lungs, "I am a woman! I am a woman!" The general impression was formed that this case was a man not in his right mind, at least from a sexual sense. The newspapers even reported that the police submitted him to a psychiatric evaluation.

---

*The investigation of the rape and murder of a young girl, Raḥel Levin, in February 1953.

He was held in jail for five days without a medical examination. At the end of this period, apparently, no legal statute was found forbidding a man to wear a woman's clothing.** Therefore, Gershon Natan (29) was charged with a different violation: that a year ago he had given a false declaration to the Haifa police.

Natan admitted guilt. A year ago, he had tried (unsuccessfully) in Haifa to castrate himself. On his way to the Magen David Adom station, he became weak, and entered the police station to ask for help. There he told them that two anonymous men had attacked him, and asked them to refrain from any further inspection. Now in Tiberias he told the truth. The justice of the peace required him to sign personal bail for good behavior, for 50 *lirot*.

Dolls Instead of Soldiers

From a journalistic perspective, the story of Gershon Natan ends here. But for Natan himself, it is not over. On the contrary, Natan, who claims that he travelled to Tiberias intending to be arrested, in order to draw public attention to his personal tragedy, fervently hopes to continue it.

The story begins 29 years ago in the city of Siegen, next to Bonn, in Germany, when a person [*adam*] whom Nature had equipped with the sexual organs of both sexes, insufficiently developed, was born. Already in those early years, he preferred to play with dolls and not soldiers, but his parents chose to raise him as a boy. Perhaps it was the case that judgement ascertained his male characteristics were more pronounced than his female ones. In cases of sexual mixture, the male side generally overshadows the female side.

Outside of the Land of Israel, Natan specialized in agriculture, and became a teacher in France at an agricultural school. But when he immigrated, seven years ago, to the Land of Israel, he could not continue in this work, because he did not know sufficient Hebrew. Instead, he went to work on a kibbutz.

No Money for Surgery

But now, his unique characteristics began to disturb him to a crucial degree. When people discovered his bodily circumstance, they began to treat him with suspicion and ill will. Many whose education in this area was lacking were

---

** Note in text: But there is a law forbidding a man to wear a woman's clothing in order to enter a place open only to women, such as showers or public restrooms.

convinced (incorrectly) that he was a homosexual. All agreed that he could not be housed in the men's dormitory, nor in the women's.

Again and again, Natan served as a member or a worker in [the kibbutzim of] Maʻagan Michael, Ashdot Yaʻakov, and Naʻan. He worked, according to his testimony, very hard, and succeeded in whatever tasks were assigned him. But in each place, he would be dismissed, not through his own fault. The essential form of his female manner aroused all sorts of suspicions.

The young man with green eyes began to struggle with his fate. He knew that in the end he had to be either a man or a woman. He tried at first to be a man, underwent treatment with the help of male hormonal injections. These injections helped him temporarily, altered his voice and his beard growth, but they did not affect his inner development. He sought surgery, but his financial situation could never permit that. This kind of treatment would cost hundreds of *lirot*.

IN THE ARMY, A SEPARATE ROOM

During the War of Independence, Natan was drafted, became a medic. When he found it difficult to find work in civilian life, after his release, he returned to the army in the same role. But in the army, too, his characteristics aroused unpleasant attention. They gave him a separate room, and in the end released him. This was several weeks ago.

Today, Natan leans more towards becoming a woman. Moving around in women's clothing is more comfortable for him. "The female parts of my body are influencing me more, perhaps because I cannot get to them," Natan explained. In the end, on the threshold of despair, he decided to be arrested—both in order to force society to take account of his situation, and also from the hope that in this manner he might receive an essential medical examination, by experts, for which he wouldn't have to pay. "Society owes this to me," Natan said. "I feel in myself so much strength. I could be able to teach here a new strategy in agricultural education, which could yield vast sums of money. But as long as I have this tension inside myself, I cannot do anything!"

On the road to Tiberias, he sat next to a male and female police officer, who began to look at him with interest. They did not suspect that he was a man, but rather the opposite. Since he had painted his lips more than necessary, they suspected that he was a prostitute.

In Tiberias itself, he no longer succeeded. The police attempted to determine whether he wore women's clothing in order to enter women's rooms in the city limits. When it was firmly established that this was not the case, they were happy to find any law at all that could permit them to move his case to court—and free the police from worrying about this strange problem.

An Educational Role

After the failure of this attempt, his situation worsened sevenfold. The publicity in the newspapers hurt his future, he said. He had wanted to return to agricultural education, "But," he asked, "who would hire a man like me in an educational role?"

His only hope—as he explained this week to the staff of *Ha'olam Hazeh*, which he visited to ask for help in explaining his circumstance—was that society might take upon itself responsibility for his situation, and help him at last by medical means to tip the balance, so that he could live either as a man or as a woman.

"Tragediyah Du-Minit," *Ha'olam Hazeh* 806, April 2, 1953, p. 7. Reprinted by permission of Uri Avnery. Translation from Hebrew by Noam Sienna. I thank Dr. Iris Rachamimov for bringing this source to my attention, and for sharing her research on Rina Natan.

Further Reading

Shapira, Avner. "Pioneering Pride: The Unsung Heroes of Israel's LGBT Community." Ha'aretz, Jun 06, 2013 (https://www.haaretz.com/.premium-pioneering-pride-un-sung-israeli-lgbt-heroes-1.5274853).

Yonay, Yuval. "Asur lihyiot homoseqsual: keitsad homo'im veha'ittonut haktuvah ḥashvu vekat-vu 'al haḥoq ha'oser homoseqsualiyyut." In *Zekhuyyot haqehilah hage'ah beyisra'el: mishpat, netiyyah minit, uzehut migdarit* (ed. Alon Harel, Yaniv Lushinsky and Einav Morgen-stern, Jerusalem: Hebrew University Press, 2016), 921–970.

104. An American Rabbi Counsels a Homosexual (Alabama, 1955)

A unique document, Israel Gerber's book *Man on a Pendulum* (1955) claims to be the case history of a former "invert" who had turned to a certain

"Rabbi Turner" for counseling. While the rabbi accepts his client without rebuking him for sinning, he still maintains that homosexuality can and should be changed, and indeed in the Epilogue his client returns some years later without having "lapsed back into his former mode of existence." In a review of the book in ONE Magazine (see source 105), the reviewer writes that they were "uncomfortable" with the emphasis on curing homosexuality, concluding that "perhaps [the protagonist] is learning how to live with other people. When does he learn to live with himself?" In his preface, Gerber notes that the biographical data of the story are true, with only names and places changed, and he urges his fellow clergy to listen empathetically and nonjudgmentally. Rabbi Israel Joshua Gerber (1918–2011) was an American rabbi and a psychologist, receiving rabbinic ordination from Yeshiva University in New York in 1941, and a Ph.D. from Boston University in Psychology in 1950. After serving as a military chaplain in the Korean War and the Army Reserves in Germany, he led Reform congregations in Alabama, North Carolina, and Virginia, and lectured at local colleges on psychology and religion. Gerber was deeply invested in religious counseling (writing his doctoral dissertation on "A Psychological Approach to the Book of Job" and its implications for rabbinic pastoral work), and this book reflects these interests. Amid the growing awareness of homosexuality in American society, Gerber's book was one of the first responses from an American rabbi.

Preface

The biographical data in this book are true. The names of the people and the places mentioned are fictitious, however, to conceal the true identity of the central figure, John Edward Collins. Collins was an invert; the past tense is used because Collins now claims that he is no longer that. The writer saw him again three years after the therapeutic process described in this book had ended, and he had not lapsed back into his former mode of existence.

The story, as it is here unfolded, comes essentially from Collins' own mouth. It presents the dynamics of a personality enmeshed in a typical homosexual experience. Some of the insights he gained during the course of interviews are included, and Collins himself has recaptured many of the conversations as they actually occurred. The narrative may sound grotesque, fantastic, unbelievable, perhaps nauseating, but truth is truly stranger than fiction. This is humanity in action! The reader should approach this story with understanding and compassion, for we are dealing with a creation of the Lord.

Shortly before the termination of our counseling relationship, Collins remarked, "The story of my life would make interesting reading." The writer responded, "Do you feel that it merits publication?" Collins reflected for a few moments and then replied in the affirmative.

Why draw this sketch? The impelling factor is that John Edward Collins rid himself of his homosexuality. Collins contends that many inverts would desert their present mode of life if interested and trained listeners concerned themselves with them. Committing this case history to the printed page would hold out hope to people like himself, who might then be inspired to seek the necessary help to free themselves of their asocial behavior.

Many inverts will identify with him, for their experiences are basically identical with his. Seeing themselves in truer perspective may prove to be enough of an incentive for them to accomplish this aim. Collins felt that should the writer take the time to write his biography, it would be a contribution, of whatever magnitude, towards decreasing the number of persons involved in this difficult and knotty problem.

The writer believes that this biography will serve as an additional object lesson to his colleagues of every religious persuasion. The problems that present themselves are considerable; the opportunities for service are numerous. The clergy must train itself to be of maximum aid to all the emotionally distorted. The clergyman cannot choose the type of problems that come his way. An autocratic Reverend Jones or a Chaplain Combs is not the answer to a mankind heavily laden with problems. To be effective, the clergyman must listen empathetically and not be judgmental; he must not be shocked by what he is told, regardless of the language used and the incidents narrated. Only then will the troubled person be willing to express himself freely and adequately...

ISRAEL J. GERBER
Dothan, Alabama

Prologue

"I am a homosexual," John Edward Collins declared in a clear, firm voice to Dr. Jeremiah Tanner, Rabbi of the Temple in Springville. "You knew it all the time." He made this confession approximately five minutes after he had entered the Rabbi's study.

It was not by mere chance that Collins walked into Rabbi Tanner's office one dreary New England Monday morning. He had heard of the Rabbi; that he had organized a Counseling Center for the benefit of all the Centerville people at the request of the local Council of Churches. The newspapers and radio had given it much publicity. The Center had proved so successful that some physicians referred patients to it who suffered from psychogenic rather than organic ills. As a result, the Rabbi's name, as that of a man of the cloth devoted to serving emotionally disturbed people, had become a familiar one in and around Centerville. People of all faiths came to him with their problems on their own volition. John Edward Collins was one of them.

No one was in the outer office when he entered. Directly ahead of him was a door with Dr. Tanner's name on it. His eyes searched the office as he walked deliberately to the door and gave it two short, weak taps.

"Come," a deep voice boomed.

He opened the door slowly. Before him sat a blond-haired man at a mahogany desk, writing. The desk had a neat pile of papers on the right side and a telephone on the left. The man raised his head and their eyes met.

"Come in," the man said with a smile as he stood up.

"Rabbi Tanner?" Collins asked hesitatingly as he took a step deeper into the room.

"Yes, I'm the Rabbi. Did you want to see me?"

"Yes…Yes…I—I know…I have no appointment…with you. But…can I…talk to you?"

No sooner did he utter these words than he regretted having taken this action. He had misgivings about being in Rabbi Tanner's presence. His previous experiences with the clergy had been unfavorable. Why should the situation be any different this time? He had made a mistake in coming. But he needed someone to talk to, someone with whom he could share the emotional turmoil that was crushing him despair. Sheer desperation had compelled him to take his step.

Rabbi Tanner looked at his wristwatch. "I have fifteen minutes until my next appointment."

"That'll be enough time," Collins replied quickly.

"Fine. Please shut the door and have a seat, Mr…"

"Collins. John Edward Collins." He closed the door noiselessly.

"Please sit down, Mr. Collins," Rabbi Tanner said, motioning to a chair that stood on the left side of his desk as he seated himself.

[…]

Unable to control himself any longer, Collins made the disclosure, "I am a homosexual."

Although it usually takes time for hidden thoughts and basic desires to be revealed, Collins was so in need of an unburdening that he was ready to unveil himself almost immediately. Without betraying any emotion, Rabbi Tanner uttered those two words so often used by psychiatrists, "I see." His expression did not change, nor did a muscle move.

Collins was even more distraught after making this disclosure. "What do you think of me now?"

"Am I supposed to think differently of you now?" the rabbi asked in the same calm tone.

"Yes," he replied in a raised voice. "You're supposed to."

Rabbi Tanner did not reply.

"Everybody who hears about it reacts in some way," Collins proceeded, gesticulating. "You're not even fazed by it."

"I am sorry to have disappointed you. Somehow, in spite of what you have told me, I still regard you as one of God's children. I regret that I cannot view you in any other light."

Collins was puzzled. What sort of a man was he dealing with, this Rabbi? He was so different from the people he regularly encountered. How different he was from his own pastor! When Reverend Jones had learned of his behavior, he had berated him, had called him a sinner doomed to eternal damnation, with no hope of salvation unless he stopped this practice immediately. Oh, how he had tried! But he couldn't. Even the psychiatrists in the Army would do nothing for him. Unlike the others, not only did Rabbi Tanner not drive him from his office, but he accepted him as he was. He even called him a child of God. Some of Collins's tension left him. At last he had found the man he could talk to; the man in whom he could confide; the man who might even help him become integrated.

[...]

"I can do no more than listen to you, Mr. Collins, and hope that perhaps I may be of some assistance to you by helping you overcome that emotional stumbling block. It is only on this basis that our relationship can begin."

Collins reflected for a moment and said, "I hardly know where to begin."

"It might be well to begin with the immediate reason or reasons that prompted you to come here."

Collins, whose head had been bowed, looked up at Rabbi Tanner and spoke with vehemence and anger. "I'm disgusted with myself! Imagine me living this way! I'm outside the law, constantly terrified I'll be found out. I don't care what happens to me personally, but the shame and humiliation it would cause my family is more than I can bear. I had even thought of suicide."

Rabbi Tanner looked at him sharply.

"Don't worry, Rabbi," he reassured him. "I rejected that idea. Suicide would mean an inquiry. They'd find out all about me. I'm trapped. I can't live with myself, and death by my own hands is no solution."

"You've been searching for a way out of your problems."

Collins nodded. "I've heard much about your counseling center and the good it is doing. After much self-deliberation I decided to come to you. The fact that you are a rabbi and not a Christian minister, appealed to me. My own pastor down in Kentucky has rejected me. Maybe you as a rabbi, can make me feel that God has not given up on me. It seems that Christianity has no place for me."

"You are seeking a solution outside of Christianity?"

"I thought I could find my way in my church, but I've been discarded by it."

"You mean you feel excluded because of your pastor."

"He speaks for the Church! Doesn't he? I was baptized a Christian and I want to live as a Christian. I want to be accepted by the church, but I don't have the feeling that I am."

"Do you want to change?"

"As matters stand now, life is intolerable. I'm terribly distressed."

"You want to abandon Christianity for Judaism?"

Collins remained silent. He squirmed in his chair uncomfortably and then changed the subject again. "You know I was released from the service not too long ago."

"Mmh."

"Yes. I finally broke with the armed forces."

"Would you like to tell me about it?"

"Well," said Collins, drawing out the word, "I don't know whether you would enjoy listening to it."

"We are not here for the sake of pleasure. Your telling me about it or anything else will be helpful to both of us. It will help me to understand you, and you may be able to see your experiences in a different light."

Israel J. Gerber, *Man On a Pendulum: A Case History of an Invert* (American Press, 1955), 7–20.

Further Reading

Meyerowitz, Joanne. "The Liberal 1950s? Reinterpreting Postwar American Sexual Culture." In *Gender and the Long Postwar: Reconsiderations of the United States and the Two Germanys, 1945–1989* (eds. Karen Hagemann and Sonya Michel, Johns Hopkins University Press, 2014), 297–319.

Minton, Henry. *Departing from Deviance: A History of Homosexual Rights and Emancipatory Science in America* (University of Chicago Press, 2002).

Waller, James. "'A Man in a Cassock Is Wearing a Skirt': Margaretta Bowers and the Psychoanalytic Treatment of Gay Clergy." *GLQ* 4:1 (1998), 1–16.

105. An American Homophile Magazine Reports on Homosexuality in Israel (Los Angeles, 1955)

ONE: The Homosexual Magazine was a monthly periodical that was published by ONE, Inc., an American gay rights organization established in Los Angeles in 1952 (the magazine ran from 1953 to 1969). This report on Israel was written by "RH Stuart," the pseudonym of Rudolf (Rudi) Hans Steinert (1911–1993), a German-Israeli gay man who immigrated to the United States in 1955. He soon became personally involved in ONE, Inc., taking its classes, contributing to their magazine, and eventually becoming a staff member. In his report, he portrayed Israel in classically Orientalist images, claiming that "conditions in Israel are very similar to those in the Orient," where it is easy "to make a friendly acquaintance by a quite obvious approach—and to know at the same time that you do so without danger." He emphasizes that, with the exception of "imports from Europe," there are no "pure" homosexuals in Israel, and no gay bars or clubs; instead, he describes a cliché vision of the Arab—including Jews from Arab countries—as sexually open and fluid, and naturally predisposed toward homosexual behavior (but without the sense of a uniquely homosexual identity which had begun to coalesce in North America and Europe by this time). Steinert also stereotypes Israeli women as masculine and active, observing that "one often sees the lesbian type in Israel, but one rarely sees a lesbian." He concludes by noting that "Israel is a very small country, and the people love to gossip as they do everywhere." Gay men and lesbians in Israel faced heavy discrimination, as well as negative depictions in Israeli media, throughout the 1950s and 1960s, and the first Israeli gay rights organization was not founded until 1975. The ban on consensual same-sex sexual acts was not formally repealed in Israel until 1988, although it was not strictly enforced after the early 1950s, when Attorney General Ḥayyim Cohen instructed courts to allow consenting private sexual activity between adults.

Many people believe that Israel is like the Orient in its reception of the homosexual. In some respects the Orient and East Asia are ideal for the gay element. Nothing is less difficult in Istambul, in Algiers, in Casablanca or in Cairo than to make a friendly acquaintance by a quite obvious approach—and to know at the same time that you do so without danger. At times, it is true, one must pay for his amusement but it is also possible to find a lasting friendship of more permanent worth.

In this way conditions in Israel are very similar to those of the Orient. The country is populated by a remarkable mixture of people—many from other places. Its atmosphere is thus cosmopolitan as one might expect. However, the culture of Israel is more Occidental than Oriental and in some ways much like that of the states of Europe.

The laws are very mild against the homosexual—one could say they hardly exist at all. Of course, if a case were to arise involving a minor, such as a boy of thirteen, both parties would be brought to trial.

Except for imports from Europe, there are not many homosexuals living in Israel. For this reason, bars and clubs, exclusively for the gay, cannot exist. What happens in practice is that most natives are either heterosexual, without taking the matter seriously or bi-sexual but few are what could be called "pure" homosexuals. Of course the younger set know all about "the question" and play along with it. No one is openly hostile, unpleasant or upsetting. On the contrary…

At the same time there are those living in Israel—a ring of people who come from the Orient: from India, Iran, Lybia, Africa, etc. These persons are Jews but in their natures are like Orientals; they are the Moslems. For the Moslem there is a law; and this law states that before his marriage he may not go with women. But the Koran does not mention that a young bachelor may not go with a boy. So this is quite simply why many of the young unmarried Moslems like to be together with boys—and often later, after they are married.

In contrast to the Oriental-Jew-Moslem mentioned above, the Oriental Jew may start very young to enjoy the pleasures of both men and women until the time of his marriage.

Among the soldiers and oftener among the unemployed men there exists a limited form of prostitution. But it is of little significance. This easy state of affairs in Israel might well be brought about by the genuine independence of the women. They are frequently found active in business, teaching and vigorously practicing law: many are even to be found in construction work and government planning. One often sees the lesbian type in Israel, but one seldom sees a lesbian. This, instead is just their manner of behavior.

Another reason for the unconcern and acceptance of homosexuality in Israel is the very basic fact of there being more men about than women. Situations of long standing between two men occur seldom for all of the customary reasons. And further, Israel is a very small country, and the people love to gossip as they do everywhere.

RH Stuart (Rudi Hans Steinert), "International: Israel," *ONE Magazine* 3:12 (Dec. 1955), 6–7. Reprinted courtesy of ONE Archives at the USC Libraries. I thank Dr. C. Todd White for sharing his research on Steinert and confirming some biographical details.

Further Reading

Fink, Amir Sumaka'i, and Jacob Press. *Independence Park: The Lives of Gay Men in Israel* (Stanford University Press, 1999).

Loftin, Craig. *Masked Voices: Gay Men and Lesbians in Cold War America* (SUNY Press, 2012).

Milo, Marva. "'But Oh! What Tales': Portraying the Middle East in U.S. Homophile Periodicals of the 1950s and 1960s." *Journal of Homosexuality* 64:7 (2017), 889–907.

Moore, Tracy (ed.). *Lesbiot: Israeli Lesbians Talk about Sexuality, Feminism, Judaism, and Their Lives* (New York: Cassell, 1995).

White, C. Todd. *Pre-Gay L.A.: A Social History of the Movement for Homosexual Rights* (University of Illinois Press, 2009).

Yonay, Yuval. "Asur lihyot homoseqsual: ketsad homo'im veha'ittonut haktuvah hashvu vekatvu 'al hahoq ha'oser homoseqsualiyyut." In *Zekhuyyot haqehilah hage'ah beyisra'el: mishpat, netiyyah minit, uzehut migdarit* (ed. Alon Harel, Yaniv Lushinsky and Einav Morgenstern, Jerusalem: Hebrew University Press, 2016), 921–970.

106. Pearl Hart, American Jewish Lawyer, Advises Homosexuals on Legal Rights (Chicago, 1957)

The Mattachine Society, founded in Los Angeles in 1950 by Harry Hay and his circle of friends, was one of the first LGBTQ organizations in the United States, and it quickly established chapters across the country. The Chicago

Mattachine operated from 1954–1958, and was then revived in 1965 as Mattachine Midwest. One of the active but discreet leaders in both incarnations of this group was Pearl Minnie Hart (1890–1975), whom Timothy Stewart-Winter calls, "the crucial figure in the emergence of the homophile movement in Chicago." Hart was born in Michigan and raised in Chicago; her father, a Russian-born rabbi named David Harchovsky, served a congregation on the Near West Side. While working as a stenographer, she took night classes at the John Marshall Law School and was admitted to the Illinois Bar in 1914. A founding member of both the National Lawyers Guild and the American Committee for the Protection of the Foreign Born, she was one of the first female attorneys to specialize in criminal law and practiced law for 61 years, working until just weeks before her death. She devoted her life to fighting for the rights of the vulnerable and oppressed, especially women, children, immigrants, and gay men and lesbians. She defended numerous clients subpoenaed by the House of Representatives Un-American Activities Committee (HUAC), and represented many gay men arrested in bar raids or police stings. Although she herself had two long-term female partners—singer and actress Blossom Churan, and writer and activist Valorie Taylor—Hart never publicly identified as a lesbian; she portrayed her involvement with Mattachine as that of a professional legal advisor. This booklet, published by the Chicago Mattachine in 1957, provides legal advice to gay men and lesbians worried about arrest and harassment, and Hart emphasizes, "People must realize that they are as they are, and whether or not they have engaged in conduct proscribed by the law at the time of arrest, they still have rights guaranteed by federal and state laws." According to Karen Sendziak, Hart once remarked sadly to the president of Mattachine Midwest that she would have no one to recite the *kaddish* (the mourner's prayer) for her after her death, but he reassured her that all the members of the organization were her children, and would gladly say *kaddish* for her.

Your Legal Rights

INTRODUCTION

Law was not created for the harm or intimidation of individuals. The primary function of the law is PROTECTION. This protection takes two forms.

First it serves as a protection of society against the depredation of individuals, and second as a protection of individuals from harassment and persecution by society or its agents. When most persons think of the law, they usually visualize the law in its first aspect, that of protecting society against individuals. The second form of protection, however, is just as important.

The founders of the government of the United States of America, wisely foreseeing the necessity for limiting the extent of the law and the methods of its enforcement, drafted the Bill of Rights. Its purpose was to protect the individual from unjust acts and from the human frailties of those who would in the future be entrusted with the enforcement of these laws. All of the States made these rights effective by enacting laws for the specific purpose of providing their citizens with such protection.

Many private citizens, through ignorance, or fear, fail to avail themselves of these laws which guarantee their inherent rights when confronted with criminal charges. Such ignorance or fear are particularly prevalent among those minority groups whose social ostracism frequently makes them feel a personal guilt or inferior status before the law. Thus a knowledge of these protective laws is essential to every citizen, for almost anyone may at some time in his life find himself charged with a crime and forced to defend himself against such a charge...

What ought to be the deportment of the private citizen when confronted by the law in the person of its enforcing agents?

Arrest or Simple Questioning by the Police

The laws protect any resident against unlawful interference with his right of privacy; a peaceful person, whether on the street, in his home or in a peaceful gathering is entitled to be free from arrest or search unless a warrant has been issued for his arrest or search by some proper authority. No one has a right to arrest on suspicion, and the corollary is that no one has a right to hold anyone on an "open charge." An officer may arrest only when an offense has been committed in his presence, or when an offense has in fact been committed, and there are reasonable grounds to believe that the person about to be arrested is the one who committed the offense. To resist such an arrest as this, even when innocent, might subject one to prosecution on the charge of resisting lawful arrest.

No police officer has a right to question a person who has committed no offense, and the law does not require the person to answer indiscriminate questioning because the police happen to be making an investigation, or because there is a so-called "crime wave."

However, the existence of regulations for the protection of the individual need not imply that he adopt an uncooperative attitude toward any officer of the law who is pursuing his duty. The mere stopping of an individual may be taken to constitute arrest at in some cases, and the word "arrest" need not even be mentioned for the act to take place. It is not advisable, when being questioned, for one to invite arrest by asking if he is being arrested. In general it is advisable not to resist an arresting officer with either force or insolence. If the individual feels that he is being falsely arrested, he should permit himself to be arrested peaceably—but only under protest—in the knowledge that he may later, upon acquittal or release, sue the arresting officer for false arrest. Such knowledge should, of course, be kept to oneself at the time. Similarly, if questioned by a police officer, even where no alleged offense has been committed, it is advisable for the individual to cooperate at least to the extent of identifying himself, although the Law does not require him to do so, and does not require him to submit proof of his identity (unless he is an alien required to register or of an age subject to selective service regulations) or submit himself to search of his person (if this is done, again, he should protest, knowing that later, on acquittal or release, he may sue for violation of his rights). And certainly the law does not require him to answer any questions which might tend to incriminate him.

PRELIMINARY QUESTION AND COMMITMENT TO THE POLICE LOCK UP OR BOOKING

Following the arrest, the arresting officer may frequently attempt to obtain statements from the arrestee, but the experience of the legal profession has taught that any statements by the arrestee beyond simple self-identification at this time, when he does not have the advice of counsel, are fraught with danger for him. He should remember that the law does not require him to make any such statements without the advice of his lawyer and he should politely remind his questioners of this fact.

Whether or not such preliminary questioning has taken place, the arrestee is next committed to the police lock-up nearest the scene of his arrest, where his name is entered on the station book, and where he may be fingerprinted and photographed for the purpose of identification (upon later acquittal or release he may demand, preferably through his attorney, that these fingerprints and photographs be returned to him). Except for possible temporary removal for more formal questioning, he is required to remain here at the police lock-up until he has been formally charged and becomes eligible for bail. The period during which he may be held without charge or hearing may not, under normal circumstances, exceed twenty-four hours.

FORMAL QUESTIONING AND CHARGING

In many cases where arrest has taken place under one of the statutes listed in the appendage to this brochure, the arrestee, in Chicago, may be removed to Police Headquarters (1121 S. State St.) for formal questioning. During this formal questioning, all that has been said of his demeanor under preliminary questioning continues to apply; the arrestee should remain polite and cooperative, but need answer no questions.

Following such formal questioning the arrestee is usually formally charged and returned to the lock-up.

COUNSEL, BAIL AND RELEASE ON BAIL

The arrestee is legally eligible for counsel from the moment of arrest and, once the formal charge has been placed, or before twenty-hours have elapsed, he has the right to notify his family that he is being so held. He should be allowed to make telephone calls to his family and to obtain counsel but he would be responsible for furnishing the funds for such calls.

In some cases the officers in charge will permit a professional bondsman to visit the accused or will inform the accused that he may request the services of such a person, who will, for a fixed fee, deposit bail bond (which is money or other security furnished to assure the appearance of the accused in court) for him. Whether or not the accused avails himself of such service will naturally depend upon his estimation of the likelihood of his being able to obtain sufficient funds from relatives or friends within a desirably short time (if bond is not posted at this time, the accused will be held to await trial, but bond may be posted anytime prior to trial).

Frequently such professional bondsmen will also offer to secure the services of a lawyer for the accused. In general, however, the best legal opinion holds that a lawyer known personally to the accused or secured through persons known to him is to be preferred.

Following posting of bond, the accused is released from custody, at which he is informed of the date of his hearing, which by law should occur at the earliest possible conditions would be twenty-four hours.

Once the accused has obtained the advice of counsel, he should confide in and follow the suggestions of such counsel. Of course, there is always the possibility that one may not be able to enlist the assistance of counsel, friends or a bondsman, due perhaps to financial difficulties, time or place. In such a case one would have to remain in custody until the time of his hearing, in which event it might be advisable to recall the existence of at least two and possibly three more (depending upon circumstances) very important rights.

In Chicago, if trial or hearing takes place in either the Boys Court, Women's Court or the Criminal Court of Cook County, one has a right to use the services of a public defender at no cost to himself. Whether or not this service exists or is utilized, there still remains the right to move for a continuance of his case (to permit time for preparation of his defense or for further efforts to secure bail bond), and the right to petition for a change of venue (i.e., for a change of judge).

Knowledge of the foregoing facts should not be considered to make the individual competent to deal effectively with the problems of his defense. In every case the individual should make every effort to secure the services of a reputable attorney. It cannot be too strongly stressed throughout all the previously mentioned steps that the primary need for many arrested persons is to eliminate the feeling of fear which so many entertain because of lack of knowledge of legal procedures. People must realize that they are as they are, and whether or not they have engaged in conduct proscribed by law at the time of arrest, they still have rights guaranteed by federal and state laws; and if they are denied any of these legal rights, they have recourse against the individuals responsible.

Pearl Hart, *Your Legal Rights* (Chicago: Mattachine Society Inc., 1957). I thank Julie Herrada from the Labadie Collection at the University of Michigan for locating a copy of this rare publication. I also thank Karen Sendziak, and Dr. Wil Brant at the Gerber/Hart Library, for their additional assistance researching Pearl Hart.

Further Reading

Sendziak, Karen C. "Pearl M. Hart (1890–1975)." In *Before Stonewall: Activists for Gay and Lesbian Rights in Historical Context* (ed. Vern L Bullough, New York: Haworth Press, 2002), 56–62.

Stewart-Winter, Timothy. *Queer Clout: Chicago and the Rise of Gay Politics* (University of Pennsylvania Press, 2016).

De la Croix, St. Sukie. *Chicago Whispers: A History of LGBT Chicago before Stonewall* (University of Wisconsin Press, 2012).

107. A Homosexual Jewish College Student Writes his Life Story (New York, ca. 1958)

This testimony was written by an anonymous undergraduate student at Columbia University, given the pseudonym "Tim" by the sexologist Phyllis Kronhausen (1929–2012), who worked as a lecturer in Health Education from 1956–1958 while pursuing her Ed.D. at Columbia (which she received in 1958). Inspired by the pioneering work of American sexologist Alfred Kinsey (1894–1956), Kronhausen taught a course in "Marriage and Family Life Education," in which she asked students to write personal histories of their sexual education and experiences; in 1960 she published her analysis of these narratives as *Sex Histories of American College Men*, co-written with her husband Eberhard Kronhausen (1915–2009). In this fascinating and complex account, which highlights the challenges of Jewish assimilation in mid-twentieth century America, "Tim" describes his experiences growing up with immigrant parents, his struggles with his dysfunctional family, and his resistance to living his mother's idea of a good boy: "to marry a nice Jewish girl, go to the temple, make a lot of money, and raise kids in the same myth and superstitions that she was raised in." Interestingly, he notes that early in his life he had wanted to be a rabbi, and describes performing mock ceremonies while wearing "those dresses"—a kind of drag, both gendered and religious. He concludes by contrasting his knowledge of himself as a homosexual with his desire to have companionship and family, hoping that "there will yet be a happier tomorrow even for me."

I am of Jewish descent and have been reared in a European fashion in many respects. My mother, who is the main cause of my problem, came to this country when she was in her teens. Here, like other immigrants, she was hoping to make a better life, for in Europe she had only known extreme poverty and hardship. She was, however, totally unprepared for life in America...My father has not led a spectacular life. Like Ma, he is from Europe. He sneaked into this country when he was in his teens. He drifted from various jobs until he met mother. She made him hold on to his jobs a little longer than he had been used to in the past. But that's about all the good I can say about him...

[As a child] I wanted to be a rabbi and used to make the vestments from rags mother had around the house. I would then perform a mock ceremony, wearing those dresses. My mother has told me that I played with dolls and wanted dolls. This I don't recall, but Ma still speaks of it with delight, telling me how "cute" I was—then!...

When I was seven, my mother enrolled me in a religious school. There I became emotionally and sexually aroused whenever a certain boy, age twelve, was in class. He wore his pants very tight which accented his buttocks and thighs...[When I was about ten] we boys began to show our erections to each other. This fooling around lasted till I was thirteen and a half. Once we entered high school, these activities ceased.

During this homosexual stage, we partook in general horseplay and occasionally assumed fellatio positions. However, we never actually indulged in it. I enjoyed myself immensely and seemed to display the greatest sexual drive.

Soon after this, I found a boy in religious school who wanted to 'fool around' (sexually). This time I actually committed fellatio—although it was never completed. I never did that again with him, but ever since then I began loitering around a men's room in the subway...

A year later, I began to fight with Ma about my working. I had no friends, no social life, no parties or dates at all. I wasn't allowed to Gentile parties, only to the dull Jewish affairs, arranged by the synagogue—'that' was my attitude.

I had Gentile friends in high school I wanted to associate with, but Ma said 'No.' She judged my friends, even though she didn't know them. Only Jews were good enough for me, she said. She also forbade me to go out with girls. Holding hands with girls, she claimed, would lead me to worse things. My 'Jewish virginity' had to be preserved. 'Good boys don't go out with girls,' that's all I heard. So I did the next best thing—and became a full-fledged homosexual!…

This friction kept throwing me into a homosexual environment. I developed an inferiority complex, especially around girls. In high school I had a crush on another boy. In my last two years, I met a few other boys in school who were homosexual, but I never had affairs with them. We just talked about our experiences and the classmates we wished to "make," or who we thought were "hep" to us.

I didn't bother to attend the senior prom. My Ma would have been quite upset at the money spent. So I didn't bother to bring it up. By now I had lost all my desire for girls. I just adored handsome, well-developed boys and men.

College was my emancipation. When I was eighteen I was finally allowed to go out on week ends. 1:00 AM was curfew. But I didn't make the types of friends I wanted to in college. I wasn't masculine enough, and the boys I wanted as friends—I wanted for sex. So I gave up on the college boys and began to associate regularly with homosexuals who congregated in the park near my home. A couple of them were going to college. But the majority of them were fags.

I was never intimate with them. They were a lot of fun to be with and offered me some companionship. My apartment wasn't too modern or nice, so I never invited any of the masculine ones over. Besides, I wasn't too sure if I could trust them, since I lived so close to the park. Most of their friends knew they were queer, therefore they were liable to also give it away to others…

Anyhow, in the past year I have dropped all my former homosexual associates and am now even more lonesome than ever. I've tried to adjust to a man's life, but I've failed miserably. Women just don't appeal to me. I've never gone through the motions with them. I feel I'm queer and lack confidence in myself. I become very tense talking to girls, especially if I've just been introduced. I'm afraid they can sense immediately something is wrong with me.

My mother lives simply for me. I've learned in the past three years that I have her wrapped around my fingers. I should have left home years ago, but then I'd be nowhere. I am now unhappy and lonesome (so are my parents). There's no question, I'm suffering from an Oedipus complex—but my mother is a Jocasta, too...

Throughout most of my early adolescence, it was I whom my mother confided in. Now that I look back, I see that I was the husband and not the son. I was also the go-between who delivered the messages from one to the other when my parents weren't on speaking terms—which was a good deal of the time. I recall a number of times my mother telling dad to leave home if he wouldn't stop gambling. One day he was outside school crying, "Mommy doesn't want me." I told him I'd see what I could do. Later I talked to Ma, trying to straighten it out.

But who stood up for me? Nobody! I was always forced to do things against my will and I had nobody to defend me. I had to join the boy scouts when I was fourteen, because mother wanted me to. Yet, I couldn't go on hikes, because I worked. I had to go to religious instructions when I was twelve. I was the only kid in my age group from the whole neighborhood who went. But I had to go so my mother could hear everyone praise her for having such a good (queer) boy. I had to do it. Always. She was the boss...

If she ever finds out what's wrong with me, I doubt if she'll understand. She says I'm lazy, no good, sneaky. She used to say, "Three times I gave birth and three times they were snakes." She doesn't dare say it any more, but I know that's the way she feels. I just can't live up to my mother's expectations. Her idea of a good boy is to marry a Jewish girl, go to the temple, make a lot of money, and raise kids in the same myth and superstitions that she was raised in...

What will the future bring for me? Even though I am a homosexual, I would like to get married. My wife would know of my past. I don't like this life of wandering and loneliness. There's nothing worse to see than an old homosexual, unloved and unwanted by everyone. It's pathetic and makes me cry.

But will I make a good marriage, a good husband, a good father? I want to have children more than anything else in the world—especially a couple of sons. God help me if I have all girls. I want to give my boys a life I never had, and the companionship with their father. But will I be able to give up this way of life and be faithful to my wife? Right now I doubt it. Will any woman accept me the way I am? It's most unlikely. What the future holds for me looks rather dim. But it is in my hands and in my mind. Perhaps there will yet be a happier tomorrow even for me.

Phyllis and Eberhard Kronhausen, *Sex Histories of American College Men* (New York: Ballantine Books, 1960), 185–197.

Further Reading

Gordan, Rachel. "Alfred Kinsey and the Remaking of Jewish Sexuality in the Wake of the Holocaust." *Jewish Social Studies* 20:3 (2014), 72–99.

Kranson, Rachel. *Ambivalent Embrace: Jewish Upward Mobility in Postwar America* (University of North Carolina Press, 2017).

Meyerowitz, Joanne. "The Liberal 1950s? Reinterpreting Postwar American Sexual Culture." In *Gender and the Long Postwar: Reconsiderations of the United States and the Two Germanys, 1945–1989* (eds. Karen Hagemann and Sonya Michel, Johns Hopkins University Press, 2014), 297–319.

Prell, Riv-Ellen. *Fighting to Become Americans: Assimilation and the Trouble Between Jewish Women and Jewish Men* (Beacon Press, 1999).

108. A Syrian Rabbi Rules on an Intersex Infant (Jerusalem, ca. 1960)

While the Talmudic category of *androginos* (see source 5) remained mostly a theoretical concept, there are occasional instances where rabbinic thinkers applied it to real-life cases of intersex people. In this case, which occurred in Israel around 1960, it seems that an intersex child was born and initially mistakenly assigned as male; the doctors then told the father that the child "was actually female" and needed corrective surgery, but before deciding, the father turned for halakhic advice to Shoshan

Kohen (Chouchan Hacohen, d. 1976), a Djerban rabbi who served the community of Eitan, a *moshav* founded in 1955 by Tunisian immigrants. Kohen, in turn, asked advice from the Syrian Rabbi Ovadyah Hedayah (1889–1969), a leading scholar and Kabbalist who served as the head of Yeshivat HaMequbbalim Bet-El in Jerusalem. Hedayah answers that surgical intervention is strongly prohibited—a stance echoed by many intersex activists today—but his rationale rests on the spiritual superiority of men, and thus in the choice between raising this child as a boy or a girl, a boy is preferable. At the same time, Hedayah's assertion that this case is in the Talmudic category of androginos is a fascinating example of using indigenous Jewish categories of sex and gender to resist the medical and scientific binary. Hedayah emphasizes, in a tantalizing and puzzling aside, that there is no worry in having a man menstruate, mentioning that "I myself know clearly that there are some men who have menses, and they are healthy and fine"—is he referring to other cases of intersex people? Or other configurations of gender nonconformity?

To my honorable friend, the great rabbi Shoshan Kohen, the rabbi of the settlement of Eitan:

Regarding a question that was brought to him, concerning a boy who was circumcised as usual, but then fell ill and was taken to the hospital, and stayed there some six months, and the doctors sent for his father to tell him that after the tests, they determined that this child was actually female, and by the age of six it would be necessary to perform surgery to allow him to menstruate, and they advised [the father] that it would be best, while the child was young and did not know right from wrong, to operate on his genitals, meaning to remove his member so that he would become female. Thus his father came to ask [Rabbi Kohen] whether there was some issue of prohibition here, or some concern, since according to the doctors the surgery would be necessary for the menses, and so it seemed there was an issue of danger, and in a case of danger we rely on the opinion of the doctors. But since [Rabbi Kohen] could not find explicit discussion of this [issue] among rabbinic authorities, for he lacks books, he therefore desired to know the opinion of this humble one, according to his knowledge of Torah.

This is my response: first, according to what is described in the question, that after circumcision the doctors declared him to be female, it is clear that this is a case of the *androginos*, and indeed there is a long *mishnah* in the fourth chapter of Bikkurim dealing with this…From all this, it is clear that [the *androginos*] is considered closer to male than female, for he can marry [a woman] but cannot be married [to a man], and he is clearly obligated in all the commandments of the Torah like men; therefore, just as castration [*sirus*] is prohibited for men, it is prohibited for the *androginos*.

But there is room for disagreement, for we know that if a full male is castrated, he will not be able to have children, but this is not the case with the *androginos*, for he has both maleness and femaleness. Thus, even if they castrate him by removing his male genitals, and make him into a woman, he could still have children if he is married to a man; this is not the same as the castration of a man, or a woman, where after castration they cannot have children, for here he can have children as I said. But in the end, males are obligated in [the commandment of] "*be fruitful and multiply*" (Genesis 1:28), while women are not obligated in this, and so by means of the castration which turned him into a woman, his obligation in the commandment of "*be fruitful and multiply*" has been completely forfeited, as indeed has his obligation for all the commandments in which men are commanded more than women. This lowers him in holiness—from the holiness of men to that of women.

Regarding the claim of the doctors that by the age of six surgery will be necessary for menstruation, meaning that they will need to remove his member to prevent some danger of female menstruation, and this constitutes a danger, heaven forbid—these things have no basis whatsoever, and there is no danger for a man to menstruate, and in fact I myself know clearly that there are some men who have menses, and they are healthy and fine, and married women and have children, and nothing has happened to them. The words of these doctors are empty and meaningless, and have no basis in fact. Indeed, in the *mishnah* of Bikkurim it says that "[the *androginos*] is made impure by a menstrual emission, like women," etc., and therefore if there was any danger in this, the [rabbis] would not have remained silent on it. Therefore, Heaven forbid that we would permit the surgery and change him to a woman, which is completely and severely prohibited…

From everything said, there is no license to perform surgery on this child and remove his genitalia and castrate him. The one who castrates him violates a prohibition and will be liable for punishment; neither will the father who permits them to do this be exempt, [since he is] assisting one to commit a sin… And regarding the claim that there is some potential danger here to the child, Heaven forbid, we have already proven that there is no possible danger, and the one who listens to us will rest securely and in peace, and he will have a blessing of goodness, and God will not bring any child of Israel to a stumbling block or to sin, Heaven forbid.

OVADYAH HEDAYAH

Ovadyah Hedayah, *Yaskil 'Avdi*, vol. 7 (Jerusalem: Yeshivat Hamequbbalim, 1979, ed. Shalom Mordekhai Hedayah), Even Ha'ezer, §4. Translated from Hebrew by Noam Sienna.

Further Reading

Gray, Hillel. "Not Judging by Appearances: The Role of Genotype in Jewish Law on Intersex Conditions." *Shofar: An Interdisciplinary Journal of Jewish Studies* 30:4 (2012), 126–148.

Gray, Hillel. "The Transitioning of Jewish Biomedical Law: Rhetorical and Practical Shifts in Halakhic Discourse on Sex-Change Surgery." *Nashim: A Journal of Jewish Women's Studies & Gender Issues* 29 (2015), 81–107.

109. A German Jew Advocates for the Decriminalization of Homosexuality (Erlangen, 1962)

The German law prohibiting sexual relations between men, Paragraph 175 (see source 72), remained in force in both East and West Germany after the end of the Second World War. The excerpts presented here are from an article advocating for its repeal, published in December 1962 by the German Jewish scholar Hans-Joachim Schoeps (1909–1980). He argues that homosexuality is natural and innate, and he denounces its continued criminalization as cowardly and discriminatory. Schoeps does not reference his own homosexual inclinations (even though he himself fell afoul of Paragraph 175 in 1964), but declares that "as a Jew, to whom maintaining justice is a vital matter," he felt compelled to speak out. Indeed, his provocative article, especially the bold statement that "for homosexuals, the Third Reich is not over yet," sparked a heated public conversation in several German periodicals over the following year. Schoeps himself was a complicated and enigmatic figure: pro-monarchist, anti-Zionist, and anti-Marxist, he had helped co-found the *Deutsche Vortrupp* (German Vanguard) in 1933, an alliance of patriotic German Jewish students who supported the rise of the Third Reich. But Schoeps soon discovered that no amount of patriotic sentiment would save a Jew from Nazis, and indeed Schoeps' own patriotic parents died in Theresienstadt. He fled to Sweden in 1938, where he spent the war, and returned to Germany in 1946. Schoeps devoted the rest of his life to fighting extremism and promoting interfaith understanding, although his past associations, and his lifelong contrarianism, often left him isolated.

Should Homosexuality Remain Punishable?

In the present legislative period, the *Bundestag* [German Parliament] will pass the draft of a new penal code presented by the Federal Ministry of Justice after several years of preparatory work by the Grand Committee on Criminal Justice, which will have tremendous significance. The punishability of a number of offenses was disputed even in the preparatory committees and remained undecided in the end. This is true above all of the ethically indicated termination of pregnancy (hitherto §218, now §157) and sexual intercourse between men (hitherto §175, now §216)…It is scarcely possible to avoid the observation that obviously, in today's public opinion, there is a sweeping lack of the open-mindedness, honesty or courage needed to take a stand on these questions independently and objectively. Indeed, anyone attempting to do so must expect to be personally suspected, slandered and degraded. In my opinion, this is not a good sign for the moral qualities of today's civic society. Before 1914, they were more advanced here in many respects.*

Even the comparison with the "roaring twenties" comes out to the disadvantage of the present, for at the time, German intellectuals were neither dishonest nor cowardly. The corruption through Hitler certainly bears a considerable

---

*Note in text: In the year 1905, 5000 reputable persons, among them 2800 physicians, signed a petition to the Reichstag in favor of the abolition of the discriminating paragraph. In the twenties, 400 public figures did the same; some of them are still alive. After World War II, no such initiative has been heard of—presumably because too few "celebrities" have the courage to lend their names to this kind of thing.

part of the blame, but the moral self-degradation which has taken place in the meantime even more so. Who would dare today to be the odd one out and truly have an opinion of his own? Those who call themselves "nonconformists" mostly are nothing but affected and pretentious busybodies who, when push comes to shove, would not even dream of hitting a hot topic and possibly burning themselves in the process. In short: in the twenties, there were more honest and courageous people. I do not believe that my memory betrays me here. The way people position themselves—or refrain from positioning themselves—with regard to homosexuality as a central societal taboo seems especially well suited for drawing conclusions about the mentality of one's contemporaries…

Amongst themselves, homosexuals are connected only by the shared distinctness of their sexual orientation, which constitutes a very superficial fact. Looking at homosexuals as a group, it immediately turns out that we are dealing with a subset of humanity as a whole, i.e., all known character types, degrees of intelligence, levels of personality and frames of mind are represented. There is no commonality among homosexuals beyond the fact that they are "different from the others" with regard to their sex life, other than common interests when it comes to defending their embattled position…

It seems fundamentally wrong to me to count homosexuality among the other sexual perversions, all of which are acquired. The Dresden physician Rudolf Klimmer rightfully states in his valuable monograph: "In general, a homosexual will view a transvestite, a sadist etc. just as incredulously and with an affective aversion, as the heterosexual."** The reason why homosexuality is different from perversion lies deeper and cannot be explained with any biological pattern. Hans Blüher aptly states, "What differentiates male-to-male sexual relationships most clearly from perversion is that they exhibit exactly the same principle as love for the opposite sex and that in turn, this sexual principle is surrounded by the same rudiments of perversion." If homosexuality is innate or something that emerges in early childhood, it is impossible to continue referring to it as a perversion; these people are capable of deep, pure love relationships, they experience their "Being Thus" vis-a-vis their fellow human beings as a naturally given "Being Different." In my book "What

---

** In *Die Homosexualität als biologisch-soziologische Zeitfrage*, "Homosexuality as a Biological-Sociological Question of Our Time," Hamburg 1958.

is Man?" [*Was ist der Mensch*, Göttingen 1960], I myself expressed myself as follows: "The fact that homosexuality is emotionally and constitutionally conditioned, that is, deeply anchored in the nature of the respective person, manifests in that the homosexual first of all is not a split personality and not an artificial product, but that his feelings run entirely parallel to those of the heterosexual..."

This, however, has been rejected by the new penal code as a "self-serving claim." It mentions the "overwhelmingly dominant view of the populace," according to which homosexuality is "something deviant, an abnormal state," and "not a normal, unobjectionable drive, for which one can lay claim to the same right as for the relationship between a man and a woman." The constitutive preamble to the draft of the new Paragraph 216 is even more apodictic in its wording: "According to the vastly predominant view among the German populace, a sexual relationship between men is to be seen as a despicable aberration, capable of ruining the character and destroying the sense of morality."

Thus, unperturbed and not to be influenced by facts and arguments, the Federal Ministry of Justice, which also disregarded the suggestions of the Grand Committee on Criminal Justice, in concealing them, clings to pre-scientific views, for whose legitimation the "prevalent view of the populace" is invoked. Apparently, what is meant here is the "healthy instinct of the people" [*gesundes Volksempfinden*], which was a stock phrase during the Third Reich. In any case, there is suspicion that the Federal Ministry of Justice is adhering to national-socialist views, since it never advocated rescinding the tightening of these paragraphs on June 28, 1935, under Hitler. Thus, jurisdiction after 1945 has proceeded accordingly. For homosexuals, the Third Reich is not over yet...

Since Holland abolished the punishment of homosexual acts between adults already in its 1886 penal code, Greece, Finland and Poland (1932), Denmark (1933), Romania (1936), Switzerland (1942), and Sweden (1944) have followed on this path. For all I know, no detrimental consequences for public morality, or testimonials on excesses which might have arisen, have transpired in any of these countries...

It is also hard to bear that even in the future, homosexual relationships between men will continue to be punishable, while between women they will not be subject to prosecution; to a layman, this appears as an infringement of the equality between the sexes, even if the Karlsruhe court did not yield to this argument. Especially disturbing is the vagueness of the elements of the crime, if the present draft, E 60, which has already been approved by the Cabinet and by the Federal Council, will adhere to the idea of declaring punishable "acts resembling intercourse" between men. Klimmer rightfully points out that this constituent fact is not verifiable unless it is freely confessed.

On the other hand, in terms of the law governing sexual conduct, a person's minority and the free self-determination of the individual must be considered as unconditionally in need of protection. The Medical-Legal Task Force of the Institute for Sex Research already in 1950 argued for the absolute necessity of penal protections against the use or threat of force, against the abuse of a relationship of dependency, against the seduction of minors of unblemished character through the exploitation of sexual inexperience, as well as against actions which create a "public nuisance," which, however, are already punishable according to §183 of the penal code (§219 of the new draft).

All these reasons lead to the same conclusion: §175 of the present penal code (§216 in the new draft presently at issue) can and should be scrapped. Even if it would be desirable to adapt the present age of consent of 21 years to today's state of knowledge and to define the problematic fact of "seduction" more succinctly, in practice, even if this wish remains unfulfilled, intercourse with eighteen-to-twenty-year-olds will be treated more leniently once at least the punishable basic fact is dropped. Of course it is clear to anyone familiar with the circumstances that social discrimination, and with that, usually also social disadvantage, will continue once the discriminating paragraph has been abolished: a homosexually predisposed person will probably always encounter the aversion of those faultless citizens who conform to the norm.

A last, national-political aspect remains to be mentioned, which up until now has not figured in the discussion at all, and which I nevertheless consider to be sweeping and decisive, if all deliberations and arguments presented here should be pushed aside and rejected. For me as a Jew, to whom maintaining justice is a vital matter, it was the reason and the actual guiding motif for discussing this touchy subject: since the persecution of the Jews in the Third Reich, the

German people is suspected, in the eyes of the world, of harboring a tendency to torture, persecute and terrorize its minorities. Of course, homosexuals aren't an ethnic-religious but rather a biological-anthropological minority within the totality of the people. Since the furnaces of Auschwitz and Majdanek burned— wide sections of the German people have long ago calmed down about it, but not the still suspicious public in the Western world—one should think twice or three times whether one should continue to subject homosexuals to exceptional laws even in the new penal code. Members of the Bundestag, as the appointed representatives of the people, who will have the final say regarding this decision, would be well advised to give room to these concerns in their hearts and in their conscience.

Hans-Joachim Schoeps, "Soll Homosexualität strafbar bleiben?" *Der Monat* 171 (Dec. 1962), 19–27. Text used by permission of Julius Hans Schoeps. Translated from German by Barbara Ann Schmutzler. Copyright © 2019 Print-O-Craft Press.

Further Reading

Donahue, William Collins, and Martha B. Helfer (eds.). *Nexus: Essays in German Jewish Studies*, Volume 2, special issue on Hans-Joachim Schoeps (Boydell & Brewer, 2014).

Evans, Jennifer. "Homosexuality and the Politics of Masculinity in the GDR." In *The Long Postwar* (eds. Karen Hagemann and Sonya Michel, Baltimore: Johns Hopkins Press, 2014), 343–362.

Nielsen, Philipp. "Disgust, compassion or tolerance: Law and emotions in the debate on §175 in West Germany." *InterDisciplines Journal of History and Sociology* 2 (2015), 159–186.

Whisnant, Clayton J. *Male Homosexuality in West Germany: Between Persecution and Freedom, 1945–69* (Palgrave-Macmillan, 2012).

110. Poetry of Edward Field (New York, 1963)

Edward Field was born in Brooklyn in 1924 to a family of Ashkenazi immigrants and grew up in Lynbrook, where he and his family faced antisemitism and discrimination. He enlisted in the Air Force during the Second World War, and served in England and France until 1945. Returning to New York, he quickly became a fixture in the literary community and the gay and lesbian scene (with much overlap between them); he even provided an interview for Alfred Kinsey's *Sexual Behavior in the Human Male* (1948). He began writing poetry in the 1950s, fighting through depression and therapy to proudly claim his sexuality as part of himself. His first collection, *Stand Up, Friend, With Me* (1963) won the Lamont Poetry Selection from the Academy of American Poets. He has continued to write and edit; his collection *Counting Myself Lucky, Selected Poems 1963–1992* won the Lambda Literary Award in 1992. In "Ruth and Naomi," Field celebrates the relationship of these biblical women, who "lip to vaginal lip / proclaimed their love throughout the land," and whose love inspired everyone to love them and each other. In "The Sleeper," he reminisces about his childhood friend Sonny Hugg, an athletic boy who saw beauty and purpose in the parts of Field that he saw as "liability and curse." Field declares that he will always remember "his foolish and delicious faith / That with all my oddities, there was a place in the world for me / If only he could find the special role." In an autobiographical essay, Field explains that "The Garden," the final poem in *Stand Up, Friend, With Me*, was inspired by the joy of meeting his lifelong companion, Neil Darrick, in 1959. Field describes their new life together as an explosion of verdant growth and flourishing, "a colony in a strange land / planting seeds and making ourselves at home," and sings his gratitude of how beautiful life can be with "a sweet creature of your own."

Ruth and Naomi

If one is a Jew who has a history
—Meaning simply to remember and be sad—
Then Ruth became a Jewess
When Naomi's kisses in her gentile blood
Turned the rumors garrulous in her veins.

How easy for men! They offer up their foreskins.
How strange she felt before this god
Who was, after all, only a voice in the clouds!
So she solved the question as later other gentiles did:
She made the one she loved her godhead.

At first the rabbis were shocked at this liaison,
But what could be done? She ate no pork,

And obeyed all the sacred laws;
So, being wise, they turned it into a moral lesson
And loved her, since she was lovable.

And when the people learned the official approval
All of Israel blessed this union
(Which they had been secretly admiring anyway)
As Ruth and Naomi, lip to vaginal lip,
Proclaimed their love throughout the land.

The Sleeper

When I was the sissy of the block who nobody wanted on their team
Sonny Hugg persisted in believing that my small size was an asset
Not the liability and curse I felt it was
And he saw a use for my swift feet with which I ran away from fights.

He kept putting me into complicated football plays
Which would have been spectacular if they worked:
For instance, me getting clear in front and him shooting the ball over—
Or the sensation of the block, the Sleeper Play
In which I would lie down on the sidelines near the goal
As though resting and out of action, until the scrimmage began
And I would step onto the field, receive the long throw
And to the astonishment of all the tough guys in the world
Step over the goal line for a touchdown.

That was the theory anyway. In practice
I had the fatal flaw of not being able to catch
And usually had my fingers bent back and the breath knocked out of me
So the plays always failed, but Sonny kept on trying
Until he grew up out of my world into the glamorous
Varsity crowd, the popular kids of Lynbrook High.

But I will always have this to thank him for:
That when I look back on childhood
(That four psychiatrists haven't been able to help me bear the thought of)

There is not much to be glad for
Besides his foolish and delicious faith
That, with all my oddities, there was a place in the world for me
If only he could find the special role.

The Garden

The plants on the window ledges are all growing well
Except the avocado which is dying

The grapefruit seeds from breakfast came up
And the watermelon are sprouting all over the window box

The mango practically exploded it looked so pregnant
Cherry, peach, apple and plum trees flourish

The potato eyes threw up weird white shoots
And the birdseed grew a good crop of ragweed

We have formed a colony in a strange land
Planting our seeds and making ourselves at home

The laws are our own to make except those of growth
Which are God's and we obey His alone

I look around this place, everything in order
The implements of living stacked

Fishes in the stream blowing bubbles like kisses
Wild cats to drag yowling from the woods

Trees to hug and roots to dig
A young horse to play around with

It is a beautiful place to have the run of
When a sweet creature of your own brings all of it to you.

Edward Field, *Stand Up, Friend, With Me* (Grove Press, 1963). Copyright © 1964 by Edward Field. Reprinted by permission of the author.

Further Reading

Field, Edward. *The Man Who Would Marry Susan Sontag, and Other Intimate Literary Portraits of the Bohemian Era* (University of Wisconsin Press, 2006).

Field, Edward. "Autobiography." OutHistory, 2009 (http://outhistory.org/exhibits/show/edward-field).

Hennessy, Christopher. "An Interview with Edward Field." In ibid., *Our Deep Gossip: Conversations with Gay Writers on Poetry and Desire* (University of Wisconsin Press, 2013), 23–52.

111. "Rabbinical Stands on Homosexuality:" A Jewish Newspaper Report (Indiana, 1963)

This article, by journalist Jeanette Rachmuth Herschaft (1924–2003), appeared in the Indiana-based newspaper *The National Jewish Post and Opinion* in 1963. The question of Judaism's stance on homosexuality had been prompted by the appearance of Reform rabbi Alvin I. Fine (1917–1999), from Temple Emanuel in San Francisco, in the film *The Rejected* (1961), the first documentary on homosexuality to be broadcast on American television. Rabbi Fine, who was throughout his life a passionate advocate for civil rights and racial justice, had suggested a lenient and welcoming approach to homosexual Jews. Herschaft interviewed other rabbis, however, who disagreed; Rabbi Aaron B. Ilson (1915–2001) from the CCAR emphasized that Rabbi Fine was not speaking as a representative of the Reform movement, and Rabbi Armond E. Cohen (1909–2007) of the Conservative Rabbinical Assembly explained that while he agreed generally with Rabbi Fine's sympathetic approach, he believed that homosexuals were, in Freudian terms, suffering from "delayed resolutions of one Oedipal complex...and therefore in need of psychiatric assistance." Herschaft closes her article with an unnamed Orthodox rabbi and psychiatrist who distinguished between "manifest" or practicing homosexuals, who are actively sinning, and "latent" homosexuals, who merely need treatment. Her piece demonstrates some of the many ways that the American Jewish community grappled with the rising visibility of homosexuality and the gay community in the 1950s and 1960s (for others, see sources 104, 114, and 119). Herschaft maintained an interest in the issue of homosexuality in Judaism, publishing a similar piece on the subject in 1968, and a longer in-depth series that ran for six weeks in the fall of 1971.

RABBINICAL STANDS ON HOMOSEXUALITY

By Jeanette R. Herschaft

NEW YORK (P-O) "Judaism today takes a different view from its biblical and post biblical edicts on homosexuals...Such persons are not criminals and should not have punitive action as atonement...Judaism believes that psychological approach is the answer..."

In making these statements on educational television (WNDT-TV, New York: "The Rejected One"), Reform Rabbi Alvin S. Fine, Temple Emanuel, San Francisco, opened up a subject that has long been taboo in the three wings of Judaism. Every rabbi faced with the problem of homosexuality in a person he is in contact with has had to decide whether to abide by the biblical injunction regarding homosexuals or attempt to use or suggest modern psychological means to treat them. To adopt the latter attitude would mean viewing homosexuality as a sickness rather than a sin or a crime.

The biblical injunction states: "And if a man lies with mankind, as with womankind, both of them have committed abomination: they shall surely be put to death; their blood shall be upon them" (Leviticus 20:13).

How does the modern rabbinate then handle the problem? Three rabbis, representative of the three wings of Judaism and who would be in a particular position to answer the question, were polled on their views.

Was Rabbi Fine's statement indicative of the position of the Reform movement on the matter? It wasn't according to Rabbi Aaron B. Ilson, Temple Sinai, Pittsburgh, the chairman of Religion and Psychiatry of the Central Conference of American Rabbis. "Rabbi Fine expressed a personal opinion and in no way did what he say reflect the view of the Central Conference of American Rabbis," Rabbi Ilson said. "It has taken no formal steps in that direction and has not made a clear-cut ruling on this issue. Rabbi Fine could not speak in the name of the Reform movement or for any Judaistic group as none has issued such a pronouncement."

Rabbi Armand Cohen, the Rabbinical Assembly of America (Conservative) chairman of Mental Health, spoke more freely on the subject.

Rabbi Cohen said the Mental Health committee had discussed the issue but has come up with no formal ruling. However, he said that he agreed personally with Rabbi Fine's statement.

While homosexuality may be a sin, it is not a crime, and therefore no punitive action should be taken, Rabbi Cohen said. Such people need medical help as they suffer from inadequacy, he said, and to consider it a crime is cruel and therefore sinful.

"The Jewish tradition regards sin as man's failure to achieve his full human potentiality," Rabbi Cohen said. "When a man sins, he expresses his spiritual inadequacy; he has somehow missed the mark."

"Within the framework of Jewish culture, homosexuality was regarded as a sin because the homosexual has failed to fulfill himself sexually," he said. "This is consistent with prevailing medical attitudes which regard psychological homosexuality as a disorder in which there is a failure to achieve positive sexual identification."

"Sometimes this results from delayed resolutions of one Oedipal conflict," Rabbi Cohen said. "Everyone has both male and female characteristics. In a normal person, fairly early in life, his native sex endowment predominates and the original conflict is resolved."

"The psychological homosexual has not yet achieved this resolution and is therefore in need of psychiatric assistance," Rabbi Cohen said. "In some, there is a physical disorder and medical assistance is needed to help determine sexual identification. But whether it be psychological or biological, homosexuality in our culture is a disorder and it should not be regarded as a crime."

A leading Orthodox rabbi who is also a practicing psychiatrist—who asked not to be quoted—drew a finer distinction on the subject.

"The topic is sufficiently clear in the Bible," he said. "It is a crime, of course, but only for the 'manifest,' the practicing homosexual. The 'latent' homosexual is the unconscious one. It is the latter that I have treated; the former rarely seek medical aid."

Jeanette Herschaft, "Rabbinical Stands on Homosexuality," *The National Jewish Post & Opinion*, May 17, 1963, p. 7.

Further Reading

Kahn, Yoel. "Judaism and Homosexuality: The Traditionalist/Progressive Debate." *Journal of Homosexuality* 18:3/4 (1989), 47–52.

McMullan, William Eugene. *Queer Witness: Religion and the History of the LGBT Movement in San Francisco, 1948–1981* (Ph.D. dissertation, UC Berkeley, 2011).

112. An American Jewish Gay Activist Delivers a Speech on the Fight for Civil Liberties (New York, 1964)

Franklin Kameny (1925–2011) was a pioneering American Jewish gay rights activist, who coined the slogan "Gay is Good" and was one of the leaders in spurring the homophile movement into political activism. Born in New York City, Kameny served in the Army in the Second World War, and graduated Harvard with a doctorate in astronomy in 1956. He was hired by the United States Army Map Service in 1957, but when his homosexuality became known, he was dismissed and his file was marked as "unsuitable" for federal employment. Kameny was one of hundreds of Americans who lost employment during the "Lavender Scare" of the 1950s, part of the larger social panic of McCarthyism around communism and other forms of social disruption. Kameny refused to accept this, and began protesting his unjust termination in the court, eventually reaching the Supreme Court in 1961—the first civil rights claim based on sexual orientation to be brought there—although it was denied. Kameny co-founded the Mattachine Society of Washington that year, and began organizing protests and pickets of the White House, the Pentagon, and other prominent locations. He also lobbied the American Psychological Association to remove the classification of homosexuality as a mental disorder (which they finally did in 1973), and was active in LGBTQ activism until his death in 2011. Although he was Jewish himself, Kameny rarely spoke about Judaism except as part of his general argument that sexuality should be considered a valuable and protected facet of identity, just like religion or race. In this speech, delivered at the July meeting of the Mattachine Society of New York in 1964, Kameny emphasizes that homophile organizations should focus on eliminating social prejudice and legal discrimination, insisting that homosexuality needs to be respected, not cured or treated, just like race or religion. He also argues that the rejection of homosexuals by religious communities was a loss to both parties, and describes his work reaching out to the Jewish community, specifically the Reform synagogue of Temple Sinai in Washington DC, to support "closer integration of the homosexuals with the religious life of their community." In 2009, the United States Office of Personnel Management formally apologized for Kameny's dismissal, and he was inducted into the Department of Labor Hall of Honor. His picket signs are now held in the Smithsonian's National Museum of American History, and his personal papers at the Library of Congress.

Civil Liberties: A Progress Report

Good evening, ladies and gentlemen. It is a pleasure and a privilege to appear before you this evening, as your 100ᵗʰ monthly speaker. My talk tonight will fall into two major parts. Because I have done and am doing my best to lead my organization—the Mattachine Society of Washington—in directions somewhat different from those traditional homophile organizations in this country the first part of my talk will be a presentation of the homophile movement as a civil liberties and social rights action movement, and of the philosophy and rationale behind what I have been trying to do.

I usually try to tailor my talks to my audience and so my talk this evening is directed to some extent to an audience which as I believe you are, is a mixture of both "in-group" and "out-group." And part of it will be directed to those active in the homophile movement.

My approach is one of strong and definite positions, unequivocally held—I feel that the nurture and presentation of controversy are not as virtuous as many in the movement would have them be, nor is the cultivation of an outward neutrality on questions upon which we should be taking a firm clear, no-nonsense stand.

Let me make it clear at the outset that, like any organization based upon strongly-held beliefs, and composed in its active part of people of strong personality, there exists a considerable range of viewpoint within the Mattachine Society of Washington on many matters directly relevant to the homophile movement. For this reason, the views I express this evening are my own, and are not necessarily those held in any formal sense by the Mattachine Society of Washington.

It seems to me that there are three primary directions in which a homophile organization can go—social service, information and education, and civil liberties—social action. These are complementary, of course, neither mutually exclusive nor competitive, and usually become matters of a difference of emphasis from one organization to another—the placing of the emphasis resulting from a mixture of the setting in which the organization finds itself and the interests and personalities of those leading the particular group.

As I understand it, the Daughters of Bilitis, for example, devotes itself primarily to social service; the Mattachine Society of New York, in the well established Mattachine tradition, emphasizes the information and education role. The Mattachine Society of Washington, from the outset (because of my own interests, and because in Washington, it seems the clear and obvious direction to take) has placed its emphasis in the area of civil liberties and social action. It is an exponent of that emphasis that I speak this evening.

My reasons for placing emphasis where I do are the following. In regard to social services: No lasting good can be accomplished by administration of social service alone. Let me give an example by analogy. One can supply virtually unlimited amounts of money, food, clothing, and shelter to the poor, but unless one gets to the roots of poverty—the economic system which produces unemployment, the social system which produces lack of education, and the one which over-produces people, etc.—one will accomplish little of lasting value. Similarly, we can refer homosexuals to lawyers, we can find jobs for those who have lost jobs, or have been denied them because of homosexuality, and we can assist them in other ways, but unless and until we get at and eliminate the discrimination and prejudice which underlies—and, in fact which are—the homosexuals' problems, we will accomplish nothing of lasting value, either, and our job will go on literally without end.

Obviously we cannot easily turn away people now in need with the argument that we are working in order that those in the future will not need; so there is clearly a place in the homophile movement for the social services and the Mattachine Society of Washington does its share—but only, I feel, to supplement work of a more fundamental nature, dealing with changes of attitude, prejudice and policy.

We come next to the area of information and education. While this is important, I feel that any movement which relies solely upon an intellectually-directed program of information and education, no matter how extensive, to change well-entrenched, emotionally-based attitudes, is doomed to disappointment. The Negro tried for 90 years to achieve his purposes by a program of information and education. His achievements in those 90 years, while by no means nil, were nothing compared to those of the past 10 years when he tried a vigorous civil liberties, social action approach and gained his goals thereby.

The prejudiced mind, and that is what we are fighting, is not penetrated by information and is not educable. This has been shown in a number of studies of the mental processes associated with prejudice, and has been confirmed by a recent study which showed that tolerance is only slightly promoted by more information: that communication of facts is generally ineffectual against predispositions: that prejudiced opinions, attitudes, and beliefs, usually change only when people are forced to change.

The prejudice against homosexuality is primarily one of an emotional commitment, not an intellectual one; and appeals based upon fact and reason will, for the most part, not be effective.

Where a program of information and education will be useful and very important is in presenting our position to that minority of the majority who are potentially our allies anyway, but who have not thought about the matter before—such as the clergy, as just one of a number of examples—who are looked to as leaders by the masses of people…

This brings us to the area of civil liberties and social action. Here, we get into an area in which we are engaging in what is fundamentally down to-earth, grass-roots, occasionally tooth and-nail politics. We are dealing with emotions of people, and the policies of officialdom, and our methods must be in accord with this…

Now, a few particular points. My starting point is one now well accepted among the homophile organizations, although still novel elsewhere—that the homosexuals make up a minority group comparable to other, what might be called sociological minorities, such as the Negroes, the Jews, etc. I think that this should be explicitly justified, however, since direct challenges to the concept are frequently posed.

I feel that a little consideration will show that aside from the obvious statistical basis, a minority group in the sense in which we speak, must possess four characteristics.

First, the members must possess, in common, some single characteristic or closely related group of characteristics, but otherwise be heterogeneous.

Second, on account of this characteristic, but not in reasonable, rational or logical consequence of it, the majority about them must look down upon the members of the group, and must discriminate adversely against them.

There is a third facet of minority-majority group relations which is a little more subtle, but which I think is always present in regard to a group which is a sociological minority. The consequences of the faults and the sins of the individual members of the minority are visited upon all members of the minority. Let a white, heterosexual, Anglo-Saxon Protestant commit a crime and he alone is blamed. Let a Jew, a Negro, or a homosexual commit a crime, and epithets and blame are depicted against all members of his minority. Let a few members of the majority be personally objectionable or ridiculous to large numbers of people, and the reactions to their offensiveness will be directed against them individually. Let a few members of a minority group be offensive or ridiculous to large numbers of people, and a stereotype will be created which will be applied indiscriminately to all those known to be members of the minority group. This is true of the Negro and Jewish minorities; I hardly need to point out that it is also true of the homosexual minority.

A fourth criterion for the establishment of a sociological minority group is a feeling on the part of members of the minority of cohesiveness, of belonging, and of identity among themselves. This does not have to imply a feeling of belonging to an organization or movement—much as the members of the homophile movement might like all homosexuals to feel—but a feeling of kinship to others whom they know to be members of this minority group. This feeling is clearly present among homosexuals, and strongly so.

With this as a starting point, I look upon the homophile organizations as playing for the homosexual minority the same role as is played by the NAACP or CORE (Congress of Racial Equality) for the Negro minority.

We cannot ask for our rights as a minority group, and I will elaborate briefly upon just what it is we are asking for; we cannot ask for our rights from a position of inferiority or from a position, shall I say, as less than whole human beings. I feel that the entire homophile movement, in terms of any accomplishments beyond merely ministering to the needy, is going to stand or fall upon the question of whether or not homosexuality is a sickness, and upon our taking a firm stand on it. I feel that The New York Times article of last December 17, and the recent New York Academy of Medicine Report have made this abundantly clear. The Question arises every time there is serious discussion of homosexuality, and I feel that an unequivocal position must be taken.

I do not intend this evening to go into a lengthy or detailed discussion of this question. Suffice it to say for the moment that reading of the so-called authorities on this matter shows an appalling incidence of loose reasoning, of poor research, of supposedly generally applicable conclusions being derived from an examination of non-representative samplings, of conclusions being incorporated into initial assumptions, and vice versa, with the consequent circular reasoning. A case in point is the recent, much relied upon study by Bieber. Not only were the homosexuals in his study all patients of his, and therefore, a priori, disturbed, but he makes the statement: "All psychoanalytic theories assume that adult homosexuality is pathological." Obviously if one assumes that homosexuality is pathological, then one will discover that homosexuality is a sickness, and that homosexuals are disturbed just as, if one assumes that two plus two equal five, one is likely to discover that three plus one are equal to five. In both instances, the assumption requires proof before it can be seriously entertained.

There seems to be no valid evidence to show that homosexuality, per se, is a sickness. In view of the absence of such valid evidence, the simple fact that the suggestion of sickness has been made is no reason for entertaining it seriously, or for abandoning the view that homosexuality is not a sickness, but merely a liking or preference similar to and fully on a par with heterosexuality. Accordingly, I take the position unequivocally that, until and unless valid, positive evidence shows otherwise, homosexuality, per se, is neither a sickness, a defect, a disturbance, a neurosis, a psychosis, nor a malfunction of any sort.

I will go further, and say that I feel so strongly that the rationale for the homophile movement rests, and rests heavily upon this position, that should evidence arise to show conclusively that this position is in error, I shall give serious thought to leaving the movement. I do not anticipate that I shall ever need to do so.

Another question which has a way of intruding itself upon any general discussion of homosexuality—much less so, of late, than it formerly did, although it still is the basis for the Federal Government's approach to the question—is that of morality and immorality. It is a point upon which I have rarely heard a straight, direct statement of position from persons in the homophile movement—even when expressing publicly their own views.

Matters of morality, of course, are ones clearly of personal opinion and individual religious belief so that, except for an affirmation of the right of all individuals to adopt their own viewpoints upon those matters, without penalty therefore, and without the official imposition of orthodox views, the homophile movement would be in error in proscribing a position.

However for myself, I take the stand that not only is homosexuality, whether by mere inclination or by overt act, not immoral, but that homosexual acts engaged in by consenting adults are moral, in a positive and real sense, and are right, good and desirable, both for the individual participants and for the society in which they live.

There is another point which comes up frequently in discussions of homosexuality: the matter of the origins of homosexuality and the possibility of re-orientation to heterosexuality. While, as a person dealing in all aspects of homosexuality, I find that these questions are ones of some passing interest; from the viewpoint of civil liberties and social rights, these questions interest me not at all.

I do not see the NAACP and CORE worrying about which chromosome and gene produces a black skin or about the possibility of bleaching the Negro. I do not see any great interest on the part of the B'nai Brith Anti-Defamation

League in the possibility of solving problems of anti-semitism by converting Jews to Christianity.

In all of these minority groups, we are interested in obtaining rights for our respective minorities, as Negroes, as Jews, and as homosexuals. Why we are Negroes, Jews or homosexuals, is totally irrelevant, and whether we can be changed to whites, Christians, or heterosexuals is equally irrelevant.

Further, as implied a moment ago, I look upon the assumption that it is somehow desirable that we be converted to heterosexuality (with the implied assumption that homosexuality is an inferior status) as being presumptuously arrogant and an assault upon our right to be ourselves on a par with those around us, as would be similar attempts for example, to convert Jews to Christianity—something which, for just that reason, has become unfashionable in this country.

There is one final point of basic approach, before I become somewhat more specific—and this is a somewhat subtle one, one which is difficult to express clearly. In reading through many statements put out by the homophile movement, there is easily perceptible a defensive tone—a lightly veiled feeling that homosexuality really is inferior to heterosexuality but that, since we have to live with it, it must be made the best of. While I do not, of course, take the ridiculous view point discussed in the recent New York Academy of Medicine Report that homosexuality and homosexuals are superior to heterosexuality and heterosexuals, I am unwilling to grant even the slightest degree of inferiority: I look upon homosexuality as something in no way shameful or intrinsically undesirable.

Now, from the civil liberties and social rights viewpoint, just what do we want? I feel that we want, basically, what all other minority groups want and what every American citizen has the right to request and to expect—in fact, to demand: To be judged and to be treated, each upon his own merits as an individual and only on those criteria truly relevant to a particular situation, not upon irrelevant criteria, as homosexuality always is, having to do only with the harmless conduct of our private lives. We wish, AS HOMOSEXUALS, to be rid of the contempt directed against us by our fellow citizens—contempt which exists without reason, which serves only to render contemptible those manifesting it, and which is reinforced and perpetuated by present official attitude and policy—and it is the latter which, in great measure, is the target of a civil rights endeavor.

In short, as homosexuals we want (to quote from a portion of the statement of purpose of the Mattachine Society of Washington) "the right, as human beings, to develop our full potential and dignity, and the right, as citizens, to be allowed to make our maximum contribution to the society in which we live." These rights are ours in fact, though we are currently denied them in practice.

I feel that with due regard for strategy and tactics, we must take a bold, strong, uncompromising initiative in working for these rights; that the established framework of authority, constituted and otherwise, must be challenged directly by every lawful means at hand...

We come now to the last of our current areas of major endeavor, religion. Last December, I gave a talk, followed by discussion, to part of the congregation of Temple Sinai, one of the reformed Jewish congregations in Washington. The talk was well received.

In January, just before one of the radio broadcasts which I mentioned earlier, one of our members telephoned every Unitarian minister in the greater Washington area to tell them of the broadcast: shortly thereafter he sent them a letter, including a copy of Cory's The Homosexual in America. This resulted in a sermon by one of the ministers. The sermon was titled "Civil Liberties and the Homosexual" and couldn't have been more satisfactory if I had written it myself. The sermon was followed by two discussion groups—both well attended—at which I was asked to preside.

Subsequently, with the member just mentioned as chairman, I formed a new committee—our Committee on Approaches to the Clergy—which has informally approached perhaps two dozen clergymen of several faiths and denominations, with a considerable and gratifying degree of favorable response. The Committee's bases of approach are two—of equal emphasis. First, we feel that the homosexual finds himself rejected by almost every religious body to the loss and detriment both of the religious bodies and of the homosexuals. We seek to remedy this by working for closer integration of the homosexuals with the religious life of their community.

Second, we wish to enlist the aid of the clergy in our battle for civil rights. Our committee has drawn up a formal statement of purpose, which, in its present proposed form, pleases me greatly. This very nicely covers all three directions of endeavor discussed above. We plan to send this statement of purpose, our Society's statement of purpose, and a covering letter to the entire clergy of the greater Washington area asking for their assistance and inquiring about their interest in participating in a conference with us.

Most recently, at his initiative, I had lunch with a high official of the Methodists' national headquarters in Washington (we have had very favorable responses from the Methodists). He had just come from a retreat in the San Francisco area, attended by members of the clergy and the homophile movement. He indicated to my pleasure that he felt that we in Washington had done far more in the direction of making contact with the local clergy than had any of the West Coast groups. He was completely with us and wished to assist. He is now rounding up a group of sympathetic ministers of a variety of faiths to meet with us in the very near future. He will try to appear on the program of our forthcoming ECHO conference.

In that connection, I might mention in passing, that the Methodists will have their 5-day national conference in Washington at the same time as the 1964 ECHO conference. Informal plans are now afoot to explore the possibility of some sort of coordination.

I feel that these activities with religious leaders are of the utmost importance because the commitment of most people to their religion and to the leaders thereof is an emotional one. They will follow the lead taken by a minister where they will not follow the intellectual lead set by other leaders and persons in positions of constituted authority. If we can get any substantial portion of the clergy to support us—and a surprising number do—and to support us openly and actively, we can go a very long way, very quickly, toward remedying some of the situations in our regard which are so badly in need of remedy.

That completes a quick accounting of our activities, past, present, and proposed, in all three areas—civil liberties and social rights—information and education—and social service. I hope that the pressures of a somewhat hasty preparation have not made this presentation too unclear, too perfunctory, or too uninteresting.

Franklin Kameny, "Civil Liberties: A Progress Report," *New York Mattachine Newsletter* 10:1 (January 1965), 7–22. Reprinted courtesy of the Estate of Frank Kameny.

Further Reading

Faderman, Lillian. *The Gay Revolution: The Story of the Struggle* (New York: Simon & Schuster, 2015).

Johnson, David K. "Franklin E. Kameny." In *Before Stonewall: Activists for Gay and Lesbian Rights in Historical Context* (ed. Vern L Bullough, New York: Haworth Press, 2002), 209–219.

Johnson, David K. *The Lavender Scare: The Cold War Persecution of Gays and Lesbians in the Federal Government* (University of Chicago Press, 2004).

Ridinger, Robert (ed.). *Speaking for Our Lives: Historic Speeches and Rhetoric for Gay and Lesbian Rights, 1892–2000* (Routledge, 2012).

113. *Totempole*, A Gay American Jewish Novel (New York, 1965)

The cover of the first edition of *Totempole* (1965), by Sanford Friedman (1928–2010), features a blurb declaring the book to be "the most audacious affirmation of the homosexual experience...I have ever seen." The book follows the life of Stephen Wolfe, a gay American Jew (and almost certainly the first gay protagonist in a Jewish American novel), from childhood to adulthood: performing in drag at his summer camp, learning to masturbate while studying for his bar mitzvah, being initiated into sex by his college roommate Leonard Gottlieb, and finally, falling in love with a Korean POW, Sun Bo Pak, while stationed as an American soldier in Korea. In this excerpt from the end of the book, Wolfe finally overcomes his struggles with his homosexual identity and allows himself to submit fully to Pak for the first time, triumphantly realizing "in the midst of his ecstatic joy" the feeling of a new birth. As Wolfe prepares to leave, Pak gives him a ring to immortalize their time together, which Wolfe proudly wears as he re-enters America to begin his new life, now at peace with himself. While perhaps not as optimistic as *Wasteland* (source 101), the relatively happy ending was still daring for its time. The explicit treatment of homosexuality, and especially the explicit sexual scenes, were shocking to some—one reviewer wrote that "the procedural detail may occasion a certain queasiness in even the most enlightened"—and the racial stereotypes are uncomfortable for modern readers, but many critics at the time found it a powerful and well-crafted, if perhaps low-brow, novel. The author, Sanford Friedman, gave Wolfe the central biographical elements of his own life: born to a working-class Jewish family in New York, Friedman studied drama and playwriting in college, and served in the U.S. Army in Korea from 1951–1953 (where Friedman was awarded a Bronze Star). Friedman continued to write and publish after *Totempole*, and lived for two decades in Manhattan with his partner, the Jewish American poet Richard Howard; his final novel, *Conversations with Beethoven*, was published posthumously in 2014.

When Stephen was naked Sun Bo took off his own clothes and lay down on his side, facing Stephen. For a long time they kissed—kissed until their kisses seemed inadequate. Then Stephen pulled Sun Bo on top of him and murmured in his ear, "Oh my love, come into me. Please, please come into me." But scarcely had the words left his mouth, than Stephen realized there was no lubricant in the room—nothing! nothing but some lukewarm sake—and his heart sank.

But Sun Bo was not deterred. Slipping away from Stephen's lips, he began to kiss him on the neck, the nipples, the navel, the thighs, until Stephen felt almost galvanized and Sun Bo turned him over tenderly and penetrated Stephen with his tongue.

So exciting was the sensation, Stephen made no effort to resist. All he could do was moan—his moans becoming more and more audible as his excitement increased. And when, in response, Sun Bo embraced him from behind, attempting to come into him, Stephen tried consciously to relax. "No, no," Sun Bo whispered, "do not force."

Stephen bit the pillow to keep from crying out. But even as he did, he understood at last that it was not a matter of submission or surrender but of self-assertion—of actively laying claim to Sun Bo, wanting him, demanding him—and his teeth released the pillow, as he took Sun Bo into himself, shouting out triumphantly "Yes! yes! yes!"

At the same moment all of Stephen's questions about the "passive" partner's satisfaction were answered by Sun Bo, who licked his hand and took hold of Stephen.

Unable to restrain himself, Stephen began to grunt. Some part of him, his consciousness, that seemed just now outside himself, was shocked by the sounds he produced. In their volume and ferocity they were reminiscent of the moose at Lobster Pond, the lions at the zoo. But as he neared his climax the grunts diminished, grew more staccato, breathy, until, for one split second, there was no sound at all, no breath, and Stephen thought his had stopped, before he heard himself let out a long ecstatic cry. Then, somewhere toward the end of it, this cry turned abruptly into laughter—loud orgiastic laughter that seemed to issue from his bowels. It was uncontrollable, he simply could not stop. And so he laughed and laughed and went on laughing, and as he did he suddenly remembered the myth of Zarathustra, about whom it was said that when he was born, instead of crying, he burst into laughter. Stephen had never fully understood the myth before, but now he did—now, in the midst of his ecstatic joy, he realized he was being born...

[Stephen prepares to return to America.] Sun Bo sat down and opened his hand. In the center of his palm he held a silver ring.

Stephen picked it up with care. The ring was in the shape of two clasped hands. On one side of the band, designed to represent an arm, was inscribed the name Sun Bo, on the other, Stephen.

"You remember spoon from mess hall?"

Stephen nodded.

"Spoon now ring," Sun Bo explained. "Why you do not put it on? I know you do not like luxury, but ring not luxury. Ring mean to represent friendship between Stephen and Sun Bo."

Stephen tried to put the ring on his third finger but it wouldn't fit, so he put it on his pinky. "I'll never take it off, Sun Bo. Never, never."

"You weep again," Sun Bo observed.

"I'm sorry, sorry."

"Why you weep?"

"Because—because—" Stephen stammered, squeezing the ring as if to keep the hands from coming unclasped, "because I have to leave you…"

Leaning against the deck rail, twisting the silver ring on his little finger and watching the shrieking gulls patrol the churning wake, Stephen felt both overjoyed and sorrowful as the troop transport, *General Miller*, steamed through the Golden Gate. Joyful to be home again, to see his family and friends again, and soon to begin his career; sorrowful not only because he had lost Sun Bo and left Korea, but also because he had lost something of himself. What it was, he could not say, but from the way in which he gazed down at the emerald water, Stephen seemed to know by instinct that he had lost it in the sea. Part of him—some central part, some fiercely personal, yet antenatal, even prehistoric part he would have thought he could not live without—was drifting, drowning there below the opaque surface, even as the rest of him was being borne back to the Pacific Coast…

Suddenly, just overhead, like a gigantic metal sea fan, dazzling in the sunlight, Stephen saw the underspanning of the Golden Gate Bridge. A little army band was on the pier again as the *General Miller* docked, and Stephen stepped of the ship, away from the water, away from the ocean, down the gangplank, onto the land.

Sanford Friedman, *Totempole* (New York: EP Dutton, 1965, reprinted by New York Review Books Classics, 2014), 372–380.

Further Reading

Bronski, Michael (ed.). *Pulp Friction: Uncovering the Golden Age of Gay Male Pulps* (New York: St. Martin's Press, 2003).

Shatzky, Joel. "Sanford Friedman." In ibid., *Contemporary Jewish-American Novelists: A Bio-critical Sourcebook* (Westport, CT: Greenwood Press, 1997), 97–100.

Stryker, Susan. *Queer Pulp: Perverted Passions from the Golden Age of the Paperback* (San Francisco: Chronicle Books, 2001).

114. The National Federation of Temple Sisterhoods Issues Resolution on Homosexuality (New York, 1965)

By the 1960s, some rabbis (starting within the Reform movement) began to advocate for more compassionate and welcoming approaches for gay and lesbian Jews, while others insisted that homosexuality was both foreign to, and incompatible with, Judaism (see sources 104 and 111). Many Jewish leaders took a middle ground, arguing that while homosexuality might be a psychological disturbance or illness, it should not be criminalized or punished. This short statement on homosexuality was prepared for the National Federation of Temple Sisterhoods (NFTS, today the Women of Reform Judaism) in 1965, in conjunction with the Biennial, the national convention of the United Association of Hebrew Congregations (UAHC, today the Union for Reform Judaism). Their resolution contrasts biblical attitudes to those of "enlightened men" today, who understand homosexuality to be a "symptom of psychiatric disturbance," which needed treatment rather that punishment; it demands the decriminalization of homosexual activity, and an end to police harassment of homosexuals, instead suggesting that "all available resources of society be brought to bear on the alleviation of this problem." According to Rabbi Yoel Kahn, this resolution was prepared by NFTS as a parallel to a similar resolution opposing homophobic discrimination prepared for the general vote at the UAHC Convention, but that resolution was never presented, and so the NFTS resolution was not implemented.

Resolution of the Women of Reform Judaism National Federation of Temple Sisterhoods 25th Biennial Assembly, 1965: Homosexuality

The Bible treats homosexuality as an "abomination" (cf. Leviticus 18:22, 20:13) and penalties for its practice were severe. Today, however, enlightened men understand that homosexuality may be a symptom of psychiatric disturbance which requires sympathetic understanding and psychiatric evaluation.

We, therefore, deplore the tendency on the part of community authorities to harass homosexuals. We associate ourselves with those religious leaders and legal experts who urge revisions in the criminal code as it relates to homosexuality, especially when it exists between consenting adults. While the young or nonconsenting person must be protected from the advances of disturbed individuals, the aberrations of such individuals must be considered as expressions of possible illness rather than of criminality. We further urge that all available resources of society be brought to bear on the alleviation of this problem.

Unadopted resolution of NFTS, as published in *Kulanu (All of Us): A Program for Congregations Implementing Gay and Lesbian Inclusion—A Handbook for UAHC Congregations* (ed. Richard Address, UAHC Press, 1996), p. 247, reprinted by permission of Richard Address.

Further Reading

Goldman, Karla. "Women in Reform Judaism: Between Rhetoric and Reality." In *Women Remaking American Judaism* (ed. Riv-Ellen Prell, Wayne State University Press, 2007), 109–133.

Kahn, Yoel. "Judaism and Homosexuality: The Traditionalist/Progressive Debate." *Journal of Homosexuality* 18:3/4 (1989), 47–52.

Nadell, Pamela. "National Federation of Temple Sisterhoods." *Jewish Women: A Comprehensive Historical Encyclopedia* (eds. Paula Hyman and Dalia Ofer; online at https://jwa.org/encyclopedia/article/national-federation-of-temple-sisterhoods).

115. A Gay Jewish Activist Advocates for Homosexual Solidarity (New York, 1965)

"Leo Ebreo" (Leo the Jew) was the pen name of Leo Joshua Skir (1932–2014), a gay Jewish activist and writer from New York. Skir was friends with noted Jewish Beat poets Allen Ginsberg and Elise Cowen (Cowen and Skir met in the 1940s on a Zionist training farm in Poughkeepsie), and was responsible for saving much of Cowen's poetry after she committed suicide in 1962. While studying at Columbia, he spent the summer of 1951 on a kibbutz in Israel, but was disappointed to find that his burgeoning sense of his homosexual identity was not welcome in the kibbutz's heteronormative environment. Skir returned to New York, and after graduating, continued to write for Jewish and non-Jewish literary journals while completing an MA at New York University; in 1975 he moved to Minneapolis, where he lived for the rest of his life. Skir published many articles, theatre and film reviews, and a semi-autobiographical book titled *Boychick: A Novel* (1971). In this article, originally published in the lesbian magazine *The Ladder* in 1965, Skir draws on his background in the Zionist movement, and his experience as a first-generation American Jew, to call for solidarity among homosexuals, linking the fight for gay rights as part of the larger national and global struggle of oppressed minorities. He castigates his fellow homosexuals for holding themselves back in a self-declared "ghetto," declaring that "when the Negro, the Jew, the homosexual, is known and a neighbor, he will cease to be a bogey," and urging the readers to join him in fighting for full integration and equality. While religion was a popular topic in gay and lesbian magazines in the 1950s and 1960s, it was almost always Christianity being discussed, and usually with negative implications. Skir's explicit and thoughtful engagement with Judaism is a unique and unprecedented window into the relationship of gay Jewish activists with the American Jewish community of the 1950s and 1960s.

A Homosexual Ghetto? By Leo Ebreo

When I was younger—about sixteen—I was an active Zionist. I believed that the best thing for American Jews, in fact *all* Jews, to do would be to go to Israel and live in a kibbutz (collective). I belonged to a Zionist "movement" and tried to get the Jews I knew to join. I expected of course that few would want to emigrate, but I thought that most would be interested in helping Israel and the Zionist movement.

This was not the case. I was met, very often, by an extraordinary hostility. It was not until years later, reading works on Jewish self-hatred, Negro self-hatred, that I could realize that I had frightened some already-frightened people.

For this fright I have still no cure. The rational arguments which I gave my Jewish friends then, I would give them now.

These arguments (both the ones they gave me and my replies) came back to me recently when I began working in the homophile movement and speaking to homosexual friends about it. When I attempted to draw some parallel between the Jew's struggle for his rights and the homosexual's struggle for his, I was often stopped short with the explanation that there could be no parallel because one was a "religious problem" and the other a "sexual problem." I tried, without success, to show how much the Negro's struggle paralleled that of the Jew, even though the Negro "problem" was a "race problem" and not a "religious problem."

As I have said, I have no rational arguments against the surrender to fear, and the rejection of self that lies behind it. This essay is not written for those who have surrendered to fear, but for the others, the fighters.

I think we need to constantly reaffirm our perspective in the fight for homophile rights, to realize that we are part of a broad, general movement towards a better, freer, happier world.

This struggle of ours for complete acceptance will probably continue throughout our lifetime, as will the struggle of the Negro and the Jew. Oceans of hatred, unreason, rejection, craven fear will continue to come from the "other" world (of the white, the gentile, the heterosexual), will continue to infect many individuals within these oppressed minorities.

And in this light, I think my parallel Zionist experience will show us both the currents of the Opposition from within our own ranks, and the answers which we must make. The objections my Jewish friends raised were as follows;

(1) "I'm not that Jewish." "Being Jewish isn't that important to me." (2) "I don't want to go to Israel." (3) "*You* are making the situation bad for *us*. There isn't any great problem. Discretion is the password. You are being offensive. You are putting us in a GHETTO, or would if we allowed you."

The answers I gave then come back to me now:

1. "I'm not that Jewish." What does "that" mean? Orthodoxy? Many Zionists are not *that* orthodox. To be Jewish does not mean a series of outward observances. It means being part of a people, recognizing their history, trying to find within that historical experience your lesson, your place.

2. "I don't want to go to Israel." Perhaps not. Perhaps not now when conditions for Jewish life are good in the United States (as they were once in Germany). But don't you want Israel to exist? Some place which will represent the Jews, to which they can go if oppressed? What other nation would try Eichmann? And if an Israel had existed in the time of Nazi Germany, could not the Jews have gone there? And, with an Israel to represent them, might there

not have been some action taken to prevent the extermination of the Jews in Europe?

3. "You are making the situation bad for *us*...You are putting us in a ghetto." Nonsense. Israel is not a ghetto. It is a place where the Jew is, if anything, more normal than in other countries, a place where he is a farmer, seaman, shepherd, rather than furrier and candy store owner.

Of course, the Jews who offered me these arguments were not convinced by my replies. They had a certain picture in their minds of what being "Jewish" was—a curious, narrow, ill-informed vision defined by an old man (always old) with a long white beard and a yamulka and a long black coat, a Yiddish accent, the boredom of prayer mumbled and half-heard on certain holy days in a synagogue. The reality of Jewish existence, history, aspirations was unknown to them. Small wonder then that they could not imagine the reality of Israel. Its youth, vitality, the variety of its peoples.

So they hung back—often, too often, proud of not being "too Jewish," changing their names to less Jewish-sounding ones, the girls having their noses shortened surgically.

And yet, as the years passed, I saw them grow more confident, less apologetic of their Judaism, because, in spite of themselves, they were proud of Israel, that nation whose growth they had at first resented.

And so. I think, it will be with those homosexual friends of mine who are now fearful, even resentful, of the homophile organizations. Their reactions now parallel, almost word for word, those of the Jews:

1. "I'm not that homosexual." Here too, the image the outside world pictures is used by those raising this objection. One doesn't have to fit the stereotype to be *that* homosexual. (Yet to a certain extent we must work with the outside world's definition of the homosexual.) The German Jews were the most assimilated, often not knowing Yiddish, often not religious, often converted to Christianity. Still they were exterminated. Similarly, too often the one who suffers from persecution of homosexuals is the respectable married man, like [Walter Wilson] Jenkins, who makes a single slip. No one trying to defend Jenkins (and there were few who did, to our eternal shame) noted that he wasn't *that* homosexual.

2. "I don't want to be a member of a homophile organization." My full sympathies. Neither do I. But I do belong. Just as I belong to the UJA, to the NAACP. Being in the Zionist movement, like being in the homophile movement, was to some extent a burden to me. It is a trial to pay dues, to attend meetings, to hear lectures, and—most of all—to have to deal with so many people and with their many, many faults. (St. Theresa, the Jewess of Avila, said that people were a great trial to her. That was the 16th century, and people are still a great trial.) But don't you want the homophile movement to exist? Don't you want to see some organization represent homosexuals, stand up for their rights?

Fighting though I was for the state of Israel, I was still—and am still—a confirmed internationalist. But to arrive at that place in history, these intermediate steps are necessary. It is not a certain good—an absolute good—that there be a state of Israel, with borders, army, taxes, ministries. But until there are no French, German, Russian, American nationalities, I think it unwise to eliminate the Jewish nationality, which all these nations have at times acknowledged (before its official creation) by discriminating against it.

The question you must ask yourself is not whether you "like" to join or at least support a homophile organization (or a civil rights organization), but whether it is *needed*. And the homophile movement is needed, as Israel is needed, *at this point in history*.

3. "Your homophile organizations make our situation worse…Discretion is the password. You are being offensive. You are putting homosexuals in a ghetto." Here again we are dealing often with homosexual fear and self-hatred and self-rejection.

This very word—GHETTO—has been used to me by homosexuals outside the movement. The homosexual who says this has accepted the negative picture of the homosexual drawn by the outside world. And, just as the American Jew may imagine a nation of candy store keepers with Yiddish accents and skullcaps, so the "assimilated" homosexual, from his troglodyte perspective, may imagine an assembly of campy ballet dancers and hair dressers.

There is already something of a ghetto pattern for homosexuals, because of the pressures put on them to confine themselves to certain vocations where they are "expected" and to isolate themselves. But the aim of the homophile organizations, like that of the NAACP, the UJA, is not for further ghettoization but for *integration*, for *equality*.

However, there is a radical difference between the situation of the homosexual and that of the Negro and Jew in relation to their organizations. The Negro can rarely "pass." The Jew might be able to, but he is under many pressures, especially family upbringing and sometimes family presence, not to. The homosexual, on the other hand, can usually "pass" easily and does not have the family pressure as an inducement to declare himself. If anything, there is another pressure, to pass for the sake of family appearances.

Thus the individual homosexual may claim that membership in a homophile organization, rather than enabling him to normalize his situation, might endanger the assimilation, the equality he can achieve with just a bit of "discretion" and silence. This argument has a certain cogency. Its limitation is that it is a solution for the *individual* homosexual.

It is the "solution" (or, to be charitable, the "path") taken by the average homosexual, especially the one outside a city, or who is not in touch with the gay community. And this is not a solution, a path, which is to be avoided. For certain people, in positions in the government, in schools, there may be no choice but secrecy at this time.

But the price can be a terrible one. It is, as I have said, an individual solution. Often, too often, it results in an isolation for the individual, sometimes a world of pathetic furtive sexuality or public lavatory sex—shameful, inadequate ridiculous, dangerous. Even when the hidden homosexual has a mate, the union still has a peculiar isolate character, being secret, disguised. Thus the homosexual who passes is often in a ghetto composed of one person, sometimes of two. An individual solution perhaps, but hardly a permanent one, or a good one.

Those of us who are active in the homophile movement feel ourselves working for those outside and fearful of joining. We are working for a day when our organizations will be strong enough, active enough, to protect the rights of those in public employment (such as teachers), in the armed services, in government. The homosexual who is accepted as a homosexual will be a fuller, better person than the furtive imitation-heterosexual who has found his individual "solution."

The aim of the homophile organizations is not to draw a small circle and place the homosexual within it. The very term "homosexual" (only 68 years old if we are to believe the Oxford English Dictionary) may not be used with such frequency in the Larger Society which we are working to create. We *are* drawing a circle—but a LARGE circle, to draw the large society of which we are a part, in. We are asking to be accepted. This acceptance which the homosexual minority needs, wants, can only be gotten when it is *asked* for—if need be, DEMONSTRATED for through groups like ECHO and their picket lines.

The drive to eliminate discrimination against homosexuals (sex fascism) is a direct parallel to the drive to eliminate discrimination against Negroes (race fascism). These minority movements are not attempts to overthrow the white race, or to destroy the institution of the family, but to allow a fuller growth of human potential, breaking down the barriers against a strange race or sexuality. When the Negro, the Jew, the homosexual, is known and a neighbor, he will cease to be a bogey.

We are working towards that world in which there will be respect for, enjoyment of, the differences in nationality, race, sexuality, when the homosexual impulse is seen as part of the continuum of love which leads some persons to be husbands and wives, others to be parents, others to be lovers of their fellow men and women, and still others to be celibate and devote themselves to humanity or deity.

In that world there will also be greater variety. Our stratified ideas of masculinity and femininity will long have been altered. (Have you noticed that men's greeting cards have either a gun and mallard ducks, or a fishing rod and trout?)

It is this world, where the barriers of nation, sex, race have been broken, this larger, non-ghettoized world, that minority groups are organizing to work toward. And it is this picture of the larger world of the future that we must hold up when we are accused, by the very existence of homophile organizations at this point in history, of wanting to ghettoize homosexuals.

*"Knock, and it shall be opened unto you."**

Leo Skir, "A Homosexual Ghetto?," *The Ladder* 10:3 (December 1965), 4–8.

---

*Matthew 7:7.

Further Reading

Esterberg, Kristin Gay. "From illness to action: Conceptions of homosexuality in *The Ladder*, 1956–1965." *The Journal of Sex Research* 27:1 (1990), 65–80.

Johnson, Joyce. *Minor Characters: A Young Woman's Coming-of-Age in the Beat Orbit of Jack Kerouac*, 2nd ed. (Penguin Books, 1994).

Sienna, Noam. "A Forgotten Gay Jewish Pioneer Rises Again." *Tablet*, January 8, 2018 (https://www.tabletmag.com/jewish-life-and-religion/252136/gay-jewish-pioneer-leo-skir).

Skir, Leo. "To Be a Jew and a Homosexual." *Sh'ma: a journal of Jewish responsibility* 2:33 (1972), 102–103.

116. A Yiddish Story of Love Between Women by Isaac Bashevis Singer (New York, 1966)

The Nobel-Prize-winning Yiddish author Isaac Bashevis Singer (1902–1991) was born near Warsaw, and emigrated to the United States in 1935, where he continued to publish short stories and novels for the next five decades in his distinctive and consistent style, setting most of them in a romanticized (or kitschy, according to some critics) Old Country. He wrote many works that engage explicitly with sexuality and gender, especially his 1963 story, "Yentl, a Yeshiva Boy" (heavily altered in its 1983 adaptation into the award-winning film with Barbra Streisand), which describes how Yentl, a masculine young woman, transforms into a yeshiva student named Anshel; Anshel's ḥavruta partner then falls in love with him, and the story ends ambiguously with Yentl/Anshel's disappearance. In a 1969 interview with Cyrena Pondrom, Singer described "Yentl" as a story in which "we have to do with homosexual people," although he did not specify to which characters in the story he was referring. Later stories deal even more explicitly with homosexuality, lesbianism, and gender ambiguity, including "Androgynous" (1975), "Two" (1976), and "Disguised" (1986). In this excerpt from "Zeitl and Rickel," first published in Yiddish in 1966, and then in English in 1968, Singer describes the relationship between two women in an unnamed shtetl, whose love for each other mystifies the other residents. The narrator recalls overhearing the two of them talking one night of their plan to get married in heaven, where "there is no difference between men and women," and where they will live together in happiness among their ex-alted ancestors. At the end of the story, Zeitl and Rickel both commit suicide, and they are buried together.

I do not know exactly how Zeitl and Rickel got together. It seems that Reb Yisroel fell ill and Rickel came to rub him down with turpentine. People said he had cast an eye on her, but I don't believe it. He was already more dead than alive. He died soon afterwards, and both girls, Zeitl and Rickel, were left alone in the world. At first people thought that Rickel had stayed on with Zeitl as a servant. But if Zeitl had never had a servant before, why would she need one now?

While Reb Yisroel was alive, few matchmakers came to Zeitl with offers. They knew that Reb Yisroel wanted his daughter for himself. There are such fathers, even among Jews. She waited on him hand and foot. If his pipe went out, she would bring him an ember to relight it. I don't know why, but he nev-er went to the bath, and it was whispered that Zeitl bathed him in a wooden bathtub. I've never seen it, but those false believers are capable of anything. To them, a sin is a virtue.

Anyway, Reb Yisroel gave the matchmakers such a reception that they forswore repeating their visits to the tenth generation. But as soon as Zeitl was alone, they were back at her doorstep. She sent them off with all sorts of excuses: later, tomorrow, it's not yet time. She had a habit, whenever she spoke to anyone, of looking over his head. Rickel had moved in with her, and now whenever anyone knocked, she would answer from behind the door chain: Zeitl is out, she is asleep, she is reading.

How long could the matchmakers keep coming? Nobody is dragged to the wedding canopy by force. But in a small town people have time, and they talk. No matter how you may try to keep away from strangers' eyes, you can't hide everything.

It was said that Zeitl and Rickel ate together, drank together, slept togeth-er. Rickel wore Zeitl's dresses, shortened and made smaller to fit her. Rickel became the cashier, and she paid the bills sent by the storekeepers. She also collected the rents. In the day time the two girls seldom went out together, but on summer evenings they went strolling down Tumah Street, along the avenues leading to the woods. Zcitl's arm would be around Rickel's shoulders, and Rickel's around Zeitl's waist. They were absorbed in their talk. When people said good-evening, they did not hear. Where did two women find so much to talk about? Some people tried to follow them and listen in, but they were whispering, as though they had secrets between them. They would walk all the way to the mill or the woods.

Rumors were brought to Reb Eisele, our rabbi, but he said: "There is no law to keep two women from walking to the mill." Reb Eisele was a Misnagid, a Lithuanian, and they have a law for everything: either it is permitted, or it's a sin.

But the talk would not die down. Naftali, the night watchman, had seen Zeitl and Rickel kissing each other on the mouth. They had stopped by the sawmill, near the log pile, and embraced like a loving couple. Zeitl called Rickel dove, and Rickel called her kitten. At first nobody believed Naftali; he was fond of a drop and could bring you tales of a fair up in heaven. Still, where there's smoke, there must be fire. My dear folks, the two girls seemed so much in love that all the tongues in town started wagging. The Tempter can make anybody crazy in his own way. Something flips in your head, and everything turns upside down. I heard talk of a lady in Krasnostaw who made love with a stallion. At the time of the Flood, even beasts paired themselves with other kinds. I read about it in the Women's Bible.

People went to Reb Eisele, but he insisted: "There is nothing in the Torah to forbid it. The ban applies only to men. Besides, since there are no witnesses, it is forbidden to spread rumors." Nevertheless, he sent the beadle for them. Rickel came alone and denied everything. She had a whittled tongue, that girl. Reb Eisele said to her: "Go home and don't worry about it. It is the slanderers who will be punished, not you. It is better to burn in a lime pit than to put another to shame."

I forgot to mention that Zeitl had stopped teaching the girls how to write.

I was still very young at that time, but something of all that talk had reached me too. You can't keep everything from a child's ears. Zeitl and Rickel, it was said, were studying Reb Yisroel's books together. Their lamp burnt until late at night. Those who passed their bedroom window saw shadows moving this way and that behind the drapes, and coming together as in a dance. Who knows what went on there?

Now listen to a story.

One summer it turned terribly hot. I've lived through many a summer, but I don't remember such heat. Right in the morning the sun began to burn like fire. Not only men, but even girls and older women would go down to the river to bathe. When the sun blazes, the water gets warm. My mother, may she plead for us, took me along.

This was the first time I bathed in the river. Men went into the water naked, but the girls wore their shifts. The roughnecks came running to peep at them, and it was impossible to drive them off. Each time, there'd be a squealing and a panic. One woman started drowning. Another screamed that a frog had bitten her. I bathed and even tried to swim until I was so tired that I lay down among the bushes near the bank to rest. I thought I'd cool off in the shade and go home, but a strange sleep came over me. Not just sleep; may heaven preserve us, it was more like death. I put my head down and remained there like a rock. A darkness seemed to fall over me, and I sank into it. I must have slept for many hours.

When I awakened, it was night. There was no moon. The sky was cloudy. I lay there, and I did not know where I was or who I was. I felt the grass around me, moist with dew, but I did not remember that I was on the outskirts of town. I touched myself; I had nothing on but my shift. I wanted to cry, to call for help, when suddenly I heard voices. I thought of demons and was terror stricken, yet I tried to hear what they were saying. Two women were speaking, and their voices seemed familiar. I heard one ask:

"Must we go through hell?" The other answered:

"Yes, my soul, but even going through hell together with you will be a delight. God is merciful. The punishment never lasts more than twelve months. We shall be purified and enter paradise. Since we have no husbands, we shall be no one's footstools. We shall bathe in balsam and eat of the leviathan. We shall have wings and fly like birds…"

I cannot recall all their talk. I gasped. I knew who they were now: the questioner was Rickel, and Zeitl gave the answers. I heard Zeitl say: "We shall meet our fathers and mothers there, and our grandparents, and all the generations: Abraham and Isaac, Jacob and Rachel, Leah, Bilhah, Zilpah, Abigail, Bathsheba…" She spoke as though she had just come from there, and every word was like a pearl. I forgot that I was half-naked and alone out late at night.

Zeitl went on: "Father is waiting for us. He comes to me in dreams. He is together with your mother." Rickel asked: "Did they get married there?" And Zeitl answered: "Yes. We shall get married up there too. In heaven there is no difference between men and women…"

It must have been past midnight. There was a flash of lightning, and I saw my clothing, shoes and stockings on the grass nearby. I caught a glimpse of them too. They sat by the river in nothing but their shifts, their hair down, pale as death. If I did not die of fright that night, I'll never die.

Isaac Bashevis Singer, "Zeitl and Rickel" (trans. Mirra Ginsburg), *The Hudson Review* 21:1 (1968), 130–133. Original Yiddish published in the *Forverts*, Aug. 19–20, 1966.

Further Reading

Hoffman, Warren. *The Passing Game: Queering Jewish American Culture* (Syracuse University Press, 2009).

Seidman, Naomi. "Reading Queer Ashkenaz: This Time from East to West." *TDR: The Drama Review* 55:3 (2011), 50–56.

Sherman, Joseph. "Scrutinizing the Shtetl: I. B. Singer's 'Tsyetl un Rikl.'" *Prooftexts* 15:2 (1995), 129–44.

Sherman, Joseph. "Upside Down in the Daytime: Singer and Male Homosexuality." In *Critical Essays on Isaac Bashevis Singer* (ed. Grace Farrell, New York: G. K. Hall, 1996), 191–208.

117. A Jewish Politician Decriminalizes Homosexuality in Britain and Wales (London, 1967)

The Sexual Offences Act of 1967, which put into action the recommendations of the earlier Wolfenden Report of 1957, officially decriminalized private homosexual activity in Britain and Wales. It was written and introduced by Leo Abse (1917–2008), a Welsh Jewish lawyer and politician, who served as a Labor MP (Member of Parliament) in the House of Commons for almost 30 years. He was often described as "eccentric" and "colorful," known for wearing silk waistcoats and analyzing his fellow parliamentarians according to Freudian psychology, although he was adamantly heterosexual himself. The Sexual Offences Act was controversial from the beginning—activists from the Homosexual Law Reform Society and the Gay Liberation Front thought that it didn't go nearly far enough, and many felt that it was was merely an excuse for increased police harassment. Abse himself discussed the Act in Parliament in ways that many found offensive, including referring to homosexual men as "faulty males" and arguing in Freudian terms that homosexuality was an arrested stage of emotional development. In oral histories done towards the end of his life, Abse expressed regret and sadness for those statements, and claimed that appealing to his colleagues' sense of pity was the only way to have succeeded in passing this legislation. Abse emphasized that he saw himself as an ally to the gay community and that he had hoped that this Act would be a first step towards more harmonious social integration. He himself became aware of the issue as a young lawyer, when he discovered that a vicar in his town was being blackmailed for homosexuality and was paying for numerous criminals' legal fees (Abse recalled that "I sent for one of the criminals and told him if I had another cheque from [the vicar], I'd get him sent down for 10 years. I [then] sent for the vicar and told him to come to me if they approached him again"). In this reflection, which Abse published just after the Act's passage in 1967, he hinted that the "imperfectly sublimated homosexual group loyalties...and repressed homosexuality" of some of his fellow MPs were responsible for their hostility to the bill, and he acknowledges that its penalties are still too harsh, but that it was a necessary compromise that otherwise would never have been passed. The Sexual Offences Act remains an important and controversial landmark in the history of LGBTQ rights in the UK.

The Sexual Offences Act

Leo Abse, M.P.

More than a decade elapsed before the House of Commons was prepared to implement the cautious recommendations of the Wolfenden Committee. Such timidity requires explanations. It may be apposite to recall Leon Trotsky's denunciation, made during a grim battle in 1918, of the "pusillanimity of an historic fatalism which in all questions, whether concrete or private, passively seeks a solution in general laws, and leaves out of account the mainspring of all human decisions-the living and acting individual." Certainly it was not the over-determined reactions of a handful of vociferous members that caused the long delay: the House of Commons was sufficiently self-conscious not to be much influenced by such manifest neurotic anxiety. But the "historic" argument against legislation was more seductive and sufficiently sophisticated to provide the rationalisation that many required. What had been done eighty years ago could not without catastrophic consequences now be undone. "Should we" asked Rab Butler in 1958 "if we were drawing up a code for the first colonists of the moon make this kind of an offence a criminal offence? I am in some doubt whether we should or should not." But he clearly had no doubts of the serious consequences if the existing prohibitions were abolished here and now. Not for the only time, Butler abdicated leadership. On this occasion it was to the Labouchère of 1885.

In many subsequent debates initiated by Kenneth Robinson and Roy Jenkins, by Berkeley and myself, first Butler plagiarised his own original thesis, and then other opponents of reform, albeit less fluently, adopted his arguments. Usually half the House failed to vote in such debates. The subject was mined, electoral opinion uncertain, and undoubtedly the whole matter too emotive to be courted. In 1962 when a Bill watering down Wolfenden was coming before the House and a Government decision was needed a prominent Minister refused to discuss the matter in Cabinet since the subject was too "disgusting," and an unhappy junior Minister was instructed to talk the Bill out. Reaction-formations of this order were not, however, widespread: but nevertheless there was a striking hesitation in the House to accept that public opinion was becoming less hostile to the Bill. The almost hermetically sealed male institution with its club and public school traditions was singularly vulnerable and sensitive to any criticism or innuendo. In an establishment where sometimes imperfectly sublimated homosexual group loyalties play a prominent part and where repressed homosexuality may often be dealt with by paranoic references to opponents, resistance to insights into the aetiology of homosexuality predictably existed. Not less relevant to the tone of the debates was the notorious character disorder which issues in a passionate striving for power and prestige masking the attempt to overcome and deny anxiety.

External power is sought as a means of protection against inner dependence and passivity. Unease among politicians, doubtless more marked than most to a dual identification with a powerful aggressor and an omnipotent provider, originally the imagos of father and mother, caused persistent difficulties to the reformers whose arguments could clearly never persuade those fearful of any passive homosexual component within their nature. The very number of debates, however, and the persistent controversy consequently aroused in the press, undoubtedly levered much repressed material to the surface and the later debates were markedly free from the earlier tensions. Meantime activation by Arran of a House of Lords anxious to maintain a progressive image teased and confused those in the Commons who were against reform but wished to identify the peers with reaction. And the Gallup polls, which, despite public denials to the contrary, are well noted by M.Ps. reassured those who always need to be led from behind. Most important to the final passing of the Bill was the entry into the House of an intake of academics and younger men to whom the traditional resistance of the more conservative was not meaningful: indeed already by 1965 the humourless speech of the main opponent to the Bill was regarded by them as caricature and was tolerantly received with unembarrassed laughter.

The Act in its final form, though substantially implementing the Wolfenden recommendations, reflected the appeasement required to assuage the irrational fears which otherwise could have overspilled and totally engulfed the Bill. The penalties attached to some public displays of homosexuality are too harsh: but the courts are, it is hoped, unlikely to apply the maximum sentences. The provisions concerning servicemen and seamen aboard merchant navy ships are unrealistic and could, if harshly administered, cause grave anomalies. More important, the interpretation of privacy within the Act, if too narrowly applied, could thwart the legislature's intentions. Vigilance will be required amongst reformers in the early years of the Act.

Its final passage was praised by Roy Jenkins, the Home Secretary, who had given much assistance in securing the passage of the Bill, as "an important piece of social legislation" and ambivalently devalued by Quintin Hogg as "a small measure which will have very little effect on our social life." It would be, however, an error to assess the value of the Act in terms of those homosexuals who were directly affected by its provisions. The ten year debate, and its conclusion, helped to make our country a little more rational. Persistent educational campaigns of this kind assist both the nation and its leaders to gain insights and to come to terms with sexuality and aggression. Those who embark upon such campaigns, aware of the force of unconscious prejudices, know the way must be long and hard: but rationality cannot ever be easily achieved.

Leo Abse, "The Sexual Offences Act," *British Journal of Criminology* 8:1 (Jan. 1968), 86–87, by permission of Oxford University Press.

Further Reading

Brooke, Stephen. *Sexual Politics: Sexuality, Family Planning, and the British Left from the 1880s to the Present Day* (Oxford University Press, 2011).

Gleeson, Kate. "Freudian Slips and Coteries of Vice: The Sexual Offences Act of 1967." *Parliamentary History* 27:3 (2008), 393–409.

Smith, Richard Adam. "The beginning of the end of discrimination." *The Guardian*, 21 Aug 2008 (https://www.theguardian.com/commentisfree/2008/aug/21/equality.gayrights).

118. Charlotte Wolff Recalls Lesbian Life in Interwar Berlin (London, 1969)

Charlotte Wolff (1897–1986) was a German Jewish physician, psychologist, and sexologist; in 1933 she fled Nazi Germany to Paris and then to London, where she lived the rest of her life, aside from a brief return to Germany in the late 1970s. She developed a theory of diagnosis through palm-reading, which introduced her to many notable artists, writers, and philosophers, including Marcel Duchamp, Virginia Woolf, Thomas Mann, and Walter Benjamin. Her first publications dealt with cheirology (the study of the hand), but in the late 1960s she turned to the study of sexuality, and began a series of in-depth interviews with lesbians and bisexual women that resulted in her groundbreaking study *Love Between Women* (1971), followed by *Bisexuality* (1977). In 1969 she published her first autobiography, *On the Way to Myself*, in which she acknowledged the role that her love for women had played in her own life, describing her nights at lesbian clubs in Berlin, and her relationship with Lisa, a Russian Jewish woman with whom she fell in love during her adolescence. Elsewhere in the book, she writes that "homosexuality in its mental and spiritual aspects is an important ingredient of the complex image of the ideal teacher," and concludes that "homosexual love is ideal twinship"—an approach that she continued to develop over the following decade of prescient and groundbreaking studies.

When we had known one another for some time, [my friend] showed me an album of photographs and pointed to a picture of a school friend she had known in Kiev who by then was living in Berlin. I could not forget that picture. I asked about the personality behind the photograph and my friend told me that Lisa was a brilliant girl and very strange. Whenever I could I looked at that photo. I dreamt of it; I knew that Lisa was a person I *must* get to know, though at that time I had no idea how to manage it. Three years later I did manage it, thus fulfilling a long-standing desire.

Why did this photograph stir me so much? Lisa had the face of a Russian Jewess, with a melancholy expression in her big eyes and the marks of a superior intelligence combined with an irresistible sensuousness. She seemed to fit my image of a desirable and glamorous woman, an image which had been nourished in my mind by Dostoevsky's novels, the German translations of which were excellent. I had devoured them all. For me, these books were life experiences. *The Idiot* was my favorite among them, and Nastasia Filipovna my ideal woman. Lisa's photo represented my picture of Nastasjia; and thus Lisa herself, reinforced by the imaginative power of literature, was an object of great attraction to me before I ever set eyes on her.

In January 1917 I visited a famous ear, nose and throat specialist in Berlin and on the eve of the Russian New Year, Lisa came to see me at the *pension* at which my mother and I were staying. My mother had gone to see an aunt of hers while my photograph and I met. Yes, it was Lisa, whom I had known for three years in my imagination. From the moment she entered hers was the face, the body, the mind, in fact everything which aroused in me wonder and shyness. I knew that the world had changed for me and that any town would be a different town if Lisa was in it. She had the body and the movements of a dancer. Her head was too large for her small stature and it appropriated all one's attention. The soft brown hair was brushed away from a high forehead with twofold protuberances, above the eyes and half-way up the brow. Her eyes were as arresting as the protruding mouth with the deep-red lips. She was the most striking human being I had ever seen: a Russian Jewess with a 'South Seas' appeal. Her friends called her Mona Lisa, and in spite of racial differences, her head and her hands resembled the famous portrait. Willi Jaeckel, the German Expressionist painter, must have thought so, because he painted her like a Russian Mona Lisa. The portrait was acquired by the Hamburger Kunsthalle and I hope it is still in their possession. Lisa fascinated everybody with whom she came into contact. Her unusual attraction lay in her combination of good, indeed arresting looks and exceptional intelligence. She was a sculptress with a wide understanding of the arts and literature, and her intellectual curiosity also extended to science and politics. A human being in the round, she had the added attraction of a complete lack of self-consciousness and vanity. Of course it was love at first sight for me. She must also have been drawn to me, because after an hour's meeting she spoke of a kinship between us. Our contact was not to cease for years to come, though it had to be mainly by letter. Our correspondence became my most precious inspiration. But in 1918 she left for Russia and again I had to suffer separation. I paid two visits to Berlin after our first encounter, two visits which made me well and ill at the same time...

In Germany's post-World-War-I period of inflation I had the time of my life. The last shackles of restraint fell from German youth, to which, as I then thought, I belonged. I studied medicine in Berlin, the metropolis which was everything to everybody, a beautiful prostitute. The mushroom growth of amusements and escapes made it the capital of erotic glamour and foreigners, much desired and welcomed for their hard currency, locked into it, either to nibble at or to drown themselves in pleasure and vice.

The generous allowance my parents gave me shrank in value to almost nothing, but I did not mind my poverty for everyone else was in the same situation, and life was good. I managed to find a number of Russian students to whom I gave German lessons to bolster my finances, but in spite of this I lived a hand-to-mouth existence.

Germany was in a state of economic siege which was as adventurous and exciting as a state of war without the bombs, and I lived with my insecurity in the real splendour of youth and happiness. Between nights in Lesbian and other night clubs, lectures at the university, studies at home, and making a living, I still had time for love, friendship and poetry.

I lived in furnished rooms in the Kaiserallee and on the Nollendorfplatz and felt at home amidst all the noise of traffic by day and of a queer life by night. I had chosen the Nollendorfplatz in order to be near everything I desired: at the hub of trams, buses, subway trains, and girls in high boots standing about and shouting at night until customers took them away for a time. On one side elegant restaurants, mainly for rich foreigners, made the square look respectable, but a few yards away, in nearby side streets, one could spend the night in a night club with a difference. Women smoking cigars received one and dancing went on between girls. At about midnight a kind of gavotte was danced under the direction of a tall woman with an aquiline nose and sombrero, mumbling words and orders which were meant to be a sort of Black Magic. We called her Napoleon and did what she said; that is, we held a drink in one hand, placed it in the other one, drank it up and finally put the empty glass behind our back. The symbolism of the performance is obvious. There and at other clubs, through evenings and nights, the tunes had that nostalgic flavor which goes with the end of an era.

A new era started when the Nazis took over Germany.

Charlotte Wolff, *On the Way to Myself* (London: Methuen & Co, 1969), 52–53 and 192–193. Copyright © 1969 by Methuen & Co Ltd. Reproduced by permission of Taylor & Francis Books UK.

Further Reading

Alpert, Rebecca. *Like Bread on the Seder Plate: Jewish Lesbians and the Transformation of Tradition* (Columbia University Press, 1997).

Beachy, Robert. *Gay Berlin: Birthplace of a Modern Identity* (New York: Alfred A. Knopf, 2014).

Brennan, Tobi, and Peter Hegarty. "Charlotte Wolff and Lesbian History: Reconfiguring Liminality in Exile." *Journal of Lesbian Studies* 14 (2010), 338–358.

Brennan, Tobi, and Peter Hegarty. "Charlotte Wolff's Contribution to Bisexual History and to (Sexuality) Theory and Research: A Reappraisal for Queer Times." *Journal of the History of Sexuality* 21:1 (2012), 141–161.

Friedenreich, Harriet Pass. *Female, Jewish, and Educated: The Lives of Central European University Women* (Indiana University Press, 2002).

Wolff, Charlotte. *Love Between Women* (New York: St. Martin's Press, 1971).

119. A Reform Rabbi Writes a Responsum on Homosexuality (Pittsburgh, 1969)

While American rabbis had made public statements about homosexuality (see sources 104 and 111) since the 1950s, this passage is the first American *teshuvah* (rabbinic legal response) of any denomination to deal with homosexuality. Uniquely, it addresses the place of homosexuality in Jewish history, rather than solely as a question for contemporary society. The question, from Rabbi Irving B. Cohen (1921–1990) of Temple Israel in West Palm Beach, asks about material in Jewish law on homosexuality for an upcoming discussion program. Was this program organized by a gay congregant? The socially-minded rabbi? A concerned parent? In any case, this suggests that, already by the late 1960s, the Gay Liberation movement had succeeded in raising public awareness of issues faced by queer people in American society of the time, including in the larger Jewish community. The respondent, Rabbi Solomon Freehof, summarizes some Talmudic and medieval legal statements, emphasizing that "it is remarkable how little place the whole question occupies in Jewish law," and concludes that "the very paucity of biblical and post-biblical law on the matter speaks well for the normalcy and the purity of the Jewish people." Solomon Freehof (1892–1990) was born in London and came to the United States as a child; he was ordained by the Hebrew Union College in 1915. One of the most prominent halakhic thinkers of the Reform movement, he served as president of the Central Conference of American Rabbis (CCAR) and the World Union for Progressive Judaism (WUPJ) in the 1950s and 1960s.

A group in the Temple is planning a discussion program on the question of homosexuality. What is there in Jewish law on this subject? (From I.B.C., Florida.)

Considering the prevalence of homosexuality in the East, one can say in general that it is remarkable how little place the whole question occupies in Jewish law. After the biblical prohibitions, there is almost nothing in the Mishnah, Talmud, and Codes on the question. The Talmud itself explains (perhaps unconscious of the fact that it is explaining it) why there is so little discussion of the question. In *b. Kiddushin* 82a it discusses the prohibition of seclusion (*yichud*) with any of the forbidden sexual degrees of relationship; i.e. a man must avoid being, or must not be permitted to be alone with a woman with whom he is forbidden to have sexual relationship. Then the Talmud says that Jewish people are not under the suspicion of homosexuality (i.e., it is highly improbable among Jews) and therefore it is not forbidden for a Jewish man to be alone with another Jewish man.

There is an interesting development of this Talmudic statement in the way this dictum (that Jews are not suspected, etc.) is carried over to the *Shulchan Aruch*. The *Shulchan Aruch* (in *Even Hoezer* 24) states the law as derived from the Talmud that since Jewish men are not suspected of homosexuality, they are not forbidden to be alone with each other. Then Joseph Caro adds: "However, in these generations when sinful men have increased, it is better to avoid isolation with another male." Moses Rifkes (Poland, seventeenth century) in his *Be'er Ha-Golah*, gives the Talmudic reference for the first part of the statement; but as for the latter part of the statement ("Nowadays when evil men have increased," etc.) he notes carefully: "These are his own words; there is no reference for this precaution in the Talmudic literature, and Joseph Caro makes the precaution on his own authority." Why should Joseph Caro have made such an extra precaution which the Talmud does not require, against males being secluded together? The *Bes Shemuel* (Samuel of Furth) explains, in the name of Joel Sirkes (Poland, sixteenth century), that in the land in which he (Joseph Caro) lived, homosexuality was rampant. But "not in our land," hence it is not required for males to avoid isolation (see *Bach to Tur*, same reference). Of course this is correct historically. The Arab lands were notorious for homosexuality and Joseph Caro knew that. But to the rest of Jewry it seemed farfetched to prohibit males to associate with each other for fear of homosexuality.

Now as to the biblical sources: They are Leviticus 18:22 and 20:13, prohibiting male sexuality with males: also Deuteronomy 23:18, which prohibits male prostitutes who were maintained in connection with the idolatrous temples. So, more specifically, I Kings 14:24, speaking of the evils of Judah when it became corrupt, says that the people copied "the abominations of the nations around them and had male prostitution." The prohibition is carried over into the Mishnah, *Sanhedrin* VII, 4, where it is briefly mentioned among the whole list of sexual relationships. Then the fullest discussion in the Talmud is in *Sanhedrin* 54b. There is a discussion whether illicit intercourse is punishable by death if it is involved with a person under the age of nine. The Rambam in *Hilchos Issure Biah* 1:14 summarizes this Talmudic discussion and says that both the active and passive partners are culpable (as the Talmud says) but the punishment of death should not be inflicted upon a boy under nine (evidently a young boy would hardly initiate such action). But Maimonides adds that although the punishment of death does not apply in this case, they should be punished by the courts. In other words, such intercourse with a boy under nine is *potur* from the death penalty, but *asur* (forbidden *per se*) and should be punished.

All in all, considering how much detail there is in the law on every kind of forbidden sexual relationship, the very paucity of biblical and post-biblical law on the matter speaks well for the normalcy and the purity of the Jewish people.

Solomon Freehof, *Current Reform Responsa* (Hebrew Union College Press, 1969). Reprinted with permission from the Hebrew Union College Annual. I thank Elisa Ho at the American Jewish Archives for identifying Rabbi Irving B. Cohen.

Further Reading

Kahn, Yoel. "Judaism and Homosexuality: The Traditionalist/Progressive Debate." *Journal of Homosexuality* 18:3/4 (1989), 47–52.

120. Poetry of Vera Lachmann (New York, 1969)

Vera Lachmann (1904–1985) was a German-American classicist, poet, and teacher. She studied Germanic languages and Greek philosophy at the University of Berlin, graduating in 1931. In 1933, as the German government began to impose restrictions on Jewish students, she opened a school in Berlin for Jewish children, and maintained it until the Nazis forcefully closed it in 1939. It was almost impossible to leave Germany at that point, but scholars in the United States petitioned Eleanor Roosevelt to grant her a special "ex-quota visa," and Lachmann was finally allowed to leave Germany in November 1939. She taught at Vassar from 1940–41, and then at Bryn Mawr, Yale, and finally Brooklyn College until her retirement. She also founded a boys' educational summer camp, Camp Catawba, in the Blue

Ridge Mountains of North Carolina; Lachmann directed the camp until its closing in 1970. In 1950, Lachmann met the woman who would become her lifelong partner: Tui St. George Tucker (1924–2004), a visionary American composer, to whom Lachmann dedicated her first volume of poetry, *Golden Tanzt das Licht im Glas* (Golden Dances the Light in the Glass), published in Amsterdam in 1969. In these poems, Lachmann recalls their travel to the village of Eressos on the island of Lesbos, the birthplace of Sappho, in 1967. Lachmann celebrates the poet who first put into words the power of love between women (see source 1), declaring: "you were handed over to the glaring light / to the threatening love force of the island sun / you, almost with too much wisdom to live. / Gods, however, desired that you sing."

Lesbos

Not the adamantine horn
of your very sublime mountain,
nor the opal twilight waters
of the bay you embrace,
not even the hundredfold roundnesses
on slopes buttressed
by walls of your silver-green olive wealth
makes you, island, so desired,
as does the hide-and-seek play
of your Undaunted One.
She quivers there awhile
in the tiny crown of a cyclamen
between broken rock,
yet before being picked
she flees into blast of mountain wind,
throws herself in sorrow
into after-glow of sea sand,
beats the ether
with slender crane wings
toward a pale-orange
large moon.

In Eressos

It was here, darling, here you opened your eyes,
where ruffled oak paints a round shadow
on pale gold of the burnt slope,
where fleecy sheep rest and munch.

For you the brilliant sea poured
monotony from brocade folds onto the gray beach.
Forms of barren shore-mountains
stood solemnly around your tiny slumber.

Your fine face lay alabaster white,
temples delicately veined—hardly unfolded
from your warm mother; moving your lips
you tasted tear-salted sea wind.

You were handed over to the glaring light,
to the threatening love force of the island sun,
you, almost with too much wisdom to live.
Gods, however, desired that you sing.

Vera Lachmann, *Golden Tanzt Das Licht im Glas / Golden Dances The Light in the Glass* (English by Spencer Holst, Amsterdam: Castrum Pellegrini, 1969). Copyright by Castrum Peregrini Amsterdam.

Further Reading

Friedenreich, Harriet Pass. *Female, Jewish, and Educated: The Lives of Central European University Women* (Indiana University Press, 2002).

Hallett, Judith. "Nunc Meminisse Iuvat: Classics and Classicists between the World Wars." *The Classical World* 85:1 (1991), 1–27.

Kantsa, Venetia. "'Certain Places Have Different Energy': Spatial Transformations in Eressos Lesvos." *GLQ: A Journal of Lesbian and Gay Studies* 8:1–2 (2002), 35–57.

Miller, Charles (ed.). *Homer's Sun Still Shines: Ancient Greece in Essays, Poems and Translations by Vera Lachmann* (New Market, Va.: Trackaday, 2004).

Suggested Tracks

These lists create thematic links between sources from different periods, connecting entries by genre, by identity, and by geography. These lists are aimed at assisting readers who wish to use this book in developing a text-based class session, writing a syllabus, or incorporating primary sources in a focused study. These lists are not comprehensive; I have included them in the hope that they open new possibilities for interconnections and creative recombinations.

Genre

How is the discussion of sexuality and gender shaped by conventions of genre and text? What themes are shared by similar kinds of texts across time?

Poetry

- Sappho and the Torah, Compared by a Hellenistic Philosopher: Source 1
- Poetry of Yitsḥaq Ibn Mar Sha'ul: Source 18
- Poetry of Qalonymos ben Qalonymos: Source 32
- Poetry of Todros Abulafia: Source 33
- Poetry of Menaḥem Egozi: Source 39
- Poetry of Sarmad Kashani: Source 46
- Poetry of Emma Lazarus: Source 61
- Poetry of Jacob Israël De Haan: Source 79
- Poetry of Sophia Parnok: Source 81
- Poetry of Anna Margolin: Source 86
- Poetry of Mordechai Jiři Langer: Source 87
- Poetry of Edward Field: Source 110
- Poetry of Vera Lachmann: Source 120

Literature and Drama

Halakhah (Jewish Law)

Identity

Whose lives have been recorded, and whose have been ignored? What commonalities and changes are there in the relationship between identity and sexuality/gender over time?

Gender Fluidity and Transition (Trans, Intersex, Non-Binary Identities)

- The Androginos: Source 5
- What Was Adam's Sex? A Midrash: Source 6
- Avraham and Sarah were Tumtumim: A Midrash: Source 12
- Dinah's Sex is Changed: A Midrash: Source 14
- Avraham Maimonides Disapproves of Gender-Nonconformity: Source 30
- Poetry of Qalonymos ben Qalonymos: Source 32
- Male Souls in Female Bodies: Source 40
- An Account of Jewish Dancing Boys in Aleppo: Source 49
- A Gender-Bending Jewish Runaway in New France: Source 51
- An Ottoman Sephardi Rabbi Rules on Gender Transition: Source 65
- "Memoirs of a Man's Maiden Years"—A German Jew's Transition: Source 68
- A Russian Scholar Describes the "Maiden of Ludmir:" Source 70
- A Jewish Immigrant's Gender Transition: Source 73
- An Account of Persian Jewish Dancing Boys: Source 74
- Jews Join the Crowd at a Drag Ball: Source 90
- Gender Transition in the Shtetl: Source 96
- American Jewish "Sex Variants:" Source 99
- First Sex Confirmation Surgery in Israel: Source 103
- A Syrian Rabbi Rules on an Intersex Infant: Source 108

- Sappho and the Torah: Source 1
- Philo Condemns "Unnatural Pleasures:" Source 2
- The Talmud on Sexual Contact Between Women: Source 11
- Maimonides Codifies Laws on Homosexual Activity: Source 27
- Poetry of Todros Abulafia: Source 33
- A Converso Doctor Describes the Origin of Lesbianism: Source 43
- A Jewish Woman with "Contrary Sexual Feeling:" Source 59
- Poetry of Emma Lazarus: Source 61
- Poetry of Amy Levy: Source 63
- A Yiddish Play Presents a Lesbian Romance Onstage: Source 69
- Magnus Hirschfeld Records Life Story of Jewish Lesbian: Source 72
- Gender Transition Revealed After Death: Source 73
- An American Zionist's Erotic Connection to Women: Source 80
- Poetry of Sophia Parnok: Source 81
- A Polish Jewish Lesbian is Deported for Obscenity: Source 82
- Poetry of Dina Lipkis: Source 85
- Practicing "Sapphic Love:" Source 89
- American Jewish "Sex Variants:" Source 99
- *Wasteland*, A Lesbian American Jewish Novel: Source 101
- Pearl Hart Advises Homosexuals: Source 106
- A Yiddish Story of Love Between Women: Source 116
- Charlotte Wolff Recalls Lesbian Life: Source 118
- Poetry of Vera Lachmann: Source 120

Geography

How are the articulations of identity impacted by cultural context? What are the similarities and differences in how Jews have understood sexuality and gender in different places?

Sephardi Lives (Jews of Iberia and its Diaspora)

- Poetry of Yitsḥaq Ibn Mar Sha'ul: Source 18
- Poetry of Ali ibn ʿAṭṭiya Ibn al-Zaqqaq: Source 23
- The Tale of Sapir and Shapir: Source 29
- Issach Salamó is Executed for Sodomy: Source 34
- Homosexual Activity in the Synagogue: Source 35
- Moshko's Sexual Escapades: Source 37
- Poetry of Menaḥem Egozi: Source 39
- A Converso Doctor Describes the Origin of Lesbianism: Source 43
- Homosexual Activity in a Dutch Sephardi Yeshiva: Source 48
- A Gender-Bending Jewish Runaway: Source 51
- Homosexual Activity in the Balkans: Source 55
- Poetry of Emma Lazarus: Source 61
- An Ottoman Sephardi Rabbi Rules on Gender Transition: Source 65
- "Sapphic Love" in Salonica: Source 89
- Poetry of Édouard Roditi: Source 93
- Sexual Deviancy Among Tel Aviv Youth: Source 94

Mizraḥi Lives (Jews of the Arab and Persian Worlds)

- Saʿadia Gaon on the Danger of Homoerotic Love: Source 16
- Singing Homoerotic Poetry: Source 17
- A Brawl in the Synagogue: Source 21
- Maimonides Codifies Laws on Homosexual Activity: Source 27

Ashkenazi Lives (Jews of Eastern Europe and its Diaspora)

Permissions

413

General Index

Bernstein, Allen (1913–2008), 296–300

Bible: ESTHER, xix, 34–35; EXODUS, 36; EZEKIEL, 36; ISAIAH, 40–41; PROVERBS, 36; PSALMS, 32–33; SONG OF SONGS, 265. *see also* Index of Passages

Bill of Rights, United States, 342

bisexuality, 181, 222, 294, 322–23, 339, 395

Bitania, 233–234

Bloch, Shimshon (1785–1845), 131–36

Blüher, Hans, 233, 235, 355

B'nai Brith Anti-Defamation League, 371–72

B'nai Brith Lodges, 194–95

Boyarin, Daniel, 35, 41–42

Brandeau, Esther / La Fargue, Jacques, 9, 11, 123–25

Brazil, 103–4

bridegrooms, 51, 75–76, 92, 128, 152, 164, 203–4, 206, 212

brides, 51, 75–76, 152–53, 164, 167–68, 206, 211

brothels, 202, 238, 286. *see also* prostitution

Buber, Martin, xvi, 266

Bundestag (German Parliament), 354, 358

burial service, 227

Burstin, Hinde Ena, 260

butch/femme identity, 7, 224, 252, 302

cabaret songs, 257–59

Caelius Aurelianus of Sicca (ca. fifth century), 107

Cain, 25, 244, 247

Canaanites, 37

Canada: Quebec, 123

Caribbean, 119

Carpenter, Edward (1844–1929), 214–16

case histories, sexual, 154–58, 301–16

castration *(sirus)*, 83, 352–53

Catalan (language), 83–84

Catalonia, xviii, 76–77, 78, 83

categories of sex, Talmudic. *see androginos; aylonit; tumtumim*

Catholics and Catholicism, 103, 178, 194, 230, 281, 322. *see also* Christians and Christianity

Cavafy, Konstantin (1863–1933), 271, 282

celebrations, 78, 117, 126–28, 132, 140, 255, 273, 278. *see also* festivals; wedding celebrations

celestial tropes: MOON, 53–56, 79–80, 99, 116, 169; PLEIADES, 56; STARS, 48–49, 64, 146, 148–49, 151, 153, 245, 268, 282–83, 326; SUN, 42, 56, 60, 66, 73, 99, 150–52, 168, 201, 242, 248, 267, 282, 378, 390, 402–3. *see also* animal tropes

Chajes, Ephraim (Ḥayyot), 136–40

Christians and Christianity, 9, 73, 77, 83, 98, 136–37, 137, 173, 239, 337, 381, 383. *see also* Catholics and Catholicism; conversions

The Chronicle of Solomon bar Samson (Shlomo Bar Shimshon, ca. 1140), 67–68

circumcision, 27–28, 128, 185, 279, 352

Civil Rights for African Americans, Jews and homosexuals, similarities, 367–70, 372, 381–86

clubs, gay and lesbian, 190–93, 252–55, 273, 280–81, 338–39, 395, 398

Cohen, Irving B. (1921–1990), 399

Columbia University, 346

Committee for the Study of Sexual Variants, 301

concentration camps, 287–89; Auschwitz, 191, 253, 314, 358; Dachau, 287–89; Majdanek, 358; Mauthausen, 288; Sachsenhausen, 258; Theresienstadt, 354; treatment of Jewish homosexuals within, 288–89. *see also* Holocaust

conversions: to Christianity, 103, 107, 124, 178, 244, 372; to heterosexuality, 178, 244, 371–72, 383; to Islam or Hinduism, 114; to Judaism, 314

conversos (New Christians, *cristãos-novos*), 103–7

CORE (Congress of Racial Equality), 370–71

Cory, Donald Webster. *see* Sagarin, Edward

Cowen, Elise, 380

cross-dressing, 75–76, 117–19, 123–25, 223–28, 253–54, 302–6, 312, 327, 328–31. *see also* dancing boys; drag culture

Czech (language), 235–237
Czechoslovakia: Prague, 235, 258, 265–66

dancing, 174–75, 229, 234, 274–75, 280, 398
dancing boys, 75–76, 117–19, 228–30
David (king), 52–53
de Castro, Rodrigo (1546–1627), 9, 13, 106–8
decriminalization of homosexuality, 327; advocated for in Germany, 353–358; advocated for in U.S., 379–80; in Britain and Wales in 1967, 391; in European countries before 1945, 356; in Israel, 338
De Haan, Jacob Israël (1881–1924), 240–243
de Thevenot, Jean (1633–1667), 117–19
Deuteronomy, Book of. see Index of Passages
Deutsche Vortrupp (German Vanguard), 354
diaspora, 104, 173, 234. *see also* suggested tracks, 409–11
dibbuq (possession by deceased spirit), 277
Dinah, xix, 44–45, 80
Dinshaw, Caroline, 5–6
divorce, divorcee, 39, 90–91, 110, 127, 129–31, 170, 184, 213, 226, 244, 277, 311, 318. *see also* get
dowries, 211
drag culture, 8–9, 190, 272–76. *see also* cross-dressing; female impersonators
drama. *see* suggested tracks, 406
dreams and dreaming, 60, 145–53, 166–67, 169, 175, 197, 198, 236, 261, 264–65, 305–6, 306, 391
Drinkwater, Gregg, 6
Dror, Benjamin (1900–1988), 233–34
Dutch (language), 240–43
dykes, 313
Dzmura, Noach, 30

Egozi, Menaḥem (d. 1570), 98–99
Egypt, xvi, 24, 35–36, 37, 47, 57, 69–70, 71–72, 75–76, 295
El'azar, Rabbi, 34, 39–40
Eliot, T.S., 281
Eliyahu, Abba David (d. 1876), 188
Eliyahu, Chair of, 279

Eltinge, Julian, 303
England, 281; Kent, 214; London, 141, 145, 174–76, 391, 395
eros, Eros (sexual appetite), 27–28, 166, 233–36, 235–37
Exodus, Book of. see Bible. *see also* Index of Passages
exorcisms, 277
Ezekiel, Book of. see Bible. *see also* Index of Passages

Fall, Richard (1927), 257–259
false witness, 38, 121, 144. *see also* witnesses
fasting, 102, 188–89
female impersonators, 190, 303. *see also* cross-dressing; drag culture
festivals, 29, 58. *see also* celebrations; wedding celebrations
Field, Edward (b. 1924), 358–361
First World War, 215, 235, 240, 277–279
folk healers *(opshprekherke)*, 210, 213
Fonrobert, Charlotte, 30
France, 78, 83, 123, 128; Paris, 190, 230, 252, 281; Perpignan, 83
Freehof, Solomon, 10, 399–401
French (language), 124–25, 129–32, 192–93, 230–33
fricatrices, 13
Friedman, Sanford (1928–2010), 375–78
Ftayya, Yehuda (1859–1942), 277–79

gaon (head of the Babylonian Talmudic academy), 47, 51, 58
Gay, Jan (1902–1960), 301
gay bars. *see* clubs, gay and lesbian
Gay Liberation Front, 392
gender fluidity and transition (trans, intersex, non-binary identities). *see* suggested tracks, 407
Genesis, Book of. see Index of Passages
Genesis Rabbah. see Index of Passages
Genizah (Cairo), 57, 71
Gentiles, 12, 77, 86, 90–91, 171, 239–40, 348

Gerber, Israel Joshua (1918–2011), 331–37
German (language), 154–58, 194–201,
217–23, 257–59, 288–89, 314–16,
354–58, 401–2
Germany, 66, 106, 153–54; Berlin, 194, 217,
257, 314, 395; Erlangen, 353; Siegen, 329;
Würzberg, 153
Gestapo, 288
get (divorce certificate), 90–91, 184–86, 226.
see also divorce, divorcée
ghettos, 111–13, 381–86
Giese, Karl (1898–1938), 218
gilgul nefashot (transmigration of souls),
100–101
Gill, Jacob, 141–43
Ginsberg, Allen, 380
G.I.s, Jewish American, 296–300. see also U.S.
Army service
Gock, Hermann (1848–1910), 154
Goldstein, Elyse, 1, 9
Goodman, Paul, 281
Gray, John (1866–1934), 9, 177–78
Greece, 92, 126; Arta, 92; Lesbos, 294, 402;
Salonica, 126, 271
Greek (language), 22–28, 271–72
Greek Orthodox, 9, 271
grooms. see bridegrooms

Habas, Brakha (1900–1968), 285
HaItamari, Eliyah HaKohen (ca. 1640–
1729), 121–23
halakhah (Jewish law). see suggested tracks,
406
Halevi, Yehuda (ca. 1075–1141), xix, 59–60
Halper, Shaun, 235
Hammer, Jill, 6
Hanukkah, 86, 250
al-Harizi, Yehudah (1165–1225), 62–63
Hart, Henry, 141–43
Hart, John, 141–43
Hart, Pearl (1890–1975), 8, 340–46
Hashomer Hatsa'ir, 233–234
Hasidism, 131–36, 178, 210–13, 234, 235
Haskalah (Jewish Enlightenment), 131, 159

havruta (study partners) and sexual relations,
41–43, 46, 119–21, 126–28, 236–37, 387
Hay, Harry, 340
Hayy ben Sherira, 51–52
Hayyim, Yosef al-Hakham (1835–1909). see
Ben Ish Hai
Hebrew (language), 15–16, 33–46, 51–57,
59–60, 62–63, 62–70, 73–82, 85–87, 90–
103, 108–10, 120–23, 126–28, 131–40,
143–45, 184–86, 188–90, 211, 233–34,
265–69, 269–70, 276–79, 280–81,
285–87, 292–96, 327–31, 329, 351–53
Hebrew Immigrant Aid Society (HIAS),
224, 226
Hebrew Octoberists, 269
Hedayah, 'Ovadyah (1889–1969), 351
HeHalutz, 314
HeHasid, Yehudah, 144
Henry, Dr. George, 301
herem (excommunication), 93–94, 97
Herschaft, Jeanette Rachmuth (1924–2003),
362–64
Heschel, Susannah, 9
Hindus and Hinduism, 114
Hirschfeld, Magnus (1868–1935), 8, 16, 194,
217–23, 292–94
Hitler, Adolf, 354, 356
Hitler Youth, 314
Holocaust, 241, 253, 258, 383. see also con-
centration camps
homophile movement, 328, 341, 365–75,
380–86
Homosexual Law Reform Society, 392
Horodezky, Samuel Abba (1871–1957),
210–14
Hosea, Book of. see Index of Passages
House of Representatives Un-American
Activities Committee (HUAC), 341
Hyman, Paula, 9

Iberian Hebrew poetry, 52–57, 59–66, 85,
98–99
Ibn Aderet, Shlomo, or the Rashba (1235–
1310), 76–78, 85

Index of Passages

This book was typeset in Caslon 11.5/16, originally cut by the Englishman William Caslon I (1692–1766) who, like John Fell before him, was heavily reliant on Dutch typefaces. Caslon's typefaces were immediately quite popular in England and remained so until around 1780, when the transitional typefaces of John Baskerville and others came into vogue; they regained popularity in the nineteenth century. Caslon gained a particularly strong following in the American colonies; the first printings of both the Declaration of Independence and the Constitution were done with Caslon type. Adobe Caslon, the interpretation used in this book, was designed by Carol Twombly in 1990. Caslon designed Hebrew typefaces, as well; they have not, as of yet, been digitized.

Introductory paragraphs were typeset in Futura, designed by Paul Renner in 1927. Subheadings were typeset in Seravek, designed by Eric Olson in 2007.

Section and chapter headings were typeset in Gilbert, named for Gilbert Baker (d. 2017), gay rights activist and designer of the rainbow flag. It is one of the first fonts to take advantage of the new OpenType-SVG "color font" format.

CPSIA information can be obtained
at www.ICGtesting.com
Printed in the USA
BVHW041024020221
599224BV00015B/2628

9 780990 515562